No More Menemies

Allison,

Hope you enjoy it

love
x

NO MORE MENEMIES

Getting beyond the fear and frustration
of the gender wars

Lori Meakin

ISBN: 1739745318
ISBN 13: 9781739745318

My unofficial subtitle for this book is 'How good would it be if we didn't feel the need to keep banging on about gender all the time?!'

Women may read that as 'Wouldn't it be great if we didn't _need_ to keep talking about all the problems we face, because gender equality had been achieved.' Men might be more likely to read it as 'Wouldn't it be great to have a respite from the constant attack from feminists who make me feel like I'm the enemy when I'm genuinely not a bad man.'

The difference in those two readings shows that there is benefit to us both, but we need to work better together to get past the gender wars and 'menemies' mindset we're stuck in. If that means using different motivations to lead us to achieve common goals, then that's fine by me. We'll never get enough men working for feminism unless they feel like feminism is working for them too. That's why this book is one woman's attempt to understand what it feels like to be a man in a world where everyone is talking more and more about gender equality.

It's intended to stimulate more positive conversations between all the good men out there and anyone whose gender means they're not top dog in the patriarchal system we all live in. Maybe that way, we can make the progress around gender equality that will benefit us all.

For Jonny, Nancy and Betty,
with all the love and thanks in the world.

And for me.

CONTENTS:

INTRODUCTION

Why am I talking to men about gender equality?

Women can't solve this alone.

============

Why am I talking to men about gender equality? The reason is simple and somewhat selfish: I want my young-adult daughters to be free to forge their path through life without having to deal with quite so much of the shit that I've struggled with for decades. But I know I can't achieve that without the help of men.

And yes, let's just enjoy for a moment the irony of the fact that I'm a woman striving to achieve gender equality, and the first thing I say is that I'm powerless without men.

Now, I've spent hours and hours having inspiring conversations about gender with all kinds of brilliant women, and creating all kinds of positive action. And that's something I absolutely cherish. But increasingly, one question kept returning to me: If I were a man, why exactly would I want to actively help build a more gender-equal world?

And honestly, I'm not even sure that I would.

I'm pretty sure that 'man-me' would think it's the right thing to do from a moral point of view. But if I really were a man - particularly a white, 50-something, successful, cis, straight man - I'd probably feel like I had an awful lot to lose. I may well feel a bit resentful at constantly being told I had too much advantage and privilege, as I'd know that I've worked hard and beaten the odds to earn the success I have in life. I'd maybe feel a bit like I'm being blamed for other men having had it their own way for centuries, and that wouldn't seem entirely fair. But of course, I'd avoid saying that to women, for fear of sounding like an anti-feminist.

I imagine that if I were a man today, even if I genuinely wanted to help create a more gender-equal world, I'd struggle to know exactly what I should do. I'd probably worry so much about doing the wrong thing that I'd feel a bit paralysed. And - whisper it - I think that secretly, a bit of me might be thinking that some feminists are over-egging the whole 'it's tough to be woman,' 'the patriarchy is holding us back' thing, that they're making mountains out of molehills, and that they might be a whole lot happier if they didn't keep banging on about gender all the time.

The bottom line is, if I were a man, why would I want to give up the privilege that women keep telling me I have? Why would I want to make my path through life harder, for me and for future generations of men and boys? And when I'm not being lectured and criticised and guilt-tripped by the feminist movement, when I'm enjoying moments of just getting on with my life… honestly, would I even think about it at all?

That's why I decided to write this book. I wanted to talk to men so I can try and answer the fundamental question: Why would any perfectly decent man (one who isn't a rampant misogynist but isn't an active card-carrying feminist either) want to help make a more gender-equal world?

The gentle art of persuasion.

I'm a professional persuader, and after 20-plus years of developing brand strategies and advertising campaigns for all kinds of brands, from Amazon to Vue, Google to M&S food-porn, BBC iPlayer to National Drugs Helpline, one thing I know for sure is that trying to persuade people to do something they don't want to do is just pushing water uphill. It's pointless.

Every successful strategy and campaign I've ever developed in my professional life has started from really understanding the people whose behaviour I want to affect. And instead of trying to tell them all the ways our brand is good for them; instead of lecturing them about why they should want it, I've always simply identified what it is that those people really value and want in their lives that also happens to help our client's business. And then encouraged them to do more of that.

So I decided I'd try the same approach with gender equality. Yes, it sounds a little bit ridiculous to me too. And maybe I have bitten off a little more than I can chew, as gender equality's certainly in a different league to Prime subscriptions or melt-in-the-middle chocolate puddings.

But maybe the same principles remain true. What if I tried to really understand what it feels like to be a man these days; and then identified some things men want to do and enjoy doing, that would also create more gender equality almost as a by-product?

The strategies that stand the best chance of working will be ones where men feel like they're gaining something, and where women feel like we're making positive change that levels the gender playing-field.

So I rounded up some willing volunteers and sat down with each of these twenty three individual men who were kind enough to let me quiz and question them, to try and understand what it feels like to be a man right now; and to see if there are things they want and value that could also create more gender equality if they acted on them more often, or in a different way. And while qualitative researchers and academics might be having paroxysms at my methodology as it's by no means a rigorously scientifically representative sample, let me just point out that I'm not in any way trying to suggest that this is the last word on the subject. These are simply my observations, understanding and ideas, based on these conversations with the men who have been willing to talk to me. I hope it might provoke more conversations for other ordinary, decent, good men who've not really explored this stuff much up until now.

But before I share what I've learned from these conversations, I must declare that I'm not a dispassionate observer. Despite years of progress, I'm still pissed off at so many ways gender inequality still exists. And I want more change. So it's only fair, I think, if I start by setting the scene and explaining a little about my somewhat complex relationship with masculinity. You might still think I'm an angry harridan, but you may at least recognise some of the things that have caused that.

Me and masculinity.

Looking back to when I was a young girl, I don't remember really noticing gender. I loved pretty clothes and dolls and long hair, but I also climbed trees, rode a bike, spoke up for myself in class and saw myself as a leader. I wanted to be a backing singer/dancer for a pop star and a high court judge. My experience of the world, which came almost entirely from TV, showed me very clearly that the former were almost always women and the latter almost always men, but I don't remember ever really noticing that or thinking about it. My sister (who, along with my mum and my daughters is one of the women I love and admire most in the world) told me that my middle name was Malcolm, the same as our dad's. Knowing that my middle initial was indeed an M, and having no idea that I wouldn't be given a boy's name, I just accepted that. For years. No, I have no idea either how I could have known the initial of my middle name but not known that I couldn't be called Malcolm, but there it is.

As I grew a little, things changed, and I started to notice gender more. I'm ashamed to say it now, but as I watched the male grown-ups around me and on TV and in the papers, I wanted to be more like them than the majority of the women I saw. So I became a bit of a tomboy in frills. And as I grew, throughout my teenage years, at some level I wanted to be a man. A gay man, actually, because even after I survived an aggressive sexual assault one winter's evening aged 18, I was still physically attracted to the male form. I tried to make myself a gay woman, but my attempts at amateur conversion therapy were to no avail. Baby I was born this way, and it was only the male body that I found attractive.

I feel the need to apologise to the gay men and women who were - and still are - experiencing homophobia at personal and structural levels, because throughout the time of Clause 28, of the AIDS crisis, of gay men and women being told they couldn't marry and shouldn't have kids, as I campaigned for the Terrence Higgins Trust and for Stonewall, all the while I secretly wished I was a gay man. I hated the femaleness of my body, where even showing just a few inches of bare calf below my long oversized man's coat was enough to signal 'victim' to a sexual predator on a dark rainy winter's evening in suburbia. As the senior policeman who investigated the attack told me, making me retrace my steps and pace up and down while he scrutinised me: 'He could tell you were an attractive young woman, even under that coat and umbrella, because of those yellow argyle socks you're wearing.'

Oh well that explains it all, then.

For years, throughout my twenties, I remained angry at being a woman. Small, blonde, young-looking, and not at all boyishly flat-chested as I'd have liked, I was regularly leered at by groups of blokes with invitations to get my tits out for the lads. And, dear reader, of course I know that these bad guys are a tiny, tiny percentage of all the men I've encountered in my life. But stuff like this isn't a numbers game, so while I fantasised about having breast reduction surgery so that I could pass through the world less noticed as a sexual being, these men would 'compliment' me with such kind affirmations as 'you could be a Page Three girl,' and the real wits might offer up 'alright love, you don't get many of them to the pound do you?' Every time, I ignored it and just walked on, head down, furious at myself for not being able to think of a riposte that would make them realise how angry and ashamed that makes a woman feel; knowing they'd go on to do it to the next young woman whose body was unfortunate enough to please them.

But as well as all this fear and the frustration at being too visible in a way I didn't want, I also felt invisible in areas where I really did want to be seen and heard.

Studying literature and film back then was a way to feel dismissed and diminished a hundred times a day. In books or films, men were the protagonists, the authors, the critics, the directors, the producers, the backers. No wonder men were the default in language too - chairmen, moneymen, masterfully lording it over the rest of us. They inherited titles, land and power. They did the looking, and women performed under their gaze.

Society and culture constantly reminded me that I was weaker - not just physically, but in every way. Less clever. Too emotional. More vulnerable. Less worthy. And so it was made clear in ways both explicit and subtle that it was my role in life to serve men - to pour them drinks, laugh at their jokes, listen to their stories, clean their clothes, support their team, move out of their way, and don't complain. No one wants a nag around.

And I hated that. Despite everything, I still wanted to be part of this male group that had all that privilege and that seemed free to enjoy life in ways that I couldn't. (I didn't recognise, of course, that my whiteness meant I already was in that privileged group in a different way. But I never really noticed that, and too often I still don't - because when you're inside the privileged group, it's often simply invisible if you don't keep forcing yourself to see it.)

So I deliberately used the few masculine qualities that I did possess[1] as a ticket to the world I was excluded from. For me, that ticket was my cleverness - a kind of cleverness that was valued by the blokes: effortless (I never really tried at school or even at uni, to my shame now); quick; sometimes cruel; and most of all, competitive - I could harness an argument in seconds that would destroy all-comers. And even though my girly voice wasn't loud enough to take up space in the room, and I had to fight for every utterance to be heard before I'd be interrupted again, my particular type of intelligence gave me a ticket to operate inside 'fortress masculinity.'

I continued to eschew my visible femininity and tried to look right running with the male pack too. No longer the tomboy in frills of my childhood, I now disguised my young adult female body in as much boyishness as I could muster. Cropped hair, oversized jeans, no make-up, big chunky shoes (from DMs to Buffalos to Nikes). I drank pints, even though I hated them. I fell in love with football (admittedly, that wasn't much of a sacrifice back then, as Arsenal in the era of Henry, Vieira and Freddy-with-his-red-hair was easy to love). I smoked. I swore like an old sailor. And I hung out with men far more than with women. I'd finally been adopted into the male world I'd coveted for years. And that felt great, for a while.

Making peace with femininity.

Things started to change as I entered my 30s. As I became more senior at work, I started to realise that younger women wanted senior women as role models in their lives - but senior women who acted like women, not like wannabe men. That felt weird to me. Coming of age in the 80's, the powerful women I saw generally displayed more masculinity than most of the men around them. (Yes, as well as the poll tax and the miners' strike, I believe Maggie Thatcher has that to answer for too.) So I had to learn that using my intelligence as an offensive weapon, talking too much, always wanting to be right, wasn't an ideal model of leadership. It's a lesson I'm still working on to this day. When I worked briefly on the makeup brand Revlon, researching colour, body language, and the social history of make-up completely changed the way I thought about my own self-expression. I started wearing red lipstick every day, as a celebration of the fact that I have something to say. And I tried to just stop caring that men might mistakenly assume I'm wearing it to look attractive to them.

Most unexpectedly of all, the feminine body I'd long hated finally made me respect it, by growing two incredible human beings. Human beings who are female. And, unlike the guy in the hardware store around the corner who'd commiserate with me each time, telling me that maybe I'd be lucky enough to have a boy next time, I could never, ever be disappointed at their being girls.

Like the archetypal Islington middle-class parents we'd now become, we deliberately bought our baby girls clothes and toys that were gender-neutral. But when they started using the Early Learning Centre drill as a hairdryer and demanding that everything be pink, sparkly and covered in rainbows, we just went with it. By this time, I'd realised femininity wasn't something to be ashamed of.

My wonderful husband, a complete 'bloke' in some ways, happily shared the childcare, being one of only two men amongst the gaggle of mums at the school gates each day. We both worked, we shared domestic duties more equally than pretty much any of our friends, and our little girls grew into young women who are both fearsome and feminine.

I now proudly embrace the more feminine qualities that I have too, and use them to help me be a better leader and mother. And I'm flying under the radar of the male gaze these days, because getting older as a woman is like suddenly being gifted an invisibility cloak. I can't remember the last time I got leered at on the streets. Which would be a relief, were it not for the fact that I know they're just doing it to my daughters instead. Which brings us back to why I'm here, writing this. We've come a long way. I've come a long way. And I'm immensely thankful for all that progress. But (and don't hate me for saying it) …

Houston, we still have a problem.

It's the 2020s, for fuck's sake.[2] I don't want my girls to go for a run and have to come back furious about what some idiot leering blokes in a van shouted about the way their body moves.

I don't want them to ever feel like they have to behave more like men have done for centuries in order to be powerful and successful, at work or in their personal and social lives.

I'm happy for my daughters to choose whatever they want to do, but I don't want them to have to take time off work to have children just because their partner's company wouldn't pay him if he shared the parental leave.

And I don't want them to watch less talented men get ahead because they're louder, more confident, or just there. (In case you think I'm being prejudiced against men for saying that, here's the data: Only 9 percent of the top jobs in the biggest companies in the UK are inhabited by a woman.[3] Expressed another way, men are nine times more likely than women to have that CEO role right now. But I refuse to believe the average man is nine times more talented than the girl he sat next to in school or at his first work desk. Or that for every talented woman in pretty much any field there are nine more talented men. In fact, exam data shows girls and young women outperform men throughout formal education years, and extensive scientific studies have shown that the qualities proven to make better leaders are ones in which women tend to over-index. And yet here I am, celebrating the nine percent but craving so much more.)

I don't want my daughters and their girlfriends to have to be ready to use their keys to defend themselves every time any man walks too close behind them at night.

I don't want the vast majority of the entertainment they watch to be directed by men with most of the main protagonists still men, and women still given significantly fewer lines to speak, even in films that tell their stories. (Again, if you think I'm being unfair, Google the Bechdel test. Or the analysis of 2,000 screenplays by The Pudding[4] who, for instance, found that even romcoms, films that we think of as definitively girly, have dialogue that is, on average, 58 percent male. Or read Brandsplaining which shows, for example, that still only 3 percent of ads show women being funny, as opposed to laughing at men's jokes; and the same paltry number had women in roles that demanded any kind of intelligence).[5]

I don't want the medical profession that's there to serve my daughters to have to run a huge government review into how far it's still overlooking women's health issues, because so much research in the past was done exclusively on the male body.

I don't want the products they and women like them might rely on for safety, from seatbelts to PPE equipment, to simply not work as well for them because they're designed to work for men.

I don't want it to feel natural for my girls to inhabit a world where men keep on taking up more than their fair share of space. Where men still talk more; interrupt more; talk louder; spread their legs and arms into their neighbour's space as if it belongs to them; expect women to get out of their way when walking and literally charge them aside if they don't.[6] Not because I think my girls are delicate little flowers. They're not. But because all of these little moments subliminally act as a reminder that the world they inhabit is one that was made for men first and foremost, and that women are still expected to fit in around that like they don't quite belong, like the world is not equally theirs.[7]

But neither do I want men to feel terrified of saying or doing the wrong thing in a post #MeToo world.

I don't want any man ever to feel overwhelmed because of the pressures on him to succeed in all those traditionally masculine ways. And with suicide the biggest killer of young men, Houston we have a huge problem here.

I don't want men (straight or gay) to be told they're not able to care for children as well as women naturally can; to be denied custody of their children unless the mother is an entirely unfit parent; or to be seen as somehow less of a man if they choose to enter a caring profession.

I don't want the 90 percent of top CEO's who are currently men to feel like they haven't earned their place at the top table, and to feel under attack or guilty simply for being male.

I don't want decent, good men to keep scaring the hell out of women (and making it easier for the tiny numbers of men who do attack women on the streets) just because they've never really been educated about women's safety.

I don't want talented directors and actors with great stories to tell, that we can all enjoy and learn from, to be cast aside just because they're male.

I don't want male doctors, who have spent their lives trying to help their patients, being made to feel like they've been failing women all along.

I don't want men to simply give up because they're so worried about what's the right thing to do, or make, or say.

I don't want men to start feeling like they don't quite belong in the modern world; like the future is increasingly made by and for women, and that men are simply dinosaurs, predators or imposters in it.

Selfishly too, I don't want to feel like a nag for saying that all of these problems still exist, a Moaning Minnie, harping on about gender again. I don't want to feel like I'm presenting women as weak, as victims. And I don't want men to think I'm using all of this as a weapon in a gender war, trying to control or punish them because they've had it too good for too long. Because I don't see women as weak victims, nor men as the enemy.

And even if I did, I know that's not the best way to help create change. And change is what I really, really want.

So, to all you good men, chaps, boys, lads, guys, blokes, gentlemen... or however you define yourself: I'm here to ask you to help me. I'm powerless to create a more gender-equal world without you.

Do it for whatever reason works best for you. Help me because it's the right thing to do, if that's what you genuinely think. Or if you prefer, do it just to give the feminists one less stick with which to beat you. I honestly don't mind.

Help me by being gender equality's saviour if you like to feel like a knight in shining armour. Whatever works. You might just discover that, as Julia Roberts' character points out at the end of Pretty Woman, a more gender-equal society ends up saving you right back.

But even if you don't believe that will happen, I just want more men and women to talk about this stuff together, to see if we can understand each other better and find a way of making a more equal world that can work in all of our favour. Without judgement. And without blame.

That's what I've spent some time doing. So what follows is a snapshot of the understanding and ideas that I got to, thanks to the generous men who gave me their time.

I hope it helps start some positive conversations for you too.

INTERLUDE:

Getting past the anger

Listening without prejudice should be the easy bit.

==============

Now before we get going, I want to establish a few ground rules, just so we all know what we're getting into here:

Food for thought, not the answer.

This project is about listening, questioning and suggesting where some possible solutions might lie, so that you can build on those yourself. You won't find all the answers here. Of course, many of the men I interviewed made self-deprecating jokes about how if I were a bloke, I'd claim to have all the answers. But sadly, I don't. Instead, I hope that each of these chapters can operate as a brief for further work from anyone who's willing to take up the mantle.

In each of the chapters that follows, I start by sharing some publicly available data, to set out the problem with a fact base that's incontrovertible. This fact base operates as the context for the reader, but it's not where my conversations with respondents started. In fact, I didn't share *any* of this data about the current state of gender inequality with the men I talked to - at least not until some follow-up conversations. Other than billing the conversations as 'I'm trying to understand what it feels like to be a man in a world where people are increasingly talking about gender equality,' we didn't talk about these gender inequality issues and facts specifically at all. Instead, my questions were about each man's experiences, thoughts and feelings in areas that I knew from the data were pertinent to gender inequality - things like being a parent, competition (with women and with other men), sex, the deep-rooted belief that 'being girly' is something inferior to being a boy, navigating the workplace and even the invisibility of many of the issues themselves. I debrief here what I discovered, and how that related to the data-led issues with which I start each chapter. Then finally, in each case, I set out a few thought-starters for where we might be able to start making positive change together.

Some of those thought-starters may resonate with you and you'll want to put them into practice, or at least explore them further; others, you'll find irrelevant, or even just plain wrong. That's fine. There are plenty of ways to skin a cat - although as a cat-lover, I do wish there were a less gruesome metaphor for multiple right answers. All I hope for is for men to feel better able to engage in conversations about gender that are a bit more productive, and for us all to start to listen to and understand each other better, so we can build a world that works better for men, women, and for people who don't identify as either of those.

It's not always binary.

Of course, there have always, in all cultures, been people who don't identify as either male or female, and awareness is now becoming increasingly mainstream of people who live their lives beyond the dominant gender binaries of man/woman, male/female. The fact that I generally talk here about men and women is never intended to diminish anyone who is non-binary or gender non-conforming, although I understand that such exclusion may well, unfortunately, feel like that. I hope that questioning and exploring how limiting and damaging traditional gender expectations are, and bringing more men into that conversation, will benefit all of us.

Additionally, in the Epilogue, I explicitly address the way that gender equality intersects with the struggles faced by all kinds of people on the LGBTQIA+ spectrum, and explore what the men I talked to understood and felt about this.

It's important that readers recognise that when I use the terms 'men' or 'women' throughout this book, I mean anyone who identifies as a man or a woman. Listening to trans women talk often leaves me awe-struck at how important their woman-ness is to them, how difficult and dangerous it is for them to live as the woman they know they are, and how often the conversation immediately defaults to questions about the state of their genitalia. I'll no more exclude my trans sisters from the idea of 'women' that I use here than I would exclude a cis woman who's undergone a hysterectomy or mastectomy. I believe it's *you* that matters, not just your body parts.

Sometimes, I'll reference data that's specifically about bodies, and other times it will be more about how we're socialised and how we perform masculinity and femininity. I hope that any trans woman can use whatever elements of the data and insight apply to her, and disregard what doesn't, at least until we have more robust intersectional data. And where I inevitably mis-speak or stumble around this issue, I hope that trans and non-binary people and activists will correct me in a spirit of mutual positivity and learning. Because I firmly believe that there's much more that unites us than divides us; and that unless we work together, the patriarchal system that damages us all will continue to flourish.

By women, I don't just mean privileged white women.

I'm a white woman, and one whose life is now so middle class that until I talk about my early childhood, I definitely pass as a fully signed up member of that elite group. I'm also able-bodied, well-educated and I live and work in the south-east of England in a creative industry, so I'm very aware that I enjoy all kinds of privilege that those women who live further from the white, cis, straight, middle class patriarchy simply don't. When I talk about women, I actively intend this to mean *all* women. We still don't have access to anywhere near enough intersectional data focusing on women of colour, for instance, but we do know that some women are significantly 'less equal than others.' Those of us with systemic privilege must keep reminding ourselves, as we read, that the issues outlined in the following pages are hugely exacerbated for women of colour, women from less privileged socio-economic groups and so on. And we must hope that soon, the people who gather all this data will start looking at these areas of intersectionality as a matter of course.

The men I've talked to.

The men I've talked to represent a mix of socio-economic backgrounds. Some are in the creative and media industries where I've worked until recently; others are in jobs whose culture and expertise is very different from that. They range in age from 20s to 60s and include different races, gender identities and sexual orientations. A healthy proportion were brought up outside of the M25, and they include some men who went to private and public schools, and more who were at very ordinary state comprehensive or secondary modern schools (remember those?) Most importantly, I assured each of the men total anonymity, so that they felt comfortable talking to me as openly as possible, knowing that nothing they said could identify them, even to friends or family who knew they were participating in this project.

So, although what I've discovered here won't necessarily be representative of what all men think and feel, what I've learned from this diverse group of men is a good start for thinking about whether or how that might apply to men more broadly.

One more thing.

There's one other thing I'd like to do before we dive into the following eight chapters that each set up the issues facing women, explore what it feels like to be a man in that general area, and think about what that might mean for how we can create change together.

I'd like to have a little rant; to get a few things off my chest, and to be listened to for a bit before I start with all the listening to my brilliant volunteering men.

A brief interlude:
Some stuff just for men to listen to and not try to fix.

Before you saddle up the white charger and we gallop off into our understanding of what it feels like to be a man so we can make real change, there's one final thing that's important. If you're a typical bloke, you're not gonna love it, because it's about talking about feelings. But don't worry, it's my talk and my feelings. All you need to do is pause, listen and try to empathise. Try to just concentrate on feeling how that feels rather than thinking about how you want to solve it or what you'd do about it if you were me. If it helps, know that listening to women is something proven to make men more sexually attractive.[1]

Importantly, too, there are some things that can't be changed, because they're in the past. Reparations can't really be made, but these things can be understood, reflected on, and not ignored. For me at least, a starting point for the help I'd love from men is to be listened to rather than immediately dismissed or 'saved'. To be understood, even just a little bit. So I'm going to indulge myself with a few minutes of asking you to listen to me before we turn the tables for the rest of this project. Neither of us will be able to solve the big stuff together if we don't start by understanding each other a little better.

That's why I've spent many hours and days and months actively listening to men, rather than telling them what they're doing wrong and why/how they should change. And I've learned through these conversations with men about masculinity and gender equality that it's hard for all of us to do that, and it may be especially hard for men. You may not recognise or even quite believe all the little ways that society is still stacked against women, holding us back, putting us at risk and preventing us having equal opportunities in many areas of life. That's not surprising, as they're things that appear natural and normal. You've most likely never even noticed a lot of them before. But I do notice them, and I know many other women notice them too. We feel them. And even when they don't have an immediately measurable negative impact on our lives, the feeling of them is a backdrop that's always subliminally there for us, and that can sometimes get difficult to bear.

So please try to battle against any logic that says, 'that's all in the past now', and don't dismiss it as over-dramatic or over-emotional when I say that despite how much progress we've made, reminders of where we've come from still really hurt. Please know that I'm thrilled if any man genuinely tries to understand the possibly-irrational pain and anger I feel whenever I'm reminded of how women have been treated for centuries, even though neither of us can change the past. And please try not to feel like the following is a personal attack, because I know you didn't do any of this!

It may seem unproductive or unreasonable to you, but I can't help feeling angry every time I'm reminded that women just like me, who were unlucky enough to be born in previous centuries, were literally owned by men, passed from one to the other and not allowed to own property or even have rights over their own children, because legally we were the property of our husbands or fathers. So it's no wonder I'm a bit touchy about the many small ways that women are still treated like a man's property now, from aristocratic women still putting up with ancestral property inheritance passing down the male line, to women being 'given away' by their fathers on their wedding day in front of a god who's invariable male, to me still being occasionally formally addressed as 'Mrs Jonathan Meakin.' (Seriously??!)

I can't just forget that for centuries, 'difficult' or 'overbearing' women whose bravery I now benefit from were brutally tortured, raped and killed for being too provocative or too outspoken. (And tragically, they still are in many places around the world.) If you think I'm exaggerating, read up on how the Suffragettes were deliberately groped and sexually assaulted by police as a way of breaking up their protests, and how the imprisoned women who went on hunger strike as a form of protest were violently force-fed by prison officers; how countless thousands of ordinary women in the UK alone were burned as witches by the state, not for acts of religious heresy, but just for just living outside the constraints imposed on their gender, for being 'difficult women'; or how throughout the 18th and 19th centuries women diagnosed as 'hysterical' by male doctors were forced to have non-consensual sex or hysterectomies as 'treatment' for a range of behaviours that included being too interested in sex, not interested enough in sex, and even simply being exhausted. So it may feel to you like I'm being over emotional when I get angry or upset about another story about terrible violence against women, or about things that might seem small and inconsequential, like women being casually slut-shamed or told that their voices are too loud or too high or too quiet, but at some deep level, from time to time the rage of my ancestors still screams within me, and it doesn't help to be told I should just forget about it.

Surely that's not the kind of thing we should just forget? I don't want to forget the trauma and fear and sacrifice that millions of young male soldiers made in wars near and far to protect the freedoms we all cherish. I don't want to forget about the genocides that have been committed by our enemies or by our Empire. I don't want to forget about the way gay men were imprisoned, chemically castrated and even killed because of who they loved. I want to honour the victims of those gross injustices, learn from that horrific mistreatment of people, and respect the trauma that still lives within their descendants, because that's how we can make sure it never happens again; and how we get the energy to keep working to eradicate the very many vestiges of those gross injustices that still remain. And surely that has to be true for the historical misogyny, abuse and gross injustices that women have endured too.

Remembering, honouring, and learning from injustice is important, and it really doesn't mean I'm just bearing a grudge. We've come a long way, but it's been tough, and there's still so far to go, and that sometimes makes me angry and scared and tired. But I try to keep focused on the positives. And to look forward. Not just because that's what nice girls are supposed to do, but also because anger and fear don't help recruit the many male allies for the work that still lies ahead. So, if you're a male reader and you're still reading, I thank you from the bottom of my sometimes-angry heart. And to all the good men out there I say: I need your help. Women need your help. We're far from powerless in general, but we're powerless to make all the changes we need without you working at it alongside us.

Now this is where things might start to feel more comfortable. Because it's time to do something to fix stuff. Time to do something that's practical and helpful and feasible and not too costly. Because I know from my professional life that building from things people already care about is most likely to make change happen. It's why that really successful anti-smoking advertising campaign that I long admired didn't tell people that smoking kills; instead, it told you that it dulls the skin and smells bad, because that's a bigger turn-off if you're someone who spends time and money on great makeup and perfume than someone telling you that you might die of lung cancer.

So I set out to try and understand what it's like to be a man. And see if we can find some things that might motivate regular guys to help create a world that has less structural and interpersonal sexism in it and more gender equality.

Buckle up. Here we go.

ISSUE 1:

That 'I've Never
Really Thought About It' Face

Exploring our blind spots in a default-male world.

===============

REALITY CHECK:
WHERE WE ARE RIGHT NOW

We live in a world that's largely designed by and for men.

That may sound like I'm being a hysterical woman, seeing imaginary problems everywhere, but it's not. Neither is it an accusation, as no man alive today created the entire system that governs our world. But it is a fact. The buildings, towns and cities we inhabit, the political, economic and social systems on which our current behaviours and practices are based, the art and literature that fills our libraries, galleries, schools and universities, the scientific and medical knowledge on which new discoveries build, even the very language we speak have all been established over centuries or millennia almost exclusively by men, in an era when women's lives were very much separated from public spaces and their contributions excluded.

So it's hardly surprising that the world we live in is designed in a way that simply doesn't take account of bodies and lives that are different from those for whom it was designed, including the half of the population that happens to be not-male.

But because it's always been that way, the very fact that the world is optimised for men and doesn't fit women quite as well is often invisible. If we're not affected by something, it can easily pass us by unnoticed. I spent years buying 'flesh-coloured' plasters, undies whose colour was described as 'nude' and ballet shoes that were pink because 'they create the illusion of bare feet' without (I'm ashamed to say) spotting the very obvious point that this is only true if your skin happens to be white. If that 'flesh colour' isn't the same as *your* flesh colour, every time one of those plasters enters your world, it's silently saying 'you're different, you're other, you're not like us, you don't quite belong amongst us.'

So if you're a man, it's no surprise that you don't notice all the ways that the world you move through every day just doesn't work as well for women. (And of course if you're a black or brown woman you'll be very aware that this issue is hugely exacerbated for anyone who looks like you).

But this 'male as default' design in all kinds of areas makes life more challenging for all women, and in too many cases it makes it more dangerous too.

Caroline Criado-Perez has literally written the book on this: *Invisible Women: Exposing Data Bias in a World Designed for Men*.[1] It's the book that won the 2019 Science Book Prize, and in it she meticulously sets out rigorous and wide-ranging evidence of the many ways that this default-male bias seriously damages women. Like how service women who put themselves in harm's way to protect us all are at greater risk of injury than their male peers because their body armour, which is supposedly 'unisex', simply isn't designed to accommodate the shape of a woman's body.

Or like how women are 47 percent more likely than men to be seriously injured and 17 percent more likely to die in identical car crashes, because women's bodies haven't been factored into car design: the size and weight-distribution of crash test dummies that are used to determine the safety of anything from driving positions to seat firmness and shape to seatbelts are still based on the male body. I know, by the fact that I literally have to use a booster cushion to make the driving seat in our family car functional and comfortable for me, that cars are designed for male bodies rather than for all the women who drive them too. I was totally shocked to discover the truth that cars being designed for the default-male doesn't just (to paraphrase Gloria Steinem) piss us off. It literally kills us.

Even in the field of medicine, which we assume to be unbiased, rigorous and scientific, we see the same thing play out. Women are at higher risk of being mis-diagnosed for heart attacks, for instance, because the conditions they present with are significantly different from the ones found in men, but medical data (which typically is derived from subjects who are solely or predominantly male) has been assumed to be universal. In her foreword to the Scottish Government's Women's Health Plan, Minister Maree Todd starts by quoting from *Invisible Women*: 'Historically, it has been assumed that there wasn't anything fundamentally different between male and female bodies other than size and reproductive function, and so, for years, medical education has been focussed on the male "norm", with everything that falls outside that designated as "atypical" or even "abnormal"' She goes on to say 'This has to change. Women are not atypical - they are 51 percent of Scotland's population.'[2] The Women's Health Plan points out too that, 'Women's health is not just a women's issue. When women and girls are supported to lead healthy lives and fulfil their potential, the whole of society benefits.'[3]

England followed suit and acknowledged the need to to address these massive oversights and blind spots too, stating in its December 2021 *Vision for the Women's Health Strategy for England*[4] that 'there is an overall need for more research into women's health, including that looking specifically at sex differences in conditions, and for greater monitoring of the diversity of research participants,' and that there's a need to 'embed routine collection of... research participant demographic data, including sex and ethnicity, and use this data to ensure that our research is representative of the society we serve.' Because still, right now, it simply isn't representative of the society it serves.

Health authorities as well as businesses are only just beginning to face up to the need to rethink hundreds of years of assumption that the default human is a male (and a white male at that), and a woman is just a smaller male body with different reproductive bits. And in case you, like me, had pretty much assumed that too, let's be clear: she's not. Both sex-specific *and* non-sex-specific conditions are often different in women versus men. Oestrogen creates big differences in immune system function and yet women (even including female mice and cells) often remain excluded from drug trials because changes throughout the menstrual cycle are seen as complications to be avoided in studies rather than realities affecting women's real lives that need to be considered. Women's feet have a shape and proportion that's different from men's, although that's clearly news to all the footwear giants whose specialist 'women's footwear' is typically designed on a smaller version of a male last. And although the temperature at which the average woman's body feels comfortable is significantly higher than the male body, most office buildings continue to set their aircon at a temperature based on the male bodies that historically dominated those spaces, mistakenly assuming that what's comfortable for men is what's comfortable for all people.

It's not just women's *bodies* that aren't accounted for.

In the design of the world we inhabit, women's contributions are often ignored or erased too. A good recent example of the bias towards male-as-default in activities and action, is the English men's soccer team at the Euros a couple of years before the Lionesses won the competition in 2022. The press was excitedly pointing out that, 'England reaching the Euro 2020 final was historic for a couple of reasons. Firstly, it is the first time they have ever reached the final of the Euros, and it's their first final, full-stop, since winning the World Cup In 1966.'[5] Except it wasn't. England actually reached the finals of Euro 2009, but the reason those headline writers ignore it is because it was the women's football team who did it.

'Yes, but football's traditionally a male sport, so of course over-excited footie fans and pundits might have forgotten about the ladies' game', I hear you say. But tennis is the biggest televised sport that features men and women pretty much equally, and we see the erasure of women's achievement happening here too. Andy Murray famously had to remind a sports journalist that women also exist when a reporter in his post-match interview asserted that Sam Querrey (who had just knocked out Murray in the Wimbledon quarter-final) was 'the first US tennis player to reach a Grand Slam semi-final in eight years.' Murray quickly corrected him with 'Male player', to be met at first with a somewhat baffled 'I beg your pardon?' and then a laugh, as the reporter shrugged it off and corrected himself. Murray wasn't laughing. And neither am I, because now I've started noticing, I see the 'default-male/invisible women' thing happening all over the place.

Nearly a century after Virginia Woolf wrote *A Room of One's Own,* the literary canon is still slow to welcome the voices of female writers who've been actively or passively marginalised for centuries. And the same is true of female visual artists of all sorts, who've been largely excluded from galleries and studios, and airbrushed from dominant versions of art history.

Within the science community, an area culturally coded as particularly male, energy is starting to be put into recognising the achievements of women who have been overlooked for too long. But there's still a long way to go:

NASA mathematician Katherine Johnson calculated the safe return for the Apollo 13 astronauts, after the famous cry for help 'Houston we have a problem.' Yet she and her fellow African American 'computers' had been largely written out of the popular narrative of (white) man's conquering of space, meaning too few people had heard of her, until Obama awarded her the Presidential Medal of Freedom in 2015 and the movie *Hidden Figures* told these women's story. Unbeknown to most, too, a team of female specialist seamstresses played a major role in enabling the Apollo moon landing in the first place, by creating the space suits that would keep astronauts alive when the male scientists alone couldn't make it work.[6] Yet we're more familiar with 'the guy sweeping the floor' than we are with this vital team of expert craftswomen when we think of NASA and the talented team 'putting a man on the moon, Mr President.'

Physicist Mileva Marić Einstein was just as precociously brilliant as her husband Albert, but her contributions to his work have been largely written out of the popular history of the loveable individual genius. We say 'Einstein', we think only of Albert.

It was Hedy Lamarr who invented the technology that forms the basis for Wi-Fi and GPS (although she remains more famous for being a beautiful actress than an inventor and pioneer), and Ada Lovelace (better known as Lord Byron's daughter) who effectively invented the basis for modern computer programming. And yet, the tech world they helped create is now often experienced as a man's world, a bro culture dominated by default-male geeks, where women struggle to belong.

Composer Daphne Oram pioneered electronic music, but it's 'man and his machine' that dominates the popular narrative of this musical genre, like so many others. Likewise, with the motor car. Bertha Benz co-invented it with her husband, Carl, but her contribution, including the fact that she was the one responsible for its intrepid and dangerous maiden test drive, still goes largely unrecognised. And cars are seen very much as boys' toys, despite early ones being very popular with women.

Even in academia, social scientists studying human behaviour fall prey to the default-male bias. Sandi Toksvig tells the story of how at Uni, her anthropology professor showed an ancient antler bone with 28 markings on it, and explained that it was long believed to be 'man's first attempt at a calendar.'[7] The professor (a woman - is that who you pictured?) made the obvious but overlooked point that it was, in fact, much more likely to be 'woman's first attempt at a calendar', an early precursor to the modern period tracker.

These aren't isolated examples. The erasure of women's achievements has gone on for centuries. Historian Dr Bettany Hughes tells us the sobering fact that 'women have always been 50 percent of the population, but only occupy around 0.5 percent of recorded history.'[8]

If the stories we tell of human achievement are this male-dominated, is it any wonder that, as Simone de Beauvoir pointed out back in 1949 in *The Second Sex,* 'Representation of the world, like the world itself, is the work of men; they describe it from their own point of view, which they confuse with the absolute truth[9].'

Even the language we use often ignores or erases women.

We see the marginalisation of women happening in language too, but often fail to notice it because it's what we've always been used to. I casually used the expression 'the world and his wife' recently with my daughter. It took us both a second to realise how we'd just verbally erased ourselves from 'the world' with that familiar bit of language. Once you're aware of it, you spot it everywhere. Morrisons were recently selling pairs of mugs with the words 'The Boss' and 'Lady Boss' on them. Even pharma companies do it, with someone recently sharing a photo on Twitter of the stated side effects of their medication, which included 'sexual dysfunction, female sexual dysfunction.' What they mean is 'Man Boss', and 'male sexual dysfunction', but they don't *say* that, because the assumption is that men are just the generic, somehow genderless and universally human. It's women who are the exception, despite being 51 percent of the population. That's why we often talk about 'scientists and female scientists'; 'professors and female professors'; 'drivers and women drivers', as if 'male drivers' and 'drivers' are the same.

A particularly galling example we came across recently was when one of my daughters was studying ancient Greek theatre: The book she was reading talked at great length about how the people of Athens gathered in amphitheatres and watched plays for days at a time; it talked about what they wore, where they sat, what they found funny... and then, added simply: 'Women and slaves were probably excluded.' What really bothered me was not just the fact of our exclusion centuries ago; it's the fact that a modern writer saw fit to use the term 'people' throughout the entire piece when he really meant men, and then casually refer to women and slaves as if they're somehow different from 'people'.

I'm sure the writer of that book, and the football and tennis journalists, weren't *deliberately* excluding women. They just didn't think about women specifically when they thought about 'people'. And it's hardly surprising we do this, of course, because it's estimated that even at its highest potential, the conscious mind's processing capacity is 200,000 times slower than the unconscious.[10] That unconscious mind makes assumptions, takes shortcuts, and carries powerful biases. So just as we've been taught that the term 'man' means 'all people', we've also been socialised to assume that 'people' generally means men, unless we're specifically told otherwise.

I've made this mistaken assumption myself, many times. One games night, a quiz question required me to name which British middle-distance runner won double gold at the Olympics, and I was thinking aloud, hesitating over whether it was Steve Ovett or Sebastian Coe, when my husband's face clearly indicated that I wasn't on the right track. So I started questioning myself - hang on, what about Steve Cram? Maybe it's him, the less expected athlete? The answer, to my eternal shame, was Kelly Holmes. In thinking about a 'British athlete', I had simply forgotten that she existed. A while ago, a couple of female colleagues and I did the same thing at work too. We had an introductory meeting set up with a very senior client of a big company, but tech difficulties had reared their head, and Zoom wasn't working. We were told that 'Alex's assistant was working it out, and would shout when it was sorted', so then when the screen came alive and the woman on screen told us it was all now working, it took all three of us women a second to realise that the woman in front of us *was* Alex, the senior corporate lawyer we were scheduled to talk to, and not the PA who'd sorted out the Zoom call. If the client had been called Susan, maybe we wouldn't have made this mistake, but without that specifically female cue, we'd simply assigned masculinity to the more gender-neutral name Alex. We felt like we'd let the side down, of course. All three of us had experienced being on the receiving end of being overlooked, diminished, ignored and marginalised like this, and knew first-hand how frustrating it feels. It's like being told you don't really matter, like you don't count in the same way that men do. Even as I write that, I can see the thinly disguised eye-rolling that always happens when I mention these things as significant issues, as if women like me are making mountains out of molehills, being over-sensitive and looking for problems where there really aren't any.

Again, let's turn to the facts.

Numerous studies over decades have consistently found that although we believe that we're talking about everyone when we're using the generic masculine (things like 'mankind' or 'Chairman' or 'guys' to encompass both men and women), in actual fact, we're not. Those terms are almost always understood as male. And this has real-world consequences.

Criado-Perez presents evidence that 'When the generic masculine is used, people are more likely to recall famous men than famous women; to estimate a profession as male-dominated; to suggest male candidates for jobs and political appointments.'[11] Then, these positions of power and responsibility being disproportionately held by men negatively impacts women's achievements, as Harvard public policy professor Iris Bohnet points out in *What Works: Gender Equality By Design:* 'Stereotypes describing how we believe the world to be often turn into prescriptions for what the world should be.'[12] Studies have shown that women who were subtly exposed to a picture of a female leader before having to give a speech were rated higher by external observers (and by themselves) than women exposed to a picture of a male leader, or no picture.[13] Interestingly, the performance of the men in the study was no different in each case. Similar studies have gathered students who are about to take an exam in a waiting room, where the portraits on the wall contained all men, or a mix of men and women. Women who'd been exposed to portraits of eminent women as well as men performed significantly better in their exams than the group of women who saw no portraits of female role models staring down at them as they waited. Unsurprisingly, the effect is seen to apply to race too, where again black women are even more disproportionately impacted.

This plays out in the world of work, as well as in education: 'Women are also… less likely to perform well in interviews for jobs that are advertised using the generic masculine.'[14] Job descriptions that use implicitly gendered language also put women off applying in the first place, as the more that women inferred a job to be male dominated, the less they thought *they* belonged there, even if they knew they were qualified to do the job.[15] And this is bad for the recruiters as well as the applicants, because studies into what motivates exceptional performance have shown that the key differentiating factor is not the desire to be better than others, but the desire to be part of an elite group of excellence. So high-performing teams that inadvertently transmit this gendered sense of not belonging are likely to be creating barriers to the most exceptionally talented women, preventing them from achieving their full potential.[16]

The fact that the *Women in Tech Report 2021* by Trust Radius found that 72 percent of the women they surveyed have worked at a company where 'bro culture' is pervasive is depressing, but not massively surprising to me. What did shock me, though, was that the issue was completely invisible to so many of the men.[17] You can't correct for bias if you don't realise it's there, but Mary Ann Sieghart in the excellent but frankly terrifying *Authority Gap* quotes a study which found that employers (by which I mean both men and women) who believed no gender bias existed offered jobs to candidates that were signified as male more than identical 'women' candidates.[18]

So, the continued invisibility of women as a significant half of the population, the mistaken assumption that we are a subset of, or an alternative to 'people', continues to damage women's opportunities, and even our safety in our world that remains largely default-male.

Let me be very clear. I'm not suggesting that if you're a man, this is your fault. All of us, men and women, have internalised these systemic biases, and we act on them innocently and unwittingly. But that doesn't mean it's not all of our responsibility to help address it. If a car accident happened, and we saw it, would we stand around ignoring the people who were injured because we didn't design or drive the car? Of course not. We'd quickly want to work out how we could help.

I spend a lot of my evenings and weekends working with women who give up their time, energy and expertise to help, even though none of us designed the system. But we can't do it alone.

If we're to expect men to help us, we need to start by better understanding what it feels like to be a man, so that we can work out *why* you guys might want to do something about it. Those motivations need to be more than just because it's wrong (although of course it is). They need to be more profound and more positive than simply because you're fed up with us nagging you (yup, there's that gendered language again). Because if we don't find those reasons and nudges that make you *want* to do it and *enjoy* doing it, it's much less likely to happen; just like when brands, governments and individuals use negative or didactic kinds of approaches to try to persuade people to eat more healthily, or to stop smoking.

How do we find those reasons and motivations? That's what I uncovered through my conversations with men.

WHAT I LEARNED
ABOUT MEN

In each of the interviews I did with men, I started by asking a question that I'd thought would be quite simple. A nice little gentle warm-up.

When I'd asked the equivalent question to women, all of them had been able to answer easily, and with a long list of 'for instances', so I'd thought the men would find it just as easy; I just expected they'd maybe have less frequent examples to call upon.

My assumption was wrong. When I asked my opening question, I almost always got the same response: silence; a slightly baffled face; and then an acknowledgement that they honestly didn't know what I was asking them (along with a few protestations of 'I thought you said these were going to be easy questions?') The question was this:

How often do you think about being a man?

Turns out that the overwhelming majority of the men who'd volunteered to talk to me had never really thought about their man-ness. So much so, that they found the idea of thinking about it really confusing and weird, even when I'd billed our conversation as being about me 'trying to understand what it feels like to be a man in a world where people are often talking about gender equality.'

Some of the men talked explicitly about how they don't think of themselves as a man, just as 'a person.' Some tried hard to consider it - 'That's a difficult question. Let me think about that for a minute. [pause]. Is this OK? Do you mind waiting while I think?' Others needed me to ask a different angle on that question in order to get the conversation going.

Interestingly, the only people amongst my respondents who were able to immediately understand and engage with the question were those who weren't straight, white men. A young gay man quickly explained 'I've felt othered my whole life', and went on to say that he spends a lot of time actively thinking and talking about 'gender identity as part of the queer community...thinking about the BTQ part of the spectrum, not just the LG. I've got years of unlearning about the trans community to do.' Another respondent explained that he's 'very aware of being a black man' (not a 'black person', notice), and that being a man who's black is 'seen as more threatening' and carries 'a whole load of stereotypical expectations and assumptions that are different from the stereotypes and assumptions about black women.' A third man, who'd recently become a father, talked about how in the parenting classes and midwife appointments they'd been together, the assumption that 'parent' tended to mean 'mother' was entirely understandable, but did often feel rather alienating: 'It makes you feel like, even though everyone's saying it's good that you're involved, going along with your partner and all that, as a man you just don't quite belong there, like you're not as important as a parent.' Now, my sample was small, so I'm not claiming this correlation would necessarily be replicated more broadly across a bigger, statistically significant sample, but it was fascinating that it was those who'd been marginalised or even ostracised because they didn't conform to the white, heteronormative, man-as-provider version of what 'being a man' means who had thought more actively about their own masculinity. Their maleness wasn't invisible to them, as it had been problematic in some way.

However, for those who *weren't* in one of those rare contexts, like parenting, where the default was female, or who *hadn't* been told that they somehow failed to be like default-male was 'supposed to be', they simply didn't seem to have the language to talk easily about their own man-ness. As renowned psychologist Esther Perel puts it 'We've spent the last 50 years discussing what it means to be a woman. Women have examined their relationships, their identity, their sense of agency, at home and at work. And now, maybe for the first time, we're at a moment where men could have the same opportunity to redefine themselves - but I worry that we aren't giving men, or women, the resources they need to get there.'[19]

The next questions I asked men, to help understand at the most basic level what it feels like to be a man, was:

Have you ever wondered what it would be like to be a woman?

The answer to the former was generally another 'no, I don't think so' or 'not as far as I remember.' Again, I was often met with the slightly baffled face. 'I've wondered what sex feels like if you're a woman,' said one, but his wondering about what life feels like for a woman hadn't really gone beyond that. One pondered for a while, then offered up 'I wish I was a woman sometimes, on a plane, when my legs are crushed up against the seat in front and the shorter women are stretching out in their seats.' But whereas most of the women I've asked tell me they've frequently wondered, with some envy, what it would feel like to walk through this world as a man, it seems that the reverse is not something the men in my sample had really spent any time pondering.

This was a big realisation for me, the fact that creating space for men to simply stop and wonder what life feels like when you're a woman seemed like a valuable and positive experience for both of us. One young man articulated in a sudden moment of realisation: 'I've never faced any issues, so I don't really think about it. I've never questioned being a man.' He found this thought fascinating, and went on to say 'I'm happy as I am, and if you're content, you don't wish you could be something else.' So of course, he says, he's never really wondered what it would be like not being a man, let alone ever wishing he could trade places with women.

And have you ever thought life would be easier if you were a woman?

This question seemed to unlock something powerful too, as it sparked a series of outpourings from many, especially the slightly older men, who have lived and worked for years alongside women that they respect and admire. They were really quite definitive, and emotional, about how much they *wouldn't* like to have to live life as a woman. These were things I'd never really heard the men I know say, before this conversation.

'I'd hate to be a woman. I'm not strong enough for it. All the stuff you have to deal with, even just your bodies, with periods and childbirth. It's incredible. I don't know how you cope with all of that!'

One told me he's always thought that 'being a woman must be an unbelievably beautiful thing', especially when it comes to bearing a child, 'that miraculous thing that men can't do.' Then he goes on to say that he feels lucky to be a man, as 'women have a really hard time, they have so many more battles to fight.'

Many spontaneously talked about how 'if I was a woman, I'd find the constant scrutiny and judgement hard. You need to try and please such a broad portfolio of men. Some'll think you're too sexy with a button undone, others too frumpy; some think you're being too confident and overbearing, others too passive or gentle.'

And even though some acknowledged that there's always been pressure on men to behave in particular ways, and that there's now increasing pressure on men to look a particular way too, the feeling from all the men I talked to was pretty unequivocal: 'It must be so hard as a woman, having to constantly walk the line, and be judged for being too this or too that.'

One man, interestingly, said he thought that things may be even harder for women now than they were historically: 'In previous generations, gender roles were simpler. It wasn't all good, obviously! But at least it felt like traditional women's roles were respected back then. Now it feels like there's little respect for women's roles in the home, and they have a tougher time at work too.'

The added burden of parenthood, in terms of the juggling act women face and the tightrope they have to walk, came up often: 'Being a dad has made it really clear to me how hard it is for women to balance work and motherhood. I'd never really realised that before. I'm lucky I don't have to face that as a parent, and I really wouldn't want that for myself.'

What most fascinated me here is that, when I've had conversations with these men (and others like them) about anything relating to gender equality in the past, they'd never articulated these things before. And yet, simply by asking them these questions, we outed an almost unequivocal admission of 'I've never once thought I'd like to trade places with women.' And *that* then enabled the men to articulate how they perceive their life as a man as being a more advantageous one, without feeling like they were being accused or under attack. It also enabled them to think about it in a very personal way, as the aspects of life that they recognised as being harder for women were the ones that they had a particular connection with. Most of all, I was struck by the respect and even awe that they expressed for women who led these lives and dealt with these issues that they didn't have to experience.

Quite a few of my respondents recognised, as we chatted, that as well as having the advantage of just being male, they'd personally been dealt a good hand too, in terms of specific qualities of masculinity, which included being 'tall', (it seems this world that's built for men is even easier to navigate when you're a tall man); 'charming'; (a couple admitted this was a quality they'd been told they had, and that helped them in life hugely); 'fast', 'funny', 'good at football and 'clever.' The way they talked about these things was quite unexpected too, because they absolutely weren't showing off - not even in a jokey way. They mentioned these things in a tone that was really humble and even, if anything, a little apologetic, like they realised they were playing the game on a playing field that was not even close to being level. Voicing a recognition of those advantages was not something I'd heard the men I knew do in our many conversations outside of these specific interviews either, and it gave some interesting clues as to how they saw masculine advantage working.

There was one area, though, where many of the men I talked to said they *were* often aware of their advantage as men, and where they admitted they had often thought how they'd hate to be a woman: the issue of personal safety.

'When you hear warnings that there's a creepy man around, I'm really glad I'm not a woman. I just walk home and never think about it. And that's just horrible.'

'If I were a woman, I'd hate the idea of not being safe and needing to be taken care of, whether it's by a bloke or walking home together with a group of girls.'

'I'm really aware of my privilege as a man walking home at night when that's not something my female friends feel safe doing.'

And a couple expressed discomfort at the way some men exploit this to adopt some kind of 'virtue-signalling, hero-complex' behaviour. 'You know, the "Don't worry, I'll walk you home" thing. I'd hate that if I was a woman.'

Most, though, seemed to just feel a little guilty, frustrated and powerless about this. Other than 'walking women home', or 'making sure they got an Uber', few seemed to know of things they could do to actively help women feel safer at night, like crossing the road to give a woman space rather than walking too close behind her or towards her; taking a position on the pavement that avoids her worrying she's about to be trapped between a stranger and a wall/alley/driveway; and not initiating a conversation with a lone woman. So of course, they'd never thought about nudging other men who are doing these things (inadvertently or deliberately) in the right direction either.

When I mentioned this kind of advice that organisations were giving to men around this, which was being shared a lot in the wake of the horrific murders of Sarah Everard and Sabina Nessa, there was a recollection of it for some, and an interest in it for all. It just didn't seem to be remotely top of mind though, versus the more traditional 'heroic man as saviour/guardian' behaviours that were more prevalent, like walking a woman home or getting her a cab; and they certainly didn't think about them on a day-to-day basis when the issue of personal safety for women still often remained pretty much invisible to them. Some told me they wished they'd been better educated about it, so they'd 'think about it as automatically as women think about these issues.' Being able to do things that weren't heroic grand gestures but that would make a real difference on this important issue seemed to offer a particular kind of pride to these men, and I'd love to know if that's true more broadly too.

There was one other area where the invisibility of women and the ubiquity of our default-male world was sometimes apparent, but where responses were a bit more polarising: the issue of language. Only one of my respondents spontaneously mentioned language being default-male. He is a gay man who enjoys actively playing with assumptions and biases around gender, including using 'Girlies' as a generic term to include both men and women. 'I just love it,' he explained, 'it's got such attitude, like in the "grrrls", "sis" sense, like in the ballroom scene…but also it feels more inviting and loving. Not like "lads" which triggers me. That word makes me feel like I'm on a rugby pitch again.' For me, there's something so positive and celebratory about the way he uses the term 'girlies' and I personally love that 'you go girl' energy as well as the more gentle, loving undertones that he mentions, but I wondered how all kinds of men around him experience it. 'Some straight men get weirded out by being called "girlies" and think it's an insult!' he explains - a notion I'll explore later in *Issue 3: The Thing Is, Boys Are Just Better*. Others, he says, seem to just be a little confused, or see it as a kind of joke. They certainly all notice it though!

The other men I talked to tended, on the whole, not to notice language being gendered. When I asked them about the term 'guys', for instance, they said to a man (sic), that it was definitely, these days, a gender-neutral term. I then tried the following test that I've seen women sharing, to help work out whether that's true:

'Do you think the term "guys" refers to men or men and women?'
[when straight men say it means both]
'So how many guys have you slept with?'

Not a single man I talked to said they'd understand that sentence as meaning 'how many men or women have you slept with?' Every time, the men I talked to were caught by surprise, and admitted that maybe the term 'guys' isn't as entirely gender neutral as it appeared after all.

They often seemed to find it fascinating and enlightening to have me point out examples of gendered language that they'd never noticed. 'The world and his wife' amazed us all. Similarly a biblical commandment that we all knew of (even those who were of another faith or no faith) 'Thou shalt not covet thy neighbour's wife', suddenly made us realise that 'thou' throughout the Bible was clearly a man: 'I'd realised religion was really male-centred in that God and Jesus and the priests and whatever are all men, and the women are Madonnas and whores,' said one, 'but no, I'd not spotted that the "thou's" are assumed to just be men too.'

However, for some of my respondents, the issue of gendered language was a more uncomfortable and frustrating one. Whilst they found the above facts undeniable, they clearly felt that 'all of this policing of language' was just making life quite difficult. Some had been actively and publicly criticised for using language in ways that they'd meant to be respectful and inclusive, like calling out the fact that a senior professional is a woman - 'female doctor', 'lady barrister' and so on. In their minds, they'd simply been being accurate, drawing attention to the fact that a doctor or barrister being female was a relatively unusual thing, as there are fewer women in these positions than men. They even seemed to have been meaning it as an act of celebration. I couldn't help but notice that their body language in this moment was (unsurprisingly) quite defensive and even a bit exasperated - all very different from the way they were feeling when talking earlier in the 'would you want to trade places' conversation about how much easier it is to be a man than a woman.

The same was true when we discussed some conventions that are gendered in ways that are often largely invisible too. I asked those who were married whether they had considered taking their partner's surname; and those who weren't married whether they'd consider doing that. Interestingly, it often took a bit of perseverance before the straight men even answered this question, as typically they'd start talking about the names of the children, rather than themselves, telling me how it was good to consider using both parent's surnames. It was clear that, like the vast majority of men, none of the straight men I talked to had considered ditching their own surname and adopting that of their new spouse.[20] And when I asked how they'd feel about doing that, some of the responses were surprisingly vehement: 'No, that would just be weird!' they'd say, and then offer up 'but I don't expect the woman to take my name if she doesn't want to', as if that meant that naming conventions were now completely free and open, as they are for gay couples where gendered assumptions don't play a role. When I pushed a bit more, and asked 'but if you decided you both wanted the same surname, how would you feel about taking your wife's name?', not one of the straight men said they'd happily do that. And their reasons? 'It's just who I am, I don't want to give up my identity'; 'people would find it too much of a statement', 'it'd just get confusing' and 'it's just always been this way, so it doesn't really make any sense to change it.'

So, it seems that in some areas, these men's sense of injustice and a desire to help create change was less pronounced. In fact, for some, simply talking about these issues felt almost counter-productive at times, creating an unspoken sense of 'it's all going a bit too far' that was at odds with the tone of much of the rest of our conversations. Clearly, if we're to create change together, that's something to be avoided wherever possible.

When, though, in follow-up conversations with some of these men I shared other elements of the data that I've written about in the first section of this chapter, they were as amazed, fascinated and horrified by much of it as I was when I initially discovered it. Importantly, it also helped them to engage in the conversation in a way that didn't feel like they were being blamed.

'Bloody hell, I had no idea!' was a common response to facts about how objects in the world are created by men, for men. The Criado-Perez examples of cars, bullet-proof vests and medical trials were big favourites, as were the sporting examples that erased women. Often, these men didn't just enjoy learning these things (in a 'wow that's fascinating' way, not a 'hurrah for the patriarchy' way!); they often responded, 'now you've said that, I can see it everywhere.' Then they'd build on my examples, for instance pointing out how Christianity 'positions God the Father as the creator of man when scientifically *every* person who's *ever* lived in the history of the *world* has been created by both a man and woman (even if in a test tube), and nurtured, grown and birthed by a woman (whether through a natural or surgically-assisted birth). And our art galleries and churches just celebrate that male creator thing without questioning it.' One enjoyed telling me that 'walking a bride down the aisle and "giving her away" is a vestige from the times when the woman was literally the property of the bloke - first the father, then the husband.' And each time, the fact that all of these examples were things that were 'not our fault' because they'd been around for centuries helped my respondents engage in the conversation in a positive way: 'No, it doesn't make me feel guilty or accused. It's not *my* fault. It's the historical system that's wrong and that needs to change.'

A cynic might point out that none of the men were immediately questioning their own behaviour, or asking what *they* could do to help make change. Now, maybe that's because they were being responsible interviewees and focusing on the conversation still to come. I hope it wasn't that they felt excused for all of this, because it's systemic stuff that's not their fault, and so somehow also not their responsibility. Because while I completely agree that any of us being 'an accidental sexist' in a whole load of areas is completely understandable, as a result of all of us (men and women) having 'grown up in a world where for generations man's view is continuously written as *'the'* view', that 'does not remove accountability for its consequences.'[21] Being able to talk about gender inequality in a way that doesn't make men feel under attack is helpful, but it's not enough if it doesn't generate action.

So how can we move from recognition that the world is accidentally sexist, to a place where more men actively help us to make it not so?

WHY MEN MIGHT
WANT TO CREATE CHANGE

Here, my lovely reader, is where you come in, because what I've gathered below are a few ideas about how we all might create change *together*.

My principle is clear - we need to stop telling men what they're doing wrong, and instead, start building from and working with things men already like and do. We need to go with the flow, build on the positives, and just redirect that a bit to help solve these big problems. That's partly because so much of this stuff isn't done deliberately, by 'bad men'; it's done inadvertently by good men - and by women too. So creating a sense of blame is often quite unfair. Moreover, though, we need to build on and work with things that men already care about and want, because it's just going to be more *effective* if we do that - just like talking about smoking's impact on your skin or your sexual prowess.

So here (and for the other seven big issues I explore), I set out five thought-starters for how we might build from what I've learned about the things that already motivate men, the things they already enjoy and want to do more of. I certainly don't have all the answers, so please don't treat these five things as the simple solution to a default-male world. Instead, consider them as briefs for you to build on with your own ideas, or just areas to explore in further conversations across the gender divide.

1. Listening to men: As so much of this damaging gender inequality goes unnoticed because we're so used to it, what if we simply start by just asking men, as I did, 'what does it feel like to be a man?', and 'would you want to trade places with women?' Opening up non-judgemental conversations, and really listening to a man's perspective feels like it helps any of these conversations start in a really positive way, often with men bringing up the areas of inequality that mean most to them - which are hopefully areas they'd be more likely to want to do something about changing.

2. Facts: Lots of data has been uncovered about the many ways that women's bodies and lives are made more difficult and dangerous than they need to be. Maybe the fact that a lot of men enjoy knowing and quoting facts might be able to help us here - as evidenced by my men pointing out more examples of default-male/invisible women in action. Can we encourage this, helping men be the 'pointer-out' of these things, gamifying it or creating a thing like a swear-jar for spotting another example of something being default-male? Can we all win points with our loved ones for changing our gendered language, for example saying, 'men & women' (or even, heaven forbid, women and men) instead of 'people' more regularly, to remind us all that 'people' must start meaning more than just men? Can we celebrate and share the facts we already know, and any more that we uncover, like some kind of living museum of invisible women; and can we think of ideas for how we can use whatever power *we* have to change those things in the small bit of the world that we can control or influence?

3. Fight the old guard: It really resonated with my men that it's hundreds or thousands of years of historical tradition that's left us with our current world, that's still built largely for men. Of course, that helps take any implied blame out of the conversation, because none of us created this system. But there may be something else we can use here too. For those men that like to position themselves as iconoclasts, innovators, nonconformists, men who like to stick it to The Man, can we make the fact that we're living in a world built for the comfort and pleasure of our *grandfathers* something to kick against? Putting up with cars that kill women more than men because the car companies are too backwards-looking to make change feels like something to get a bit fighty about, if fighting the system and championing innovation is your thing.

4. Fair play: I was always really impressed when the men I talked to recognised, and felt comfortable talking about, how the odds in life are stacked in their favour in many areas that we often simply don't recognise. They were bold enough to say, 'I have this advantage that's unfair', and I think that made them look stronger, not weaker. Can we celebrate the men who do that? And can we make men who *don't* admit it look like they're a bit cowardly, or even cheats, refusing to admit that they're playing the game of life with loaded dice? Data shows that a sense of fair play is a primary differentiator for men who actively champion gender equality[22] so there must be scope to build on that.

5. Use humour to turn the tables. Every one of my conversations demonstrated what we all know - that it's easier to accept a different view of the world, deal with difficult issues and recognise things we take for granted if it's done with humour. So I'll leave the last words here to @ManWhoHasItAll, a satirist whose Instagram and Twitter feed is full of his arch observations on how the world is default-male, including gems such as: *'I'm interviewing a male investor about what it's like to be an investor at the same time as being a man. What shall I ask him?'* Maybe humour can even help us address some of those issues that felt most challenging to my respondents, like language being gendered. @ManWhoHasItAll does this brilliantly too, in my humble opinion: *'"The term spokeswoman is obviously gender-neutral and covers both men and women. The world has too many problems to be offended by nouns" says Stefan, male spokeswoman.'*

And finally…

As with every one of the issues in the chapter that follows, my biggest ask is that we all just talk about these things more, in a spirit of openness, trust and learning about each other: This is the beginning of us exploring this issue, not the end. Go forth and have conversations! And if you want to share your ideas, conversations, learnings and explorations on social media so that others can benefit too, please do that at @MenemiesNoMore.

ISSUE 2:

Aren't We
Nearly There Yet?

Why it's easy to think gender equality's all done and dusted.

==============

REALITY CHECK:
WHERE WE ARE RIGHT NOW

We've come so far, haven't we?

We've just seen that we've still got a lot of work to do to put right the centuries of default-male design in everything from products to medicine to spaces to language; but surely in terms of professional, personal, and social *relationships*, we're pretty much sorted on the gender front? If anything, hasn't the pendulum swung the other way to the point that it's tough being a straight white man these days? That's certainly how life feels for all those angry young men who are generating billions of TikTok views for Andrew Tate's videos where he openly expresses his aggressive misogyny as an antidote to a world where women are taking over; and it's what some angry older men, like their cheerleaders-in-chief Piers Morgan or Jeremy Clarkson, bemoan as they dismiss conversation about gender and racial equality as 'woke nonsense' while positioning themselves as victims of 'feminazis' who at best overlook men like them, and at worst vilify, cancel and punish them.

It seems to me that even though the way they express their anger is often completely inappropriate, those men's underlying *feelings* of

47

disempowerment are quite understandable. A lot has changed in the last generation, and men don't always feel well-equipped to deal with many of these changes, so it's no wonder that they resent them. Women *do* have more power in workplaces and relationships than at any time in history. Could these angry men even be right that the pendulum has swung *so* far that in some areas, the world really does now work in favour of women, at the expense of men? Let's turn to the data.

Leadership remains male-dominated.

Of course, gender equality has made huge strides over the years, and we're now a world away from the dark days of the late eighteenth century when women were not even recognised as legal entities. Not since the 1980's have UK banks demanded that women be accompanied by their husbands in order to open a bank account. And even though some American and British men still wrongly think that women give irrevocable sexual consent at the altar, it's actually been two decades since the UK's Sexual Offences Act 2003 clarified that rape was rape even if the perpetrator was your husband; and marital rape has been illegal in all states of the US since the 1990s. For decades now, women have been allowed to have proper careers as well as having kids, no longer being forced to leave their jobs when they married; and we increasingly see women doing all kinds of things that would have been unthinkable a generation or two ago, from flying planes and rockets, to captaining ships and leading countries. Every few weeks we seem to hear another 'the first woman to…' story being celebrated. So it's no surprise that for many middle-aged men in management, and for young men just entering the workforce, there's the distinct feeling that 'women are everywhere now', being hired and promoted over men left, right and centre.

But while momentum towards a more gender-equal world is undeniable in these areas, the numbers show that we're still a long way from equal representation yet.

While it may *feel* like women are dominating business these days, the numbers of women leading companies are still far from representative of women's prevalence in the population, and their proven intellectual, practical and leadership abilities. In 2022 the government lauded recent progress in the UK, celebrating the fact that 'nearly 40 percent of UK FTSE 100 board level positions are now held by women, compared with 12.5percent just 10 years ago.'[1] But that still means that for every 10 women on a Board, there are 15 men. I don't know about you, but it doesn't seem very 'we've gone too far' to me. And those are some of the best numbers. The same government data shows that men still outnumbered women two to one in leadership roles overall, and four to one in Executive Committee roles. But the real killer comes when we look at who's the ultimate boss of our leading companies.

Despite all the recent progress and the government's celebrations of a 'sea-change', only a tiny five percent of FTSE 350 companies here have a female CEO; and not a single one of the eight female CEOs in the FTSE 100 was a woman of colour.[2]

The picture is no more encouraging in the US. Rachel Thomas, the CEO of LeanIn.Org, who published along with McKinsey the 2022 *Women in the Workplace* report said that 'despite women being ambitious to lead, only one in four C-suite leaders is a woman, and only one in 20 is a woman of colour'[3]. Women account for only nine percent of CEOs in the Fortune 500, and we see 'the promotion of women of colour lag across the indices which include the Fortune, S&P 500 and Private companies.' She also points out that women leaders are leaving their companies at 'the highest rate we've ever seen', and the gender leadership gap starts early: just 87 women for every 100 men are promoted from entry-level positions to management, and for women of colour the number is only 82.[4]

And it's not just at the top of the big, established companies that women remain underrepresented. Female entrepreneurs face massive under-investment versus men, even though women are estimated to own 40 percent of all companies in America, with Black and Latina founders starting businesses in record numbers. In the hugely important tech market, for instance, 2021 data shows that globally, female-founded private fintech firms received just 1 percent of total fintech venture funding[5] and according to Bloomberg in 2022 the funding disparity is widening for UK female fintech founders, as start-ups founded by women made up just four percent of total investment.[6] A chronic underrepresentation of women is clear in politics too, as in 2022, only 28 out of 136 countries have female leaders. That's just 21 percent, which means that if we maintain the current rate of change, UN Women predicts it will be over 130 years before we see gender equality in this space.[7] Similarly, the World Economic Forum's *Global Gender Gap Index 2022* report tells us that based on the world's current rate of progress, we still have to wait 132 years until we reach true gender parity globally across the four key dimensions of Economic Participation & Opportunity, Educational Attainment, Health & Survival, and Political Empowerment.

Looking beyond those global averages, even in countries with the narrower gender gaps, unless we speed up the pace of change we won't reach equality in my lifetime: at the current rate it will be 59 years before we close the gender gap for North America, who place 27th in the world rankings; and it will be 60 years for Europe, where Iceland, Finland, Norway and Sweden are all in the world's the top 5, but the UK ranks 22nd globally and doesn't even make it into Europe's top ten.[8]

So while we may notice the progress, if we look at the facts and not just the feeling that 'women are taking over', we can see that gender inequality is stubbornly continuing, often unnoticed, in business, relationships and leadership in all kinds of areas.

Sexual violence and harassment continues.

Now it's true that we've come a long way since the days when women's sexual liberation was completely non-existent; and I'm beyond thankful to have been brought up in a culture that's largely free from gender-based atrocities that are still legal today in some places in the world such as the prosecution of rape *victims*, female genital mutilation or 'honour killings.' And personally, I'm immensely privileged that I journey through life in this western democracy without the sexism I suffer being exacerbated by structural and interpersonal racism, ableism, homophobia etc. But for all of us, even for privileged women like me, some alarming data demonstrates that we've not yet reached the promised land when it comes to sexual equality.

Sadly, the growth in the numbers of women in positions of authority carries with it a terrifyingly violent backlash from some extreme quarters. Studies show that women are 27 times more likely to be abused online than men for posting the exact same content, and many women in public life have received shockingly graphic rape and death threats seeking to silence her and punish her for what Mary Ann Sieghart[9] memorably describes as having the dangerous combination of 'an opinion and a vagina.' Yet despite the strongly gendered nature of these horrific threats of sexual violence, misogyny is not yet legally classified as a hate crime in the UK, even though 70 percent of the population believes that it should be one;[10] whereas in the US, hate crime *does* include gender in 35 states and at Federal level, but 'out of the 7,314 hate crime incidents recorded in 2019 across the country, only 0.9 percent were categorised as being motivated by gender bias.'[11] Meanwhile, deep fake technology and VR are also allowing the sexual harassment that's always existed online to operate in a way that feels even more devastating for victims, but is often dismissed as 'not real' and therefore nothing to worry about[12].

As I write this, adverts throughout the London Underground tell men and boys that they shouldn't be upskirting or sexually harassing women. I guess in some ways it's great that something is being done to educate here, but I find it more than a little disheartening that we still have generations of men and boys who need to be told that this is not an acceptable behaviour. Millions of men and boys remain unaware that every day, women calculate the potential danger of walking home versus getting into a taxi alone at night, avoid wearing their hair in a dangerous ponytail, carry keys to use as a defensive weapon and reassure each other when they arrive home safely.

Obviously, the vast majority of men will never be perpetrators of sexual violence so it's very much 'not all men.' But women aren't being overly-dramatic when they say they can't afford to take the risk, especially considering that 1 in 4 women in England and Wales has been raped or sexually assaulted as an adult[13] with an estimated 300 women being raped every day in England and Wales;[14] and that one woman is killed by male violence in the UK every 3 days.[15] Despite these scarily high rates of violence against women, UK charging and conviction rates are now among the lowest since records began, with only around one percent of rapes resulting in a charge, let alone a conviction; and prosecution and conviction rates for rape victims from a minority ethnic background are even lower than for white women.[16]

But trusting those who are supposed to protect us isn't easy, as numerous shocking issues of misogyny as well as racism and homophobia have been discovered in our UK Met police. Wayne Couzens, the serving police officer who abducted, raped and murdered Sarah Everard in London in 2021, had been nicknamed 'the rapist' within group chats that were long dismissed as just 'banter' by police colleagues. And he wasn't the only cause for concern: A recent investigation into abusive behaviour at London's Charing Cross police station uncovered many messages within groups of up to 17 officers which were 'highly sexualised and/or violent and discriminatory... but were claimed to be a "joke" or "game", or just a "misunderstanding."'[17] One Met officer said in 2019 about a female colleague 'She will use me as an example. Lead me on then get me locked up when I rape and beat her! Sneaky bitch', while another boasted about detaining a 15-year-old girl with what he famously described as a 'struggle snuggle',[18] and in 2022 'three Met police officers were facing criminal prosecutions: two for rape, one for unauthorised meetings with children.'[19]

Much as we might think and hope that it's gone away, sexual violence against women and girls is in no way just a thing of the past. It's a systemic problem right here and now.

Women's abilities remain underestimated and under-valued.

For centuries it was decreed that men and boys were cleverer, and that thinking was inappropriate or even dangerous for women and girls. I had assumed that those ideas would have died out amongst younger generations, but today's children *still* tend to think that boys are cleverer and more competent than girls. When researchers asked six- and seven-year-olds to imagine 'someone who's great at their job, who knows all the answers', both girls and boys are more likely to imagine a man. Similarly, boys aged six or seven are more likely than girls to be chosen for 'games only for really smart people'. And that bias continues even when people are shown proof that at every age group, where there is a gender difference in ability, it's generally girls who are the cleverer and more competent.[20]

This belief that boys are just better plays out even in areas we may think of as relatively progressive, like the world of art. The most expensive painting ever sold by a female artist, Georgia O'Keeffe, fetched an enormous $44.4m,[21] but there's a long list of male artists with at least one painting that achieved twice that value, including Mark Rothko, Thomas Eakins, Francis Bacon, Andy Warhol, Jean-Michel Basquiat, Robert Rauschenberg and Kazimir Malevich. And it's easy to find over 70 paintings that have sold for significantly more than the value of O'Keefe's, every one painted by a man - including a 1955 painting by Willem de Cooning that sold for $300m.[22] Meanwhile, down at less stratospheric price-points, there's a 10:1 disparity in the value of men's vs women's art. Helen Gorrill, the author of *Women Can't Paint*,[23] has studied the prices of 5,000 paintings that have sold all over the world, and found that for every £1 a male artist earns for his work, a woman earns a mere 10p.[24] You may well be thinking, 'but maybe that's because men are just ten times better at art than women.' Renée Adams, an Oxford Professor of Finance, explored that very question when she showed a sample of 'affluent men who visit galleries' (the classic profile of art collectors) a painting created by AI, and randomly assigned it either a male or female artist's name. If the collectors were told it was painted by a man, they said they liked it more than if they were told it was painted by a woman. As she puts it: 'The same artist, the same painting.' No wonder that in the real world, a woman's signature being ascribed to her painting actually makes it *less* valuable than if it had no signature at all.[25]

Women's voices remain marginalised.

Male characters, voices and points of view still disproportionately dominate the narratives of our everyday lives. Not surprisingly, the vast majority of children's storybooks that are already in print are male dominated, but amongst books that are newly published, we might expect a proportionate 50 percent to feature lead characters who are female. We may even suspect that things have swung even further in favour of female characters, in order to accelerate a better overall balance. But not so. Because in *new* children's books, male lead characters still outnumber female leads by around 2:1, with just 31 percent being female,[26] so it's set to be a long time before the stories on children's bookshelves properly represent the population that reads them.

Meanwhile for grown-ups, less than 20 percent of the best-selling fiction books that are written by women are read by men, whereas the readership of top male authors is much more gender balanced, at 55/45 percent male/female readership; and that's despite evidence showing that when they *do* read them, men enjoy books by women authors just as much.[27] In the media, only 19 percent of quoted experts are women,[28] and studies show that on Twitter, the accounts that men follow and retweet are 90 percent male. In real life as well as in the written word, men dominate the conversations too, with analysis of everything from business meetings to the US Supreme Court, and televised presidential debates all showing that men disproportionately talk over and interrupt women. Importantly, these things aren't just annoying; there's proof that these micro-aggressions (such as being interrupted, ignored, and underestimated) have as big a cumulative impact in the workplace as more obvious bias: 'Although its ambiguous nature may make it seem innocuous on the surface, an abundance of empirical evidence suggests subtle discrimination undermines employee and organisational functioning, perhaps even more so than its overt counterpart.'[29]

Damaging gender inequalities continue in all kinds of areas.

Back in the 1960's, when children were asked to draw a scientist, 99 percent drew a man. Now, despite all the big pushes to get more women into STEM, the number that draws a man remains surprisingly high, at 72 percent.[30] No longer do we assume that doctors will almost inevitably be men and nurses women, but still, female patients have worse outcomes than men when they're treated by male surgeons,[31] and are regularly gaslit by doctors when reporting symptoms or pain.[32] Yet again, that's even more extreme for women of colour. The tech world largely remains an inhospitable place for women. For instance, 48 percent of gamers in the US identify as female,[33] but still only 24 percent of game developers are women, as the norm of female characters being hypersexualised leaves many qualified female developers feeling that the industry is simply not a place they want to work. Inequalities remain in the domestic sphere too. As well as doing more paid work outside the home than they did in bygone times, inside their homes, women still do much more of the household's domestic labour than their male partner, including the 'disproportionate amounts of the worrying and caring that needs to be done in the domestic realm.' And not because that's somehow just the way women are, as there's 'little data to support the centuries-old idea that women are just wired in a way that makes them worry and care more.' [34]

Moreover, although this 'domestic CEO' role involves carrying most of the family's mental load, leading the household's operations, and managing everyone's health, happiness and success, this work is not generally valued by employers nor by society in the same way that those leadership skills and abilities are within the paid workplace. On the contrary, working mothers generally suffer a 'motherhood penalty' at work whereas working fathers benefit from a 'fatherhood premium',[35] and when women do try to push against prevailing stereotypes, they get punished for it. 'Sixty-three studies [show that] women who assert their ideas, make direct requests and advocate for themselves are less liked. They're also less likely to get hired - and it hasn't improved over time.'[36] Maybe the most damning evidence of the continuing gender imbalance for straight men and women in domestic and working relationships is this rather depressing summary of London School of Economics longitudinal data: 'The healthiest and happiest population subgroup are women who never married or had children... And they are more likely to live longer than their married and child-rearing peers. If you're a man, you should probably get married; if you're a woman, don't bother.'[37]

In some areas, we're now going backwards.

COVID is proven to have set back progress towards gender equality, at work and at home, with women bearing disproportionate amounts of the work such as home-schooling and losing or having to quit their jobs at a higher rate than men. But many men in straight relationships assume that domestic life is now more gender-equal than pre-COVID, simply because they are doing more domestic work than they used to do, prior to lockdowns. What they fail to realise is that their female partner is doing a much greater share of the 'more' that's fallen to the household in lockdown.

Thanks to the overturning of Roe v Wade, there's been lots of coverage in the US, UK and across the world about women now feeling like our bodies are increasingly coming under attack again, with long-established rights being rolled back, because while the emotive subject of abortion rights appears, at face value, to be about the life of the unborn child, it's actually a debate centred on the woman's body. This becomes clear when we compare it to other life-or-death situations. No one could insist they have a right to use any part of your body - blood, organs, etc - to keep someone else alive, even if giving those things did you no physical harm whatsoever; but in many places now, if another body[38] needs a woman's *uterus* to stay alive, that woman's right to bodily autonomy suddenly doesn't exist. In some places, that remains true even if it might kill the woman to use her body in this way. Just imagine if the state could decide that, if a baby needed your heart or one of your kidneys to survive, you *had* to give it to them, even if you died as a result? We simply wouldn't accept such a violation of someone's bodily autonomy; and yet, many people do accept that when it comes to women's reproductive function, where things are often seen very differently.

Importantly, that's not just because we make different rules when it comes to reproduction either, because the idea that the state might deal with unwanted pregnancies by passing laws making men have reversible vasectomies until they actively choose to become fathers would seem ridiculous, and women who've even jokingly suggested the idea have been subject to angry and often violent trolling.[39] Clearly, there's an assumed bodily autonomy around men's reproductive organs that just doesn't seem to apply to women.

Perhaps most alarming of all, because so much of the content we consume now is driven by algorithms that deliver more and more of what we've previously expressed an interest in, there's a growing subculture of angry misogyny that's increasingly being served up to men and boys. Andrew Tate is the current poster-boy for this kind of attention-grabbing, hostile sexism that positions itself as man-to-man support, and attracts millions of likes for expressing 'outrageously misogynistic views, including beliefs that ...assaulting women for cheating is OK, and [that] men should date women who are 18 or 19 rather than women in their mid-20's, because they can "make an imprint" on them.'[40] Some of Tate's more infamous quotes include: 'If a woman dates a man, she belongs to that man', 'You can't be responsible for a dog that doesn't obey you (...) or a woman that doesn't obey you,[41] 'If you put yourself in a position to be raped, you must bear some responsibility', and 'Stick to the serious definitions and stop pretending normal male behaviour is rape...If I left a million dollars outside my front door - when it got stolen, people would say "Why was it there? Irresponsible."'[42]

Despite being banned from various social platforms, Tate 'remains omnipresent on the internet, thanks to fans who continue to share his misogynistic views', and while many will dismiss his outbursts as click-bait posturing, there are without doubt dark corners of the web where incel groups fantasise about, and plan, violence against women as retribution for the way they feel men are now ignored and disempowered. In March 2022 the US Federal government investigated violence linked to misogynistic extremism, releasing a study on 'the growing terrorism threat from men who call themselves "anti-feminists" or "involuntary celibates" and draw motivation for violence from their inability to develop relationships with women.' They go on to say that 'since 2014, attacks inspired by the "incel movement" and spanning the U.S. and Canada have left dozens dead [and represent] ... a pattern of gender-based, ideology-driven attacks calling for violence against women.' 2020 alone saw an alarming number of incidents linked to incel terrorism: 'a shooting at an Arizona mall targeting couples, a machete attack at a Toronto massage parlour and a 23-year-old Virginia man who blew his hand off while tinkering with a bomb that federal authorities believe was meant to target a cheerleading performance', as well as 'a self-described "anti-feminist" lawyer and fervent "men's rights advocate"' whose killing of a District Court Judge's son was 'motivated by a belief that 'manhood is in serious jeopardy in America.'"[43]

This picture is terrifying; it certainly won't right itself; and women simply cannot solve it alone. Most men would probably agree that those with the greatest power are most able to create change, which means that 'in a male dominant culture, it is the men who need to recognize it and commit to changing it... You have over 90 percent of the leadership of the world, so *you* decide what happens and what doesn't.'[44] But although many men will hopefully now agree that things need to change, and will find much of the above just as distressing as I do, we're not yet making change that's fast enough and deep enough to reverse the backward steps, and to accelerate progress. So how might we encourage more good men to take action?

To answer that, let's put all of this information aside for a moment, and start, once more, by simply listening to and understanding what it feels like to be a man right now.

WHAT I LEARNED
ABOUT MEN

It's important to remember that I talked about none of the above with my male respondents, because I wanted to get a clean read as to what life felt like currently from their point of view, so we can build together from *their* start-point. Here's what I learned:

How close to equality do you think we are now?

When I asked this question, what I found wasn't a huge surprise: pretty much all of the men I talked to believed that, although some issues stubbornly remained, such as the 'unfair' gender pay gap[45] and the 'disgusting' risk of sexual assault, most of them thought that because we've made so much progress in recent years that we *must* be close to gender equality in most areas. In the age-old tradition of 'asking for a friend', many of my respondents who perhaps didn't want to admit it themselves told me that, 'quite a few guys I know feel like we've probably gone a bit too far in some areas' when it comes to gender equality. Only after we'd established a feeling of complete trust and an absence of judgement did some of them feel comfortable enough to admit that they themselves sometimes feel that too - although they all said they'd avoid saying that out loud in public, for fear of being accused of misogyny, and so cancelled.

Most commonly, they expressed this worry that things had 'gone too far' about the world of work. Whether they already worked in professional jobs or were still students, many of these lovely, kind men that I chatted with seemed to feel quite keenly that, 'these days, if you're white, straight, middle class and male, you know you're probably at the bottom of a recruiters wish list.' They weren't necessarily suggesting that talentless women (and others who are marginalised in different ways) were being promoted simply by showing up and not being white men. The tone of our conversations felt much more measured and considered than the ones I had a lot when I was at uni, or just graduated, where (I kid you not) mainstream men would happily 'joke' about how 'unless you're a black one-legged lesbian, you've got no chance, mate.' My straight, white, male respondents all acknowledged that, 'when you look at the grand scheme of things', their current experience was something entirely just: 'It's the scales balancing themselves, to compensate for the unfair promotion and dominance that men like us have enjoyed for centuries.' Another used an interesting analogy: 'It's like mixing colour. If you've got red, and you want to get to orange, you're gonna need to add a serious amount of yellow. If you just add the orange that you want to get to, it'll never happen.' The trouble is, this isn't just a theoretical question of fairness and balance; it's personal, because despite that sense of overall justice, if you're red but yellow seems to be in higher demand right now, it's really tough. 'You feel a bit unlucky… which is a terrible thing to say, because I'm not saying I wish we were back in the times when men dominated business. But in future, the correction will have been done, so things might be a bit more 50/50, whereas now, it does feel like people are looking to bring in more women, so if you're a man, you're at a disadvantage today.' However much the broader picture of rebalancing felt important and justified, the personal impact still hurt.

At this point in the conversation, some of the men seemed to worry that they might be sounding a bit 'hostile sexist', or like they're 'having a pity party', and so would quote me statistics and examples of recent female promotions or recruitment in their company, to try and prove their point. Interestingly, they quoted examples of how things were 'enormously skewed in favour of men in the past', and of how many women were being recruited and promoted today, but none of them spontaneously mentioned how many leadership positions or jobs were still held by men in their companies right now, even though for all but one of them, men still remained the majority.[46] That's not at all surprising, of course. We know from excellent work done in the area of Behavioural Economics that loss aversion is a hugely powerful force, with humans appearing hard-wired to fear losing something even more than we desire gaining something of the same value. Maybe that helps explain why the men I spoke with tended to measure the current gender balance at work in terms of there being fewer opportunities for men now compared to how it was for previous generations of men, whereas the many women I talk to about the same matter are more likely to contrast the number of women in jobs or leadership roles with women's prevalence in the general population. These different contextual framings create very different feelings about the same reality.

Language matters too. I witnessed some visceral discomfort, and even resentment from my respondents at the term 'privilege'. Interestingly, they were happy to apply it to powerful men in the past, but the idea that *they personally* were enjoying 'male privilege' seemed to make them feel defensive and frustrated. That's because every one of them could talk about some aspect(s) of their life where they felt anything but privileged, and they thought that the word 'privilege' implied that they'd never really had any challenges in life, it suggested 'being posh, being born with a silver spoon in your mouth' and 'never having to work hard for anything'. Even the men who, by objective standards, genuinely *were* posh didn't really want to identify as privileged, because each of them had a palpable sense of pride at overcoming some obstacles in their lives, of working hard to succeed, of making progress; and language that undermined this sense of pride - including the loaded word 'privilege' - more often than not just made the shutters come down.

Outside of the world of work, there was also a strong sense amongst the straight men I talked to that things are harder now than they used to be when it comes to relationships with women. They recognised the huge importance of 'not doing things that are out of order', and so they felt a constant need to 'be careful'. All of these men were adamant that women have the absolute right to feel secure, that they shouldn't have to deal with 'men being sleazy', men 'coming on to them all the time' and 'idiots not reading the signs.' Thankfully, none of them felt any resentment at all about this. I heard no hint of 'female empowerment has gone mad', no reactionary lamenting of the old days, when women knew their place. None of them seemed to be harking back to the good old days when men could come on to women in whatever way they liked, because women were at your beck and call. In fact, many of them specifically pointed out how they were glad for their daughters, their girlfriends and/or their girl friends that those days were long gone. However, while there was a strong sense that we're in a better place now from that point of view, they did also acknowledge that we're in a more complex place too. 'It may not have been good for women, but things were simpler in the old days', and 'there were more fixed roles, and so less difficult negotiation needed.' The current situation seems to feel like a bit of a minefield to most, because despite their best intentions, they didn't always know what was appropriate and what wasn't, so they worried about how their behaviour could be misconstrued. 'I know at the extremes, obviously. It's not about behaving like a Weinstein and not realising that's wrong. It's about the more subtle things, like is complimenting a woman on her dress or her make up OK, or will I get cancelled for that?'

As we continued talking about those kinds of 'more blurry-lines areas' of behaviour, a few of the straight men seemed to believe, at some level, that women - especially when they're dressed up a bit for a night out - must be flattered by male attention and are probably actively seeking it. Again, this was absolutely not a 'they're asking for it' endorsement of any kind of male sexual harassment. But I had a fascinating realisation that many of the men assumed that women were seeking male 'appreciation' when they were dressing to go out, and that they thought 'women do that much more these days than they ever used to.' They'd say things like, 'Look at people like the Kardashians, there are more and more women now who dress in really revealing clothes that no one would have worn in my generation, to attract likes and follows and to get talked about.' A few of the men across all ages, from students to grandfathers, also suggested that 'some women do play the system' and 'use their feminine charm to get noticed and progress.' Some also thought that 'it's not right that they should have to, but some women clearly seem to think, "if that's the system, I'll use it to my advantage." And I probably would if I was them too.' I explore this whole area in more detail in *Issue 6: 'Let's Talk About Sex'*.

Is masculinity now broader or more constrained than in the past?

In these conversations, all of the straight men I talked with articulated their current reality as a more constrained, limited one than previous generations had enjoyed. They spoke a lot about the things that men 'quite rightly aren't able to get away with doing any more', and some of the more mature men talked explicitly about some of the ways *they'd* routinely behaved in their younger days, which 'I'm really embarrassed about when I look back.' They gave me examples like, 'I remember all of us [men] would applaud an attractive woman when she came into the bar we went to for drinks after work.' Another recalled how 'we used to cat-call women on the street, on public transport, in bars, anywhere really. It felt like a bit of a laugh, and we genuinely meant it to be flattering. I now realise how that's so disrespectful. Those women must have felt really self-conscious.' Interestingly, repentant and reflective as this man was, he still didn't seem to realise (either then or now) that those women might have felt scared, angry and/or humiliated at being objectified in this way, not just self-conscious. The important big point to note, though, is that whatever specific examples they gave, each of the men focused on a range of acceptable behaviour that was (quite rightly) narrower for them than it had been for other men in the past.

The queer men I spoke with were different though. They talked about their lives having a broader range of possibilities of what 'being a man' can mean than previous generations enjoyed, and they felt this as a profound personal benefit. One talked eloquently about how, despite identifying as male, he just doesn't 'see myself as a "man" in that "be a man, man up" kind of sense.' After we'd talked for a while about what he considered 'being a man' meant, he did go on to say, 'if that's what we mean, then yes, I am a man, but just in a broader view of what 'being a man' means.'

When I prompted the straight men to think about all the ways that they felt masculinity might be getting either broader or narrower these days, they too all told me that there's 'more freedom and breadth of expression and experience' nowadays, but then always added that this was 'for trans and non-binary folks' or 'for the LGBT community.' These broader possibilities of what being a man can mean seemed to be for others, not for them. But this changed a bit as our conversations progressed, and the younger men did acknowledge that men like Harry Styles were pushing the boundaries of what masculinity means for straight men too: 'It's probably easier, now, to wear nail polish, and make-up, and feminine clothes, and still be attractive to women these days.' Generally, though, they didn't seem to think this was so attractive or so free from stigma that they themselves felt like giving it a go.

Similarly, straight men of all ages went on to mention historical examples of men expressing themselves in ways they interpreted as more typically feminine, including how 'hundreds of years ago, men were the biggest peacocks, wearing frills and colour and feathers and as much extravagant bling as the ladies.' A couple of the men in their 50s and 60s didn't have to plunder such historical depths to find examples of outwardly straight men who were 'famously sexy as far as the ladies were concerned, but who dressed in ways that would be deemed too feminine now, like Marc Bolan and Mick Jagger.' They went on to explain that men like these 'wore incredibly girly clothes and make-up, and even moved and spoke in quite an effeminate way but we all loved them and wanted to be like them.' Others mentioned 'Steve Strange and the whole New Romantic era', pointing out that 'whereas Boy George created that massive "who is that, are they a man or a woman?" thing on *Top of the Pops*,[47] the Duran Duran and Spandau lads dressed in a really feminine way, but we never questioned their sexuality or gender. They were straight men, in frilly shirts, make-up and big bouffant hair, who were dating supermodels and actresses, and were massive sex symbols for all the girls at school. If we see men dressing like that now we'd assume they were probably gay or trans.' In each of these cases, they did acknowledge that 'even then, rules for pop stars were a bit different from your average bloke' and 'your average small-town lad had to be pretty brave nipping down the local high street dressed like that.' But they also said that these men from the 70s and 80s were 'way more out-there than most straight men would get away with wearing today.'

Most importantly of all, as the straight men started to talk about how this area of masculinity is more constricted for them than it used to be for men in the past, a fascinating point emerged: unlike their fear of being cancelled for not treading the right line in their relationships with women, this specific narrowing of what's an acceptable way of 'being a man' wasn't driven by what women might think or do. When it came to fashion and self-expression, they were primarily worried about the judgement of other men. Here, the sense of 'what you can get away with doing as a man these days' was much narrower than it used to be simply because of what other *men* might think, how your mates would judge your expression of adequate masculinity: 'Women might like a bloke in frills, but imagine wearing that around your mates when you're watching the footie! I don't think so!' This is an area I explore in more detail in *Issue 4: 'It's dog eat dog, and I'm nobody's bitch.'*

The other big area that we ended up exploring in many of these conversations about what's deemed acceptable masculine behaviour these days was around 'being more comfortable showing love, empathy, vulnerability… those more feminine emotions.' The younger men tended to articulate this through the lens of mental health: 'A better thing about masculinity these days is, it's easier to admit when you're not OK. People won't immediately think you've failed at being a man if you admit you have vulnerabilities, worries, like they did in previous generations. We're not always brilliant at talking about emotions, but at least we don't laugh at other guys for feeling them… Well, we might laugh a *bit*, but laughing about difficult stuff makes it easier for us to open up sometimes.' A couple of the more mature men who'd experienced, and sought help for specific mental health difficulties articulated it in this way too, with one reflecting on the differences between his father's view of mental wellbeing, his own and what his son's might be as he grows up: 'My generation feels like it's in a transition point, stuck between the residual World War II values and attitudes of our parents, with the stiff upper lip, "know your place", don't show weakness etc; and the next generation's, who'll be all about expressing yourself, being who you are, talking openly about mental health, relationships and whatever. They'll hopefully feel a lot less isolation and loneliness than my generation, and less shame or confusion too.' All of the men who were parents or grandparents recognised and welcomed this broadening of what constitutes acceptable masculine behaviour now too, although they tended to articulate it in terms of what it means to be a dad. All agreed that 'it's a positive thing that dads these days are expected to be a bigger part of their children's lives now.' A couple of them expressed some regret about how, compared with the way many dads are now, they themselves had not been very involved in the caring duties when their kids were babies, and one man who's now a grandparent talked with beautiful, heartfelt power about 'the utter joy' of being able to take an active role in caring for his grandchildren: 'It's the best thing ever. It's magical. Just you wait.'

In these conversations about how far we've got with gender equality, we touched on one final point that was a difficult one for them to articulate, but quite a clear feeling: Even though the risks they felt of being cancelled if they put a foot wrong were very strong, and the threat to their career from gender equality were very real, they also thought, 'hasn't gender equality just fallen down the list of things to care about and work on these days?' Their overriding sense that lots of progress has been made for women, and for the LGBTQ community, combined with lots of other problems that seemed more visible in the news and on men's social feeds, all added up to leave them feeling that 'women's issues (Roe vs Wade aside) just don't really feel like that big of a deal right now.' One articulated it in very binary terms, saying, 'after Black Lives Matter, shouldn't we be focusing on fixing systemic racism instead?' Others reflected a similar idea that there can only be one big issue that we should all focus on, asking 'what about the fact that we're busy destroying the planet?' or 'there's the widening gap between rich and poor, COVID, the war in Ukraine and economic difficulties plunging millions of people into real poverty while the most privileged get even richer. I'd rather focus on that.' Interestingly, evidence suggests that cultures where more women hold positions of power tend to do more work around diversity and inclusion than more male-dominated teams, so a rising tide of gender equality should help raise all boats. But setting that aside, I believe it's incredibly important that we avoid pitting different forms of systemic inequality against each other, and instead ensure that we always apply an intersectional lens to each of them, gender included.[48] Out of the long list of issues to fix in society, some people will have a different start-point, and that's healthy and helpful as long as whatever the primary lens, we always look at how different marginalised groups intersect with that too. It's not either/or, we don't need to choose between fixing different kinds of oppression as if we must concentrate on one at the expense of others.

So how *can* we ensure that gender inequality remains high on men's list of things to fix, whether it's as an intersectional angle on another issue, or as the main focus? How do we ensure it isn't simply treated as a done deal, dismissed as a marginal issue, or thought of as something that's a danger, but ultimately an issue that's 'not for me'?

WHY MEN MIGHT
WANT TO CREATE CHANGE

To make progress, we need everyone to understand and believe the scale of the problem; and it seems in theory like the data that's set out in the *Reality Check* section of this chapter should help with that - but it only will if we use it in the right way. If we start with those facts, trying to convince men that they've got it all wrong and that we need to go further and faster, there's a real danger that it will simply be dismissed or ignored; partly because none of us likes to change our deeply-held beliefs; and also because, in the context of our current gender wars, these facts could easily feel like an attack on men. We should use the facts to help us understand where the problems are, not to try and just persuade men that they should feel differently about everything. To make change, we need to start with what we've learned about how men see the world, about what motivates them in this area, and then use *that* to identify ways that men might want to solve any of these problems with us. So here, like with each of the eight issues I cover, are five more ideas that any of us might want to explore further together. They're briefs to build on, thought-starters for further conversations, so please do share anything you learn about what works for you at @MenemiesNoMore.

1. Use 'whataboutery' for good. Men notice the progress we've made in gender equality at work and in leadership much more than they notice the problems that remain, so it's not at all surprising that they think the job's done. But many men do like to be that guy who knows better, who puts other people right, who adds a different perspective. So, could we encourage men to use this desire to add a 'yes but what about...?' to the conversation when it comes to gender, but in a way that helps us make progress? So when someone's talking about how ground-breaking it is to have reached 40 percent women on a leadership team, can we celebrate the man who says 'yes but we're still not at 50 percent' or 'yes but what about women of colour?' When a group of guys has a bit of a moan about all the things men aren't allowed to do or say any more, can we laud the smart man who says 'but what about the things men in earlier generations weren't able to do that we now can? 'And when a man suggests that walking a girl home is the heroic answer to women's safety on the streets, can we salute the guy who adds 'but what about educating boys about what we can all do to help women feel safer?'

2. Make confusion a badge of pride: When it comes to relationships with women, men are acutely aware that they have to 'be really careful these days', but often they don't know exactly how to avoid a damaging mis-step, and that can make them feel resentful at being put in this position. Even younger men compare this situation to how things were in the past, and envy those 'simpler times.' But instead of envying that 'simple' past, can we help men feel good about distancing themselves from it, because they're smart enough to realise that in some ways, it wasn't actually as great as it looks? Back then, women needed men for social and economic security, whereas now, it's harder to know what a woman might want from you because it is a want, and not a need. Can we encourage men to feel proud to be feeling a bit of confusion, as it's a sign that you're not going through life assuming some kind of masculine entitlement that makes you blind to what women really think. If you're feeling a bit confused, that's because you're thinking about it, and that should be something to be really proud of.[49]

3. Femme straight men are sexy: One area of the past that men recognise has been lost is the ability to express a broader spectrum of what masculinity looks like without being ostracised or judged for it. Cis, straight men might think traditionally feminine expressions and qualities are OK for queer men now, but still reject this broader version of masculinity for themselves. But they want to be attractive to women, so can we remind them that many straight women find these more expansive versions of masculinity sexy, and use that as a defence against the policing of other men - if the ladies find this stuff attractive, surely straight men should embrace it? Witness Harry Styles, from his pearls to his defending of girls' opinions; Trevor Noah using empathy-fuelled humour against white male dinosaurs; Dwayne Johnson showing how you can be a rock physically but be soft as hell; Keanu Reeves' thoughtfulness and respect for women making him even more attractive than his beautiful face. If a straight man wants to be more attractive to women, it's clever to use those kinds of men as role models, and to care more about what the women you want to attract think than what other men might think.

4. The competition is other men, not women: Inevitably, we'll continue to see more and more women moving into leadership, in business and in society more broadly, which makes many men feel like they're in competition with those women, and that being a man is actually a disadvantage now. But this is something we can reframe, because no-one is looking for a women-only world, where every job and position of responsibility is taken by a woman. There will be plenty of room for men too, albeit just not as many as there are right now. So ambitious men don't need to feel they're competing against the women; they just need to be better than the other men. I'm reminded of a joke my dad used to tell, where a lion has escaped, and two men have to run from it. One man stops to put his running shoes on, and the other asks, 'why are you doing that? You'll never out-run a lion?' The first man answers, 'I don't need to out-run the lion. I just need to out-run you.' If gender equality feels like a lion's on the loose, becoming the man who actively works to create gender equality can be your running shoes.

5. Empathise about walking the line: The feeling of not knowing what women want and how you're supposed to behave is unsettling for men; as is the belief that being a straight, white man now puts *you* at a disadvantage. Of course, that can feel unfair, particularly when you have areas of your lived experience that have been a real struggle, so for many men, this can create anger and resentment, and make them see women as the enemy, even if they don't want to say that too openly for fear of sounding a bit 'Andrew Tate'. But men and women have lots in common here, as we no doubt all feel we've experienced some personal injustices in life, as well as knowing we ought to acknowledge our own privileges in specific areas; and we all have some ways in which we feel powerful, and others in which we are really vulnerable. Could we make these feelings something that connects men and women, rather than being what sets us against each other? Can we encourage a bit more empathising with each other's feelings, including in areas where men feel overlooked and undervalued, such as caring and parenting, or talking openly about mental health, or feeling free to adopt more typically feminine forms of expression. Helping men in areas where *they're* the ones who are marginalised was a strategy that RBG famously used to accelerate gender equality, and we all benefit from that still[50], so I for one am happy to take a leaf out of her book.

Taking a more empathetic approach, and working together for the benefit of all, is much easier to do if we start from an issue where you already have a strong personal interest, or where you might already see some problems. So, now that we've established the big picture, let's move on to some specific ways in which gender inequality manifests. Feel free to read the chapters that follow in any order, if some feel more pertinent to you than others. Because working from what interests *you* most is the best way to create change. And there's still a lot that needs changing…

ISSUE 3:

The Thing Is,
Boys Are Just Better

Addressing the masculine superiority myth.

===============

REALITY CHECK:
WHERE WE ARE RIGHT NOW

We've grown up being told that girls are simply second-rate.

In my first chapter, I talked about the guy in our local hardware store who commiserated dolefully when, after each pregnancy full of hope and expectation (on his part, at least) I broke the news that I'd 'only' produced a girl. The shame! What a disappointment I was. But however much his response incensed me, I knew that he hadn't intended his comments to be such a slur. He was blissfully unaware that what he'd said was an enormous insult both to me and my baby girls. I also know that, even today, two decades later, he's far from alone in feeling that way, even if more people might think twice before saying it so boldly these days. I'd grown up with that feeling all around me though; so much so, that I'd completely internalised it, believing that boys were so far superior to girls that I'd spent years trying to behave more like one. As Lily Singh puts it, 'from the moment I came into the world I was already a disappointment to so many people,' and it's therefore 'a lifetime mission to try and prove to *myself* that I am enough.'[1] I knew that all the dads on the Dagenham council estate where I grew up really wanted at least one boy. That wasn't just so they had 'someone to have a kick-about with'; it was because, at some primal level, their job as a father didn't seem quite complete until they'd had a son and heir.

Henry VIII has a lot to answer for in that department. I remember lots of us council-estate kids being weirdly fascinated by Henry VIII's story. Hundreds of years of English kings and the only one we knew anything much about was the guy with eight wives and a habit of beheading as often as divorcing the ones who troubled him. I was especially intrigued by the audacious Anne Boleyn, fascinated that the girl she bore had a star power that echoes down the ages, eclipsing most subsequent kings. But it wasn't lost on me that Anne Boleyn was executed for her failure to produce a male heir, and it all felt like some kind of lesson in what happens when women get ideas above their station. Even today, with exceptions like the musical *Six*, I still hear more talk about how ruthlessly this king disposed of his many wives, than how fundamentally ridiculous it was in the first place that the church and state endorsed the overriding need for a boy child. And despite a 2013 change in the laws of primogeniture that made Charlotte our first princess to maintain her place in the royal line of succession despite the birth of a younger brother, in other British aristocratic families, the title, power, property and a seat in the House of Lords are still passed down the male line.

But this male superiority narrative doesn't just exist in the past and in our out-of-touch British aristocracy. Nor is it something only men believe. The sense that men and boys are naturally superior to women and girls remains all around us, driving all of our behaviour in ways we may not even be aware of. Like the default-male bias about the way our world is designed, this belief in some inherent male superiority has grown up over thousands of years, and it remains so deep-rooted that often we don't even notice or question it. But again, once you start to notice it, you see it everywhere - an assumption that men are superior in all the areas that really matter, alongside a parallel devaluing of things that women are generally deemed to be better at than men. Think I'm being silly? That in itself is some kind of proof... but if you need more hard evidence, here it is.

We mistakenly believe that men are smarter.

Although we've come a long way since the days when people believed that our delicate female brains were so ill-equipped for thinking that it was dangerous for us to even try, we still - women as well as men - often believe that men tend to know more than women, and are the better thinkers. Mary Ann Sieghart's enlightening book *The Authority Gap* contains hundreds of data points demonstrating how men are regularly accorded more authority than women because we still tend to over-value men's achievements, interests, talents and attributes versus women's, even when there's hard evidence to the contrary.

It starts alarmingly early too, as parents have a tendency to think that their sons are cleverer than their daughters. 'British parents, when asked to estimate their children's IQ, will put their son, on average, at 115... and their daughter at 107, a huge statistical difference. Why they do this is a mystery, as young girls develop faster than boys, have a bigger vocabulary, and do better at school.'[2] And it's not just an issue for us deluded Brits: 'American parents, meanwhile, are two and a half times more likely to Google "is my son gifted?" than "is my daughter gifted?", even though girls make up 11 percent more of the gifted and talented programmes in US schools.'[3] Note, too, that 'parents' means mothers as well as fathers - without even realising it, we're all complicit.

This then results in boys growing up thinking they're cleverer than girls, and girls believing they're right. We saw in *Issue 2: Aren't We Nearly There Yet?* how when children were asked to choose team-mates for a game for 'really, really smart' children, both boys and girls were more likely to select boys. And even though young girls are proven to be just as good at maths as boys, studies show that children as early as five believe boys are better. No wonder that, when researchers ask both men and women to estimate their own IQ, 'adult men will, on average, put their own IQ at 110, while women estimate themselves to be just 105. Yet we know that, except for at the far extremes of the IQ curve, women's and men's IQs are distributed identically.'[4]

In educational attainment as well as in IQ tests, studies show that boys simply aren't better than girls. A report back in 2015 by the Organisation for Economic Co-operation & Development found that, by a considerable margin, 'in all sixty-four countries studied, girls outperformed boys in reading and writing... By comparison, the gender gap in mathematics is [smaller and] shrinking; [and] in science, girls and boys perform about equally.'[5] 2021 data confirms that 'in formal learning, females outperform males at every level and every age group, from the early years through to SATs, GCSEs, A-levels, university admissions and degree classifications. It happens not only in the UK but in every developed country, with few exceptions.'[6] And it found that even at the very upper end of the distribution curve in maths 'this year was also the first in which more female students got A* grades in maths than their male counterparts, albeit marginally.'[7] Despite common myths about boys being cleverer, and girls being a distraction, the educational experience for all is improved when girls are around: 'studies estimating peer effects in classrooms suggest that while girls may well benefit from single-sex classrooms... boys benefit from being surrounded by girls.'[8]

We wrongly believe that men perform better in other ways too.

This fundamental but misguided belief that boys and men are smarter has a powerful knock-on effect, as men often mistakenly believe that they're superior to women in other ways too, and we don't listen to women who dissent from that view - because men know better, of course. So, in all kinds of areas, from leadership to driving ability to tennis skills, men have been proven to overestimate their own abilities, whereas women are more likely to either estimate theirs correctly, or to underestimate their own abilities. The results are occasionally hilarious, for instance when YouGov found that one in eight men optimistically think they can win a point off Serena Williams in a tennis match.[9] SportBible entertainingly documents the reality, whereby 'Tennis legend Serena Williams humiliated five men at the same time, as they collectively failed to score a single point against her.'[10] Yes, that's five guys on the court *at the same time*, and still they couldn't take a point off one of the world's greatest ever champions. Go figure.

Men's erroneous assumptions about their always-superior strength and resilience start surprisingly early. A study into how men and women respond to the cries of 3-month old baby boys and girls found that 'men who are told that a baby is a boy tend to perceive greater discomfort in the cry of the baby'[11] because, even though there is 'no actual difference in pitch between the voices of girls and boys before puberty,' men assume that a baby boy should have a deeper-pitched cry; so then, they think that the poor little guy must be in greater distress than the baby girls around him, otherwise he wouldn't be crying at such a high pitch. Interestingly, 'There was no equivalent finding for women.'[12] Similarly, although we're right to assume that the average adult man's body tends to be bigger and have superior muscular strength, there are many ways in which women's bodies are at least as impressively strong as men's.

Women's life expectancy is often better than men's, so for instance, out of the 43 people in the world who've made it past the age of 110 years, 42 are women.[13] A study conducted at McGill University found that women have a higher threshold for pain.[14] And according to a study published in the journal of the National Academy of Sciences, 'women are more likely to survive tougher conditions such as famines, extreme climatic changes, and disease epidemics as compared to men - and have a stronger immunity too.' They found that particularly 'when mortality was very high, women lived longer on average than men' and their data suggests this can't be attributed to environmental factors because 'under very harsh conditions, females survive better than males, even at infant ages when behavioural and social differences may be minimal or favour males.'[15]

We saw in *Issue 2: Aren't We Nearly There Yet?* how identical paintings are valued much more highly when people think they're created by men, and similar assumptions about male artistic superiority have been identified in the world of music too. Like many orchestras, the Boston Symphony had noted how it was enormously male-dominated and wanted to ensure it wasn't unfairly rejecting women at auditions. So, they set about conducting an experiment using blind auditions where 'the musicians would be playing behind a screen, in an effort to remove all chance of bias and allow for a merit-based selection only,'[16] which might, they speculated, increase the number of women in the orchestra. They were surprised when their initial audition results still skewed male, so 'then they asked the musicians to take off their shoes. The reason? The sound of the women's heels as they entered the audition unknowingly influenced the adjudicators. Once the musicians removed their shoes, almost 50 percent of the women made it past the first audition. The moral of the story? Overcoming unconscious bias isn't as easy as one might think.'[17] Especially because once we've established an unconscious bias, our minds tend to work in such a way that we convince ourselves we're right - so-called confirmation bias. And so, we keep on reinforcing the belief in male superiority, even when confronted with proof of the opposite, such as how 'research shows that houses listed by female estate agents sell for higher prices, female lawyers are less likely to behave unethically, and patients treated by female doctors are less likely to die or be readmitted to hospital.'[18]

We reinforce this myth by belittling anything 'girly'.

We don't just mythologise male superiority; we also denigrate things that women and girls are seen to excel at (such as empathy, nurturing, emotional open-ness), as well as things that women and girls are often more interested in, like dancing, fashion and beauty, or netball and gymnastics. Ask most cis, straight guys if they'd want more boys to play netball in the same way that more girls are now playing football and rugby, and you'll see it viscerally, the subliminal judgement that women can and should want to adopt men's interests and attributes; but don't expect it to work the other way round. Why should it, when the feminine is clearly so inferior? So despite the fact that empathy and inclusion are proven to be valuable leadership skills, and that research 'shows that dolls can teach empathy and prevent bias in children of all genders,'[19] a Pew survey in the USA showed that 'while 72 percent of men say girls should be encouraged to play with traditionally boys' toys, only 56 percent say the same about boys playing with girls' toys.'[20] Liz Plank marvels at how 'we're more comfortable with the image of a boy playing with a toy gun rather than a boy playing with a toy doll, because we're more comfortable seeing a boy hold something that kills rather than something that cries', and concludes that 'this uneasiness with boys playing with anything that could be attributed or associated with girls relies on a steady fundamental belief that cuts across society: that being feminine is a weakness.'[21] Global research commissioned by Lego in 2021 reinforced this, finding that 'seventy-one percent of boys surveyed feared they would be made fun of if they played with what they described as "girls' toys"', and that's a fear shared by their parents. 'Parents are more worried that their sons will be teased than their daughters for playing with toys associated with the other gender,' because 'it's also that behaviours associated with men are valued more highly in society... Until societies recognise that behaviours and activities typically associated with women are as valuable or important, parents and children will be tentative to embrace them.'[22] It feels to me that saying parents are 'tentative to embrace them' is something of an understatement when we consider how *Still Failing at Fairness* found that when middle school boys in the USA were asked what's the best thing about being a boy, their second-highest answer after sport was 'not being a girl'.[23]

This belittling and outright rejection of qualities associated with the feminine results in the very word 'girl' being used as an insult, as the Always *Like a Girl* advert back in 2014 demonstrated. In it, a young girl explains that when people say you're doing something 'like a girl', it 'sounds like you're trying to humiliate someone'.[24] She looks bemused, as if that doesn't seem to make any sense to her, largely because she's still too young to have completely internalised the myth of feminine inferiority. But Laura Bates, founder of the *Everyday Sexism Project* catalogues those messages that are still all around us: 'It feels a bit like a punch in the stomach every time I read an *Everyday Sexism* entry about girls being told, unequivocally, at such a young age that they are somehow by definition inferior to their male peers.' She explains that despite pre-pubescent girls being, if anything, bigger and stronger than boys, a boy being beaten by a girl is positioned as a humiliating failure: 'One mother tweeted to tell us: "My 11yr old just won a cross country race. As she passed the boys, a teacher shouted 'Come on, don't be beaten by a girl.'"[25] And that's no anomaly, as 'eighty-two percent of boys have heard someone tell a boy he was "acting like a girl," which they interpret to mean behaviour that is emotional, crying, sensitive, weak, feminine, and moody/dramatic.'[26] Clearly, they don't mean those things as compliments. Of course, reinforcing the masculine superiority myth by denigrating all things feminine is nothing new. In fact, it can be traced back as far as the very beginnings of the written word in western culture: 'In Euripides's tragedy Herakles (first performed in 416 BCE), the hero, even while heartbroken and facing the deaths of his children, resists shedding any tears lest he be seen as less masculine. When he is overtaken by grief, Herakles describes himself thus: "And pity me, for I am pitiful indeed as I lie sobbing and moaning like a maiden! No one living has ever seen me act like this before; for I have never groaned at my misfortunes till now, when I have proved to be a mere woman."'[27]

This ancient notion of the 'mere woman' still plays out in many areas, from art to psychology to our language, with the feminine belittled or vilified throughout history. Freud famously wrote about 'penis envy' as if the male sex organ is inherently superior; and although his theories are no longer taught with the same unquestioning awe that they were when I was an undergrad, the same implication remains commonplace today. We call bold, brave, strong behaviour 'ballsy' and tell people they need to 'grow a pair' when they need more courage. If I were feeling cruel, I *could* point out that 'ballsy' might better describe something that tends to shrink away at the first sight of trouble and is rendered powerless by one simple hit. I've heard many women joke that if awards were given out for high-functioning, can-deal-with-almost-anything body parts, surely it's women's reproductive ones that are due the accolades? Because in reality, the burden of the creation of life, that is borne by women's bodies from gestation to birth to feeding, is often brutal, bloody, painful and dangerous. (It remains particularly dangerous for women of colour, as systemic racism piles problems on top of the ones white women in our society face). Yet in western, Christian-dominated culture, we're told that all life was created by God the Father from Adam's rib, as if it wasn't countless billions of women's wombs, and either their vaginas or some major abdominal surgery that actually delivered the miracle of life. We use the phallus as a symbol of power and triumph, heroicising 'big dick energy'; and even when we call someone a 'cock' or a 'prick', these disparaging terms retain some power, whereas the go-to word for being weak and pathetic is 'pussy' (or the rather comedic 'vag'); and the c-word is not only seen as the most offensive swear word, it's also generally used to infer that someone is the lowest of the low.

We're so used to 'girl' being a proxy for 'worthless' that we rarely notice it unless it's challenged, like Harry Styles did in an interview with Rolling Stone magazine. Teen Vogue reports that 'when asked about if he ever feels pressure to prove himself to an older audience given his young, mostly female fan base, Harry said, "Who's to say that young girls who like pop music - short for popular, right? - have worse musical taste than a 30-year-old hipster guy? That's not up to you to say."'[28] But more often than not, our culture is dominated by men's rejection of things that are popular with women and girls, as Katrine Marçal catalogues in *Mother of Invention: How Good Ideas Get Ignored In An Economy Built For Men*. My personal favourite examples include how in the early days of motoring, men rejected electric cars that were popular with women, preferring the more 'manly' petrol versions with dangerous crank-handles; and men refused to embrace wheels on suitcases for years because, as their inventor says, 'there was this macho feeling. Men used to carry luggage for their wives.'[29] Marçal also observes, interestingly, that 'as we saw with the [computer] programmers and the secretaries, an industry often diminishes in status when more women enter into it.'[30] Nowadays, there's a lot of talk about encouraging more women and girls into the world of STEM, which is now male-dominated; but we see less encouragement for men to move into the traditionally 'feminine' and therefore less economically and socially valued caring professions. Importantly, all of this mythologising that men are superior, and that anything girly and feminine is worthless, has all kinds of negative ramifications, for men as well as for women.

This has damaging consequences for us all.

The false belief that boys are smarter and more competent has real-world impacts on girls from an early age, with parents treating their sons like they are simply entitled to more than their daughters. The gender pay gap starts long before entering the world of work, as a Santander study found that parents give boys 50 percent more pocket money than girls 'for carrying out household chores', and boys get a financial uplift of almost 100 percent versus girls when pocket money is 'paid for good behaviour.'[31] No wonder younger generations still rate male leaders more highly than female ones, but most troublingly, the long-standing bias against women in leadership is now increasing, according to a 2022 international study. I find it more than a little depressing that 'the study revealed younger generations have less progressive views about women in leadership roles than their parents or grandparents', and 'perceptions of female leaders declined last year for the first time since they started collecting data in 2018. Across the G7 countries, which include Canada, France, Germany, Italy, Japan, the UK and the US, fewer than half of respondents (47 percent) said they were very comfortable having a woman as the CEO of a major company in their country, down from 54 percent a year earlier. And female politicians weren't perceived as any more suitable for leadership than CEOs. Only 45 percent of those in the G7 felt very comfortable with a woman running their country, down from 52 percent in 2021. While women viewed female leaders slightly more positively than men, women still revealed substantial bias against their own sex.'[32]

Much technology that's becoming increasingly mainstream isn't helping us here either. It's not exactly new news that tech generally, and AI specifically, has a tendency to reflect and amplify both racial and gender biases; so now, with voice assistants in hundreds of millions of homes, UNESCO's Director for Gender Equality Saniye Gülser Corat warns that those biases 'reflect an attitude that almost condones a "boys will be boys" attitude and it magnifies gender stereotypes.'[33] She explains that 'the female voices and personalities projected onto AI technology reinforces the impression that women typically hold assistant jobs and that they should be docile and servile.' Importantly, these stereotypes do matter because 'they come back to affect how young girls and young women see themselves and the way they have dreams and aspirations for the future.' 'It's almost like going back to the image of women that was held in the 1950 or 1960s.'[34] Then, of course, that all plays back into the default-male thinking we explored back in *Issue 1: That 'I've Never Really Thought About It' Face.* A 2022 scientific analysis of nearly three billion web pages found that people 'tend to think about women more in gender-stereotypical terms, and they tend to think of men just in generic terms... They're thinking about men just as people who can do all kinds of different things and thinking about women really specifically as women who can only do gender-stereotypical things.'[35] So it's no wonder that the glass cliff phenomenon[36] exists, where when a female leader (be it CEO or Prime Minister) is set up to fail, her failure is seen as symptomatic of her female-ness whereas a white man's failure is assigned to his individual human qualities, not his gender; all of which, in a vicious circle, then helps reconfirm our belief that women just aren't as good at all this important stuff like thinking and leading. And so it goes on.

Our belief in the masculine superiority myth hampers women's prospects at work, no matter how unbiased and scientific employers may *think* they are. Mary Ann Sieghart recounts an experiment where scientists at top universities were sent identical applications for a lab manager job, with some applications being identified as male applicants and others female. 'The professors rated the 'male' applicant as significantly more competent and hireable than the (identical) 'female' one. They offered him a higher starting salary and more career mentoring. The stereotypes in these professors' brains were playing havoc with their rational, scientific judgement...Their unconscious bias created an authority gap where none should have existed. What is more, the female professors were just as biased as the male ones.'[37] In some areas, men have additional biases where women tend not to. For instance, a study that constructed a performance-based algorithm found that 'the algorithm rated men and women equally for similar performance, as did women' but a worrying '70 percent of men rated men more highly for achieving the same goals as women, rising to 75 percent for men in senior positions.'[38] And even though qualities traditionally seen as feminine, like collaboration, vulnerability and empathy, are now well-proven to make better leaders,[39] men still believe in their own innate superiority at work: 'A meta-analysis examining perceptions of leadership effectiveness across nearly 100 independent samples found that men perceived themselves as being significantly more effective than women did when, in fact, they were rated by others as significantly less effective.'[40] Our conviction that 'boys know best' throws additional barriers in women's career paths too, like the 'mansplaining'[41] that is an everyday reality for most professional women. Quantitative and qualitative analysis published in 2021 by Stanford University shows that 'female speakers are interrupted 12 percent more than men' and that 'roughly two-thirds of these [interruptions] are questions asked by men.'

Moreover, 'women receive more hostile or paternalistic questions than their male colleagues.' The result, researchers say, isn't just annoying. Having to deal with multiple clarification requests, especially from male colleagues, can regularly 'undermine the female speakers or belittle them from a personal and professional point of view.'[42] Data from a 2022 study bears this out, with one in three women saying they often feel undermined at work. And as 'the key word in this sentence is often', it's clear that 'this isn't a passing issue for some women, it is a major and career-defining barrier felt by almost a third of the 2,352 professional women we surveyed in the UK.'[43]

The deep-seated belief that men's *bodies* are superior to women's has some terrible real-world consequences too. Our tendency to believe that boys and men are stronger and braver means that women's pain is regularly underestimated and gaslit by the medical profession. Women are more likely to suffer from chronic pain than men,[44] yet women are also less likely to be prescribed painkillers than men;[45] more likely to be told their pain is psychosomatic;[46] and women have to wait longer in the ER to receive pain management medication.[47] As long ago as 1991, so-called 'yentl syndrome'[48] was identified, proving both in Europe and the US that 'women are only treated seriously if they are perceived to be as sick as a man, or pretend to be one', and in the NHS, women are on average diagnosed 4 years later than men.[49] As ever, this overall picture tends to be even worse for women who are marginalised in other ways too. Although data is scant, anecdotal evidence suggests that trans and nonbinary people suffer even more medical gaslighting than cis women; and we have known for far too long the utterly inexcusable fact that black women die at four times the rate of white women in childbirth.[50]

Finally, although it sounds like the masculine superiority myth is a great thing for boys, there's evidence that the way that we socialise boys to reject the feminine damages them too. Men make up the vast majority of murderers, with more than nine out of 10 killers being men.[51] In the UK, since the mid-1990s three-quarters of registered suicide deaths have been men[52], and men now account for about 80 percent of all suicides in the US.[53] Laura Bates adds to the 'long list of issues which disproportionately or exclusively impact upon men [including] different patterns of physical and mental-health problems; drug and alcohol abuse and addiction; underachievement in education; homelessness; criminal offending and the workings of the judicial and penal systems.'[54] No wonder the American Psychological Association issued guidelines in 2018, warning about the dangers of what it called a 'traditional masculinity ideology' that pressures boys and men to conform to 'a particular constellation of standards that have held sway over large segments of the population, including: anti-femininity, achievement, eschewal of the appearance of weakness, and adventure, risk, and violence.'[55]

It's crucial that we understand all of this data, so we're clear about what problems we're trying to solve. But the anti-smoking ad I mentioned near the start of this book teaches us that even people knowing something's going to kill them doesn't necessarily motivate them to change; so it'd be naive beyond belief to think that telling a man 'I have empirical proof that you're not as good as you think you are' is ever going to land well. Men will reject that. And why wouldn't they - the human brain is designed to reinforce what we already believe, and doesn't accept such wholesale change readily. It's taken me years of researching and discussing all of this to start to overcome the biases and assumptions that I myself have in this area, and I've had the advantage of fifty years of secretly believing that maybe I'm a bit smarter, stronger and more capable than all the people who patronised or belittled me gave me credit for. We can't expect boys and men who have, all their life, been told that they're naturally superior in all kinds of ways to suddenly believe that it's actually just a myth, a falsehood. Especially when they're being told by a woman What do we know? And we would say that, wouldn't we?

So how can we get to the point where men are ready and willing to really take on board these uncomfortable truths that I've just set out, that damage them too?

WHAT I LEARNED
ABOUT MEN

None of the men I talked to initially made any suggestion that the male superiority myth is just that - a falsehood masquerading as fact. On the contrary, there was lots of indication that they genuinely seemed to believe it, albeit with less extreme fervour than their forefathers had. They were proud to tell me, for instance, that of course not *all* women are weaker than men; that women are much cleverer than people *used to* believe; that *some* of them can do things like play football *almost* as well as men; that some even run countries and companies even better than some *incompetent* men. Step forward Megan Rapinoe, the Lionesses and Jacinda Ardern… But my respondents showed no spontaneous awareness of any of the evidence we've just explored about women's parity or superiority in various areas. When prompted, each of the men I spoke with told me they had at least one woman in their life who has occasionally countered the idea that 'boys are just better' with a stat or two that they'd read online, but while none of them wanted to look like they were rubbishing that notion, when I'd asked them to tell me what they thought of those arguments, they'd generally suggest that this figure was a bit of an outlier; or that it was complex and the data could probably be explained another way; or they'd question specific data points, often demanding to know the sources of studies to ensure they were robust.

So, I'd hear things like 'yes, but maybe the data suggesting girls do better at school is because girls tend to want to people-please or are better at sitting still. It doesn't necessarily suggest they have a higher IQ than boys;' or 'but women probably out-live men because their lives tend to have less physical challenge and hardship than men;' and even 'yeah, what is that book though? Is the author even a proper scientist?' Each time, they pointed out that although they believed women aren't *always* inferior, we were undoubtedly wrong in this specific instance. The tone and body language in their responses suggested that they believed we were simply mistaken rather than mischievous or malevolent, but - as to be expected - still wrong.

This isn't the first time I've seen this impact of the 'boys are cleverer' fallacy, and when I observe or engage in these kinds of conversations in the real world, when a woman tries to counter the first fact being refuted with some additional data and evidence, it generally doesn't help, and the game for the guys quickly becomes 'prove that I'm right and win this exciting debate.' What's more, when I've witnessed women mentioning some of the different areas where women's bodies excel, such as pain tolerance, longer life expectancy or resilience, most men don't seem to be able to avoid the allure of bringing the conversation back to pure muscular strength, and often start challenging women to see who can lift the heaviest object or open a tough lid on a jar.

But let's rewind for a moment, because as always, I didn't start my conversations with men by talking about these problems, let alone sharing this evidence of them. I started simply by getting them talking about themselves, and this took us in some directions that might prove more fruitful than just debating who's smarter or who has the strongest hand grip.

What are we teaching our kids? And does it cut both ways?

I started this part of the conversation by asking each man how he feels about people engaging in what's traditionally seen as inappropriate behaviour for someone of that gender. This proved easy for them to talk about, as each man happily regaled me with examples of how 'it's great that girls are now able to do loads of things that would have once been frowned upon or forbidden.' 'Girls have an absolute right to be educated just as much as boys. It's outrageous that there are still places in the world, like Afghanistan now, that think girls' education is wrong.' 'Of course, women should be able to have good jobs and successful careers, just as men always have. Not every woman is happy staying home and looking after the kids, so anyone who wants to be a career-woman should be able to.' 'I love seeing more and more girls taking up STEM subjects, studying to be engineers and coders. They're awesome.' And 'I saw a little girl today skipping around town dressed in a spiderman costume. She looked so cool! I love how you see more and more little girls dressing up as superheroes, not just as fairies and princesses.'

So, girls behaving more like boys was all hunky dory for this lot, and they clearly felt good about themselves for that, like veritable gender equality fanboys - which is helpful to note as it shows that being a male feminist does seem to have some bragging rights. However, when I turned the tables and asked how it feels to them when they see it the other way - when men or boys display what are generally seen as 'girly' characteristics - they generally reflected what the data has already told us, that 'boys worry about being seen as girly, but people think a girl being a bit of a tomboy is cool.' They didn't immediately make the leap to realising that that's because we think of the feminine as just generally inferior, though. More often, they'd start to reflect on how this question had impacted them personally... and that generally meant another trip down memory lane to tell me, often with lots of affectionate laughter, about how they behaved as a young child: 'I had a female best friend when I was little, and we both used to mess around and dress up in girls' outfits. We never really recognised they were different, and I was never made to feel bad, my mum was never worried about it. Then I just got to an age when that was no longer appropriate, and it just... stopped.' 'When my girls were little, they had a friend whose brother used to want to play with their stuff. He'd dress up in princess and fairy costumes, and play with My Little Pony and everything. He was still a proper boy as well though, he'd just be kicking a ball around dressed in those little princess shoes with heels that don't even have a strap at the back. I don't know how he didn't break his ankle!' And 'I used to love playing with my sister's Barbies as well as my own Action Man. I wasn't aware of society's expectations, and my Mum just thought it was funny, so it was never a problem.' When I asked about how long this went on, generally the answer was something like 'I just grew out of it, I guess.'

It's straight men who do 'being better than girls' best.

It's important that the men I'm quoting here are all cis, straight guys, and for each, there seemed to be a strong undercurrent permeating the conversation about the notion of 'harmless innocence'. One, who'd talked about enjoying playing with girls' toys and dressing-up costumes, explained: 'It wasn't, like, about being gender-nonconforming or anything. I know these days people would probably be saying "oh they might be gay or non-binary" or something if a kid is dressing as a princess and playing with Barbies, but for me it wasn't that. It was just that I genuinely didn't know that boys didn't really do that.' There was a sense that once a boy is 'old enough to know better', if he *still* wants to dress in feminine clothes and play with girls' toys, it's likely that 'he's probably LGBTQ, even if he doesn't realise it yet', and while all of them stated explicitly that they were really happy that queer kids didn't now have to suffer in the closet the way they once did, again when you unpack what they're saying it's clear that they're actually just re-affirming some very narrow boundaries about what is appropriate masculine expression for 'regular' cis straight boys and men, just like in the previous chapter when we were talking about historical changes in gender expression. Their unwritten code of masculinity seems to be: very young boys are 'allowed' to break the rules and do some girly things, because they're 'innocent' and 'don't know any better'. Queer people breaking the rules is also increasingly 'accepted', they believe, because we are a 'less homophobic and more inclusive' society nowadays; but still the overwhelming feeling among the straight men, young and old, that I talked to is that straight men and boys just wouldn't (and probably shouldn't) want to emulate girls. Really importantly, even though they said it with an affectionate laugh, they often made it clear that in their opinion that's not just because society has created those conventions; it was because 'girly stuff is just a bit rubbish, isn't it? As you grow up a bit, you think, who'd wanna prance around in a tutu playing make believe when you could be racing your perfect little Ford Mustang toy car across a dirt track dressed in the new Chelsea kit?'

A few did laugh self-deprecatingly at themselves and other adult men too, when they recognised their blanket dismissal of the feminine in really obvious and, frankly, silly ways, like 'when you have to hold your wife's handbag and you hold it like it's a grenade that's gonna explode any second, just so no-one thinks you're comfortable with it;' or how 'we have to have hair and skin care stuff FOR MEN that looks like it belongs on a construction site or in a war zone to make us feel super manly while we moisturise.' Even so, they had a clear sense that men's interests, including how they approach clothes, were generally superior to women's; and they enjoyed telling me this, with lots of laughs, but in all seriousness too. 'Honestly, can anyone argue that netball is a good game? Seriously? And don't get me started on gymnastics. I know it's hard, but it's not a proper sport, is it?'

An interest in fashion and beauty was seen as archetypally feminine, and that often came in for a real kicking too: 'All that focus on hair and clothes and make up that women are taught to have, it's just a bit frivolous and distracting. Give me the Obama and Steve Jobs approach - no nonsense clothes to free your mind to focus on the more important stuff.' Each of these grown-up, cis, straight men talked about their approach to fashion as being more rational and practical than women's, more about quality and cleverly-designed functionality; and they seemed proud of this, as if it conferred greater intelligence and readiness to do 'important things.' But as Grayson Perry points out in *The Descent of Man*[56], these men were often sitting there dressed in clothes that were an homage to soldiers, or athletes, or survival experts; all camo and dark colours, with their shorts, shirts and bags laden with a million pockets and utility straps, all made from fabric and rivets capable of withstanding attack in a war zone or wilderness, and wearing trainers that deploy more technology than their bodies will ever need as they're carried by trains and cars from their soft sofas to their ergonomic desks and chairs. But just don't suggest that regular straight, cis men might indulge in the childish silliness of playing dress-up, like women do. No, men are *much* more grown up, sensible and intelligent than that.

Is there nothing about women's interests that you envy or admire?

The closest I got to any of these cis, straight men acknowledging that 'girly stuff' might have anything to recommend it was when one guy reflected on a gender-nonconforming guy he'd seen around in the neighbourhood a few times. 'He's built like a rugby player, with a hairy body and really gnarly legs, but he dresses in these little strappy tank tops and short, flippy skirts that he really kind of swishes as he walks. He looks like he loves the way it feels, and it reminded me that when I was little, I used to love running around in a Zorro cloak my granny made for me. I'd leap off walls and swish it dramatically - that felt so cool, I was invincible in that thing!' This was something that the gay and non-binary men I talked to often mentioned, and what I found most interesting was not so much that they (like the straight guys) had loved playing with girls' toys, and dressing up in feminine outfits as a child; what I found really fascinating was how it made - and still makes - them *feel*. A young gay man summed it up beautifully as he showed me a new, elegant leather tote bag he was carrying that was 'a *women's* handbag, according to the shop, but fuck that! I'm a proud gay man carrying it, and it gives me such power! A real feminine energy that's just, like, so beautifully strong. I love it.' Another, who spends a lot of time in what he describes as the 'rarefied world' of the LA creative industry, tells me that within the families that populate his social circles, 'little boys are encouraged to be flamboyant, to cry, to express emotions and to just be themselves which feels really healthy' whereas 'in the real world, for most people, that behaviour would be looked on with horror.'

Things got even more interesting when the conversation moved on from feminine interests and expressions, and we began to explore qualities and characteristics that are seen as traditionally feminine. Because this was the first time that I saw the straight men really acknowledge that, despite these qualities being things in which women generally over-index, they were impressive things to which men could, and should, also aspire.

A better kind of intelligence.

I found that the most commonly and enthusiastically talked about 'feminine' quality was 'emotional intelligence'. It's telling that even the term 'emotional intelligence' was the popular way to talk about it, possibly because it chimes with these men's established idea that intelligence is already right in their wheelhouse, so adding a 'new and improved' kind of intelligence felt (ironically) rational, sensible and very different from 'being in touch with your emotions', which sounded a bit - you guessed it - girly. Fascinatingly, each of them talked about how they felt that they themselves had more empathy, emotional open-ness and a better emotional radar than your average man, even if women generally tended to be better at this stuff.[57] I can't know, of course, whether the majority of mainstream men who aren't actively misogynist would consider themselves above average in this regard too, or if it's just that my sample skewed in this direction; but in any case, I sensed a strong degree of pride as they gave me anecdotal examples of their excellence in this area compared to the average man, many of which were actually very moving. One such moment came when a very successful man in his 50's talked about how, even though his isn't an enormously demonstrative 'lovey' family and he doesn't 'throw the world "love" around like some people do,' he'd told a male friend recently that he loved him, because 'he's having a tough time and he really needed it.' He also talked with both great pride and real sensitivity about how being able to read people's emotions and show empathy had been a hugely valuable asset throughout his career.

Generally, the examples these men gave of their own emotional openness and empathy were things that occurred when they were helping others, rather than being helped themselves. Sport and war operated as huge role models here, with many admitting to shedding a tear (or at the very least, getting a lump in their throat) when watching war veterans talking about giving emotional support to their brothers in arms; and when they'd see great sportsmen showing emotional support to each other - from Federer and Nadal, to the England team after yet another disastrous penalty shoot-out, to the captain of the team they follow consoling his devastated young team-mates after a particularly painful loss. Some academics suggest that this kind of emotional openness in men is still too limited as it's only really deemed appropriate because the man is in the position of power (the one doing the comforting, so not the really vulnerable one) and/or because displaying excellence in a super-masculine endeavour like sport or combat 'earns him the right' to express a vulnerability and emotional openness that would otherwise be vilified as girly. However, while I understand that argument, after witnessing the genuine empathy and openness that my respondents displayed in these kinds of situations, I'd definitely take this as a win in this area, rather than making men feel that even this isn't enough. I honestly believe that the world would be a better place if every man, for instance, listened to Arsenal legend Ian Wright expressing true emotional vulnerability on Desert Island Discs[58] and got a bit tearful along with him. One step at a time - we don't need to tell men they're failing if they're not yet ready to be the one who's expressing the vulnerability so openly.

Beyond men using their 'emotional intelligence' to support a more vulnerable man, or empathising with hyper-masculine heroes in moments of their vulnerability, there was one other kind of role-model that my respondents talked about a lot: family or loved ones. Here, only a couple of men said they were lucky enough to have fathers or father-figures who displayed really great EQ, who were full of an empathy and emotional openness that they now emulate. More often than not, the men told me that they had actively chosen to live their lives differently from the men of the previous generation: 'In my family, we didn't really cry, cuddle, tell your kids or your parents you loved them or anything like that. But having the girls [his daughters] has made us do that all the time, and I love it now. It made me start telling my mum and dad that I love them, before it was too late. I'm really glad I did that.' Another went on to say how, unlike his own father, he was a dad who was 'huggy and proud'. However, every single one of the men talked with power and passion about a specific *woman* in their life - mother, sister, cousin, daughter, or a good friend - who was a really positive role model when they were growing up or when they became a parent, and from whom they were proud to learn. There was a really strong sense that 'I was really lucky to have a woman like that' as a loved one; someone who showed them the value and strength of emotional intelligence and empathy; and they displayed a real pride in emulating her.

Quite a few went on to say how sad they find it when they see men who aren't able to express this sort of emotional openness. One mentioned a young man in the Netflix docu-series *Cheer* who was much talked-about amongst his mixed gender friendship group. This young man was clearly a very talented athlete/gymnast, but was struggling because he 'had *so* internalised the idea of "never showing any emotion that might be perceived as girly" that he literally couldn't smile while performing'. The man who brought this up talked about it in a really touching way, simply saying it made him 'feel really sad, if that's what we're doing to young men.' Importantly, these men often made it clear that there are many places where they wouldn't necessarily say any of these things out loud, because other men might judge them for it. We'll explore that further in the next chapter, *Issue 4: It's Dog Eat Dog, And I'm Nobody's Bitch*.

'Femininity' flips from a weakness to a superpower for some.

I can't end this section without acknowledging that for a few of my respondents, the masculine superiority myth and its vilification of anything 'girly' had inflicted real trauma and difficulty in their past. Thankfully, each of them told me that they'd managed to overcome it, but not without work and not without pain. They also recognised that not everyone in their position had as happy an outcome, and expressed a heartfelt wish that youngsters in future won't have to face the same degree of struggle that they did in this area.

The men whose sexuality or gender identity wasn't what society told them it was 'supposed to be' had much to say on this. Their childhood stories were heart-breaking, such as one man talking about 'little me, standing in front of the mirror wanting to be "a man" but knowing I would never be, not like they meant. I knew that being girly or feminine was seen as weak and wanting to be like that was just wrong, and I hated myself for it at the time and tried so hard to be "better."' But now, thankfully, it's very different, as he talks about being 'proud to be the gay man that I am' and having a 'strange relationship with femininity... it's like a superpower to me.' Another talked about the viciousness of the homophobic attacks (physical as well as verbal) that he was subjected to as a young man for 'challenging their ideas of what a man should be. It was like, because I thought that the feminine was appealing, and I admired anyone - including drag queens - that walked the planet like a powerful woman, I was an idiot, a freak, a traitor, and just plain wrong.' One told me that as he grew older and more confident in his own queer identity that he used it as 'a form of protest, like an attack on their dominant system', and that 'gave me strength.'

Beyond these men whose gender identity or sexual orientation had been judged by society to be feminine and wrong, a couple of men who'd struggled with their mental health had been actively vilified for that in a way that was clearly gendered. 'We never talked about feelings and emotions, and I was taught to never do that, just push it all down. Being weak and emotionally vulnerable might be OK for girls but it wasn't what boys were supposed to do.' 'I had to have therapy to address things because my family and my school [a traditional all-boys school] never asked 'are you OK?' It would have been seen as weird and weak, and I couldn't afford for the other boys to see me like that.'

These boys who didn't fit in to the dominant notion of what it means to 'be a man' and didn't display the expected markers of masculine superiority now, as men, talked openly, easily and in beautiful ways about, for instance, the power of 'feminine energy' and the way women are in many ways 'different beasts, with more nuance and complexity.' They recognised it as a complementary kind of strength, and one that all of us might well value more, in a way that it took the straight men with uncomplicated mental health histories a lot longer to get to. I genuinely hope that in future, young men and boys won't have to suffer this kind of trauma before they arrive at such an understanding; and that all of us can learn from their experiences.

WHY MEN MIGHT
WANT TO CREATE CHANGE

Depending on each man's individual areas of interest and how the masculine superiority myth manifests for him personally, some of the following ideas may work better than others. Listening, without trying to 'fix men', is always a vital first step, but in this area, it feels even more important, if we're to avoid being dismissed as silly women, as well as coming across as judgemental, critical, and as if we're belittling men. The most effective strategy will be to lean into the positives that exist already, such as encouraging men to feel pride in the valuable, supposedly-feminine qualities or interests that they already have, that are wrongly denigrated by society. Ideas 1 to 3 all adopt this strategy. Any approach that involves men having to confront hard evidence that they're not as great as they've been led to believe poses a tougher challenge, but there are a couple of thought starters that may have the potential to do that, depending on the individual man in question. These are set out in ideas 4 and 5 here.

1. Build on the 'innocence of childhood'. As these men were so often drawn to the 'girly' things they used to do as 'innocent young boys' before they 'knew better', this could be a useful place from which to build. Could we ask men about whether they once enjoyed playing things that then became 'inappropriately girly', and marvel at how society tells boys they need to stop doing that when it's clearly not harmful. Could we then encourage them to stop vilifying that in others, and even find one of two 'safe spaces' where they can engage in some of that even as grown men, from crying in front of and hugging the kids or their team-mates in tough times; to messing about, dancing a bit more, dressing in fancy dress for parties once in a while and indulging in some sweet, innocent, child-like fun.

2. Position emotional intelligence as the superior intelligence. Instead of trying to tell men they're not as clever as they think, can we reinforce how clever they are versus your average man for having a great emotional intelligence? We could give them facts that rationally support how valuable that is too. That could mean, for instance, encouraging them to celebrate their empathy or active listening skills, which are proven to make more successful leaders; or celebrating how they're strong enough to display vulnerability and emotional open-ness, reminding them that if more men were able to do that, we may not have such a male mental health crisis and shockingly high male suicide rates. It could even mean encouraging men to enjoy buying flowers for the house, knowing that they release chemicals in the brain that are proven to make you happier, which makes it all the more ridiculous that for most adult men, the first time they're likely to be bought flowers is at their own funeral. And we can lean into this rational comfort zone by using the term 'emotional intelligence', as intelligence is something they feel happy to own.

3. Position compassion as the mark of a strong leader. The other way to encourage men to enjoy being better at traditionally feminine stuff relies less on a rational argument that's framed in cleverness, and more on their personal history and ideas of leadership. These men said that they proudly emulate the strong woman in their young lives who taught them an unusual ability to empathise, nurture and be emotionally open; so can we celebrate how they follow in that woman's footsteps by helping people in their life who are feeling vulnerable, by offering this nurturing strength and powerful compassion - be it in their sport, work, or social life. That may, in time, start to create safer spaces where they can express their own vulnerability too, without seeing that as a weakness.

4. Stop the bias for the next gen: As the masculine superiority myth starts so young, maybe we can encourage men to create change amongst future generations by spreading an understanding that young girls aren't actually inferior to boys in terms of intelligence, speed, muscular strength etc; and that even as girls grow into women, they have at least equal intelligence, and different physical strengths such as immune system strength and resilience. It might also help to add some economic and social context that makes it easier to counter the compulsion to heroicise muscular strength as such a defining symbol of masculine superiority: for instance, in ancient communities that sort of strength may have made men seem superior, but mechanisation and robotics now means it's simply not such an advantage these days. By focusing on the future like this, it hopefully feels less like we're telling men that they're wrong or inferior.

5. Make it about 'facts vs myths', not about men vs women: Bearing in mind that in many areas, women believe the masculine superiority myth too, could we use our *common* biases as a start-point? It's easier to agree with 'many of us have been wrongly taught to believe x' than it is to be told 'you wrongly believe x'. This would then free us all to enjoy playing spot-the-bias, together, myth-busting, sharing surprising evidence and enjoying the powerful, enlightened feeling of 'we've all been conned for generations, but you and I now know better.' Doing this shifts the superiority opposition from 'men vs women', to 'those in the know vs those still believing the myths', which is surely a more helpful place from which to build.

Re-drawing this axis of opposition opens up even greater opportunity in another area too, because overcoming the 'boys are better than girls' belief is only the start. The masculine superiority myth is just one half of this battle for power, and the real challenge comes in addressing another battle to be top dog: boys vs other boys. That's what we'll explore in the next chapter.

ISSUE 4:

It's Dog Eat Dog,
And I'm Nobody's Bitch

How men police each other's masculinity.

===============

REALITY CHECK:
WHERE WE ARE RIGHT NOW

We're often so focused on reinforcing the men vs women narrative that we can fail to notice the real gender war that's going on right beneath our noses: men vs other men. The manosphere is busy blaming 'liberated' women for 'emasculating men'; incels feel enraged that they're less likely to get chosen as a mate or date thanks to women's increased life choices; meanwhile, misogyny and hate swirl around the internet, pubs, classrooms and workspaces (including our government and our police), as frustrated men young and old fixate on putting women 'back in their place.' Yet all the while, we may overlook how men regularly try to tear down and dominate each other; to be 'man enough'; to 'man up', to be the alpha.

As we've seen, men's rights activist Andrew Tate, the self-styled 'King of Toxic Masculinity' is famed for his misogyny, but in reality, despite positioning himself as a self-help guru for his male followers, he actually demeans them in spectacular style too in order to assert his alpha male dominance. He's told his followers, for instance: 'You are poor, you are unimportant, men do not fear you, your woman disagrees with you. Your lives are shit.' He mocks the 'brutally mundane existence' of the men who follow him, and claims 'If you have less money than me even by a single cent you're a fucking brokey, a wagey, a peon, a peasant, a nobody.'[1] It's clear that women (who are positioned as mere possessions) are not just there to bring pleasure to their male 'owner' but to signal success and superiority to other men.

Likewise, incels are full of hateful resentment at the sexually-successful 'Chads' as well as the unattainable 'Stacies'; they are 'angry at life and society for not being structured in a way where they are closer to the top of the sexual hierarchy, and have made a villain out of the archetypal man who they believe is inhabiting this rung of the social/sexual ladder.'[2] Inevitably, the Eve complex means that these men loudly lay the blame at the feet of women, often with very damaging consequences; but whether these men are fighting to maintain their position as top dog, or they're full of hurt and hate for not being so, the real fight for masculinity that's going on all around us is not really men vs women at all; it's dominant vs 'weaker' men.

Masculinity is a competition against other men

Justin Baldoni writes and speaks about this pressure that men and boys put on each other to be *Man Enough*[3] - 'brave enough', 'big enough', 'smart enough', 'successful enough'[4]…the list goes on. He shares one example from his own childhood where his friends were all jumping from a high bridge into the water beneath and, despite his fear of heights, he jumped too 'not because I was suddenly struck by a bolt of courage and inspired to face my fears… [but] because more than being scared for my physical safety, I was scared of being seen as a "pussy"'[5] We see the masculine superiority myth from the previous chapter at play in the language here, but more than that, we can also see how brutal is his overriding worry about what the *other boys* will think of him. For the young Baldoni, failing that specific 'brave enough' masculinity test would have been much more painful than any bodily injury he might suffer. And he's not unusual in this regard. A 2018 survey by Plan International found that 'Boys are challenging each other, shaming their male peers as a way to not be the target of the exact behaviour they fear if they reveal softness or sensitivity or anything resembling feminine characteristics.'[6] In the classic bullying cycle, in order to prove their own superior masculinity and hide anything that could be seen as weakness, boys and men shame each other for not being masculine enough. And so the competitive masculinity cycle continues.

Men's policing of each other's masculinity is something Grayson Perry explores in *The Descent of Man*,[7] his ability to operate both within the world of competitive masculinity and as an outlier making him brilliantly placed to notice how, in men's interactions with each other, 'the need to play out some kind of dominance does leak out. In every walk of life, men have what I call the "dogs sniffing arses conversation", a kind of conversational Top Trumps. A thirty-year-old man at a lower-middle-class wedding might ask what car their companion is driving; artists might ask, "Where are you showing at the moment?"; cyclists who meet on the road might just enquire, "Come far?" In those questions there is a challenge: how successful or rich are you? How serious are you? How fit are you?'[8] He also laughingly highlights the way men, guided by the invisible but always-present 'Department of Masculinity' tend to behave as if they're always ready for battle with an invisible foe, as if they have to show to each other that they're constantly in 'preparation for an imaginary apocalypse... It used to be elaborate swords that were never drawn, or stately homes with battlements; now it is a car that will go from 0 to 100 in 5 seconds.'[9] For men and boys, being a man feels, as Liz Plank puts it, 'less like an identity and more like a job or a reward you received only after going through excruciating circumstances... Being a man was something you earned.'[10]

This constant earning and proving of manhood manifests in the way men speak to each other which, studies show, are distinctly different to the dominant conversational model that's more often observed between women. Linguist Deborah Tannen explains how 'often women will walk away from a conversation asking "did this bring us closer or push us further apart?" whereas men are more likely to respond to the question "did this put one of us in a one-up or a one-down position?"'[11] Tannen notes that this fundamental difference - men often approaching conversations from a 'who's up, who's down?' standpoint and women being more about 'are we close or distant?' - frequently leads to miscommunications across the gender divide. But more pertinently for our focus in this chapter, it highlights how far masculinity operates as a competitive endeavour against other men, even in something as simple as everyday conversation.

This is apparent when we look at the kind of humour that is generally considered more masculine, such as banter, the king of conversational battle for dominance, that's about scoring points off each other, laughing at (as opposed to with) your opponent, however affectionately done. There have been notable exceptions to this dominant model of masculine humour, such as the multi-award-winning *Ted Lasso*, but for the average guy in the pub, humour is more often an exercise in putting other men down than lifting them up. Meanwhile, western political and judicial discourse is modelled on the masculine combative model too, a battle to defeat the opponent rather than a nuanced and productive discussion seeking out areas of mutual agreement. It seems to me that encouraging boys and men to approach conversation primarily as competition seems like a questionable strategy for happiness too as, by definition, for every winner there always has to be at least one loser.

The dangers of men's quest for dominance over other men.

In fact, socialising boys and men to battle each other for dominance in order to 'be a man' has some hugely damaging consequences not just for women but for men too. It's most alarmingly apparent when we look at violent crime data. As we'll see later in a *Issue 6: Let's Talk About Sex*, male sexual violence against women is a huge issue, and we must never underestimate or ignore that; but men's violence against other *men* is a devastating issue too. In fact, 2021 UK data showed that men were twice as likely to kill another man as they were to kill a woman.'[12] And yes, it's men who make up the overwhelming majority of the UK's homicide perpetrators: whatever the gender of the victim, where a suspect had been charged, that suspect was male for an enormous 92 percent of homicide victims.[13] In the US, just like in the UK, perpetrators of homicide are disproportionately male, and men dominate US gun crime (a crime we rarely see in the UK) as victims and as perpetrators too, with an enormous 98 percent of mass shootings in the USA committed by men.[14]

The intersectional data around male victims of male violence are shocking too, as black men make up 52 percent of all victims of gun homicide in the US, despite comprising less than 6 percent of the population[15] and men (particularly black, native American and Latino men) are much more likely to become victims of police killings than women.[16] And while access to guns means America's gun homicide rate is 25 times higher than other high-income countries, the gender proportions remain similar to other countries, as men commit about 90 percent of murders worldwide.[17] Whether these men are using weapons to aggressively dominate other men or to try to protect themselves from other men, the consequences are catastrophic and the destructive cycle of male-on-male violence continues.

The way we socialise boys and men lies at the very heart of this. A recent study at a US university found that 'peer pressure and a threat of being seen as "unmanly" ... plays a huge role in young men conforming to toxic masculine behaviour.'[18] In an experiment, 'participants were asked a series of questions associated with stereotypically gendered interests [and] were then told if their scores were higher or lower than the average person of their gender. Women did not feel threatened by being seen as unwomanly. However, when men who received a low score were told that they were less manly than an average man, they expressed more aggressive tendencies such as completing the word fragments '*ki...*' as 'kill' and 'kick', or '*g...*' as 'gun'. They were also 'more likely to choose to participate in an aggressive activity such as boxing rather than doing jigsaw puzzles after they felt their status as a man was precarious or being judged negatively.'[19] This is because 'men are socialised to respond aggressively... when their manhood is threatened, in order to regain their threatened status', which perhaps explains why violent domestic abuse incidents increased by 38 percent when England lose football matches.[20]

This social pressure is greatest amongst younger men, who feel the need to be 'more aggressive in confirming to the masculine script'[21] which could even account for the fascinating fact that 'men with baby faces are more likely to display hostile behaviour and commit crimes.'[22]

This need to prove their masculine dominance over other men also suggests why male victims of sexual violence can struggle so much. Again, it's vital to acknowledge that female victims of male sexual violence suffer in all kinds of profound and complex ways, as do non-binary people, so the following must never be seen as a competition for superior-victim status. However, dominant notions of masculinity can create particular issues for men who are unlucky enough to become victims of male sexual violence, where they feel that they've somehow failed in man's essential mission of being dominant over other men. One male victim of sexual abuse sums this up when he heartbreakingly admits that 'the hardest thing to get over was being a victim. I am a man, a strong man. Men don't get abused.'[23]

This no doubt contributes to men under-reporting sexual assault by other men, as well as explaining why so few men seek help when they have suffered sexual abuse, because they are victims of this damaging pressure to always appear 'strong and powerful - physically and mentally [and] in control - not showing any vulnerabilities.'[24] In fact, feeling like they've failed against this masculine script in all kinds of areas, including being the provider, can be a great source of shame for men; and the horrifying statistics around male suicide attests that too often, that shame can result in terrible harm to the man himself as well as to others.

The desire to dominate other men plays out in many areas.

Outside of this incredibly damaging male-on-male violence, men's competition with each other manifests in other ways too, which Liz Plank catalogues in *For The Love Of Men: From Toxic to a More Mindful Masculinity.*[25] Cornell University researchers, for instance, explored how men will engage in behaviour that permits them to 'show off that they possess extraordinary skills, advantages, and/or surplus energy in degrees that are superior to other men.' Rather comically, they discovered that this can even show up as competitive eating, as, 'when male subjects were in the presence of women, they ate 93 percent more pizza. That's almost twice as much pizza eaten to (most likely unconsciously) impress women.'[26] Women, on the other hand, 'ate no differently whether they were in the presence of men or women.'[27] I don't know about you, but I'm now seeing Joey from *Friends'* relationship with food in a whole new light.

Washington academics explored how men respond to their masculinity being threatened by telling men that they scored lower than they did when they tested their handgrip strength. Those men responded to their apparent weakness versus other men by immediately asserting superiority in other ways, including being more likely to 'report a higher amount of past romantic conquests, identify as more aggressive and athletic, as well as stay clear of typically feminine consumer products.'[28] They even claimed to be taller than they were, despite this claim being a verifiable lie. Meanwhile, Florida researchers explored how men respond to carrying out tasks that are perceived as feminine: While a control group of men braided rope, the test group were given the task of braiding someone's hair, and then afterwards, each man was given a choice of whether to hit a punching bag or make a puzzle. The results were astonishing, as not only were the men who performed the 'feminine' task of braiding hair more likely to choose punching over puzzles; they also punched the bag harder than those men who had chosen that activity after they'd been braiding rope. Most worryingly, the researchers found that even 'the most liberal, non-homophobic men in our studies were just as uncomfortable braiding hair as those who hold very traditional beliefs about gender roles.' And although again, we can detect the masculine superiority myth in their responses, (they code hair-braiding as feminine and therefore something to be vilified), the pertinent fact here is that all kinds of men, regardless of their apparent world view and social/sexual politics, unwittingly used aggression as a 'manhood-restoring tactic' when they felt that their masculinity has been threatened in front of other men. As the researchers point out, 'women are not the main punishers of gender role violations.'[29] It's other men that are the primary source of these men's worries.

We know only too well that this desire to beat other men can have all kinds of damaging consequences for men, from the obvious dangers of 'bro-culture' traditions like hazing; to men killing themselves and others as a result of feeling pressured to drive too fast; to the unwillingness of men to cry in front of each other and so missing out on the physiological and psychological benefits of a perfectly natural human behaviour. 'Crying is an important safety valve, largely because keeping difficult feelings inside - what psychologists call repressive coping - can be bad for our health. Studies have linked repressive coping with a less resilient immune system, cardiovascular disease, and hypertension, as well as with mental health conditions, including stress, anxiety, and depression.'[30] The overriding need to 'show no weakness' around other men and 'be a man's man'[31] also suggests why men's friendships are more likely to be what psychologists describe as 'shoulder to shoulder' (doing things like watching sport together that focus around mutual competition and avoid talking about how you're feeling), whereas women tend to have more 'face to face' friendships that are more explicitly about supporting each other.[32] Sadly, despite the proven health benefits of friendship, numerous studies confirm that men have fewer friends than ever; and this is 'harming their health [as] the percentage of men with at least six close friends fell by half between 1990 and 2021… [and] one in five single men say they have no close friendships.'[33]

Every competition inevitably has losers, so the great irony is that masculinity being a never-ending competition for dominance over other men means that many of them are almost-constantly left on the losing side. But it's not only men who lose out. Men competing at masculinity with each other often sees women ending up as collateral damage too.

Competing is a man's game, so women aren't invited.

We're often told that if women want to get ahead, they just need to *Lean In*[34] to this world of masculine competition and play men at their own game. But a look at the data shows that this simply isn't the case, because women who do compete in this way do so with a massive disadvantage: women are penalised if they display the competitiveness that's expected of men. In *What Works*, author and Harvard Professor Iris Bohnet recounts how when it comes to mediations and seeking promotions, men are happy to work with 'demanding men' but they don't want to work with 'demanding women' which, bearing in mind that men still hold the majority of positions of power in the world of business, puts significant barriers in the way of women who try to adopt the masculine competitive model at work. Women, incidentally, prefer not to work with demanding people regardless of their gender.[35] Women also seemed to instinctively recognise that men don't like them being 'too competitive', as in negotiations, women who had a male evaluator were less demanding than when the evaluator was female. Men behaved the same in each case.[36]

It's important to note that women's reluctance to put themselves forward is not necessarily timidity, as we're often led to believe, but is often an awareness of this backlash that plays out when women are 'too demanding' or 'too competitive.[37] If they're perceived to advocate for themselves or consider themselves superior to those around them, women are much more likely to be vilified, for what we term 'diva' behaviour.[38] This notion of being inappropriately competitive and asserting your superiority over others is so gendered that there isn't really an equivalent masculine term. There are, though, a whole range of feminine ones to choose from, with 'princess,' 'drama queen,' 'overbearing' and 'ball-breaker' being just a few. Even when women are unquestionably superior, and in a field like sport that actively demands competitiveness, women still face this backlash. Just look at how Serena Williams and Simone Biles have been viciously trolled for having the temerity to talk proudly about their own irrefutable greatness. Biles explains reactions to her 'GOAT' leotard by saying 'Everybody can call you the GOAT, but then if you acknowledge it once, they're like, "Oh my god, I hate her! She's not that awesome!" I don't think it's fair that you can stand behind the computer and talk all that smack, and I just take it as an athlete. So it was kind of just to push back.'[39] And Williams, who is subject to much angry debate around whether she deserves to be called one of the greatest of all time, explains: 'I think being a woman is just a whole new set of problems from society that you have to deal with, as well as being black, so it's a lot to deal with - and especially lately. I've been able to speak up for women's rights because I think that gets lost in colour, or gets lost in cultures. Women make up so much of this world, and, yeah, if I were a man, I would have 100 percent been considered the greatest ever a long time ago.'[40]

Faced with all of this data, there's often a binary debate about whether men should back off or women should fight harder. Some argue that women should just stop moaning and 'man up' even more, ignoring the backlash or even hatred they'll receive; others say that men need to accept women behaving more like traditionally competitive men, and stop punishing women for it just because it's seen as unfeminine. However, both of these responses assume that competing to win is the ideal model of success - but is outright competition always the best answer?

Competition isn't always a winning strategy.

Although out-and-out competitiveness may help some elite sportspeople to compete at their best, in many areas, it's simply not true that we get better results by letting the most competitive people lead the charge. In experiments where one group got paid a piece-rate for each problem they solved, and a different group used a 'tournament' style approach where each person was paid more if they performed better than others, men and women performed about equally in the piece-rate scheme, but men worked harder and did better in the tournament setting.[41] Importantly, although rewarding actively competitive behaviour works well for those competitive men, it doesn't achieve better results overall because it ends up with 'too many of the low-performing but overconfident men and too few of the high-performing but less confident women choosing to compete' which inevitably 'leads to inefficiency.'[42] Some analysts point to financial market crashes, as well as some recent damaging behaviour by politicians, as classic examples of the very real consequences that overly-competitive cultures can create, for which the majority of us often pay dearly.

Interestingly too, the dominant cultural narrative positions men as intrinsically better-suited to competition and success, because men are supposedly more balanced and dispassionate, less emotionally unstable. But that's not actually true, as former derivatives trader John Coates explains, 'when things go well, male traders seek ever more risk; when things go badly, they become overly risk averse. Women, however, seem to be largely immune to this winner's effect'.[43] The work of academic Alexandra van Geen supports this too, as she finds that 'men who have just won a lottery are more willing to take on risk than men who just lost, while winning did not matter for women.'[44] Moreover, Grayson Perry observes that 'because men on the whole are less aware of their feelings, they characterise their often angry, mocking, combative view of the world as dispassionate.' Of course it's not. And, as we've just seen, neither is this overly-competitive behaviour really effective, damaging men as well as women. As Grayson Perry points out, 'every moment of every day is emotional for everyone; we can't turn our feelings off,' and pretending to do so 'not only discriminates against others but also inhibits men themselves from having a fulfilling time on the planet.'[45]

Fortunately, it's not inevitable that it continues. It's something that can be changed, if we want to.

It's a learned behaviour, so it can be changed.

Even though testosterone does play a part in competitive behaviour, it's simply not the case that men 'can't help acting on Impulse', as the famous ad campaign once said. Recent research suggests that it's defeatist to simply sigh and say 'boys will be boys' as if there's nothing we can do to change men's hormonal, emotional responses, because 'contextual effects' (nurture rather than nature) can be more powerful than we may realise. Studies where the same competitive task was carried out by people in cultures with very different attitudes to gender bear this out. In one highly patriarchal society, where 'women are said to be less important than cattle', responses broadly mirrored US studies with men twice as likely as women to want to compete in a task that rewarded winners and gave nothing to the losers; but when the same task was given to people in 'a matrilineal society in which women are the heads of households, [the study found that] more than half of the women decided to compete, while men were about 15 percentage points less likely to enter a competition.'[46] This suggests that societal power and privilege might well affect people's appetite for competition even more than their testosterone levels. In fact, the causal link we often assume between testosterone and aggression is increasingly being called into question, with studies suggesting that higher levels of testosterone are perhaps more likely to be a *result* of aggression than the cause of it.

So, if gender expectations are driving competition and aggression in men more than their own male hormones do, that's something that's within all of our power to change. Fathers seem to have the most room to create change here, because although there is 'a tendency for both parents to encourage submissive emotions in girls,' when it comes to 'conversation with their sons, (heterosexual) fathers were more focused on achievement, using active words such as "win", "top", "proud"... Mothers, meanwhile, were seen to be more encouraging of positive emotional expressions in their children of either gender, compared to fathers.'[47] So as well as socialising men to be competitive, we encourage women to be the opposite, to accommodate others rather than compete against them. In *Hysterical: Exploding The Myth Of Gendered Emotions*, Pragya Agarwal tells us that 'A quick Twitter poll reveals that "Smile, it might never happen" or "Cheer up, darling, it can't be that bad" are commonly heard phrases by women, whether it be on streets, public transport or in a bar....A 2019 survey showed that almost 98 percent of women had been told to smile at some point in their lives by complete strangers, and for more than 15 per cent this happened regularly, almost twice a week.' By contrast, 'Men are rarely asked to smile.'[48] I know for a fact that a more gender-equal world where men aren't constantly pitted in battle against each other, and where women aren't told to be men's sweet, supportive audience would make me smile much more than unsolicited advice to cheer up.

Finally, as we're talking about winning and losing, I think it's vital to recognise that increased gender equality isn't just a win for women. On the contrary, it's proven to benefit men in all kinds of ways. Writing in *Time* magazine, Mary Ann Sieghart points us to the 'reams of academic research [that] shows that everyone in a heterosexual family, including the man himself, gains from a man sharing in a more egalitarian partnership. The woman … is happier and healthier. So are their children, who also display fewer behavioural difficulties and do better at school. But, best of all for these purposes, the men themselves are also happier and healthier: they are twice as likely to be satisfied with their life, they smoke less, drink less, take fewer drugs, suffer less mental ill health, are less likely to get divorced, have a better relationship with their children— and they get significantly more frequent and better sex. What's not to like?' Anyone still not convinced of *What's in it for Men?* might benefit from reading the academic paper with that name by sociologist Øystein Gullvåg Holter[49] where he sets out the benefits that men in more gender-equal European countries and more gender-equal U.S. states enjoy. As Sieghart summarises, here men 'are less likely to get divorced. Their chances of dying a violent death are almost halved. The gap between male and female suicide rates is narrower. Men are also less likely to be violent against their partners and children, which in turn reduces the children's risk of being violent in later life. Best of all, though, they are happier. "It is a common misunderstanding that increased gender equality provides benefits and privileges for women at the expense of men's benefits and privileges", he says. In fact, he finds, men in more gender-equal countries and U.S. states are twice as likely to be happy, and nearly half as likely to be depressed. This holds true whatever their class or income.'[50]

Without a doubt, it helps all of us if we stop expecting nice girls to prioritise accommodating men, while boys focus on defeating each other; and it's something that we have the power to change, because it's not just the natural, biological order of things. So how can we encourage more men to take action that will benefit us all?

WHAT I LEARNED
ABOUT MEN

Am I better at this than your other men?

'I hope he wasn't *too* good. He'll make me look bad.' That was what one of my respondents joked after I told him that I'd been interviewing another man earlier that same day. He wasn't alone in expressing that thought, as many of my conversations contained at least one moment where the man would subtly or explicitly let me know that he wanted to be 'better than the average' or even my 'favourite interviewee'. They always expressed this in a jokey, self-deprecating way, but there was typically a strong hint that they were truly motivated to perform well, as the 'How am I doing? Am I winning?' joke let them simultaneously laugh at themselves for wanting to beat the other men, whilst also expressing a genuine desire to be valuable and to succeed in the task at hand.

I reassured each man that he was doing a brilliant job ('it's all about you, your thoughts, your experiences, and no-one can tell me about that better than you'), and this seemed to make each of them feel good, although it's interesting to speculate how badly the conversation might have gone had I said to any of them at that point, 'actually, the other men were much better at this than you.' And they'd have had every right to be upset if I'd have said that, of course, just as any of us would be. Which immediately makes me think that seeing the masculine competitive 'instinct' (which isn't an entirely a natural instinct) as a request for reassurance may be more helpful than seeing it as a simple desire for dominance over other men. I know that some feminists would argue that men already have more than enough confidence and need to become more self-questioning rather than getting even more positive affirmations from society/from women, but getting positive feedback about what they're doing well seemed to be genuinely appreciated by each of these men, just as it is for many women too. So I now remind myself to give micro-affirmations to men when they use their competitive tendencies in a way that feels net-positive, even if it's still fundamentally motivated by a desire to be better than other men. After all, this entire project is about finding motivations that men already have and using them for good, rather than trying to 'change men'. If you think it's manipulative and even Machiavellian to harness the very masculine competitiveness that society has encouraged in men for centuries, and use it to help create a more gender-equal world, then I stand guilty as charged. But in mitigation, I'd remind everyone that the more gender-equal world I seek is one where men stand to benefit as well as women, so it really is a win for all of us. And anyway, I think we all need a bit more positive feedback when we're doing a good job.

Beyond the 'am I as good as your other men?' jokes, each of my respondents had a moment early in the conversation where he experienced a very genuine 'Oh no, am I failing at this?' moment. It was when I asked my first proper question, the one that created the expression that we explored in *Issue 1: That 'I've Never Really Thought About It'* Face. Each time a respondent realised the very first question was unexpectedly difficult, he would look a bit crestfallen, sometimes embarrassed or awkward, clearly feeling far from the 'top respondent' he was aiming to be; and he'd generally immediately seek reassurance that the other men had found that question difficult too. Interestingly, every one of them navigated that moment with humour and humility, never once resorting to the kinds of 'compensatory masculinity' responses that psychologists' studies have seen when men feel inferior to other men. Maybe that's because there were no other men around during our conversation and it's easier to 'fail' when the 'superior' men are not visible? If so, that would suggest these kinds of conversations are better done one-on-one rather than in a group setting. Or maybe my sample is skewed and the men who took up my invitation to talk are simply less likely than the average man to display those compensatory responses when their masculinity feels momentarily undermined? Maybe there's even something about the way the whole conversation was framed that meant it somehow escaped the usual challenges of masculine competitive conversation? Their joking about wanting to be better than other men clearly indicates that they realised that kind of competitiveness was inappropriate in this context, as the conversational approach I'd established from the very outset was clearly adopting the 'feminine' model of 'how do we understand each other better' rather than the traditionally masculine 'who's up vs who's down' model. I was surprised at how quickly and easily that competitive drive became focused on something positive, like gaining a better understanding of each other; and how much easier it seemed for them to 'get it wrong' (which of course is a prerequisite for any learning and growth) here than in a more combative or competitive conversational context.

Everything's a competition, at work and at play.

I asked each of my respondents how competitiveness has played out for them in their life, whether in childhood or as grown-ups, and three key arenas kept cropping up: sporting, academic and work/ financial competition. Within each of these areas, there was a degree of nuance in their responses that is worth unpacking.

Sport was often the first stop when asked about competition, and here, even the men who weren't particularly into the big, popular men's sports would wield *that* as a way of asserting their superiority without questioning the whole 'sporting competition is intrinsically masculine' belief. They'd say, 'I'm into hockey, not football', or 'that's not my sport' with that same tone of superiority that music fans reserve when they mention the obscure band they follow. It's saying, 'I see your sport and I raise you a specialism,' playing the same game but trumping the 'entry level' sports fans. Very few said they rejected sport entirely, and one that did told me spontaneously, 'Yeah, people see it as really unmanly that I just don't really like competitive sport. It's like I'm failing my caveman ancestors, by not loving watching men trying to defeat each other. Honestly, it's that whole 'sport as sublimated warfare' thing. Not my cup of tea. And they always assume it's because I'm queer… like queer men can't love men grappling with each other in the mud!'

On the whole, then, sport plays a big role in many of my respondents' competitive lives, whether as players, fans or just vaguely interested by-standers; and it acts as a valuable metaphor for other key areas of their lives too, as the conversation played out in a similar way despite these men having some quite different backgrounds: 'I went to a traditional English boarding school, and competition was drilled into you really brutally. On the sports field. In the classroom. In the world outside that you were being trained to go and conquer. Everywhere.' Schools that weren't overly competitive were no exception, as 'the teachers tried to play that ridiculous "it's just the taking part that matters" game, but the lads weren't having any of that! And some of the girls too, of course. But yeah, definitely, I always wanted to win.' For the men from more challenging socio-economic backgrounds too, competing to win, particularly through physical dominance, was a big part of life as a boy: 'I went to a really rough school in a rough neighbourhood, and the only way to survive was beating the other boys. If you couldn't do it in fist fights or football, you *might* just survive if you could do it through comedy or music, if you were good enough. And being smart was sometimes a win, it was looked on as a way out, but you could only play that card if you were exceptional and if you didn't behave like a nerd.'

Although similar stories were told by all of these men, some expressed an alternative to this 'real men don't try hard' narrative, proudly admitting that they worked hard to achieve their academic results, or their body, or their business success. The language was telling here, though - they talked about *'working* hard', not *'trying* hard'. Doing 'hard work' sounded like an assertion of superiority over other men who 'don't have the strength for the struggle', whereas 'trying hard' sounded more like an admission of wanting to please others, of weakness. Given that so much of this masculine competitiveness is an attempt to impress other men, it's ironic that 'being a try-hard' is clearly not seen as winning at masculinity; but trying hard still can still seem strong and manly if it's framed as fighting to succeed.

Moreover, talking about sport overall surfaced two key principles that make up the code of masculine competition in all areas for my respondents, which could be best summarised as 'don't be a dick, and don't be a sore loser.'

Winning at all costs isn't cool.

Many of my respondents spoke really disparagingly about men they knew who so badly wanted to win that, as one put it 'he was just a wanker'. 'This one guy I played against a lot would always try and get away with cheating whenever he could, rolling around on the floor and calling foul when he was barely touched. That's not sporting behaviour, it's being a spoilt child.' Being too selfish in the sporting arena was often positioned as unmanly too. 'He was an idiot, so full of himself that he'd never pass the ball. I think he thought he was some kind of gifted genius who could do it all single-handedly, even when his teammates in a better position would be screaming at him to release the ball. What a dick.' The sense of anger and frustration that men quickly felt was really palpable when they were describing these people who didn't play fair or weren't good team players. And there was a clear view that if you couldn't play fair, you shouldn't play at all. None of them identified with this kind of behaviour, of course, and if anyone accused them of behaving that way themselves, they'd have been furious.

This value of 'fair play' also manifested when they were talking about academic or workplace competition. One young man, who's still studying, explained, 'we have a healthy competition with each other but when it comes down to it, we all help each other out too. When you work together you get to a better answer, so just trying to go it alone the whole time is just dumb. But it's not cheating, there's a big difference between working together and cheating. One's sensible, the other's stupid and selfish.' A few of the men admitted - almost bragged, in fact - that they often needed to work hard to keep their competitive spirit in check and stop it getting out of control. One young man laughed immediately as soon as I asked the question about competitiveness, and told me he was 'still working on not letting my competitive spirit get out of hand' in both sporting and academic environments. Others were proud to tell me that they 'don't have that "win at all costs" mentality... I do have a keen competitiveness, it's like a basic instinct so I embrace it and enjoy it, and play as hard as I can for the team. But when it comes to individual sports, I don't care enough to want to destroy my opponent. Sometimes when I win, I just feel a bit sorry for the guy who lost too.' Another succinctly put it: 'If all you care about is winning, and you'll do anything to get that, you're actually a bit of a loser.'

So masculinity isn't just about winning, it's about winning fairly; and whenever the game is a team one, it's also about being a team player.

Learning to lose well matters too.

However much these men were programmed from boyhood to want to win, there was something beyond simply losing that they sought to avoid at all costs, and that was being a *bad* loser. They recognised that losing is inevitable, at least some of the time, but interestingly, when that does happen, being able to lose with dignity was actually, for these guys, a sign of manliness too. Of course, when they lost a match or a game they'd joke about it, how they'd 'let you win', but all of them seemed to take pride in being one of those men who's able to lose well when it does happen: 'When you don't win - and even I can't win *every* time - you've gotta be able to take it on the chin.' The phrase 'they were just better than us' is often used by sports fans as a mark of being a good loser, and those words don't seem to be read by men as any sign of weakness. Quite the opposite, in fact. And just like with the notion of fair play, being able to be a good loser remains true in the world of school and work too. 'When you lose a bit of business you're competing for, it's maddening but you just have to admit that the others were better than you on the day. If you spend all your time thinking you're perfect, like you're invincible and everyone else is an idiot, you stop learning and working on your weaknesses, and that's really dangerous. You've got to have some healthy respect for the competition, and be humble enough to learn from them sometimes too.' The only exception to this - as per the rules of fair play - is when you're beaten by a cheat. Then, it's OK to rant and rail about it, and begrudge their win. However, even in the case of losing to someone who didn't play fair, expressing anger *in the moment* seemed to be acceptable manly behaviour, but bearing a grudge just wasn't. There's a point at which that anger has to subside, and a man just has to accept it and move on. The rules and codes about what's the right way to compete, to win and even to lose were very clear; and interestingly, in the competition that is masculinity, you even have a chance to win at losing, if you do it right.

The best winners help losers cope with their loss.

Just as we discussed in the previous chapter, in sport and in work (whether academic or business), sometimes these men would enjoy using their status as a winner to help other men who were suffering with their out-of-control competitiveness; or to lift up rather than beat down other men who were struggling to deal with having lost at something important. In the business context, that meant some of the more senior men telling me how they'd openly admit when they'd messed something up or didn't know an answer, because 'if I can show that, it helps all the other blokes in the room who didn't know either, but didn't feel able to say.' For someone else it meant 'helping him find a way of dealing with his anger issues, so he doesn't just end up damaging himself as well as the rest of us.' One, very poignantly said it meant 'putting your arms around his shoulders and letting him cry without shame.' Whether literally or metaphorically, offering your own broad shoulders for other men to cry on them in times of need felt like advanced-level masculine 'winning' for some of these men; and the lack of judgement they had around the men they were helping feels to me like a really powerful testament to work that's been done in recent years around men's mental health: 'feeling a bit broken sometimes is understandable; showing you're devastated is a much better way to deal with it than just bitching about who beat you, and being a sore loser. We have to help each other out.' Here's to that.

Sex and violence are a whole different ball game.

When it comes to sex and relationships, the straight men made it clear that the dating/mating game comprised two areas of competition:

'Winning the girl' was one form of competition; and winning the status of having 'done well' in the eyes of other men was the other. Clearly, this latter area was all about the opinions of other men, not women. But even when it comes to the first point, competing with other men to 'get the girl' in the first place, these men often paid as much attention to what other men thought as they did to what the girl in question thought; and even, at times, to what they themselves wanted - so much so that some admitted having lost a potential 'conquest' by showing off to or listening to their mates in a way that was a complete turn-off to the girl.

They recognised that, unlike the average nature documentary, to which some of my respondents laughingly refer, in the heterosexual dating game these days, the 'conquest' is often unimpressed by an alpha male whose seduction technique is to beat the male competition. As one astute observer noted, 'some straight men are still fighting each other like gorillas to win the "prey", but the prey these days has other ideas! Most of the girls I know think blokes that behave like that are creeps.' Although they also noted wryly that this 'hyper-masculine neanderthal behaviour is alive and well in the queer community too, causing as much damage there as it does in cis, straight lives.'

The straight men would tell me that thinking more about your mates' opinions than what appeals to the woman you're hoping to date is a pretty dumb dating strategy, but even so, I did encounter some residual belief that women are secretly impressed by a man who fights other guys to win her, believing 'that's what women really want though. They say they hate neanderthal men, but I know girls who say that and then still date the big, successful guys.' Most seem to concur that 'it's hard to know what women want these days', and told me that some men are responding to women's increased empowerment by playing the competitive game in new ways, such as by adopting what one respondent called a 'faux-feminist fuckboy strategy' where the man in question 'shows off about how much he hates misogyny, to really impress a girl, but then goes and brags to his mates about what he did with her afterwards and moves on to the next one.' Women's worries about the threat of sexual violence when walking home alone at night was fertile territory to demonstrate one's (real or strategically adopted) recognition of the burden women have to bear, so 'instead of trying to do something about it, they'd just use it to win brownie points and look more thoughtful and sensitive than other men by offering to walk her home. I suppose trying to be the hero is better than *not* trying to keep women safe, but really they're just capitalising on women's vulnerability and using it for their own ends.' This whole issue of women's sexual safety is explored in more detail in *Issue 6: Let's Talk About Sex*.

It was clear that a big part of male competitive chat about 'who's got the best girl' revolved around the power dynamic in your romantic/sexual relationship. Effectively, it's about 'do you wear the trousers, or does she?' At its most basic, that might be about some men showing off about 'what she lets you do'. (Again, more on consent in *Issue 6: Let's Talk About Sex*) However, when I asked 'would you rather someone referred to your wife/girlfriend a "bird" or 'the missus"?' the response supported this notion that even men who claim they'd never engage in those kinds of chats with their mates still appeared more worried about losing face with other men than they were about their woman being treated as inferior, as a sex object. 'Obviously it's a bit disrespectful to call her a bird, but that's just a bit of banter, maybe a bit of jealousy, and it's a compliment in some ways. They wouldn't do it if they thought she wasn't attractive. But I hate it when people call her "the missus" and behave as if I'm a hen-pecked husband and she's some kind of nagging battle-axe. I think that's really disrespectful to both of us.' When push comes to shove, it's probably no surprise that many men would rather be complicit in a bit of 'harmless' sexism than they would be positioned as someone who's under the thumb of a controlling woman. That feels to them like a double-whammy 'loser' scenario - losing the power game with other men because you can't even win the power game with your woman.

Talking of pushing and shoving, each of my respondents could tell me stories of men and boys in their lives, especially when they were younger, who often used physical violence as a way of winning the battle to be top dog. No doubt for many men who live and work in more challenging environments than most of my respondents, the real and present danger of male violence remains throughout their adult lives too, but with my sample, the conversation tended to focus on their experiences as boys and very young men. 'As a working-class boy in a rough school, fighting was just normal. When I look back, I never empathised with the victim. You always associated with the victor.' The same seemed to happen at the most exclusive boarding school too, and every school in between. 'Boys in my [boarding] school would be beating each other up all the time. And we felt we got off lightly, because for my father's generation, the teachers would be beating the boys with belts and canes as well. At least we were only fighting each other!' As we can see, even when it comes to violence, the rules of fair play still reign supreme: 'Beating up on someone obviously less powerful than you' is not, according to all my respondents, the mark of a man. 'That's a sign of cowardice.'

Even though most of them weren't the ones picking fights as boys and young men, none of the men I spoke with seemed to have been able to avoid fighting entirely, however much they may have wanted to. 'I don't remember ever starting a fight. I wasn't one of those lads who'd use violence as a first response. But I did end up being in lots of fights, just because you had to be able to defend yourself. We all did. It's funny looking back too - being big and tall, I seemed to make the hard boys want to fight me to prove how tough they were.' However, a couple of them admitted, with some shame and regret, that in their younger days they'd used aggression and violence as their stock-in-trade. One tells me 'I was a little a shit back then. A real horror, and I didn't care who I was hurting.' I was surprised to learn this, as the mature, professional, well-respected man sitting in front of me seemed a million miles from the man of his youth, so I asked what brought about such a change in him. 'I got sent to borstal,[51] and that scared the shit out of me' was his answer. 'It showed me a life I didn't want.' His *Sliding Doors* moment is more dramatic than the other men I talked to, but all of them touched on its central theme in one way or another: that the biggest competition of all is with the worst aspects of yourself.

Competition with yourself.

Some of my respondents talked about trying to win the ongoing battle with their own demons, whereas others articulated it more as being engaged in an ongoing competition with their past or current selves. In each case, winning seemed to be less about external measures of success and more about getting to a place of greater fulfilment and happiness. One very successful man told me: 'I don't define myself by big flashy cars or anything, but I'm really curious, so I've learned to love being scared, as then I know I'm learning. Being creative means being vulnerable. *Not* knowing is what will take me somewhere I've not been.' Another talked about how he used to be much more status-driven than he is now, but since becoming a father 'I'm less about crass competition with others in terms of position and promotions, and I'm doing less of that old fashioned alpha male slightly toxic competitiveness at work.' I won't necessarily assume that those men would always say the same things in an all-male 'locker room' environment, but maybe some would. And in any case, I found it really powerful to see them defining winning in their own terms in this way with me: 'I know that being a man now means having to express my feelings. That's something I've made massive progress on since my childhood when I couldn't express myself at all in that way. Although, ha ha, my wife will probably tell you I've still got a way to go.' Frequently these men talked about themselves as a work in progress, rather than feeling the need to position themselves as the finished article, and a few talked with beautiful compassion about being kinder to themselves on this journey: 'When I was little, I never quite believed I'm clever. I always thought "oh god, I'm failing in maths, why am I stupid?" I felt really inadequate, I'd get grumpy with other people and with myself. But now I can say "actually I am quite clever." In fact, I now know enough to realise I have *so* much more to learn!'

The vulnerability question.

Based on all the reading and research I've done over the years, I had expected the men I talked with to find it relatively difficult to express vulnerability. What I hadn't anticipated was that it would be difficult for many of them to even *remember* a time they'd felt really vulnerable.

Because although eventually they did get to the kinds of things I've described above, for many of them, it took a little while to get there. And that was not because they didn't know how to express it or whether to share it; it was more that, unless they were black or queer, they genuinely had to think for a bit before they could recall the last time they'd felt truly vulnerable. I found that incredibly unsettling, because it's no exaggeration to say that whenever I've asked that question to women, I see every one flicking through a mental file of moments, from childhood up to that very week, where they'd felt unsafe. Amongst my male respondents, it was only the men who were marginalised on account of their race, sexual orientation or gender expression who immediately had that same response. 'As a boy, I remember feeling really vulnerable when other boys and men would ridicule my choices for being too feminine - my toys, my clothes, my voice, even the way I moved. Before that I'd felt really free, but then I knew I needed to start masc-ing up to protect myself in some situations. But now I'm living life as me and being free again. Being in love with my fiancé has taught me to be vulnerable again. And although we're always aware, just walking around, that someone might want to attack us for that, and we'd love it if the word wasn't like that, we both feel it's a price worth paying to be who we are.' Similarly, that sense of vulnerability that many women describe about being out in the world was expressed by all of the men of colour I talked to, such as 'in some places or situations, you're always a little bit on edge. Like you're relaxed and having a good time but there's still this bit of you that's on high alert because you know that trouble can kick off in a moment and you could end up in trouble.' But the white, straight men I spoke with had to dig a bit deeper - even if only for a few seconds - to find those moments where they felt real threat, real powerlessness and a sense that the pitch they were playing on was fundamentally designed to not work in their favour, in some quite dangerous ways.

Once the straight, white men had racked their brains for a bit, they could all come up with a few moments where they'd felt a similar sense of powerlessness, but it tended to be specific and contextual rather than systemic. One mentioned finding himself in an area of town where 'I knew I didn't belong and was out of my depth. I'd taken a couple of turns off the main road and suddenly I was in a place where I knew a posh boy like me stuck out like a sore thumb. I had to keep my eyes down, try to look like I knew where I was going and just hope that I didn't run into trouble.' Another talked about how he'd felt unable to confront a group of young lads who were behaving badly because 'they may well have been carrying a knife. Loads of young blokes do these days. I'd be happy to take them on if a fist fight kicked off, but you've just got to be sensible and not get involved if you could end up getting stabbed. I hate that feeling of not being able to step in, feeling really powerless to do what's right.' Another went back to his childhood, talking about how at bedtime he used to feel 'scared of intruders, so I used to build a wall with my cuddlies to keep them out. But other than that, I don't think I've ever had a moment of feeling really vulnerable, which is weird to say.'

Aside from being mugged, stabbed, or murdered in your bed, there was one other area that nearly all of the men said they had felt pretty vulnerable, and that was being involved in recent conversations about gender. 'It's hard, when you really don't want to offend anyone, you're trying to understand and you want to help, but you know that if you say the wrong thing it could all blow up in your face.' And whereas in many other areas of work and at play, competing in high-risk situations felt exciting and adrenaline-fuelled, walking the gender conversational tightrope was not a game they felt at all comfortable playing, let alone excited. So how might we take all we've learned here about men being so powerfully socialised to compete with each other, and use it to help other men like these to become a bit less reluctant to help build the gender-equal world that makes winners of us all?

WHY MEN MIGHT
WANT TO CREATE CHANGE

This entire project centres on the fact that however hard women try, we can't create change on our own, and we need more men to lean in and do things to actively accelerate gender equality, and that applies to all eight of the big issues I explore here. But if there's any area where men leaning in and making change was even more important than the others, this one is surely a strong contender. Men spend so much time and energy competing against and trying to impress each other, and they can frequently care more about what other men think than what women think, so it would seem logical that this is one area that men *really* need to work on with other men. Maybe in reality this will work best when women step right out of the way and leave men to work on this alone, together. If so, it will require men to find both the motivation and the fortitude to fight for their position as top dog in a way that avoids falling back into typical 'locker room' one-upmanship. Maybe, on the other hand, it's easier to unlock those motivations and stimulate action with individual men when they're in a one-one conversation with a woman, where the 'team' they feel they're on in that moment is different, and where the competitive man-vs-man desire to win can more easily manifest in different ways. If so, they'll need to be able to get past the performative focus on what they're 'allowed to say' around women that has become so entrenched in recent years, and open up about some of the nuances and vulnerabilities we've discussed here.

As we can't yet be sure what's the best way, some of the thought starters below might be best suited to one-on-one or small group conversations between men and women, whereas others might be best done by men together but apart from women. Whichever is the case, if you explore and learn things that we could all find useful, please do share on @MenemiesNoMore.

1. Redirect the competitiveness: For years, men have been socialised to compete with each other, and they often enjoy it, so let's not tell men that man-vs-man competition is intrinsically wrong. Instead, can we simply help redirect it, so they're competing with each other to be best at things that are less damaging and more helpful, both to women and to other men? Like empathy. If that were a competitive sport, I know so many men who'd immediately become world class at it! Or listening. There's an example I love where a guy posts a TikTok laughing at how 'women don't ever say what they really mean,' using The Spice Girls song *Wannabe* as his proof point. But he then gets roasted by another man who points out that of course 'they do tell you what they really really want' and laughs at the first guy for not actually listening, including the unforgettable burn 'they're not asking *you* to zig a zig aah. They just want you to respect *their* wishes to do it.'[52] The prize is worth competing for, as we know that gender equality creates healthier, happier and more successful lives for us all, so can we position 'being good at accelerating gender equality' as the ultimate new sport that men can compete with each other to win at? When a man uses his masculine competitiveness in this way, it makes him a winner in all kinds of ways, both as an individual who beats other men, and as a great team player too.

2. Play fair: Every one of the men I talked with was very clear that 'playing fair' was a hugely valuable quality in a man (and in all people), both in sport and in life. They all felt proud to embody fair play, and were happy to actively police it in any men who tried to get ahead either by deliberately cheating or by benefiting from things that accidentally gave them an unfair advantage. So is there an opportunity to reframe gender equality in the language of 'playing fair'? There are so many ways that the playing field isn't level and that women (particularly women who are marginalised in other ways too) are fighting with one hand tied behind their backs to get to a place where everyone has the same opportunities. And of course, the same is true for men who are marginalised because of their race or sexual orientation. Can we encourage men to police 'unfair' behaviour in other men with even half the energy that they use to call men out on this when it happens on the sports field? In a world that's systemically stacked in men's favour, could we position the guys who are focused on maintaining their unfair advantage over women as looking a bit weak? It would need to be done in a way that doesn't position women as delicate little flowers who can't stand up for themselves, of course, but maybe the language of fair play makes it easier for men to hold misogynists to account in a way that doesn't make the man who's challenging feel like he's 'under his woman's thumb'? As masculinity thrives on men competing against each other, let's find ways for men to play each other at their own game, but with gender equality as the winner.

3. Don't be a sore loser: Closely aligned to the notion of 'playing fair' is the idea that being a sore loser is a sign of being weak and childish, and most men want to avoid other men thinking of them like that. So could the idea of 'not being a sore loser' help us talk men's language whenever they feel like they're losing something as we move towards a more gender-equal society? We should, I believe, always use facts to challenge the harmful notion of the zero-sum game and keep pointing to the ways that gender equality benefits men too. But every man in some individual moment is likely to feel that he (not just men generally) has lost out; so as well as enabling men to express those feelings of vulnerability, it feels like it could be helpful to encourage any man in that situation to not behave like a sore loser, and to not bear a grudge. It could even make him feel heroic, in the poetic way beloved of sports montages: 'If you can meet with Triumph and Disaster/And treat those two impostors just the same... you'll be a Man, my son!'[53] After all, sore losers are the ones most likely to engage in the kinds of angry backlash that just damages us all.

4. The real competition is with yourself: If our overall strategy in this project is to build from the things men already care about and value rather than trying to change them, then this 'personal growth and self-improvement' angle on masculine competitiveness feels potentially very helpful. Rather than competing against other men on terms others have imposed, this shows that men can feel they're *really* winning when the man they're competing with is 'me yesterday or me today, and not anybody else.' Not only does this stop the unhelpful comparisons with other men that can trigger more hyper-masculine compensatory responses; it also encourages men to set their own individual criteria for success, instead of just going with the flow of what success has looked like for men historically. Can the winning behaviour we celebrate be that sense of self-governance, of breaking from the past and making progress on the things that matter to you? Thinking about the ultimate masculine competition as being a competition with oneself might focus competitive men on progress towards a better future too, and away from the things men were 'allowed to do' in the past, where it's easier to fall back into an unhelpful, loss-aversion mindset.

5. Make non-competitive conversations comfortable: It's clear that men generally feel more at home in conversations whose model is 'who's up vs who's down' as opposed to the model that women more often adopt - 'are we closer or further apart?' And as the strategies I suggest here are about not trying to change them or tell them they're wrong, but instead, working with the things men already enjoy and value, it might seem odd to say that we could encourage men to adopt this traditionally feminine conversation model more often. But the fact is, these men who were able to do it definitely seemed to enjoy it too. Many of them commented on how interesting and even liberating our conversation felt. Assuming that they weren't all just excellent actors or very good liars, maybe we could try finding ways of inviting men into more conversations like these, knowing that they can not only be good at it, but also enjoy it. And be better than most other men at it. If we do take this approach, though, it's imperative that we make sure it's about really listening to men, going at their pace, and working hard to understand them, or we won't get the shared trust and understanding we need to move forward together.

ISSUE 5:

Taking Up Space

How 'manspreading' isn't just a physical thing.

===============

REALITY CHECK:
WHERE WE ARE RIGHT NOW

There was a standing joke in my family when we were young that not all halves were equal, as we experienced a phenomenon known as the 'Debbie half.' This was an affectionate dig at my wonderful sis, because whenever we had to share anything between the two of us, Debbie would somehow always make sure that her 'half' was significantly bigger than mine. And although our parents would pull her up on it from time to time, the truth is, it actually made a lot of sense to us kids. After all, as the older sibling, she'd not *had* to share before I came along, so her giving me my 'little half' felt pretty generous. And it was easy to rationalise why she deserved more. She was bigger than me. She was smarter than me. She was older than me. And maybe my half wasn't *that* small anyway? Surely that's just how things ought to be?

I don't tell this story here to heap shame on my sister. Far from it, as I love her and admire her endlessly; and neither do I intend any blaming and shaming as I share the following data and examples, although it may feel like that to men who read this. But it's important for us all to recognise that right now, men are unwittingly enjoying their very own

'Debbie half' in all kinds of areas of life, taking up more than their fair share of the space. And whereas it didn't do me any lasting damage to receive a smaller share of a break-time Wagon Wheel or occasional cream soda, the fact that women are currently only getting a smaller 'half' of the spaces we share in the world does have a significant impact on women's safety, success and happiness. So where does this happen, and why does it matter?

Sharing physical space.

Love it or hate it, we're all familiar with the term 'manspreading', but what many don't realise is that it's not just a casual moan - there are studies proving how men tend to take up disproportionate amounts of physical space. Men are more likely than women to: 'Take up more space in public - spread bags over seats, sit with their knees apart, take up elbow room, spread books and papers over larger areas of tables, spread newspapers wider in crowded situations... Men are far more likely than women to stop in the middle of a walkway and stand there, letting traffic stream around them. They're also less likely to take pains to get out of the stream of traffic [and they] assume that others - especially women and lower-status men - will make space for them without being asked'[1]. Not only are men 'less likely to notice that they're in the way' but even 'when a man moves aside, he's likely to move less than a woman. This seems to correlate to status as well as sex; high-status men often need to be asked to move two or three times before they make enough space.'[2] Unsurprisingly (and inexcusably once we're made aware of it) white people are more likely to do this too, so once again we see women of colour disproportionately impacted. There's even a phenomenon that Beth Breslaw coined 'manslamming' after her 2015 experiments showed that not only were men much less likely than women to move out of the way when approaching a woman on the street; they would actually physically body-slam women who didn't step aside for them.[3] This behaviour is almost certainly learned rather than being innate, as we can see when a trans man in one experiment talked about having to *learn* that he 'had to walk down the middle of the sidewalk, through crowded spaces such as clubs, etc., with his head up, eyes directly ahead, without saying 'excuse me' or worrying about bumping into people'[4]. It's clear that men dominating physical space like this isn't just about thoughtlessness or a general sense of entitlement, it's also 'a way of performing maleness, so that NOT doing these things marks one as less than manly.'[5]

This male domination of shared space starts young, as studies of boys' and girls' use of playgrounds demonstrates. I'd long accepted the folk wisdom that girls simply engage in less physical play than boys, but when I look at the research as well as my own childhood, it's clear that that's not quite the case. *Make Space for Girls* have looked more closely at playground use, and they note that while the traditionally male ball-sports tend to dominate the playground, activities favoured by girls, such as gymnastics, dancing and more imaginative and creative play exist too but are pushed to the edges.[6] Moreover, we see a real sense of entitlement to space amongst the boys, as when playground use was split in two, with half dedicated to the typically-male games like football, and half dedicated to typically feminine types of physical play, the girls were generally delighted at being given 'so much space' whereas the boys were often furious that so much of 'their space' had been 'taken away.' Most fascinatingly of all, the boys don't need to feel aggrieved, as when parks were created that included space for more of the 'feminine' types of play too, many of the boys enjoyed those more diverse kinds of play just as much as the girls did. Transpose that into grown-up spaces and it makes me wonder how nights out would feel if pubs regularly had a dedicated dance floor just as often as they had a sports screen and pool table or dart board. It's worth noting that women, of course, can enjoy these traditionally male activities, *and* that far from being an innate sex difference, this feminisation of dancing is socially constructed too, as we can see many other cultures, subcultures and eras where the dance floor isn't or wasn't a female-dominated space.

But enough about my fantasies of pubs with dance floors being as ubiquitous as sports screens… Let's get back to the data about how other physical spaces that men and women both inhabit aren't yet shared in a way that works equally well for women. It's time to talk toilet queues;

and this summary of the current state of affairs from Caroline Criado-Perez is worth quoting at length because although on average women take twice as long as men to use the toilet, it's not just because men pee faster and more efficiently as they stand up at urinals, like we often assume. 'Women make up the majority of the elderly and disabled, two groups that will tend to need more time in the toilet. Women are also more likely to be accompanied by children, as well as disabled and older people. Then there's the 20–25 percent of women of childbearing age who may be on their period at any one time, and therefore need to change a tampon or a sanitary pad. Women may also require more trips to the bathroom: pregnancy significantly reduces bladder capacity, and women are eight times more likely to suffer from urinary-tract infections.'[7] Most buildings, though, have historically, been built by men who may not be aware of these issues and who think that 50/50 toilet space is fair; and I've always just sighed in silent fury when queueing again for the bathroom, rather than talking to designers and architects about periods and urinary tract infections. Some women may not feel comfortable talking about these issues to the men in their lives, but we really do need everyone to see the problem before we can solve it.

Some cities including Glasgow, Barcelona and Vienna have recently identified how town planning hasn't traditionally taken account of the way many marginalised people - particularly women - use public space, and they have adopted a 'feminist town planning' approach to address this. The common misunderstanding that 'feminism' means 'female dominance' rather than 'gender equality' may make feminist town planning sound alarming, but it simply means things like making pavements wide enough to be accessible for double buggies, providing adequate toilet facilities for all, thinking more carefully about safety issues like street lighting and clear lines of sight, and ensuring public transport routes accommodate people with caring duties who have different travel patterns to those who simply go to and from the office each day. These are all things that are proven to benefit all people regardless of gender, of course, but right now, because cities don't actively plan like this, because they just rely on the historically male-centric design lens, their default design has a disproportionately negative impact on women.[8]

Sharing cultural space.

As well as dominating our shared physical spaces, for a whole bunch of historical and other reasons, men still take up disproportionate amounts of space in our cultural industries too. Despite the enormous importance of technology to all of our lives, under 30 percent of people in tech are women, and only around 11 percent work in high positions.[9] Most cultural spaces that help shape our understanding of ourselves and each other remain male-dominated too, as only around 20 percent of behind-the-scenes jobs in top grossing film & TV are occupied by women.[10] Recent figures show that 92 percent of broadcast and streaming programmes had no women directors of photography, nearly 80 percent no women directors, around 70 percent no women creators or editors, and 65 percent no women writers. Unsurprisingly, this male domination of space behind the camera gets reflected on screen too where men are overrepresented, especially as they age, so that male characters aged 60+ appear twice as often as female characters of the same age. Similarly, on broadcast television, general ageism means that the number of major male characters drops a little from 35 percent in their 30s to 28 percent in their 40s, whereas for major female characters it plummets to only 15 percent; and a similar decrease was observed for streaming services too.[11] Similarly, in movies, out of the top 100 grossing films in 2019, only 12 percent of directors were women, 20 percent of the writers, two percent of the cinematographers and 19 percent of the exec producers,[12] and of the top 100 grossing films of 2021, only seven included a woman in a lead role who was over the age of 45.[13] Search the 'Smurfette principle' and the 'Bechdel test' too, and you'll see this over-representation of men replicated across all age groups, starting with content for the very youngest children. The data I found most shocking was that we're so used to the dominance of male characters and voices in the content we consume that we fail to notice how they take up the majority of the space even in stories that we think of as being female-led, such as Disney's mega-hit *Frozen*. Even in this radically female-centred story about sisterly love, with two female leads, Virginia Mendez tells us that the majority of the lines - 59 percent - are still spoken by male characters.[14]

Over in advertising, men tend to appear four times more than women in ads, and have seven times more speaking roles;[15] and the women that *are* featured often don't reflect the reality of women's lives: Despite a recent study finding that women in every age group put 'sense of humour' and 'intelligence' in the top three characteristics that define them, in only three percent of ads were women shown being funny, or shown doing something that requires intelligence of some kind. Women over 50 are one of the biggest, fastest-growing and most affluent demographic groups on earth, and yet women of that age feature in only ten percent of adverts with women in them.[16] And when we look at the biggest advertising event in the world, despite 75 percent of American women saying they will be watching the big game, over half of Superbowl ads in 2023 still featured a male-only lead cast.[17] Meanwhile in music, only 13 percent of 2022 headline acts at the 50 the biggest festivals in the UK were an all-female band or solo artist compared to 75 percent who were an all-male band or solo artist.[18] And it's even more skewed in some genres such as dance music, where less than one per cent of the dance music played on UK radio is made by a female solo artist or all-female band, contributing to women accounting for just five percent of dance hits.[19]

It happens beyond these areas of entertainment too, as men also take up disproportionate space in our news media. The 2020 Global Media Monitoring Project reviewed thousands of stories and found that 'women were only 25 percent of the persons heard, read about or seen in newspaper, television and radio news', and while representation of women had increased in the preceding 5 years, that rise was just one percentage point, meaning that 'at this rate, it will take 67 years to reach numerical gender parity.'[20] No wonder the World Economic Forum recently advised that 'there is a need for both expanded coverage of women's issues and gender inequalities in various areas... as well as a 'horizontal' approach - or a gender lens - applied across all news beats.'[21] Although the US news media landscape has the highest proportion of economics/business (60 percent) and health editors (71 percent) who are women among the six countries studied, women of colour yet again are disproportionately underrepresented, with women of colour being 'more marginalised in news leadership in the UK than in any other six researched countries in the report.'[22]

It's easy to think that sport is now a notable exception to this issue of men taking up disproportionate amounts of space, as we've recently seen more high-profile coverage of women's sporting success. However, even there, the picture is mixed at best. In the UK, the good news is that in a six-week period in summer 2019, in what the BBC termed its 'summer of women's sport', nearly half of the BBC Sport website's homepage stories featured women's sport, and women's sport also made up over half of the 'most-watched' video clips. However, on closer inspection, 'It appears that when we have seen positive shifts in the volume of women's sport coverage, it's often when men's sport is absent. This was the case in the summer of 2019. When the men's football season restarted in August it was business as usual.'[23] And at a broader level, that 'business as usual' is pretty dire, as 'researchers have looked into the proportion of coverage allotted to women's sport by both print and broadcast media and found it to average about four percent. This abysmal level has been persistent, rarely creeping over ten percent despite fluctuations seen during exceptional moments such as the Olympics and the World Cup.'[24] US studies find a similar picture where not only was '95 percent of total television coverage, as well as the ESPN highlights show SportsCenter, focused on men's sports in 2019', but they also note that 'on the rare broadcast when a women's sports story does appear, it is usually a case of "one and done" - a single women's sports story partially eclipsed by a cluster of men's stories that precede it, follow it and are longer in length.'[25] Moreover, this study included the period of the Women's World Cup, and even so, women's sport coverage only rose to five percent for local television affiliates and 5.4 percent of the airtime on ESPN's SportsCenter. In addition, 'eighty percent of the news and highlights programs in our study devoted zero time for women's sports.'[26]

This over-representation of male sport has an unexpected knock-on effect too, where because search algorithms prioritise what's popular rather than what's objectively correct, internet search results often serve up inaccurate content that prioritises sports*men*. The excellent *Correct the Internet*[27] campaign highlights this, and prompts people to help report these inaccuracies so that the tech companies can correct them. For instance, they say: 'Search "Which tennis player has spent the longest time ranked number 1?" The facts say Steffi Graf. The internet says Novak Djokovic. This is just one of many incorrect search results out there', and they point to many examples of internet searches serving up incorrect male answers to sporting questions, including which team has won the most basketball World Cup titles, who has scored the most FIFA World Cup goals, which boxer has the most title defences, who has won the most Olympic medals in rowing and when is the next football World Cup. As the team behind the *Correct the Internet* says, 'Many of the world's best athletes are women. And many of the world's sporting records are held by women. But due to human bias, our search engines have learnt to prioritise sportsmen in our search results, even when the facts put sportswomen first. We want to change that.'[28]

It's probably no surprise, then, that men even account for disproportionate amounts of statues in our shared public spaces. Australian cricket star Belinda Clark had captained her nation for 12 years and won two World Cups, but recently she apparently became the first female cricketer in the *world* to have a statue made, standing at the Sydney Cricket Ground.[29] The issue goes way beyond Australia and cricket, or even sport in general, as 'in the US and the UK, there is a staggering lack of public statues of women', with only around 13 percent of UK statues and seven percent of statues in the US depicting historical women. It goes without saying, too, that people of colour are massively under-represented and inappropriately represented as well, once again leaving women of colour the most disproportionately impacted. And because our female statue numbers in the UK are boosted by the fact that we've had a few renowned Queens, researchers looked to see how far royals skewed the UK figures. Shockingly, when you exclude statues of royalty, we were left with just 25 statues of historical women compared to 498 of historical men.[30] That's around five percent. Women are clearly a very long way from enjoying an equal share of the plinths as well as the spaces we share in real life and in news, tech, sport and entertainment.

Sharing conversational space

It's not just in media content such as news, music, movies, TV, films and adverts that men's voices take up disproportionate space. It also happens in real life conversations; and just like with 'manspreading' and 'manslamming' in the physical world, we have a popular term associated with this too: 'mansplaining.' I'm increasingly aware that because this word makes men feel vilified, it polarises the debate in ways that are never helpful. Moreover, because it's now used so often as a casual slur, it's easy to dismiss it as an unjustified accusation, which can hide the fact that when we look more dispassionately at the data to see who has the lion's share of conversations, it is, in fact, highly gendered, so it really is something we shouldn't ignore.

Rebecca Solnit lit the blue touchpaper on this phenomenon in her essay *Men Explain Things to Me*, which includes examples that still resonate with many women and girls today: She recently said, 'People often recount the opening incident in that almost 15-year-old essay, in which a man explained a book to me, too busy holding forth to notice that I was its author, as my friend was trying to tell him.'[31] It resonated hugely with many women who have since recounted experiencing the same thing, such as this example from a NASA scientist who says, 'At a NASA Earth meeting 10 years ago, a white male postdoc interrupted me to tell me that I don't understand human drivers of fire, that I def needed to read McCarty et al. I looked him in the eye, pulled my long hair back so he could read my name tag. "I'm McCarty et al."'[32] Cue 20,000 re-tweets. Not surprisingly, these stories also generate a flurry of 'not all men' responses, and of course that's true too. So how representative of the way men share conversational space is this 'mansplaining' behaviour? Is it just a few rogue men who interrupt women, telling them they're wrong and acting as if he has a right to command the conversation like this; or is it something more systemic?

We've already identified how the masculine superiority myth, that's often believed by women too, contributes to the 'I know better than you' element of so-called mansplaining. But there's something else going on here too, and it's the verbal corollary of the data we saw earlier about men learning to take up more than their fair share of space on sidewalks, seats and so on, often without even noticing that they're doing it. A study at George Washington University found that when men are speaking with women, they interrupt 33 percent more often than when they're speaking to men. That's 2.1 times per three-minute conversation. This experience is a frequent frustration to women, as testified by sales of the 'I'm speaking' t-shirt that honoured Kamala Harris's response to being so frequently interrupted during the US presidential debate. However, most men seem blissfully unaware that they tend to interrupt women significantly more than they interrupt men; and although it's rarely intentional, that doesn't mean it's not real. In fact, it happens because, as Justin Baldoni explains to his fellow men, 'we've been trained to believe that our voices matter more and we deserve all that space'[33]

The uncomfortable truth is that people accorded higher status in any given situation tend to talk more, often without meaning to or even realising it; and as we've seen through work such as Mary Ann Sieghart's *The Authority Gap*, much of the time it's still men who are accorded that higher status. So it's not a huge surprise that white men are often so used to dominating conversations that they underestimate how much they talk, and over-estimate how much space women (and others with less social power) take up in conversations. Research from the 70s by Dr Dale Spender is often quoted in this context, where she analysed mixed-gender university classroom discussions to see how much the men and women thought they spoke, versus how much they actually spoke. She found that the women in her study had pretty accurate perceptions about who talked more in a given discussion, whereas the men perceived the discussion as being equal when women talked only 15 percent of the time; and they believed the discussion was being dominated by women if women talked for just 30 percent of the time.[34] Although arguments rage about the robustness of Spender's study and whether, all these decades later, this would still be the case, those numbers do have an interesting echo of a narrative we often hear about women in business, where we're told we're 'pretty much equal these days' even though less than ten percent of top CEO's are women; and we hear that women are 'taking over' when in reality women account for around a third of senior managers.[35] Back to conversational space, though, and we see from 2017 data that women on average talk 25 per cent less than men in meetings; that in two-way conversations, women were far more likely than men to be interrupted; that female doctors were interrupted by patients more often than male doctors were; and that boys called out in the classroom eight times as frequently as girls.[36]

Most worryingly, there's mounting evidence that in public life right now, women in leadership are subject to horrific threats and trolling that seek to intimidate them into silence. After Jacinda Ardern's resignation as PM in early 2023, researchers reported that they had just witnessed 'the most significant increase in violent, vulgar, vicious, venomous commentary against the PM since the start of our study in mid-August 2021' and that 'the vocabulary… has migrated from implicit and elusive references to her murder, assassination and rape now to explicit calls for it.'[37] Anyone who retorts that 'sticks and stones…' clearly doesn't understand how terrifying and silencing these threats can be when they regularly feature rape and sexualised murder fantasies, often with a specific focus on women's mouths, as is often the case for women who are deemed too vocal or too powerful. Another study reports that 'gendered abuse is an issue that pervades the whole online ecosystem: it is not confined to one topic or one platform', and although 'gendered abuse disproportionately targets women… gendered abuse of both men and women draws on stereotypes that are rooted in misogyny.'[38]

As ever, we see more marginalised women really bearing the brunt here too, as 'women of colour in the U.S. running for office were four times more likely to be targeted with violent abuse than white candidates, and were more likely to be on the receiving end of sexist abuse than white women running for office.'[39] It may only be a small proportion of men engaging in this behaviour, but few women who've put their head above the parapet and been seen to be 'too mouthy' have escaped this kind of silencing. Clearly, if women are to feel safe and free to take up their fair share of leadership conversation and political debate, it's imperative that we eradicate these violent attempts by some angry men to silence powerful female voices.

Sharing other kinds of space.

So ingrained is our belief that men should take up more of our shared space on a *physical* level, that we can often put men under enormous pressure to do so. Of course, the average man is bigger than the average woman, but societal expectation then heaps on top of that a pressure on men to be even bigger, to take up even more space in the world. We've long witnessed disordered eating and body dysmorphia amongst women and girls, and that's now rising amongst men too, which is far from the kind of gender equality we're seeking. But in what some refer to as the *Love Island* effect, UK data shows a rise in the number of men under 24 using anabolic steroids to bulk out,[40] as well as 'evidence to suggest that body image issues in men are becoming more pronounced, and increase the risks of poor mental health', especially as 'men also can find it more difficult to talk about their mental health and to seek help.'[41]

We only need to see the media fascination with relationships like Zendaya and Tom Holland, where the woman is taller than the man, to realise that this male expectation to take up space is about height as well as musculature - because, of course, this 'be bigger' pressure on men's bodies is about celebrating muscle and bone, not fat. Being 'too fat' is a way of taking up space that still tends to be vilified for all, regardless of gender, despite the sterling work of body positive activists. And although it's interesting to note that women's bodies remain subject to the vagaries of fashion, with the most desired female body veering from curvy to 'heroin chic' and back again, there's always a strong expectation that whatever their shape, a woman should generally be smaller than her man.

Notwithstanding these increased pressures on men to be sex symbols too, we've still not entirely eradicated the dominant idea that women's bodies exist in space (whether real space, or in art and media spaces) primarily for the viewing pleasure of men, whereas men's bodies exist to have agency, be active, to control and dominate the world that they move through. Half a century after Laura Mulvey's work on 'the male gaze,' it is still very much alive and kicking, as women's appearance is still scrutinised in a way that men in leadership and public spaces generally escape. There's a very narrow space that it's deemed acceptable for women to occupy as 'according to a 2016 study... women who put more effort into their appearance often make more money. On the other hand, though, women who are perceived as putting too much effort into the way they look are seen as less qualified, a 2014 study found. Women are not only more likely to be judged on appearance, but they are still expected to stay within certain boundaries.'[42] There's more on the male gaze in *Issue 6: Let's Talk About Sex*.

Finally, there's another important area where men disproportionately dominate the space: our names. For centuries in Western patrilineal culture, a woman's family name has disappeared when she married, which means that women are less visible and harder to find than men in everything from legal and historical records to current social media and search. And even though we see some rise in double-barrel and portmanteau names when couples marry these days, today, 'even among couples who share progressive gender politics, it's rare for men to give up their surname.'[43] All because in many nations, 'the legal construction of marriage... is modelled on coverture, the set of domestic laws imported from England by early colonists, which decreed that a married woman's identity and existence was legally "covered" by her husband. Her money was his money, her body was his to do with what he liked, and her name no longer existed.' The obvious result of this is that 'the woman's identity is essentially erased.'[44]

But, I hear you ask, beyond a few hurt feelings, how much does any of this really matter? What are the real-world effects of men taking up much more than half of the physical, ideological, verbal and cultural space that we share?

Why that matters.

A young girl who was talking about the unfair way that playground space is shared summed up its impact on her by saying simply, 'it feels like you're less important than the boys.'[45] Sad as this is to hear, young girls aren't alone in feeling 'less important than the boys' in the physical spaces that we all share. As grown-ups, many women change their behaviour just to keep themselves safe from harm, with 31 percent regularly making sure they're not alone, 28 percent regularly avoiding certain areas and 25 percent regularly avoiding being out at certain times.[46] That's millions of women not sometimes but *regularly* moderating their behaviour in public spaces in order to keep themselves safe. And this 'better safe than sorry' mindset feels entirely understandable when we consider that one in four women has been raped or sexually assaulted as an adult. I certainly wish that 'younger me' had listened to my instincts and moved to the other side of the street before the guy who turned out to be my assailant 'innocently' walked right up next to me and asked me the time, because then, maybe he wouldn't have been able to grab me by the arm as I looked at my watch, and drag me down that dark, deserted lane. It's sobering to realise that there are five million of us in England and Wales alone who, like me, have learned the hard way that we can't take our own safety in public spaces for granted.

This doesn't mean that we think every man is dangerous; but often, we don't want to take the gamble when the stakes are so high, and so women often spend their time silently assessing how far we should be on alert in any given space, especially after dark. No wonder that a monologue from the TV show She-Hulk went viral in 2022 where she tells her cousin the [He]-Hulk: 'Well, here's the thing, Bruce, I'm great at controlling my anger, I do it all the time. When I'm catcalled in the street, when incompetent men explain my own area of expertise to me. I do it pretty much every day, because if I don't, I'll get called "emotional" or "difficult" or might just literally get murdered. So I'm an expert at controlling my anger because I do it infinitely more than you!'[47] Director, Kat Coiro explained why she thought the speech resonated with millions of women, saying 'She-Hulk is a fantasy, a wish-fulfilment for a lot of women, where you don't have to be polite to that guy in the bar who hits on you. We are polite because we're conditioned to be polite, but we're also polite because we're afraid for our safety, and She-Hulk takes that totally out of the picture.'[48] Sadly, until our shared spaces feel as safe and free for women as we'd all like, it's hard to see how we can change the current situation where women regularly feel afraid or angry, and innocent men feel upset or offended by what they perceive as women's rudeness to, or rejection of them.

Women not enjoying equal ownership of the space we all share isn't just about safety though; it's about opportunity and fulfilling potential too. For instance, the data about women being under-represented in statues, films and TV may sound a bit irrelevant in the real world, but that's not actually true, because women are proven to behave differently when they're exposed to more positive images of women. A University of Washington study found that female students' associations between women and careers in computer science were strengthened simply by swapping the male-dominated Star Wars and Star Trek images that had decorated a computer science classroom for gender-neutral art and nature pictures instead.[49] It certainly doesn't take a lot of change to make a difference, as another study 'subtly exposed people either to a picture of Hillary Clinton, Angela Merkel, Bill Clinton, or no picture before they had to give a public speech. Women who had seen a picture of a female leader gave longer speeches that were rated higher both by external observers as well as by the women themselves than those who had seen a picture of Bill Clinton or no picture.' Importantly, this positive impact on women did not come at the expense of men, as the men 'did equally as well, whether exposed to Bill or to Hillary Clinton or to no picture.'[50] Just imagine how much negative impact is currently created for women simply because the typical images that tend to dominate schools, businesses and public spaces are of the men who, for centuries, have held most positions of power.

Women taking up less than their fair share of space in the world impacts their opportunities in other ways too. The lack of media coverage of women's sport suppresses investment and sponsorship, which in turn limits the opportunities for sports women to succeed. The England Women's football team famously recently beat Germany in the final of a major international competition and became the ones to 'bring football home', but their sponsorship and support is a fraction of what the men's game gets, and only 40 percent of UK secondary schools offer girls the same access to football as boys.[51] Sport isn't the only area where women suffer under-investment versus men either, as VC funding of business demonstrates. In 2019 in the US, even after years of increases, less than three percent of funding went to women-led start-ups. In fact, 'the 2.8percent figure, while paltry, was an all-time high' and it has since fallen again.[52] It's also almost three times the UK figure too, as, 'for every £1 of venture capital (VC) investment in the UK, all-female founder teams get less than 1p, all-male founder teams get 89p, and mixed-gender teams 10p.' Importantly, it's not caused by applications from women representing that miniscule a percentage. All-male teams only represent 75 percent of pitch decks reaching VC firms, but receive almost 90 percent of funding.[53]

Unsurprisingly, the silencing of women's voices relative to men's has major consequences in the real world too. A study found that in 2021 'among political candidates in the U.K. facing harassment and intimidation, women were more likely than men to modify their campaign strategies out of safety concerns. These adjustments - such as cutting down on canvassing or social media - tended to negatively affect their chances of success.'[54] And it happens way beyond the world of politics, as 'women online are being driven out of communities they value and subject to daily abuse: there is an overarching sense that they are not seen as deserving to exist safely in these spaces…and "online 'humour" is threatening women's safety.'[55] We only need to look to the police and fire service in the UK to see the damaging and sometimes disastrous impacts this can have on women's lives and, sadly, women's deaths too.

And this won't be easy to counter, as, alarmingly, we're now witnessing a rise in fear about speaking out in support of gender equality specifically too. In 2023 'the proportion of Britons who say they are frightened to champion the equal rights of women in case they face reprisals has doubled since 2017, up from 14 percent to 29 percent.'[56] And Britain is not unusual, as this 'growing sense of fear is in line with the direction of travel elsewhere in the world [where] looking across 22 nations for which trends are available, the proportion who say this applies to them has risen from 24 percent to 33 percent since 2017.'[57]

The fact that I find most concerning of all is that 'younger generations in Britain tend to be most fearful, with Gen Z (38 percent) around twice as likely as Baby Boomers (19 percent) to feel this way.'[58] As if this weren't enough, the relative silencing of women compared to men also ends up making women less likely to be chosen for leadership in the first place, even when they do put themselves forward. Adam Grant tells us that 'the person who talks the most is the most likely to become the leader [because...] regardless of intelligence and expertise, groups elevate those who command the most airtime.'[59] And that's despite the fact that evidence suggests that the people who are likely to talk less, who often have less status and authority, may actually possess a really valuable skill, because 'people with less power are better at reading the minds of the powerful.'[60] We'd all do well to stop underestimating the impact that this silencing of women and other marginalised groups clearly has.

It's a missed business opportunity too.

Men taking up much more than half the space in our media represents a missed business opportunity, because huge audiences for women's stories are currently being underserved. Despite men dominating movie roles, 2018 analysis of the highest grossing films across the preceding few years found that female-led movies outperformed male-led ones at every budget level, and 'every film that surpassed $1 billion in global box office also passed the Bechdel Test, in which (1) the film has to have at least two women in it; (2) the two women speak to one another in the film; and (3) they speak about something other than a man.'[61] So much for the received wisdom that 'chick flicks' aren't great business...

Men are missing out on opportunities to enjoy stories written by women too, as analysis of reader ratings shows that men actually marginally prefer books written by women to those written by men, and yet male readers only make up 19 percent of readers of the top ten bestselling female authors, whereas the top ten bestselling male authors achieve an almost-even gender readership split.[62] Meanwhile, in the world of news, a 2022 report commissioned by the Bill & Melinda Gates Foundation found that 'if the gender gap were to be addressed and women better represented in the news media, the industry could grow female audiences exponentially' and it estimates that 'closing the gender consumption gap could generate as much as US$83 billion over the next 10 years.'[63] Work in the real world bears this out too, as when The Guardian launched the newsletter *Her Stage* to cover issues relevant to women, but in a way that is also accessible to men, analysis revealed that its average open rate was 65 percent, versus an industry average of between 15 percent and 25 percent.[64] Similarly, in Norway 'data scientists found that the most gender-balanced newsrooms and those that write most about women's issues deliver the best audience and financial performances.'[65]

The underrepresentation of women in ads means brands are missing out massively too, as a whopping 91 percent of women in a recent study said that advertisers 'don't understand them.'[66] That's a very expensive mistake to be making, considering McKinsey calculates that women already control approximately $11 trillion in assets in the US alone, with that number is forecast to grow to $30 trillion by 2030.[67] The buying power that female consumers represent is enormous, with analysis in the US finding that women hold huge purchasing power across all kinds of categories, making or influencing over 90 percent of new home purchases, interior decorating and holidays as well as the more expected 93 percent of OTC pharmaceutical and grocery purchases. Women control the majority of spending in what are often still seen as male categories too, including almost two thirds of cars and computers, over half of consumer electronics as well as 80 percent of sports apparel and 89 percent of bank accounts.[68] As if that weren't enough, women are starting new businesses at a faster rate than men; women's earning power is growing faster than men's;[69] and 70 percent of U.S. mothers can expect to be primary financial providers before their children turn 18.[70] The picture is not dissimilar in the UK, where 'women make the decision or influence the purchase of 92 percent of holidays, 65 percent of cars, 93 percent of food, 91 percent of homes and 61 percent of PC's.'[71] No wonder Forbes asserted that 'women are the world's most powerful consumers,' explaining that 'women's engagement has the power to move markets' and 'women are a compass for a changing world [as] women are driving changes in the consumer marketplace that younger generations not only appreciate but also expect.'[72] In this context, brands and advertisers continuing to marginalise women seems like a business decision that only the ignorant would support.

It's clear, then, that women are still being marginalised in all kinds of ways, and that enabling them to take up their fair share of space in all kinds of areas could often benefit men too. So how do men understand the way they take up space in the world? Do they recognise these issues and the way women often feel about them? How do they feel about the privileges and pressures of inhabiting all of these spaces as a man? There was a lot to learn from my respondents.

WHAT I LEARNED
ABOUT MEN

Am I really mansplaining?

I asked my respondents whether they think they tend to take up more or less of their fair share of space in the physical world and in conversations, and most of them quickly leapt to conversations rather than the physical world. None of them wanted to be accused of being 'a mansplainer', and they'd immediately joke about it within our conversation as a way of recognising and yet diffusing the difficulty around this. All of them had heard a female partner or friend complain about being interrupted, talked over and not listened to, so they recognised that it was clearly a real issue for women; and most of them had seen other guys do it too, either in real life or online: 'The other day a girl on my course was talking about how one of her tutors just never lets her finish a sentence. It's bad enough when some of the mouthy lads in the group do it, but you'd think the tutor would know better.' Interrupting women, not listening to them and talking over them is clearly seen to be far from ideal behaviour, and these men saw it as especially misguided when the person doing it already has senior status, like in this example with the tutor, or when men are simply bystanders to a conversation, which they also notice happening regularly, especially online: 'You see those reply-guys who just happily jump into a conversation they're not even invited to, to tell a women that she doesn't know what she's talking about. Honestly though, the arrogance of them. It's almost admirable in a way, if they weren't so deluded.'

The term 'mansplaining' frequently cropped up here, and is clearly problematic, firstly because these men generally saw it being used not just to describe a man unnecessarily explaining something to a woman who's more of an expert than him (it's original and 'true' meaning); but also, it was often being used as a blanket term for any kind of male domination of the conversion. So our discussion here tended to bounce around between how much is being said by men versus women; and what/how things are being said, which often just confused both issues. Moreover, because 'mansplaining' is understood as a gendered slur, it's often read as a blanket anti-male criticism, which then elicits a challenge back, like 'is that really fair though? I know a lot of women who interrupt men too or talk so much they don't let anyone get a word in edgeways.' It's important to recognise that 'accusations being bandied around' that 'you take up too much of the conversational space' often just feel to them like an unjustified criticism of men; and when men feel they're facing blanket and unfair criticism, it's no surprise that they respond by defending or launching a counter-attack, as a few do by referencing the classic idea that 'women are gas-bags who can't stop talking', that has dominated popular culture since their childhood. Quite a few of these men told me that they genuinely think women take up much more of the talking time than men: 'When you lot get together, there's no stopping you! I've never seen a bunch of men talk as much as women do when they get together', although when I asked in what kinds of contexts that happens, they did tend to say 'in general chat' rather than in meetings, or 'actually, that's the case when a group of women are together but when men are there too, like in the pub, it may be true that we talk as much as they do, if not more. We definitely talk louder anyway!' A few, it should be noted, expressed the opinion that women ought to stop complaining about men dominating conversations and just join in, like some 'feisty' women they admire do.

In short, although they know it's an issue that women are annoyed by, and they could spot it in other men, none of my respondents self-identified as a man who took up more than his fair share of space in conversations; and because the idea of men taking up conversational space tends to be attached (in their minds at least) to the term 'mansplaining', that implies that men's domination of conversations is always done in a way that deliberately undermines and patronises women, which made it even easier for these men to reject the idea that they dominate conversational space, because patronising and correcting women is 'not something I do'. Even when a few of the men asked me if there's any proof that men are more likely to do this than women, they remained disinclined to believe the data I showed them, which comes as no great surprise, bearing in mind how cognitive bias works, and how the fact that men are socialised to compete (as discussed in *Issue 4: It's Dog Eat Dog, And I'm Nobody's Bitch*) means that conversation can very easily turn into 'a debate that must be won'.

Things felt much more productive, though, when we shifted the discussion away from a simple question of 'men vs women, who talks more?' and into more nuanced issues about who's good at leading conversations, not just participating in them. Here, as we talked more about who holds the power, who's leading and who's responding, it's important to note that, just as in so many areas, the men who were marginalised through their race, sexual orientation or gender expression reported having to work harder to be accorded the same space and respect that cis straight white men naturally seemed to enjoy. Character and interests also clearly play a role that shouldn't be overlooked too, as men who were naturally more introverted or less happy to express themselves in words said they let others dominate or lead conversations more often. Interestingly, though, many of my respondents came to the realisation that, while they neither want to be talked over, nor to be 'one of those bores who takes up too much air time without realising it', there's a third conversational mode that's actually 'really cool' and even 'a bit of a power play... in a good way!' and that is when someone does less asserting and more questioning. 'That really gives you the high ground, makes you the leader of the conversation without you being the person who's doing all the talking. It's like the therapist, or the old Socratic wise man, you can lead the conversation by letting other people do more of the talking, but being the person who guides where the conversation goes.'

Coupled with active listening, and a tone that was open rather than accusatory or patronising, a questioning conversational model seemed like a more evolved form of dominating conversations than the classic 'talk more, talk louder' approach that the boys had often developed in their school days. A couple of the men were also quick to point out that it's an approach that women and men seem to be equally good at, especially as it requires good listening skills and 'a lightness of touch. It's not about dominating conversations through brute force of words, it's more about leading by listening and guiding.' Each of the men who talked about this named both men and women they admired who used this ability well, and said they wanted to emulate that more in future.

Finally on the subject of conversational space, these men observed that there's a type of conversation where women almost overwhelmingly tend to dominate right now: discussions about difficult emotional issues. For these men, this included anything from dealing with sickness and bereavement, to worries about how to help friends or loved ones who were going through a difficult time, and even how to deal with personal feelings of anxiety or vulnerability. It was often the men who were parents or grandparents who brought this subject up, as well as those men who were more interested in issues of mental health and wellbeing; and they each told me that it really bothered them that men in general were often notable by their absence in these kinds of conversations, and that they'd love men (themselves included) to feel more comfortable and be more active in them. Initially, of course, there was a bit of joking around about how much better women were at talking about emotions, and how women's conversations were full of emotion even when they appeared to be talking about something quite practical: 'Just look at your text messages, they're full of kisses and emojis even when they're just about the shopping list! Ours tend to be much shorter and to the point. If one of your girlfriends sent you a message that looked like mine, you'd wonder what the hell you'd done to upset her!'

However, once we got to the 'but seriously' point, the laughing stopped and there was something very poignant about how each of these men said that they envied the ability women seemed to have to feel comfortable in these kinds of conversations. 'Even though my parents were good at encouraging me to talk about how I was feeling whenever I was stressed or having a tough time, us boys all felt there were huge areas that are no-go zones for us, even though our sisters were happy to spend ages talking about that kind of stuff.' One even added that 'I do sometimes feel a bit left out when the kids go to my wife whenever there's something difficult that they need to talk about, because they know she's better at that emotional stuff. But I want to be able to help too, and think I'd do an OK job.' Another dad tells me how 'the irony is, I'd get better with practice, but I don't really get the chance to practise as I can't just barge into those conversations if I'm not really welcome there.' There's more on this idea of welcoming men into traditionally feminine caring spaces later, in *Issue 7: The Daddy Of All Roles*.

We share our physical space fairly.

Discussions about the sharing of physical space followed a similar pattern to the 'conversational spaces' one we've just seen: a questioning of the idea that men take an *unfair* share; some defensiveness and confusion in the face of what's perceived as an attack in this area; and a reluctance to identity as one of the men who does take an unfair share himself, even when they acknowledge that other men do it. We then, though, got into some interesting discussions about a few physical spaces where women tend to dominate and where men don't feel comfortable - or even safe.

There are a couple of reasons why the men I talked to don't seem to believe that they take an unfair share of physical space. One is to do with their physical size, whereas the other is much more about cultural norms and assumptions about whose space it actually is. Let's deal with the physical size issue first, which can be summed up as 'But we're bigger!' That's especially important for men who are above average height: 'I know women complain about blokes manspreading on public transport, but I don't think that's always fair. I'm a tall guy, so seats on trains, buses and planes are actually a lot smaller for me in real terms than they are for the average woman' and, 'Sometimes it's literally impossible for me to fit my legs into the space that's allocated to a single seat, so I try and be as considerate as I can, but if I can't get an aisle seat, I can't help but use some of the space that technically belongs to whoever's sitting next to me.' When I asked the men who said these things if they thought that *all* men were as considerate as they were, some did recognise that 'actually you're right, there are those blokes who aren't that big but love to sit with their legs ridiculously wide apart, like some kind of primal show of dominance.'

Others told me that they'd had female friends or partners point out classic 'manspreading' behaviour: 'When we're on the tube, my girlfriend will surreptitiously point at men in the carriage who are spreading their legs and elbows right into the space that belongs to the woman sitting next to them.' They tend to find it comical, ridiculous, and pretty inexcusable, but few seem to think that it really matters. Some also just suggest, 'I don't know why women put up with that. If I was sitting next to a bloke like that and he didn't move, I'd just push him out of my space.'

When it came to taking up more space on pavements, and even barging women aside rather than giving way to them, none of the men I talked to was spontaneously aware that studies had observed men unwittingly doing this. However, when I did introduce the evidence to any of the men that asked for proof, there were looks of bafflement and disbelief. Partly, that was because each of these men knows that he's a good, decent, thoughtful man, so he simply can't imagine himself being 'guilty' of this kind of 'utterly dickish behaviour.' Many of my respondents had a very real sense that 'I'm not an arsehole', which is proof indeed that we need to shift conversations from criticising 'men behaving badly' and start to adopt a more inclusive approach that's less accusatory and alienating. Only this, it seems to me, will avoid men hearing the evidence as an accusation that 'you're one of the bad men' and so dismissing it, because clearly, they're not.

But there's another reason that some had a problem believing that they themselves (or even men in general) might be unwittingly marginalising women in physical spaces, and that was that 'I don't treat men and women any differently, I treat everyone as just a person', and also that 'there have been some real mixed messages on this kind of stuff over the years.' One of the more mature men elaborated: 'In my grandad's day, men were expected to stand aside for women, open doors for them, walk between them and the traffic when you're sharing the pavement, do all that kind of gallant stuff. Then in my dad's generation, the Women's Lib lot in the 60's would crucify a man for holding a door open, as if it meant men thought women were weak and incapable. Now it all feels less angry and more like everyone treats each other the same, so if you get to a door first, you might hold it open for someone just to be polite, but both men and women are happy to be either the holder or the... holdee, if that's even a word! But now these researchers are saying men are literally shoulder-charging women off the pavement? I don't really believe it.' Another says a similar thing, adding 'and anyway, I bet that if we did too much standing aside and giving way to women now, we'd look like creeps or we'd be accused of being patronising.'

This highlights two really fascinating, deep-rooted ideas that lay beneath a lot of what these good, kind, thoughtful men were saying. The first is something that they never vocalise, and don't even seem to recognise consciously, but give away in some of their conversation: the sense that the space belongs more to them. As we've discussed in *Issue 1: That 'I've never really thought about it' face,* they generally realised that women face danger when walking home alone, and they also tended to feel genuine pride at being one of the good, thoughtful guys who offers to 'walk a woman home to make sure she's safe', with no ulterior motive. And we've seen that they had little to no awareness of the simple actions any man can take to help women feel safer, such as not walking too close to her, not initiating a conversation with a lone woman and so on. But the interesting thing for the purposes of this chapter is that when we talked about what happens when another terrible attack hits the news, their responses were very much along the age-old lines of 'lock up your daughters.'

A father of teenage daughters told me, with real, heartfelt concern, 'It makes me sick to my stomach. I hate it when she's out at night. I wish I could just keep her indoors, like when she was little'; and a younger man speaks for many when he tells me, 'It's just horrible when you hear something like that. It makes me even more aware of making sure I make sure my girlfriend and my female friends are safe.' But when I ask, as a thought-exercise, 'how would it feel if *men* were asked to stay home at night after an incident like that, so that women could still go out freely and safely?' there's often a mix of confusion and a bit of nervous laughter. Some showed a little resentment along the lines of 'yeah I sympathise and everything, but you can't punish all men just because one sicko has done terrible things.' Only after a little reflection did a couple of the men say that 'I guess it's no more unfair than making women stay home… but then very quickly added 'but it just seems *really* odd, though, to even imagine men doing that.' Unless you're a black man, of course, where the sad truth is that 'when there's been a crime committed by someone who looks like me, you do hear people - the police included - tell us we're somehow "asking to be treated as suspects" if we're out on the streets. Even if you're just walking to the shops or the pub... because good black men and boys are supposed to stay home whenever a black man is a major suspect, so we don't look guilty.' Clearly, the assumption of the inalienable right to roam doesn't apply to all men, and is the product of deep-seated systemic prejudices. But however tolerant, kind and thoughtful all the men I spoke with were, there's still a residual, subconscious belief that the streets somehow belong to men more than they do to women, and so restricting regular (white) men's perceived right to that space seemed in many ways to be utterly anathema to them.

The second deep-seated but often unspoken idea that sat beneath the surface in these discussions was the spectre of fear; although it was a very different kind of fear to the one women experience. My cis, straight white respondents didn't express any generalised fear of attack by other men (despite the very real danger of male violence for men too), unless they were in some unusual scenario like being 'in a part of town I shouldn't have been in' or 'in a pub full of opposition supporters getting a bit riled up.' Only one straight white man told me he'd been a bit shaken up when a male friend 'got into a really vulnerable situation after he'd drunk far too much', and told me 'That was worrying, that could have ended really badly.'

As ever, the gay and gender non-conforming men in my sample expressed some of the same kinds of issues about sharing physical space as women tend to experience - fear of attack, frustration at being marginalised and 'constant subtle reminders that you're not supposed to be proudly occupying your own space. If you have to be out (in all senses!) in public, you should at least have the decency to do it quietly and in the margins. Like we did in the playground where I'd be the one skipping and doing cartwheels with the girls in the corners, hoping we didn't get hit by a stray football!'

None of my respondents said that they felt any fear of physical attack when they found themselves in spaces where they were outnumbered by women. Whenever they'd found themselves in the firm minority like that, the queer men told me they felt a 'blessed relief, like I'm home now!' and the straight men simply seemed to feel a bit of awkwardness, and a sense of not quite belonging. One of my respondents summed up that feeling for many when he described being sent to ballet class as a young boy: 'Before class, the girls would all sit around and talk and giggle, and the boys would just run around nervously, not knowing what to do.'

Many of my straight respondents, though, did express one important fear about being in female-dominated spaces, but this wasn't about what might happen in reality; it was about what others might *think* had happened. One father of a young daughter told me sadly that 'when we're out in the park or whatever and she's playing with her friends, I'm sometimes a bit self-conscious about being alone with the girls. And I definitely avoid doing anything that people might construe as dodgy behaviour, like if one of her friends fell over, I wouldn't pick her up or give her a completely innocent cuddle like I would to my own kids, because you're just too scared of what you could get accused of.'

A young man talked about how in pubs or at parties, 'if a girl has been drinking, you're especially wary about finding yourself alone with her, because if she accused you of something, you can't prove your innocence', and a couple of men mentioned the fear they sometimes feel in the office, saying 'if you spend time alone with one woman you work with, in the office or travelling or whatever, you do worry that other people might start whispering about it, and that could screw your entire career.' This fear of false accusations was a significant concern for these men, with a few telling me that they'd heard a story of someone who'd been falsely accused, and it had 'ruined his life.' The fear of false rape allegations is something I pick up again in *Issue 6: Let's Talk About Sex*, but it's important to note here that, because of the actions of a minority of men, women are regularly moderating their behaviour in order to avoid attack, while innocent men are moderating theirs too, out of fear of being falsely accused.

Finally, there's one area where all the men I spoke to said they'd seen a notable increase in the numbers of women taking up space, to the point where many of them felt that women are starting to 'dominate' both in terms of sheer numbers and in terms of what's acceptable behaviour: the world of work. 'There are definitely more and more women at my level at work, and all the men watch their behaviour a bit more these days' and 'there are things you don't say and do any more that you would have gotten away with even just a few years ago.' This clearly felt concerning for many, a bit of a threat, a constraint on what they're 'allowed' to do and say, and there's more on this in *Issue 8: Danger, Women At Work.*

However, some did also paint a more positive aspect to this story too, saying that nowadays they could enjoy some things that they'd never have done when the workspace was much more male-dominated. 'It's actually quite nice to have a bit of a different energy around us. It's not always full of macho bullshit posturing and dodgy strip clubs like it was in the old days, which is probably much healthier.' Another tells me that 'when we have a work event, we often go somewhere with a dancefloor too instead of all standing round at the bar or having a poker night. We'd probably not do that if the girls at work didn't encourage us, but I do actually enjoy it', while another says 'doing some more girly stuff in the office and on nights out is good actually, it's a bit of a laugh, a release. Even just making cakes for someone's birthday and people doing meditation or yoga classes… It's kind of freeing in some ways.' That's not, though, something that he'd readily say outside of our private conversation, as other men would probably find it a bit 'unmanly'.

So, even the good men are taking up more of their fair share of all kinds of spaces, and there are clearly some benefits to making everyone feel that they have an equal opportunity to use and enjoy the space we share. How, then, can we get over the significant barriers that include men feeling they somehow have more of a right to dominate; men not quite accepting the data, because if you're a good guy, you surely can't be part of a problem here; and men feeling confusion about mixed messages, and even some resentment about the problems that men also experience?

WHY MEN MIGHT
WANT TO CREATE CHANGE

Whether we're looking at the physical, conversational, or cultural spaces that men are used to dominating, we'd be wise to work with the strong feelings and beliefs that men already have, rather than telling them to change everything about who they are and how they've been socialised. None of us wants to be told to be quiet, talk less, make ourselves smaller, get out of the way; and decent, regular men with a strong sense of fair play genuinely don't *believe* that they're sharing space unfairly right now. So asking (let alone telling) men to be smaller, quieter, less physically dominant in our shared spaces probably isn't the most effective route, and it may even be counter-productive, making men feel like yet *more* rights are being taken away from them, more freedoms being lost, more things they mustn't do or think or say.

So here are a few initial thought-starters about how we might work towards shared spaces that work better for all of us, in a way that doesn't trigger massive loss aversion before we even start. If you have other ideas that you discover work well, please do share them with us at @MenemiesNoMore.

1. Make space for women's safety: Hopefully we can all encourage each other to share physical space, like seats and tables and walkways, more equitably, with a feeling of mutual respect rather than entitlement or anger; including when a man being physically bigger makes it impossible or uncomfortable for him to squeeze into a space that's too small for him, *and* when men who are in someone else's way are asked to make space for someone else. But the bigger issue in physical spaces is around women's safety. If men already think offering to walk a woman home is decent, thoughtful behaviour, can we encourage men to see actively making space for women after dark in a similar way? Maybe we can make it feel like a thoughtful, protective thing to walk on the other side of a dark road to give a lone woman some safety space; a gallant, powerful gesture, not a sign that men are being side-lined. And maybe we can also remind privileged white men that the reason they need to do this at all is because only a few men are truly dangerous, but those men often look just like the good guys.

2. Conversational gold mines: Loss aversion is powerful, so instead of focusing on telling men they should talk less, can we put energy instead into the *benefits* of listening more. Anyone whose voice isn't as powerful as others can be a great source of learning, so knowing and understanding more about people who are marginalised doesn't diminish a dominant man's status and power; it augments it, both professionally and socially. Can we encourage men to use conversations as a chance to better understand women's (and other marginalised groups') voices, then, because understanding a woman's perspective as well as their own will help them become more knowledgeable, and much more interesting than when they are more on 'transmit' mode. It's like having insider knowledge - you can use active listening to create more success for yourself as well as them.

3. The questioner holds the power: Currently, talking more acts as a show of authority and dominance, so it's no wonder that the 'shut up and share fairly' strategy that I've seen some women adopt isn't too effective. So could we give men a cleverer and cooler way to be the leader in conversations, by making the real conversational power-play not being the one who talks most, but being the one who steers the conversation, who asks the questions and listens carefully to the answers, playing the group like a conductor plays an orchestra. This should feel like less of a challenge to their subconscious entitlement to dominate, but would still result in bringing others in and creating more fruitful and inclusive conversations for all. We just need the men who do this to remember that, like the great comics, conductors and actors, it takes excellent listening and body language skills to really lead a group well in this way.

4. Be broad-minded in your entertainment: Even though they're not the things we're all surrounded by most often, there are all kinds of brilliant films, TV shows, art, writing and music by and about women that men could really enjoy too. Can we encourage more men to be bold and open-minded enough to seek out content by and about women, challenging the dominant assumption that female content isn't really for men? After all, it's a good look to be a bit of an entertainment explorer, a guy who's broad-minded enough to try things that other more cautious men avoid. And because research shows that men generally *do* enjoy it when they give it a go, it's a way of looking really open-minded and exploratory without actually having to take many risks.

5. Help men feel welcome in girly spaces: The fact that men feel unsafe in some female-dominated spaces because they're worried about what people might say is an issue we ought to address too. So instead of simply laughing at men's awkwardness and discomfort in a display of schadenfreude at how men feel in environments that are more feminine (in numbers and/or in energy), could women actively help make men feel a bit more welcome in those spaces? Whether it's the dance floor or a deep and meaningful emotional conversation, we know that men can enjoy those things if we all just try a bit harder to include everyone. It's clear that we'd all benefit from men feeling more able to join women there. And who knows, if we see more men being trusted, positive, equal contributors in those spaces, maybe some of the fear and suspicion that men fear about women's false accusations might subside a little too.

Sharing fairly can never work unless it goes both ways, so it needs to be done with genuine empathy for each other, as well as with an honest recognition of all the ways we can't currently enjoy the spaces we share with equal freedom and belonging. But sometimes, the forces that affect how we share space can just feel so big, complex and incendiary that it's hard to know how they can ever be overcome - as we can see in the great fear of false sexual assault accusation men have if they're alone with women and girls. It's time to grasp the nettle and talk about sex.

ISSUE 6:

Let's Talk About Sex

How power and pleasure prioritise men.

===============

REALITY CHECK:
WHERE WE ARE RIGHT NOW

For much of the modern era, sex has been one of the great taboos. People giggled about it, whispered about it, secretly sought out advice and information about it; but other than jokes and euphemisms, mainstream society just didn't really talk about sex, and it certainly wasn't something nice girls did. But in the 80s, the then-deadly AIDS epidemic forced governments, schools and the health service to talk a little more openly about safe sex, and the *#MeToo* movement has put the language of consent firmly on the mainstream agenda today. The growth of the internet, too, has transformed sexual content in recent decades, and now anyone can consume porn as easily as we can consume cute-animal videos, life-hacks and our household groceries; and we can be informed - and misinformed - about sex as readily as we can find out how to contour, cook a nice pasta or put up a shelf. But not only is sex talked about and watched more often than it used to be, it has also become a new front in the ongoing 'battle of the sexes.' Every day, people engage in all kinds of conversations about consent, or the lack of it. People talk about the prevalence of rape culture and sexual abuse, and the terrifying spectre of false allegations that can ruin lives. Some women bare their flesh in an act of female empowerment and others tell us that women who dress 'provocatively' are 'asking for it.' While some bemoan the sheer ubiquity of porn, the sex-positive movement encourages less prudishness and more pleasure, and others warn about the kinds of sexual relationships that porn is normalising and even teaching.[1] Girls are still slut-shamed if they have 'too many' sexual partners, while some are concerned that too many boys are remaining virgins for too long because girls are becoming 'harder to get.' Meanwhile, the battle for control of female reproductive systems rages on, powered by the post-60's sexual revolution and policed by increasingly draconian legislators. And that's just in the cis straight sex world. So what's going on here? What damage is really being done? Is the sex conversation something we should just leave to personal preference, or are there significant issues that ought to be addressed at a broader level?

It's not my job here to talk about what people get up to in wholly consensual, private sexual relationships where they're fully informed, free to choose and mutually fulfilled. But anyone who recognises the 90s song[2] that my chapter title refers to will know that the girls urged us to 'talk about all the good things *and the bad things* that may be.' Here, I'll start by focusing on the bad, because there are many issues around sex that desperately need fixing, and where more understanding and less judgement across the gender divide could really help.

The reality of rape and sexual assault.

Chief amongst the issues around sex that really need fixing is the prospect of sexual violence which, according to a 2019 UK study[3], 'permeates women's day to day lives in a way that it does not men's.' For instance, women are ten times more likely than men to say they 'often or always feel unsafe' getting a taxi/ride-share by themselves, and five times more likely than men to say the same when it's just them and a tradesperson in their house. The vast majority of men, nine in every ten, say they've *never or rarely* felt unsafe in those situations. Similarly, a massive three-quarters of men said they'd rarely or never felt unsafe when going on a first date, whereas women are more than twice as likely as men to say they've '*often or always* felt unsafe in that situation.' The reason women feel this way is that we're currently experiencing an 'epidemic of violence against women and girls.'[4]

It's impossible to get wholly accurate figures, as many women who experience sexual violence don't report it to the police,[5] but in May 2022 the Shadow Home Secretary told UK parliament that 'today in England & Wales it's estimated that 300 women will be raped.'[6] That equates to one woman every five minutes, or twelve more women by the time the average person has finished reading this chapter. Sadly, Britain isn't an outlier here as in the US, hundreds of thousands of women are raped or sexually assaulted each year, with young Americans being at greatest risk of sexual violence, and one in three women in the US experiencing some kind of sexual violence in their lifetime.[7] Even the institutions that are meant to keep us all safe are 'at best failing, at worst actively harming women,' as a horrifying litany of offences in the UK police force includes revelations that 'two officers took and shared selfies with the bodies of murdered sisters Nicole Smallman and Bibaa Henry… Met officers had joked about rape, killing black children and beating their wives. Whistle-blowers have spoken about police officers raping women they have arrested, and harassing victims, [and 15-year-old black schoolgirl] Child Q was strip-searched by police officers without her parents being notified, or an appropriate adult present.'[8] Then in 2023, a Met police officer joined the ranks of the UK's most prolific sex offenders, pleading guilty to 49 offences against 12 women including 24 counts of rape, with Commissioner Sir Mark Rowley saying: 'David Carrick's crimes were unspeakably evil. The detail is harrowing.'[9] We also learned that Wayne Couzens, the serving police officer who kidnapped, raped and murdered Sarah Everard, had previously been accused of indecent exposure on at least two occasions, including three days before he murdered Sarah, but it wasn't investigated.[10]

Across the Atlantic, a Senate investigative report revealed that 'widespread sexual abuse of female inmates continues to plague federal prisons, and accountability measures for staff have not contained the scourge of such violence,' with women being 'abused by prison staff in at least 19 of the 29 federal facilities that held female inmates since 2012.'[11] And in the US military, a report recently found that 'sexual assault rates are up, the percentage of people reporting sexual assault is down and trust in the military when it comes to protecting victims is at an all-time low' with 8.4 percent of female service members reporting that they've experienced unwanted sexual contact.[12]

Rape and sexual assault is so big a problem that a UK police watchdog report in 2021urged that 'violence against women be given as much priority as counter-terrorism.'[13] And this parallel with terrorism is no accident, as the UN has reported that misogyny and gender-based violence are among the most reliable indicators of terrorism and conflict,[14] as well as the Anti-Defamation League highlighting a 'robust symbiosis between misogyny and white supremacy.'[15] As journalist Amanda Marcote explains, 'white nationalists and other authoritarian groups figured out years ago that an effective way to lure men into the fascist cause is by appealing to their resentment toward women. The internet has created a bunch of different misogynist communities that fascists latch onto, looking for new recruits.'[16]

Of course, whilst rape and sexual assault predominantly affects women and girls, we must acknowledge here that men also become victims of sex attacks, with one in 20 men in England and Wales having been raped or sexually assaulted as an adult.[17] Even though men comprise the minority of victims (the figure for women is 5 times as high as men, with an enormous one in four adult women having been raped or sexually assaulted), still five percent of UK men becoming victims of rape or sexual assault adds up to more than a million men[18], with every one of these being a personal tragedy. In the United States, over 20,000 men were raped or sexually assaulted between 1993 and 2020 alone,[19] and in the US military, even though it happens to women around six times as often as men, unwanted sexual contact was experienced by 1.5 percent of service men too.[20] Moreover, for some communities of men, the figure is disproportionately high, with a Survivors UK study in 2021 finding that nearly half of gay & bisexual men in Britain have been sexually assaulted,[21] and men in the US who are marginalised because of their sexual orientation or gender identity are much more likely than other men to suffer sexual attacks, with reports claiming that 2 in 5 gay men will be sexually assaulted in their lifetime, and half of transgender Americans will experience sexual violence.[22]

Looking beyond the most serious crimes of rape and sexual abuse, we see that sexual *harassment* is almost ubiquitous for women. 81 percent of women in the US say they've experienced some kind of sexual harassment during their lifetimes[23] and an enormous 97 percent of UK women say the same.[24] These 'less serious' offences are sometimes positioned as an annoyance rather than a real problem, but that's not the case as 'there is a big picture here that we are just repeatedly missing. There are connections between the normalised daily behaviours that we brush off, and the more serious abuses,' and 'there is enough data to know that men who kill women do not suddenly kill women, they work up to killing women.'[25] Imagine, for instance, how different the outcome might have been had Wayne Couzens' indecent exposure accusations been taken more seriously. Yet we often miss the big picture and assume that sexual harassment is just something that women have to learn to deal with.

Even the very language we use reinforces this normalisation, implying that sexual violence is something that just happens: Jackson Katz explains that 'the term "violence against women" is a passive construction - there's no active agent, it's a bad thing that happens to women,' so we subliminally hear it as if "nobody's doing it to them."' Similarly, we talk about women 'being raped', not a man having raped a woman. That kind of language, Katz says, 'shifts the accountability off of men, and the culture that produces them, and puts it onto women.'[26] By focusing on the victim and their gender in this way instead of shifting our focus to who's *committing* these crimes, we continue to mask the sobering but vitally important fact that in the UK, an enormous 98 percent of sexual offences are committed by men,[27] and in the US nearly 99 percent of perpetrators of rape & sexual assault are male.[28] Why is it men who are so disproportionately likely to adopt this behaviour? And why do we behave as if it's just a normal part of life?

It's about power, not just sex.

Oscar Wilde is credited with the aphorism 'Everything in the world is about sex, except sex. Sex is about power', and he's certainly right when we look at sexual violence. Sex as power explains, for instance, why sex is used so often as a weapon of war, as UN ambassador Angelina Jolie attests: 'This is rape and assault designed to torture, to terrorize, to force people to flee, and to humiliate them. It has nothing to do with sex. It has everything to do with the abuse of power.'[29]

It's a pattern we see from UK police officers bragging about how 'struggle snuggles are always useful... good skills!'[30] to rape being used systemically to punish protestors, as we're witnessing right now in Iran.[31]

The insight that sex is about power is also evident when we look at hyper-masculine environments like locker rooms, frats and sports clubs, where men have often been found to use sexual assault as a way of asserting dominance over each other, as well as over women. Hockey Canada, for instance, made a multi-million dollar settlement after a woman told how she was gang-raped in 2018 by five World Junior hockey players; only then did it emerge that 'many men have also recently come forward with horrifying details of being tortured, sodomized, raped, assaulted... while they were players in the league during initiations.'[32]

From gymnastics to football to rugby; in universities, schools and professional, high-performance teams; in clubs and societies; from date rape to hazing; in Hollywood and in pubs and bars, we've become painfully used to hearing more revelations about men using rape and sexual violence as the ultimate-power play. In fact, in in the world of hockey alone, it's reported that 'accusations against players were so frequent that millions of dollars were set aside in an undisclosed fund, exclusively used to settle sexual assault lawsuits.'[33]

The threat of sexual violence is ever-present online.

Although it remains unseen by most of us most of the time, violent, sexualised misogyny is rampant in the online 'manosphere.' A 2023 Channel 4 documentary discovered that there are thousands of men in the UK on the most extreme incel forums, where content that's shared includes apparently genuine videos of women being brutally assaulted and even murdered.[34] Film-maker Ben Zand describes how 'extremely lonely men' get recruited through the so-called 'blackpill ideology' that entices and then radicalises them with the message that 'to get the same level of attention that a two- or three-out-of-ten woman gets, you need to be a ten-out-of-ten male yourself.' Increasingly, rape and femicide fantasies then become a way of addressing what this community perceives as an imbalance of sexual power that's now working unfairly in favour of women. According to research from the Centre for Countering Digital Hate, posts about incel-perpetrated mass murders have increased by nearly 60 percent in the last year, and members on one incel forum spoke about rape every 29 minutes.[35]

It's no wonder, then, that when a woman who is perceived to be in a position of power expresses her opinions or exercises her autonomy, it often triggers an enormously disproportionate, violent response from the men who inhabit these online spaces. MP Jess Phillips, for instance, told parliament that she received 600 rape threats in one night alone, and was threatened with violence and aggression every day simply because she speaks 'from a feminist perspective.'[36] Mary Ann Sieghart recounts how the campaign to have a woman featured on the back of a British bank note saw Caroline Criado-Perez get so many rape and death threats that when police gathered just one weekend's worth, they filled 300 A4 pages, and included such delights as 'Shut your whore mouth... or I'll shut it for you and choke it with my dick. OK?' and 'Women that talk too much need to get raped.'[37] Founder of the *Everyday Sexism Project* Laura Bates has bravely published some of the horrific abuse she's personally received from online trolls, and they too make terrifying reading: 'Laura Bates will be raped tomorrow at 9pm... I am serious.' 'LAURA BATES... I am seriously going to RAPE and KILL you TODAY at 8pm near your house... Are you ready to get FUCKED?' and 'Anyone involved in a feminist movement today needs to have a penis put in their mouth and shoved up their arse.'[38]

Nothing a woman says can justify these kinds of threats, of course, but it's also worth noting that women don't even have to be saying anything particularly provocative to trigger such violent responses. In fact, back in 2006 researchers entered online chat rooms using fake accounts with both masculine and feminine sounding names and discovered that 'accounts with feminine usernames incurred an average of 100 sexually explicit or threatening messages a day. Masculine names received 3.7.'[39] The police consider some of the threats women receive from trolls as genuine intentions to rape and kill, but even if most are 'just' fantasies rather than statements of real intent, we'd be wrong to assume that reading or listening to a torrent of sexual violence like this doesn't harm the victims. This abuse is intended to intimidate, traumatise, terrify and silence the victims, and in many cases it does exactly that.

Even if they're not directly threatening the woman herself, men just talking with each other about extreme sexual violence can really amplify women's fears when those private, men-only conversations come to light. A few UK universities were recently faced with many fearful and furious young women after male classmates were discovered to have been sharing rape fantasies together 'as a joke' in WhatsApp groups. Jeremy Clarkson triggered enormous anger amongst women by recounting - in a national newspaper - his hate-fuelled fantasies about Meghan Markle's public, sexualised humiliation (complete with heavy racist overtones), as well as accusing her of 'bewitching' Prince Harry with 'some vivid bedroom promises.' And millions of erstwhile Johnny Depp fans were left reeling after discovering that he admitted to writing texts to Paul Bettany saying: 'Let's burn Amber!!!...Let's drown her before we burn her!!! ...I will fuck her burnt corpse afterwards to make sure she is dead.'[40] To be clear, I'm in no way suggesting that any of these comments were an expression of a genuine *intention* to carry out those actions; and we know that the men involved often plead ignorance or 'banter', explaining that they 'didn't mean any harm'. But it's important to recognise that when women discover men (especially men we know and like) expressing hate for a woman through fantasies of sexual violence, it's just really troubling, even though we know they're not intending to act out those fantasies in real life. And when those men remain loved, valued and rewarded despite sharing those fantasies, it feels a bit like we're telling women that sexual violence is no big deal, that it's just a joke, that 'boys will be boys' and that laughing dismissively about it is just part of life. At least these celebrities' employers seem to think so, as Dior demonstrated in spectacular fashion when, despite these disclosures, they renewed Depp's contract as the face of *Sauvage*.

Women can sometimes find it hard to articulate their anger and frustration about this too, as they can very quickly be accused of overreacting and getting things out of proportion, or of fanning the flames of the gender wars and advocating cancel-culture. This plays right into something that's particularly alarming to many men, because there's a big fear that *men* have that gets triggered in any conversations about rape and sexual assault: the fear of innocent men being wrongly accused of sexual misconduct.

The fear of false accusation.

The *#MeToo* movement that started in 2006[41] but gained global fame in 2017 unleashed a tidal wave of women speaking up about rape and sexual assault that they had not reported or even spoken about publicly before, with the accusation, prosecution and conviction of wealthy, powerful men such as Harvey Weinstein and Jeffrey Epstein filling headlines all around the world. But *#MeToo* brought men's fears of false allegations right into the spotlight too - and that's unsurprising, given how horrifically damaging accusing an innocent man of rape can be.

One such false accusation hit the headlines in 2023 when Eleanor Williams was jailed for eight-and-a-half years after falsely claiming that she was groomed, raped and trafficked by multiple men, most of whom were South Asian. Her lies to the police and on social media caused horrific harm to the innocent men she accused, with the court hearing that 'three men Williams falsely accused over a three-year period tried to take their own lives after being targeted and suffering "hell on earth."'[42] One of those men, Mohammed Ramzan explained that he and his family were targeted 'in the most horrendous way' and says, 'I still bear the scars to this day', explaining that he has 'had countless death threats made over social media from people all over the world because of what they thought I was involved in.'[43] Another man who was charged as a result of Williams' false claims, Jordan Trengove, faced the trauma of spending 73 days in prison, sharing a cell with a convicted sex offender.

There's absolutely no disputing how damaging false accusations can be for any man unlucky enough to fall victim to them. However, it's vital we all recognise that false allegations like this are - thankfully - much less prevalent than many men assume. In fact, accusations that are proven false, like Williams, make up just 0.62 per cent of all rape prosecutions, which means that 'the average adult man in England and Wales has a 0.00021281 percent chance of being falsely accused of rape in a year, according to 2018 data. That means that a man is 230 times more likely to be raped than be falsely accused of it.'[44] Some men have critiqued this figure, saying that we shouldn't just count accusers who are convicted of making a false accusation in our calculations; so Channel 4 fact-checkers recently made similar calculations using a much broader definition of 'false accusation' and they still found that the risks of men being a victim of rape are significantly higher than the risks of being falsely accused of rape: 'Imagine for a second that you believe that every single one of the men prosecuted for rape in England and Wales in 2016-17 was falsely accused. Even if that unlikely scenario were true, there would still have been more adult male victims of rape (8,000) than men prosecuted for those rapes they "didn't commit" (5,190).'[45] A Scottish Rape Crisis briefing paper agrees that it is a 'misconception that false allegations of rape are common' and notes that these fears 'have sometimes been amplified by individual police officers, by the men's rights movement, and by popular culture, where references to women "crying rape" have gained much credence in recent years.' They point out that 'there is no research basis for these assumptions' and that 'research undertaken in recent years has revealed that false complaints are no more common in cases of rape than they are for other crimes.'[46]

Another way of understanding the risk of false accusations against men is to look at it from the other end of the telescope, and consider how many women are attacked but don't report it - in effect, the number of men who commit rape or sexual assault and 'get away with it' so entirely that they're not even reported, let alone prosecuted or convicted. Only 56 percent of the estimated 300 women that are raped each day in England & Wales report it to the police, and a tiny one percent of rapes that officials understand to have happened make it as far as a court of law.[47] USA 2022 data shows that only 28 percent of sexual assault victims report their experiences to the police, meaning that nearly three quarters of perpetrators there face no official accusation, let alone prosecution;[48] and in Australia, where 30 per cent of men believe that 'women who say they were abused often make-up or exaggerate claims of abuse or rape,'[49] it's estimated that an enormous 90 percent of sexual assaults go unreported.[50] In Britain, one officer commenting on Baroness Casey's 2023 official report that found the Met police to be institutionally racist, misogynist and homophobic went so far as to lament that 'so few rapists are brought to justice that effectively, rape is legal in London.'[51]

The institutional and cultural failings within the police force aren't the only reason why rape and sexual assault consistently go so under-reported though. Experts also point to the fact that 'women are scared of retaliation for speaking out, or they fear the stigma associated with sexual violence.'[52] Many rape survivors feel a misplaced but deep sense of shame, and often don't feel strong enough to face what know will be a gruelling process if they do report the crime, as this survivor so powerfully articulates: 'I felt like I was being blamed for what happened to me. It was really difficult - I felt like I was being abused all over again and I found myself actually doubting whether I was doing the right thing by taking legal action against my abuser.'[53] It's a complex issue, of course, and the law must always assume that an accused person is innocent until proven guilty. But too often in the case of sexual assault and rape, that results in the victim who reports a rape being aggressively accused of lying, even in the face of overwhelming evidence. One rape survivor, who secured a conviction thanks to having incontrovertible audio and written confessions from the perpetrator, noted that, even in *this* case, despite the overwhelming evidence of his guilt, the jury's verdict was still not unanimous, leaving her to comment 'I think that says a lot about society.' [54]

There are two other important factors that are worth noting at this point, as they both contribute to the low numbers of prosecutions and convictions for perpetrators of rape. Firstly, some behaviours that are entirely reasonable and commonplace in women can make securing a conviction incredibly difficult, because they leave victims open to accusations that they must have wanted sex with the perpetrator. Those behaviours include the woman knowing the accused; having had a relationship with him previously; being dressed in a way that's seen to be 'provocative' or 'revealing;' having had sex with other men; or having been drinking. Each of these things affect a victim's chances of securing a conviction and increase the amount of victim-blaming she'll suffer, even though legally, sex without consent is rape regardless of any of those factors. Secondly, most people believe that when a woman is attacked, if she doesn't actively fight back or try to run away, she must have been consenting. Sadly, this is another very dangerous example of the default-male thinking we explored earlier in *Issue 1: That 'I've Never Really Thought About It' Face*, because psychologists agree that although 'fight or flight' is men's most common response to threat, there are two others that are more likely to be seen in women - 'freeze', where someone is unable to move or act against a threat; or 'fawn' where the person under threat immediately acts to try to please to avoid any conflict.[55] So unless a woman embodies what society thinks a perfect rape victim should look like - a virginal, sober, demurely-dressed young white woman who physically fights the rapist who is a stranger to her - she will struggle to get a jury of men and women to believe her.

All of which brings us to the thorny question: if rape or sexual abuse isn't just a violent attack by stranger out of nowhere, where the modestly-dressed woman physically fights back, then what is it? The simple answer, of course, is whenever there's sex without consent. But what exactly *that* means is not always such a simple matter.

The matter of consent.

I'm optimistic that everyone reading this knows the basics of consent. Hopefully you're already well aware that it's not consent if you just assume 'Surely you must want it because other girls like it.' Nor if you think 'Well you dress like a girl who'd be into it, so what do you expect?' Nor if you heard that she did it with someone else, so she must be happy to do it with you too. Nor even if she consented with you previously, so 'She must still want to this time'. We've surely all watched the cup of tea consent analogy video; and if you haven't, go watch it now before we carry on.[56]

But even with all the information and advice that exists in schools, universities, workplaces and online, there's still little understanding of what constitutes consensual versus non-consensual sex. In fact only 34 percent of female university students felt that all of their sexual partners 'had fully understood what "consent" meant,' [57] and a 2018 YouGov study found that 'a third of men think that, if woman has flirted on a date, it generally wouldn't count as rape, even if she hasn't explicitly consented to sex.'[58] Moreover, 'a third of men also believe that a woman can't change her mind after sex has started. Almost a quarter think that sex without consent in long-term relationships is usually not rape. And 40 percent think it is never or usually not rape to remove a condom without a partner's consent.'[59] Even a judge in the UK recently proclaimed that he 'cannot think of any more obviously fundamental human right than the right of a man to have sex with his wife,' seemingly oblivious to the Sexual Offences Act 2003 which clarifies that as marriage no longer constitutes irrevocable consent, men don't have a 'right' to sex with their wives any more than they do with any other woman.[60]

One reason that consent is so often misunderstood is because it's not simply about someone explicitly saying yes or no. The Rape Crisis Centre clarifies that with any sex act, 'even if someone doesn't say "no" out loud, that doesn't automatically mean that they have agreed to it' and explains that 'if someone seems unsure, stays quiet, moves away or doesn't respond, they are not agreeing to sexual activity.'[61] What's more, consent is even more nuanced than that, because a sexual partner who is behaving like they're 100 percent comfortable with what you're doing can't be deemed to have given consent unless they have 'both the freedom and capacity to make that choice.'[62] So obviously, if someone's asleep, unconscious, been spiked, under age, or they've had physical force used against them, that means they don't have the freedom and capacity to agree to the sexual activity; but what's less well known and well understood is that legally, a person doesn't have the freedom and capacity required by law if they have a mental health disorder or illness that means they are unable to make a choice, or if they're drunk, or if they're being pressured, bullied, manipulated, tricked or scared into saying 'yes'. And importantly, that pressure, manipulation, or fear is based on what *they* might legitimately feel, not just on what you may or may not have intended.[63]

So it's true that with anything sexual, no means no, and that should never be ignored; but it's absolutely not the case that an absence of 'no' automatically means it's a yes. In fact, even an explicit 'yes' doesn't legally mean consent if it's given by someone who doesn't have the freedom and capacity to give it. No wonder all of this can feel like such a minefield for men as they navigate hooking up sexually; and this doubtless adds to their disproportionate fears of false accusation of sexual misconduct too.

Later, we'll share some ideas that might help address men's fears, both about false accusation and about inadvertent offences resulting from a lack of understanding about consent. First, though, we should explore some of the things that men have been conditioned to believe about entirely *consensual* sex, because we won't get to answers to all of this without questioning and re-thinking some of those deep-rooted ideas and beliefs too.

.

Women exist for men's sexual pleasure.

Now I'm not suggesting that men think the *only* reason for a woman to exist is to be the object of a man's sexual gratification, but compelling evidence shows that when it comes to sex, the dominant way that we - men and women - have been conditioned to think about it is very much from the point of view of the man. Or more accurately, from the man's penis. For centuries we've lived with the implicit understanding that sex is something men do to women (and sometimes to other men too). Sex historian Kate Lister explains that historically, many thought that lesbian sex didn't really count as sex because there was no penis involved, so the authorities didn't worry about gay women in the same way that they did gay men, assuming these women to just be very good friends. Others, like Freud, warned that female sexual pleasure that's not centred on the penis is positively dangerous. But whether sex-minus-the-penis was simply dismissed or seen as an active threat, the assumption is clear: sex equals penetration, and penetration is what men do.[64]

The language we use gives us away again here, as Sophia S Galer points out: 'The term penetration implies (and reinforces) the idea that sex is from the male perspective' and she goes on to consider how we might think about it differently: 'The opposite might be envelopment or enclosure. Can you imagine how different life would be if that's how we referred to sex?'[65] Moreover, 'vagina' in Latin literally means sheath for a sword, so linguistically 'the vagina is a receptacle, or holder for the penis. It exists to serve the sword.'[66] This language, reinforcing the idea that sex centres the male experience, mirrors how we've long associated sexual agency with the masculine, and passivity with the feminine: 'Romans saw women who were more sexually active (rather than passive) as being more manly, for example.'[67] But these issues aren't just a fascination for linguists and historians, because the unquestioned assumption that sex is about men doing the penetrating and women (and others) being penetrated can impact the real world today.

This assumption that straight sex centres on men's pleasure fuels the porn industry, as Cindy Gallop explains: 'Mainstream porn's entire purpose is to get the man off - which, with porn acting as default sex education in the absence of discussion of real-world sex - results in men and women growing up believing the entire purpose of sex is to get the man off.' She goes on to explain that because porn, like most other industries, is 'a closed loop of white guys talking to white guys about other white guys', the result is that 'women's needs, wants and desires go unacknowledged, unappreciated and unfulfilled.'[68] And unless something changes significantly, this normalisation of straight sex centring male pleasure looks set to continue, as the average age that children see porn is 13, but nearly a third have seen it by 11,[69] and over 40 percent of 18-29 year old men watch porn 2-3 times a week or more.[70] Moreover, a study amongst 11 to 16 year olds found that the majority of the boys as well as nearly 40 percent of the girls assumed porn was a realistic depiction of sex, although almost all of them said that pornography failed to help them understand consent. Dr Elena Martellozzo, who co-led that research, warns that, 'if boys believe that online pornography provides a realistic view of sexual relationships, then this may lead to inappropriate expectations of girls and women', adding that 'girls, too, may feel pressured to live up to these unrealistic, and perhaps non-consensual, interpretations of sex.'[71]

Those fears seem well founded when we consider that a recent analysis of the most-watched porn found that 88 percent of scenes showed physical aggression, and around half showed verbal aggression, with 94 percent of the aggression being aimed at female performers.[72] Researchers have noticed a normalisation, particular amongst Gen Z, of what were previously considered quite niche sexual practices, including anal sex in straight couples and rough sex including asphyxiation. In a recent US study, 58 percent of female college students said they had experienced choking during sex, and when a UK study explored consent in this area, it found that 'a third of women under the age of 40 have been non-consensually choked, slapped, gagged or spit on during sex.'[73] Similarly, 71 percent of men polled by the BBC said they engaged in rough sex, with a third of them admitting that they didn't ask their partner if they wanted them to do it.[74] A growing 'normalised coercion' of anal sex has been noted by experts too, with a 2022 British Medical Journal report showing that heterosexual anal intercourse among 16 to 24 year olds more than doubled, from 12.5 percent to 28.5 percent over the past few decades, with similar trends being seen in the US, where 30-44 percent of men and women report experience of anal sex.[75] Importantly, as well as saying they're driven by 'pleasure' and 'curiosity', young women are also citing 'pleasing male partners' and 'coercion' as motivating factors. In fact, 'up to 25 percent of women with experience of anal sex report they have been pressured into it at least once.'[76]

Technology, too, is enabling new ways of serving porn to men and boys that can have incredibly damaging real-world consequences for women. In 2019, a company which detects and monitors deepfakes found that 96 percent were non-consensual sexual deepfakes, and 99 percent of those featured women. There are large numbers of easily-accessible and affordable services that use images from a woman's social media feed to make deepfake porn to order, featuring whomever the user requests.[77] 'Nudification' is a huge industry, as one website, for example, received 38 million hits in the first seven months of 2021. Its bio reads: 'Undress any girls with any dress. Superior than Deepnude. The threat to girls.'[78] As of April 2023, only four US states have passed legislation specifically about deepfakes,[79] and as I write, the UK has only just removed the need to prove in law that images like these were created with the intention of causing harm - a which is important, because as well as so-called 'revenge porn', men often men create this non-consensual sexual imagery for pleasure, for laughs or just to make money.

There's clearly lots of work to do to curb the making and sharing of such imagery, because just knowing that anyone could be making and sharing this kind of non-consensual sexual imagery of you is disturbing enough; but when the imagery has circulated online and come to the attention of the victim, it is often incredibly traumatising. One woman explained to a *Glamour* journalist: 'It has the power to ruin your life…it is such a level of violation… because you are violated not only by the perpetrator, but you also feel violated because society doesn't recognise your harm.' She describes it as 'a very isolating, degrading and demeaning experience – it's life-ruining.'[80]

Phallocentrism - the centring of the male sexual point of view - also lies behind the assumption that women dress to be attractive to men, and are therefore signalling sexual availability if they dress 'provocatively'. We see this played out in everything from movies to music videos to sports kits, where women's bodies are frequently displayed and sexualised in a way that men just aren't; although we're now seeing sportswomen like the German gymnasts and the Norwegian handball team taking control over their own clothing and covering up in a refusal to conform to the sexualised expectations of the male gaze. Interestingly, we're also simultaneously seeing many prominent women in art and entertainment refusing to conform to the male gaze in a very different way, not by covering up, but by challenging the very idea that exposure of skin is a sign of sexual availability.

Typical of this attitude amongst women is a much-shared social post where a woman says: 'Men think women dress for them… Dude please, we dress according to our waxing schedules, periods, mood swings, location, season, matching shoes, matching bags, matching lipstick, availability of suitable underwear. You're not even on that list, so chill.'[81] Caitlin Moran talks brilliantly about this too, declaring that we'll have reached 'Feminist Utopia' when women can dress as they choose without their exposed skin being read as a signal of sexual availability, when 'everyone will be able to wear exactly what they want, without fear of judgement or reprisal. It will be understood that a teenage girl, on a hot day, wearing short-shorts and a crop-top, is no more demanding to be catcalled, harassed and assaulted than a toddler, dressed up in a nurse's hat and apron, is volunteering to give passers-by a tetanus booster and a leaflet about cholesterol.'[82] Unfortunately, we seem to be a long way from that right now.

The normalisation of women and girls as sex objects.

Experts agree that 'so much harassment - the uncomfortable staring, the catcalling, the lewd gestures, the public masturbation - is seen as simply normal nuisances that women have learned to put up with.'[83] As Laura Bates tells us, 'the idea that boys will inevitably harass, that girls are responsible for "protecting themselves" and that female bodies are to blame for making boys act badly are all conveyed to young people at an impressionable age by their own educational institutions.'[84] In fact, sex attacks on women are so normalised that anti-spike drinks covers are sold on Amazon with this jolly copy: 'Protect Yourself - This NightCap scrunchie drink cover is a dual functional scrunchie that can be used to cover over most cups and glasses to prevent pills and powders from being dropped into a drink…Simply wear the scrunchie drink protector on your wrist or hair. When ready, pull the drink cover out of the hidden pocket, place it over the drink, pop in a straw and enjoy.'[85] While it's helpful that these kinds of things exist to make it easier for people to protect themselves, surely we should be working harder to solve the troubling problem of spiking in the first place?

Despite all the recent education about consent, a 2021 UK study examining sexual violence found that over 11 percent of male university students admitted that they had committed sexual assault, rape or another 'coercive and unwanted incident' in the past two years alone.[86] One in five young women say they aren't equally willing as their partners the first time they have sex, with nearly 40 per cent of young women saying they don't feel that their first sexual experience happened at the right time.[87] And yet, perhaps most worryingly of all, in 2023 a quarter of male UK university students thought their uni is now 'doing too much to tackle misogyny among students.'[88]

The picture is no less positive amongst even younger age groups. A 2023 study in the US found that sadness and hopelessness in teen girls has shown a dramatic rise in the last decade, and is double that of boys. 'While all teens reported increasing mental health challenges, experiences of violence, and suicidal thoughts and behaviours, girls fared worse than boys across nearly all measures.'[89] The study also reports 'ongoing and extreme distress among teens who identify as lesbian, gay, bisexual, or questioning.'[90] Meanwhile, UK schoolchildren told government inspectors that 'in schools, sexual harassment, online sexual harassment and online sexual abuse are such a routine part of their daily lives they don't see any point in challenging or reporting it. Girls suffer disproportionately, complaining of sexist name-calling, online abuse, upskirting, unwanted touching in school corridors and rape jokes on the school bus. Boys share nude pictures on WhatsApp and Snapchat "like a collection game"'[91] with some girls saying they're contacted by up to 11 boys a night asking for nude images.[92] As the Chief Inspector of Schools concludes, 'it's alarming that many children and young people, particularly girls, feel they have to accept sexual harassment as part of growing up. Whether it's happening at school or in their social life, they simply don't feel it's worth reporting.'[93]

What about women's pleasure?

We may all be conditioned to think about sex as something done by men to women, but that's not always true in reality. There have always been women who have sexually agency, who aren't just passive recipients, even if they've suffered everything from being slut-shamed to being accused of witchcraft as a result; and these days, our social feeds may be full of sex-positive women of all sexual orientations celebrating their sexual agency, asserting it as something that's powerful, not shameful. These women are challenging millennia of cultural pressure that says women should conform to standards of modesty and subservience that aren't demanded of men. They're also challenging a belief that it's 'only natural' for men to be full of sexual desire, but that there's something wrong with women who seek sexual pleasure, because women are believed to 'not be as into sex' as men are. A study of over 2,300 women initially seems to confirm that long-held belief, as it found that when women engage in sex with a heterosexual partner, only 57 percent usually have orgasms, compared to 95 percent of men. However, when we look at the orgasm rate among lesbian women, the figure rises to 75 percent,[94] so the enormity of the 'orgasm gap' in straight couples isn't because women are 'naturally' only half as likely to orgasm as men. It's because 'in a society that presents us with a male-centric, heteronormative vision of what sex is, it is all too easy for that to become internalised and to manifest itself in unsatisfying sexual relationships that prioritise men's desires over women's pleasure.'[95] A 2020 study bears that out, as it found that the average penetrative sex session length was 5.4 minutes, even though it takes women on average 13.46 minutes from the beginning of arousal to orgasm.[96]

This phallocentric approach to sex, combined with a historic culture that taught us that women's sexual pleasure is shameful or even dangerous, has left millions of people not really knowing how to do sex better. Sophia Smith Galer points out that we're all often quite shockingly unaware of how our own bodies work, let alone each other's. 'A survey published in 2021 showed that a high proportion of British women and men are completely incapable of labelling all the parts of the vulva. Over half couldn't correctly identify that women have three holes and, regardless of their gender, half of Britons couldn't identify the urethra and 37 percent mislabelled the clitoris. This builds on what other researchers have found. A US study revealed that 46 percent of women surveyed couldn't point out the cervix, and a quarter didn't know where their vagina was.'[97]

Smith Galer laments this sorry state of sex education that misses any information about female pleasure: 'I should have been taught less about saying outright no and more about how to know what I want, ask for it and be prepared to make new choices if I was denied it...And yet "not being raped" is still what sex education and mass media offer when they talk to us about good examples of consent. We deserve so much more - and our wellbeing and public health depend on it.'[98] Smith Galer also advocates for better understanding that even when fully consensual, sex doesn't always go well. 'When young people reflect on how well their education prepared them for sex going wrong, 42 percent of men and 47 percent of women wish they had known more about psychosexual topics at the time they first felt ready to have sex. Awareness about sexual dysfunction - be it pain, premature ejaculation or a seeming inability to orgasm - has still not penetrated the school curriculum, despite so many people asking for it when surveyed. As a result, many of these early problems are not only destroying young people's first sexual experiences, they are going on to affect their lifelong sexual function, wellbeing & happiness.'[99]

However, there is room for hope. These huge gaps in knowledge and understanding about sex might become an opportunity to encourage better and more informed conversations about power, control, respect and pleasure, which could enable people to enjoy more equitable sex lives; they might reframe conversations about consent, from the pretty low bar of 'do I have permission to do this to you?' to a place where it's the norm for both parties to engage in ongoing dialogue about what they find pleasurable together.

What's attractive anyway?

We're told that 'beauty is in the eye of the beholder,' and at a personal level, that may be largely true for sexual attraction too. But dominant cultural narratives and expectations mean that living up to society's dominant standards of attractiveness can be more challenging for some groups than others. Women have long talked about the pressures of the impossibly-small sweet-spot they're expected to inhabit: the right degree of curvy or skinny, in all the right places, to satisfy what's currently deemed fashionable; and clothes, make up, body language and behaviour that signal enough sexual availability to ensure you don't look like a prude, but not so much that you risk coming across as *too* available. Now men too are increasingly talking about pressure *they* feel to conform to unrealistic or even impossible ideals, with a University of Chicago study finding, for example, that shorter men need to earn significantly more money in order to be deemed as attractive as their peers on dating apps.[100]

Dr Jamie Hakim researches queer intimacy in digital spaces, and recognises similar pressures there too, including a bias against gay men who present with more feminine traits on apps such as Grindr and

Instagram. 'There is a persistence in gay culture of eroticising particular forms of masculinity… It can cause lots of anxiety and a sense of failure for those who don't feel they match a certain image.'[101] Of course, all of this intersects with different racial and ethnic groups' attractiveness standards too, as we see from all kinds of people, including the iconic Frieda Kahlo and the *Black is Beautiful* movement from the 60s onwards, rejecting the white, colonial patriarchal beauty standards that have long dominated western mainstream culture.

Historians note that a culture's dominant idea of what's attractive shifts over time as well, because it responds to what kinds of people are accorded higher or lower social power and status at the time. Carol Dyhouse and Kate Lister explain how you can 'look at women's life chances in any historical era' to see what kind of life-partner they'd be looking for: in the 1950s, much TV and literature featured doctors as heart-throbs because their social status as providers was paramount at a time when women were being forced back into the home after the war; whereas in war time it generally tends to be soldiers whose qualities as protectors are loved and lusted over, from the red-coated soldiers of the Napoleonic Wars in Pride & Prejudice to the sexy American GI's with good teeth and chewing gum in the Second World War.[102] Today, as we see more and more women working outside the home, filling leadership positions and becoming entrepreneurs (as well as a greater mainstream awareness of the spectrum of sexual orientations and gender identities), it's perhaps no surprise that heterosexual male 'heartthrob' tropes are broadening to include a more 'feminine' version of masculine attractiveness, as the popularity of icons like Harry Styles, Timothée Chalamet and even Dwayne Johnson in full daddy-mode demonstrate.

Finally, it's worth sounding a note of caution that amongst all this growing acceptance of different tastes and types of attractiveness, there's one thing society still seems unable to tolerate, and that's adults not being sexual at all. Who you love (or who you lust after) is a protected characteristic across a spectrum of sexual orientations… except when you lust after no one. In fact, asexuality is often pathologised, not protected, especially when it manifests in women. Model and asexual activist Yasmin Benoit explains that there's frequently a belief that asexuality is a symptom of fear or past trauma, rather than a legitimate sexual orientation, and recounts how she often faces confusion and anger because she presents as a beautiful woman, and people (particularly men) don't seem able to grasp that she's not looking that way to be literally 'attractive' to others; she's doing it simply to please herself.[103] Additionally, if we go right back to where we started this chapter, we see that a perceived inability to be attractive to women lies behind the radicalisation of young men into the incel movement, and it's fuelling the dangerous misogyny of the manosphere, which in turn then manifests as concerns in more mainstream spaces about the dangers of an epidemic of male virginity.

How, then, might we better navigate this world of changing sexual power dynamics? It's a world where women have more social and economic power than ever, but still suffer an epidemic of sexual violence; where men and women have little understanding of consent and of their own bodies, but are still sold a version of sex that positions men as active or even predatory; Where women are seen as either passive good girls or active sluts who are 'asking for it' and 'deserve all they get' while men are sold dangerous visions of how they're expected to perform sex; a world where pleasure and power are rarely talked about, despite them both being ideas that could help break this destructive cycle. How might we approach sex in a way that's less damaging and more fulfilling for all?

WHAT I LEARNED
ABOUT MEN

First, a caveat: When it came to sex, I didn't talk about their own *personal* experiences with all of my respondents. For the gender queer respondent in my sample, for instance, sex wasn't something they felt comfortable talking about with me at all, beyond sharing their frustration at 'society's obsession with the state of my genitals.' They were clear that 'what I do or don't do with them is not anyone else's business, frankly, as long as it's all consensual. And believe me, when you're trans or non-binary, consent is something you think about probably *waaaaay* more actively than the average cis-het guy.' Even for the cis guys, whether straight or gay - particularly the respondents that I knew personally - talking about their own sex lives and practices generally just felt too intrusive. So these men talked instead about conversations they've had with friends, and in some cases lovers too. But far from hampering my learnings, this in itself is an important insight: despite the prevalence of sex online and in real life, and the casual way it fills jokes and banter, men still seem to prefer not to talk about it with people they know. When the topic of conversation is sex, it seems that it's easier for most to be open with strangers.

For all these reasons, strange as it seemed to me at first, the place that many of my respondents felt most comfortable talking about sex turned out to be the issue of sexual abuse and sexual violence - because that was 'about other people, not about me' and so it felt like a relatively safe zone for them.

The demonisation of sexual predators.

Mention sexual assault or abuse to any of the men I talked to, and I was met with a genuine wave of powerful emotions including horror, anger, disgust and outrage. 'It's disgusting what women have to put up with. Honestly, makes me really worried for my girls' was the kind of sentiment that many shared straight away, whether talking about their daughters, granddaughters, wives, sisters, or girlfriends. And this was often closely followed by something along the lines of 'it must be really hard to be a woman, having to navigate life constantly watching out for creeps and psychos in a way that you just don't when you're a man.' The empathy was palpable, as well as, for many, the feeling of guilt-tinged relief that cis, straight men, generally escaped this horror.

When I prompted them to think about the perpetrators as well as the victims of sexual violence or abuse, they rightly assumed that they were likely to be men, and often asked, in sickened exasperation, 'what's wrong with those guys? Who could ever want to do that?' They would wonder in horror at 'how could anyone be aroused by scaring women?' and 'what kind of sicko gets off on the idea of a woman not enjoying it? It's just unimaginable.' None stopped to really try and answer that question, though, as their focus quickly moved on to how women need to be better protected, and how we ought to punish sexual predators more harshly because 'too many of them get away with it for too long, like this recent bastard Carrick. He deserves all he's going to get in prison.' It's interesting that focusing on these famously horrific crimes and perpetrators, and talking about them as almost demonic, allowed these men not just to express solidarity with women in a shared hatred of sexual offences, but also served to distance these monstrous abusers from the good men like themselves: 'They really are the lowest of the low.' 'You've gotta be some sick monster to do things like that. The only thing that's worse than that in my book is when they go after kids. It literally makes me shudder.' This kind of talk is entirely understandable, and very supportive of women victims, but it doesn't open up any space for more complex and nuanced conversations about the broader cultural conditions that enable these extreme cases to happen; so unsurprisingly, there was no mention from these men of how sexual abuse, power and consent work more broadly and systemically in both men and women's lives.

A few of these good, thoughtful, kind men that I talked to found talk of sexual violence so troubling that they looked for reassurance that these men were rogue anomalies, monsters that were as rare as they were troubling. When they asked me for figures, I shared some of the relevant data, such as the prevalence of rape and sexual assault, or the numbers of men sharing rape and femicide fantasies in incel groups, and they generally found that quite hard to process. One admitted: 'I don't want to diminish it, but I really want it to be just a small, really marginalised group of men', and then, after I told him, he summed up the feelings of many when he replied simply, 'Oh god, is it really that common? Shit. I don't know what to say. Sorry.' Some even questioned the data's accuracy or recency, so reluctant were they to believe that sexual violence perpetrated by men could still be that big an issue.

Thinking about male sexual violence as a systemic issue rather than a few rogue monsters was really hard for all of these men, not least because the perceived threat to their loved ones suddenly amplified, and their self-appointed role as protector suddenly seemed massively more daunting and difficult. But it also conjured up some very challenging and complex emotional territories for them too, with a mix of fear, confusion, guilt and resentment all swirling around our conversations, particularly about porn and about consent. This difficult reckoning is something I return to later.

It's impossible to know what we're supposed to do these days.

As soon as the conversation moved away from 'evil' sexual predators and 'perverts' and on to sex, consent and relationships as it applies in their own lives, it became very clear that fear and confusion reigned supreme, often with a side-order of resentment thrown in too. They tended to start by focusing on how women dress these days: 'It's hard to know what to do and even where to look sometimes. Women dress in really revealing, skimpy clothes that are screaming "look at me!" but then they make you feel like a pervert if you find them attractive.' Many expressed some cynicism about famous women like Kim Kardashian and Emily Ratajkowski, saying that 'these women talk about how it's empowering for them to be virtually-naked, but then if you make any comment about them being attractive, suddenly it's as if you're behaving like a rapist!'

The younger men seemed to have more of an acceptance that consent and sexual expression have some nuance around them, and that 'women being sexual isn't the same as women asking to be sexualised,' whereas older generations of my respondents frequently talked about 'mixed signals' and women dressing 'provocatively' with a sense of exasperation. All ages, though, seemed generally quite confused, frustrated and a bit fearful, because they understood that respecting women's right to express themselves is vital, but they felt unsure about how to do that in reality when they're surrounded by women whose clothes, make up and body language seemed to be inviting their sexual attention. The straight men in my sample seemed to subliminally assume that when a woman presents as sexually attractive, she was signalling sexual availability, even if they later question that. One of the gay men had noticed this amongst his straight friends: 'The idea that "this woman is attractive, therefore she must exist for my sexual pleasure" is just so warped. It's incredibly arrogant. Why do you think she's displaying herself for *you*?!' Another admits that 'I do think men are a bit more straightforward and I find it harder to read the signs women give off, but I would suggest that if you're a straight bloke, assuming every attractive woman is trying to attract *you* is probably a mistake.'

The bottom line is that it's hard for most of these lovely, decent men to escape the assumptions that have been reinforced over thousands of years, that women are displaying themselves for men's gratification; that they're seeking male affirmation; and that they must then surely see male attention as a compliment. That's why it seems unfair, and sometimes even deliberately unkind to them, when a woman repels the sexual attention that straight men have been taught to believe she's asking for.

But there's even more to unpack when we start talking about power too, because although women tend to see men's assumptions that a woman is displaying herself for him as evidence of masculine power and entitlement, when it comes to sex and relationships, these men seemed to feel anything but powerful.

Women hold all the cards. We're pretty powerless.

What I discovered was blindingly obvious in some ways, but was not something I'd ever heard men voice so clearly and consistently: that when it comes to sex, these days straight men feel incredibly vulnerable in all kinds of ways.

Firstly, it's evident that they worry about not being seen to be good enough, both by women and by other men. In fact, it often sounds, when they talk, as if this fear of being found lacking is what drives their obsession about getting girls just as much as their physical desire does. It's as if securing a sexual partner is not just about physical pleasure to them; it's also a marker of their success or failure as a man. 'Being friend-zoned is really humiliating. You put yourself out there and you failed, and you know your mates are either laughing at you or pitying you. I can't decide what's worse.' Another admits that when he's rejected by a woman 'I know this is probably the wrong thing to say but it does feel emasculating.' They feel the social pressure and competition from other men too, with many of the younger men telling me that 'it's not just women who are expected to look stunning these days. Lots of men I know have issues with their weight, they worry about their looks, and they feel judged really harshly by girls.' Others feel that 'girls don't have to look amazing to get loads of male attention, but if you're not a ridiculously hot guy, you're made to feel like a bit of a loser.' Ironically, the very attention that women frequently find so frustrating and even frightening is exactly the kind of attention these men seem to be craving. It's like they're silently screaming 'please find me attractive!' even though they also admit to suffering from being increasingly judged by unattainable youth-and-beauty standards. It's worth noting, too, that this isn't just an issue for straight men, as holding men to impossibly high standards of physical attractiveness is something that gay men often do too: 'Sex and beauty is *everything* in the gay community. It's really unforgiving.... don't you dare be old and ugly if you're a gay man!'

One man was unusually open about articulating an area of vulnerability for men that I certainly hadn't fully understood: 'Everyone from Freud onwards talks about men being obsessed with their penis, and we all laugh at men building rockets and skyscrapers and cars to symbolise our phallic power, or more likely to compensate for the lack of it. But it's a bit more complex than that, because most of the time we're not just worrying about if our dick is big enough, we're worrying about whether it's gonna behave itself.' He goes on to reference a few well-known scenes from *The Inbetweeners*, and laughs as he tells me 'You spend half your life as a bloke hoping you're hard when you need to be, and the other half praying to god that you're not hard when you shouldn't be!' He then immediately worries 'I'm sorry, have I said too much?!' But this insight that young men in particular constantly worry about involuntary erections was echoed in what a couple of other men told me about the policing of women's bodies, particularly at school. 'It's wrong, I guess, that the girls at school were told not to bare their shoulders because it distracted the boys. But when girls do dress like that - and I'm not saying this is their fault - it's just a natural reaction, especially when you're a teenager, but you'll just end up with a class full of erections. And that's so humiliating for the boys.' Another told me that 'in some cultures, being fully naked isn't seen as inherently sexual, and in others an uncovered head is massively erotic. A bare ankle used to be taboo but that seems ridiculous now. So it's not true to say men just can't control themselves when they see women's bare flesh - unless you're a complete sex pest who needs some serious help, we can control ourselves. But we can't always control what our willies do, and we don't want people to see that.' I'd never quite realised that society's policing of women's bodies to the extent that it does, imposing all kinds of modesty standards on women and girls, is not just to protect women from sexual predators; we also do it to protect men from the embarrassment and social humiliation of involuntary erections. And of course, that judgement and ridicule of men is something that's within all of our power to change. Importantly too, although embarrassment may sound like a trivial emotion, we should acknowledge here that embarrassment at being a disappointment, along with an inability to deal with that disappointment, has been found to be a key factor in male suicides; so male embarrassment is certainly not something we should ever dismiss or trivialise.[104]

My respondents touched on two other areas of vulnerability when it comes to sex. The first was something they acknowledged is very rarely spoken about: that men can be victims of rape and sexual assault too. A couple mentioned cases that had made the national news of boys and young men being sexually abused by sports coaches, teachers or religious leaders. One talked about a man he knew who'd had his drink spiked and suffered sexual assault, telling me 'He really struggled with his mental health afterwards, just like women do when they're usually the targets. In a way it was even worse... no sorry, that sounds terrible, I don't mean it's a competition to say who suffers more. But he was saying there is something about men being raped, straight men especially, that makes them feel like they're less of a man or something.' He was clearly a little bit ashamed about the homophobic undertones of his comment; and it was clear to me (although not, I think, to him) that his remarks manifested the age-old idea that sex should be something done by men to women, and that the woman's position as the person being penetrated is inevitably inferior.

All of my respondents, in fact, seemed to see 'being fucked' as powerless compared to being 'the fucker'. There was one place where they did all seem to recognise that non-consensual penetration was about power as much as it was about sexual desire, and that was when they referred to prison dramas on film and TV, which many seemed to see as the purest example of this. They had huge empathy for the fictional men who became victims in that environment, recognising that they were living an almost inconceivably stressful life with this constant threat of sexual assault; and they recognised that these male victims of prison rape would struggle with complex guilt, shame and anger afterwards. One made an interesting connection, only half-jokingly: 'Thinking about it, that's probably not that far from how girls feel if they're out in a club full of fuckboys.'

One of the gay men talked about how straight men would often shout 'backs to the wall' around gay men because, as well as seeing gay men as feminised, they also, paradoxically, saw male homosexuality as an 'even more hyper-masculine sexuality than the straight version', one that, they assume, seeks to penetrate any man at any moment. Again, there's that implicit belief that the person being penetrated is the one lacking in power, and that being made to adopt the feminine position is the ultimate shame for a man. 'Even within the gay community,' one man tells me, 'There's a lot of judgement about the tops versus the bottoms. That whole power dynamic is a bit screwed.' Interestingly, the only time any of my respondents talked about penetration and sexual power in a way that didn't reinforce the 'penetration as power' narrative was when one man mentioned 'that scene with the Duke, in Bridgerton, where he wants to withdraw, and she makes him finish inside her without his consent. That kind of blew my mind. I don't think I've ever seen a consent, abuse kind of scenario working that way round.'

The last area of vulnerability that my respondents talked about regarding sex was the fear of false accusation. Again, many of them referenced news stories, film and TV, but all of them immediately started projecting 'imagine, though, if that did happen to you. If you did something that you thought she was into, where she was giving you all the signs that she was, and then afterwards she accused you of rape. There's no one there who can say for sure what happened because it's just the two of you, so it's a case of *he said, she said*... but what *she* says will inevitably be believed, and then you're screwed, your life's over.' When I asked the men who talked about false accusations like this to explain the resulting Armageddon scenario that they all imagined, the picture they painted for me tended to be less about ending up in jail (although was a concern for some) and more about what other people would think, and what that would do to their relationships, jobs and mental health. 'You'd just be hated, wouldn't you? And rightly so!' said one. 'You'd never work again. Who'd employ a rapist? And that's what you'd be to them. They'd be thinking there's no smoke without fire.' Another man, a father, tells me 'You'd lose the kids, the wife, you'd get beaten up in the street. You'd probably never sleep at night for worries that your house is going to be petrol bombed. All because one woman could say she didn't give you her consent. I don't think women realise the power they have over men now, after *MeToo*.'

Some told me that in recent years, their behaviour, or that of friends, had been affected by these worries. For some it meant they were less likely to approach women because 'you don't want to be known as the guy who's "a bit rapey," and I've heard girls say that to someone just for dancing too close to them after a few drinks.' For others, it seemed to have the opposite effect, where 'if you give off vibes that say you're scared of women, some of my mates think you're more likely to get accused, so they've become even more over-confident around women. It does seem to work too. The ones who act like they don't really give a shit about consent complexities seem to attract women who just go along with it.' For the men with children or grandchildren, there was a different, specific area where a fear of false sexual abuse accusations came into really sharp focus. 'It's one of the things I hate about being a dad, that you have to be so careful about what you do around the kids - your own and other people's. God, even saying that makes me sound like a paedo!! But it's like, when the kids are at gymnastics or dance, the mums all go and help them get ready, and when you're the dad you're not allowed anywhere near that. And I know that's right. I wouldn't want one of the other dads being backstage while my little ones were getting changed. But it's a bit sad, isn't it? That we have to assume every man might be an abuser just to be on the safe side. And so dads like me miss out on a whole load of things that mums are allowed to do, just to keep them safe.'

I must confess, I found all these conversations about the vulnerabilities that men feel around sexual relationships and sexual assault or abuse heart-breaking in many ways. To repeat the man from earlier, this mustn't ever become a competition about 'who suffers more'; and it's clear from the data - as well as my own personal experience - just how much difficulty and danger women endure when it comes to the mis-placed and selfishly-used sexual power and pleasure of men. But I was left with an overwhelming sadness at the realisation that these lovely, decent men are currently walking through life carrying a huge amount of fear and worry every day, just like many women do, even though it's often coming from the polar opposite position. I find it tragic that men who've been victims of abuse feel the same misplaced shame and guilt, as well as the burning rage that women victims do, *and* they generally find it even harder to express. It saddens me that men may feel scared, embarrassed, powerless and a bit out of control about their bodies and their sexual performance, even though they rarely admit it. And I feel a huge sense of frustration that men think that women just don't get it, and they feel despair - just like many women do - when they see the opposite sex getting more and more entrenched, angry, hate-fuelled and judgmental, accusing and cancelling each other. But this does give me a surprising amount of hope too, because all this fear and despair and anger means that there are some common emotions that men and women are feeling, even if for quite different reasons. And if we approach it in the right way, that just *might* be a basis for more empathy and conversation, which could help drive change.

Some uncomfortable reckoning.

Some of the men who were fathers of grown-up children had heard about the prevalence of sexual violence in online and tech-enabled porn, and really worried about how it was 'miseducating an entire generation'. One father of young adult children told me 'I don't have a problem with pornography itself. It's just that whereas my generation was excited to find a copy of Penthouse or Razzle or whatever, now the lads my daughter might be seeing are all watching stuff with strangling and spitting and... that's just horrifying. My boy tells me that not all lads are doing that, and I shouldn't worry about her as she can take care of herself, but it really bothers me that she might be pressured into doing stuff that she doesn't want to do just because that's what everyone is watching and thinking is normal.' Interestingly, as they talked through their worries about girls now being pressured into behaviour that they may not have chosen otherwise, they each acknowledged that when they were younger, they themselves often put girls under a bit of pressure to 'go a bit further than they might have intended to.' This was quite a troubling reflection for many of them, with one saying: 'Bloody hell, when I think back to how we all behaved when we were in our early 20s, it was just normal to pressurise your girlfriend into doing things she didn't really want to... obviously I never assaulted or abused a girl, but I do think if you judged my behaviour then based on today's rules about consent and the whole *MeToo* thing, I might be found guilty of something really hideous.'

As we talked about consent and coercion, a couple of the younger men also had a moment where they examined things they did through a new lens, and had the uncomfortable realisation that they may be 'guilty of doing stuff that, in the cold light of day, is not quite as consensual as it felt at the time.' One admitted 'when you really fancy someone and you've all been drinking, I think you do, as a bloke, put a bit of pressure on. You keep going until you're told no or actively pushed away. Obviously, it goes without saying that if a girl's so drunk that she clearly doesn't know what she's doing you'd always stop. But every man I know, myself included, has probably done something that breaks the rules of consent.' He went on to explain how that leaves him feeling confused, that on the one hand he and his mates are (in a reverse of the fear about false accusation) 'technically guilty' of things they were 'lucky to get away with.' But on the other hand, 'it's hard to say this 'cause I don't wanna sound like I'm supporting rape culture, but if guys, including me, trying our luck and going as far as a girl will let us, means we're legally sexual abusers... it feels a bit like the world's gone mad, because we're not, like, dangerous. We're just trying to get laid, going as far as we can before a girl says no.' Some had difficult personal reflections around consent too when they talked about image-based sexual abuse, with one man mentioning a gamer on Twitch who'd very recently got into trouble when he accidentally revealed deepfake nudes, after which a number of female gamers discovered images of themselves on porn sites too. 'He was an idiot to show that to the world. But it did make me realise I've never stopped to say, 'hang on a minute, is that something that woman's consented to?' when someone shares something with you. You just watch it. That's probably wrong, isn't it?'

But really, what's the big deal?

Most of the men, though, were a little bit perplexed as to 'why does this even count as abuse, especially when it's not footage of the actual woman? Like if someone's secretly filmed you screwing, and then releases that on the internet where your workmates and family can see it, I get it. But if someone puts your face on footage of a porn star and jerks off to that, it's not ideal, but is it *really* that much of a problem?' Others even argue that 'sometimes girls agree to be filmed and then afterwards say they don't want anyone to see it, which I get... but if they were that worried, why did they let him film it in the first place? You've gotta be aware that that might end up in the wrong hands.' A couple even admitted that 'with some women, I'm convinced they do it deliberately, to get fame or notoriety.' Part of the issue here seems to be an attitude that 'well I wouldn't mind if it was me', which makes them think that unsolicited dick pics are not a big deal as they'd enjoy it enormously if it were the other way round: 'Listen, most blokes would love it if a random girl on a train sent them a sexual photo of themselves.' Clearly, most of the time these men simply don't recognise the power play at work around these kinds of issues, as evidenced when I asked a couple of them if they'd see it differently if it were a man doing that to another man. Then, the old prison-rape trope appeared once again, suggesting, fascinatingly, that men may find it easier to see the threat and power in male sexual abuse of men than they do when the victim is a woman.

They all revealed a few unquestioned 'boys will be boys' beliefs too, applied both to themselves and other men they knew. One such belief was that outside of 'sex crimes' (which they abhor), when it comes to things like gently pressurising women, sending dick pics, making inappropriate jokes and so on, there was a strong sense that 'that's just what men do', and moreover, they often expressed a belief that 'that's what a lot of women want them to do too'. One married man told me 'I know it's not what you're supposed to say these days, but still at some biological level things haven't changed that much, have they? Men still go through a phase where they try to shag anything that moves, and women are a bit pickier because they're more about wanting to pin a man down, especially when they're in their late 20s and their biological clock is ticking.' Some of the younger men talked to me with pride about how they're different from others, 'the lads at uni who didn't go to mixed schools that were as progressive as mine, they see girls as just a piece of meat'; and how they recognise 'it's a compliment if a girl says you're nurturing or emotionally intelligent or cuddly.' But they do still appear to worry that 'whatever they say, a lot of the girls are more sexually attracted to guys who aren't all cuddly and empathetic.' One of the gay men described what he sees as a hilarious paradox, observing that 'loads of straight guys get jealous of my relationship with girls, the ones they fancy, because they think I'm flirting with them, even though they know I'm gay. They rant about how the girls are all over me, but they never stop to realise that they could act a bit more like that and maybe the girls would be more interested in them. You don't need to be gay to enjoy stuff that girls are into. You just need to think about what a girl enjoys instead of trying to impress her with your old-school manliness.' And inevitably, even though the Gen Z men were often happy to tell me that 'the social hierarchy is different now, and a lot of people look down on the idiots who are all about clinging on to those old versions of masculinity,' a few still recognise that there are different societal standards for girls and boys, and that they themselves are not immune to them: 'Even though I recognise it makes me a hypocrite, I do judge women who sleep around differently from men.'

Perhaps most importantly of all, the way they talked to me for the purpose of this research is no doubt very different from the way they talk about all of this around their mates, where the banter and masculine competition reign supreme, and even the most thoughtful and progressive men feel the need to walk the line and succumb to peer pressure to behave like a proper bloke. As one man so fittingly put it when he described this conundrum: 'As long as you've got decent mates and you have any kind of self-confidence, I think it's just an excuse to say you feel under pressure to behave like a dick…Although, to be fair, you never want to look like a complete pussy either.'

Quite. So, what do we do about any of this? How can we create change that will make sex less damaging and more pleasurable for all?

WHY MEN MIGHT
WANT TO CREATE CHANGE

I could easily, at this point, write a long list of things that I wish more men would do, including not treating women as if they're there for your viewing or sexual pleasure; acknowledging the gendered relationship between sex and power; questioning your own behaviours around consent instead of separating men into evil monsters and good guys; not judging women who enjoy sex, and not assuming that she's available for sex with you just because she enjoys sex with other people; understanding the nuances and complexities around consent; challenging it if your mates seem to have hateful and dangerous ideas and fantasies masquerading as banter; seeking out less violent, phallocentric porn that's always consensual; and so on… But that's pretty pointless, because telling men what they're doing wrong is more likely to create barriers and backlash than it is to create change.

So forget I said all of that! And let's look instead at how we might use the things about sex that really matter to men, that already motivate them; and let's work from those, to create change that's in everyone's interests. As always, I've added five thought-starters here that occurred to me in the process of listening to my respondents, but please share on @MenemiesNoMore any that you have discovered in your conversations across the gender divide too, so that we can all learn from each other.

1. Point to the perpetrators: Regular, decent men have an absolute abhorrence of rapists and sexual predators, and desperately want to protect the women in their lives from 'monsters' like that. Can we use this instinct in a helpful way, by celebrating the smart, enlightened men who don't talk as if 'violence against women' just exists, and who call out that the problem is the perpetrators, the sexually violent men that commit these acts. This could even include encouraging men to show off a superior knowledge of facts, like how the data proves that men are more likely to be raped by another man than they are to be falsely accused by a woman. This way, the good guys clearly differentiate themselves from the problem men, and that has a double benefit: it helps point society at the real problem and away from the blaming and shaming of victims; and it also repositions the issue as one about good men vs the bad guys, rather than an issue of men vs women.

2. Sexy 'supporting character' energy: Men want to be attractive to potential sexual partners, to be seen to be successful amongst their mates, and to be good in bed. Ironically though, these very desires often cause straight guys to do things that achieve the opposite result to the one they desire. So can we help more straight men understand that if they want to attract the girls and impress their mates by being known to be good in bed, they ought to think less about 'being attractive' and try centring the woman's experience and pleasure instead. Think 'fucking with' (in a positive sense!), not just fucking. Imagine you're the support act, not the main character and ironically, you'll end up being more in demand. Importantly, if you concentrate on generating pleasure, not just seeking permission, you'll have the added bonus of making consent a much simpler thing to navigate too, so that's a double win.

3. Flirt with women like a gay guy: Thousands of years of assuming that women exist to please men is hard to overcome, so it's no wonder that straight men still believe (subconsciously or more actively) that women who look good are making themselves 'attractive' to men rather than wearing and doing what makes *them* happy. Again, men's desire to be attractive to women could be the motivation to build on here. Can we help straight men believe that they'll be more attractive and successful if they treated women more like gay guys often do? Share women's humour, enjoy their interests, be flirty in a way that doesn't feel like an expression of the masculine power or entitlement that they'll be feeling even if you don't feel that powerful. Recognise the vulnerability and also celebrate the joy, power and playfulness that being a woman can entail. And try not to worry about other blokes' judgement - those judgments might change once they see the results you experience anyway.

4. The power of self-deprecation: If sexual success is not just about seeking pleasure but is also about competing with other men to show your masculine superiority, can we use that instinct in a helpful way too? Rather than using humour and banter as an enabler of misogyny, maybe modern men could use their humour and wit to show off their superiority to their mates in a different way. Imagine if men laughed about the vulnerability of involuntary erections; if they joked about how tough it is, now that girls want to actually *like* a man rather than just needing him for financial security, like previous generations did; or if they corrected men who assert that women aren't really into sex, telling them that they are if you're doing it more like a lesbian, as the orgasm gap data shows.

5. Shared emotions, if not experiences: Men feel confused, fearful and powerless around sex, and are especially terrified about falling victim to false rape allegations, whether deliberately malicious or ones that arise out of a more innocent lack of understanding, as consent seems such a complex and difficult area to navigate. But even though men's worries and fears are different from women's (and in some cases are the exact opposite), the fact is that both men and women are experiencing many of the same powerful emotions. Can we use those common emotions to open up conversations about some of these difficult areas of sex that are too often fuelled by anger and judgement, and find ways of understanding and even empathising with each other a bit more instead?

There's so much work to be done in this area, and it can be an uncomfortable topic for many people to even talk about. So let's leave it for now, and move on to what might be the consequence of some of that sex, for some... parenthood.

ISSUE 7:

The Daddy
Of All Roles

How making parenting less gendered would benefit us all.

============

REALITY CHECK:
WHERE WE ARE RIGHT NOW

Parenting is one of the few areas where women typically hold more of the cards. We assume that parenting is naturally 'women's work' and treat men who want to lean into parenting as more of an exception - or, in some circles, even an aberration. This dominant narrative hides a more nuanced history, though, because although nurturing has long been seen to be the traditional domain of women, the English common law principle of coverture meant that for many centuries in many nations, it was fathers, not mothers, who were deemed to have ownership of their children. In this staunchly patrilineal system 'a wife... had no rights over her own body. Her children didn't belong to her.'[1]

In weddings today, we still see vestiges of the idea that fathers literally own their children, as the father-of-the-bride 'gives away' his daughter, echoing the old legal reality that 'a woman was effectively passing from her father to her husband.'[2] It was only in 2021 that the UK government corrected what it called a 'historic anomaly' and included mothers' names on their children's marriage certificates as well as the father's.

But despite ceremonies and admin being dominated by ideas of paternal ownership, in reality, when it comes to custody, the pendulum has swung the other way now, and pressure groups like Fathers 4 Justice are having to campaign hard 'to give fathers equal rights to see their children after separation', arguing that 'no child should be denied their human right to a father, yet nearly one in three children now lives without a father in the UK – that's nearly four million fatherless children.'[3] The toll this takes on fathers who want to be part of their children's lives is devastating, as is the way that pregnant women's bodies are being fought over in ever-more-extreme culture wars. Meanwhile, millions of women are finding the task of combining motherhood with work outside of the home increasingly difficult, and calling for fathers to step up and bear a greater share of the parenting workload.

So what is really going on, and how can we make parenting work better for mums, dads, and their children?

The danger zone of pregnancy and childbirth.

Despite maternity often being portrayed in popular culture as a sweet, soft, cuddly thing, the reality is that pregnancy and childbirth has always been a bloody and brutal business. As long ago as 431 BCE, Euripides' character Medea famously said 'I would rather stand three times with a shield in battle than give birth once,'[4] and as late as the nineteenth century, one European woman in every 200 was dying from childbirth, with death rates in maternity hospitals, ironically, being ten times higher than that.[5] History is now repeating itself, as in 2022 'the number of women dying in pregnancy or shortly after giving birth in the UK has risen sharply' with evidence of widening health inequalities contributing to the fact that 229 women died during pregnancy or up to six weeks after in 2018-20, a 19 percent increase on previous years once Covid deaths were excluded.[6] This overall picture hides the dreadful truth that black women are almost four times as likely as white women to die in childbirth in the UK,[7] and in the USA the picture is just as alarming, as 'staggering racial disparities in maternal and infant health' mean that 'Black women remain between three and four times more likely than their white or

Hispanic counterparts to die from pregnancy-related complications', with a new study finding that even 'the wealthiest Black women and their new-borns experience worse outcomes than those from the lowest-income white families.'[8]

Since the overturning of Roe vs Wade, being pregnant in the US has become dangerous in an entirely different way too, with millions of women now being unable to access abortion by the time they realise they are pregnant, sometimes even without exceptions in the cases of rape and incest. Pregnancy may become even more deadly too, as despite abortion remaining legal in the case of a medical emergency or serious health risk for the pregnant patient, there's worry that doctors may be forced to act in ways that are not in the best interests of the patient, in order to avoid leaving themselves open to accusation of carrying out unlawful abortions. For instance, 'News reports and court affidavits have documented how health care workers sometimes deny women abortion procedures in emergency situations [such as] a woman who was initially not treated for her miscarriage at an Ohio ER, though she'd been bleeding profusely for hours' and 'a survey by the Texas Policy Evaluation Project found clinicians sometimes avoided standard abortion procedures, opting instead for "hysterotomy, a surgical incision into the uterus, because it might not be construed as an abortion."'[9]

Women in the UK are starting to worry about their rights to bodily autonomy too, as 'technically, in England and Wales, abortion remains a criminal offence, because the government has not repealed a Victorian law - the 1861 Offences Against The Person Act - which still supersedes the 1967 Abortion Act'[10]; and recently, 'sixty-one Conservative MPs voted against government efforts to expand abortion access in Northern Ireland, including Jacob Rees-Mogg [the influential Old Etonian Tory politician who has] previously said that he is "completely opposed" to the right to abortion, including in the cases of rape or incest, and is also patron of the anti-abortion organisation Right to Life.'[11] As journalist Ash Sarkar puts it, 'hearing about an abortion ban when you're the owner of a uterus is a bit like hearing about a plane crash while in a queue at the airport. The sudden awareness of your own vulnerability, the deep sense of threat, is hard to shake off.'[12] Straight men clearly benefit from their partners being able to avoid forced childbirth; there is virtually no gender gap in the support for abortion rights; and yet, where abortion and some forms of contraception are criminalised, a man sleeping with a woman now poses 'an existential threat to them,' whether he intends to or not.[13] So it's disappointing that, unlike the *anti*-abortion lobby, when it comes to speaking out in *support* of women's bodily autonomy, we tend to see relatively few men stepping up.

Moving beyond the battleground of pregnancy and women's bodies, though, surely things look a bit more positive? Once a child has arrived safely, we seem to have come a long way over the last few generations in terms of more equal parenting, so it's natural to assume we must be in a better place there. How much more do we really need to do to make parenting genuinely fair and inclusive?

Men can nurture too.

It's true that increasing numbers of men are leaning into parenting in ways that would have been utterly unthinkable for previous generations. Pew Research Centre estimates that in 2021 in the USA, 2.1 million men were stay-at-home dads. That's up eight percent since 1989, with the increase 'attributed, in large part, to women out-earning their male partners.'[14] Even as long ago as 2016, dads made up 17 percent of all stay-at-home parents in the U.S. and they had become much more active parents over the preceding 50 years, spending about triple the time on childcare that fathers did back in 1965.[15] In the UK, between 2005 and 2017 the number of fathers taking paternity leave shot up by 70 percent to an all-time high of over 200,000 men; and despite cost of living pressures in 2020-21 causing the figures to slip back to 2009 levels with only 176,000 men taking advantage of their right to take paternity leave, evidence shows that 'new dads still desperately want to spend time with their babies, particularly after COVID enabled them to spend more time with their families than they'd been used to.'[16] Almost two-thirds of UK fathers in two-parent households reported a better father-child relationship following lockdown, and that rose to 73 percent for dads who were full-time at home. These fathers said that lockdown had increased the closeness they felt with their children, improved their relationship with their partner and had a positive impact on their mental wellbeing too, with Black, Asian & Mixed Heritage fathers in two-parent households having even more positive experiences than white fathers on these measures.[17] So there seems to be significant numbers of fathers wanting to play an increased role in parenting, and even to play the role of primary carer.

When we look at the science, that makes perfect sense, because there's now a growing body of evidence to support what some of us are lucky enough to witness first hand: men can be just as good at parenting as women, despite old assumptions that only women are naturally predisposed to nurturing babies and children. For instance, studies amongst straight couples throughout the woman's pregnancy show that fathers' bodies prepare for parenthood alongside the mother's as there's evidence of correlations in hormone levels happening for both.[18] Studies also show that the act of taking care of a child teaches the adult how to be a carer, regardless of gender: Neuroscientists have long known that pregnancy can alter mothers' brains in ways that appear to help with caring for a baby. Now researchers have identified changes in new fathers' brains, too, with the main changes occurring 'in regions of the cortex that contribute to visual processing, attention and empathy toward the baby.'[19] The more active and engaged in parenting the man is, the more his brain, just like the mother's, also undergoes what neuroscientists call 'experience-induced brain plasticity.' Similarly, new fathers' heart rate, skin conductance and blood pressure were measured as they interacted with their new-borns, and they rose at the same rate as women's.[20] This lack of physiological differences in responses between the mothers and fathers, suggests that our neurobiological mechanisms prime all of us for parenthood, and the differences we observe in reality are 'about time spent with the baby, as opposed to being either a man or a woman' and that 'the only thing that differs between men and women is that men take a step back in the presence of their wives.'[21] This also explains why when we compare parents of the same gender - in this case, gay male fathers - it's the 'fathers who are primary caregivers [who] show stronger connections between parenting brain regions when viewing their infants, compared with secondary male caregivers.'[22] It shouldn't surprise us, then, that when researchers compared both fathers and mothers who were the primary or equal caregiver, they found no difference in the competence of the men and women as parents.[23]

Both the process of pregnancy and the social conditioning women experience from a young age may prime women for parenthood in a way that's different from the preparation men and boys have, and that might explain why one study found that the brain changes they observed in fathers, although hugely significant, were still around half the magnitude of the changes observed in the mothers. Clearly, much more research is needed in this area, but it seems to me that the key learning from all of this scientific study is that fathers' aptitude for parenting appears to be linked with how much they interact with their baby, not with their gender. So, if society keeps wrongly assuming that men aren't 'naturally cut out' for nurturing and caregiving, we're creating a self-fulfilling prophecy that prevents men from fulfilling their evident potential as active, caregiving fathers. Conversely, the more we enable and encourage men to do the work of parenting, the more their brains and bodies naturally adapt to the task, just like women's do.

And that feels like something that's often overlooked or misunderstood too: women's brains and bodies have to *adapt* to parenting. It's not the case that we're simply 'born nurturers' and that parenting is something women instinctively know how to do. However loving and wonderful the experience, it's work, and it's learned, through the experience of doing the physical and emotional labour of rearing a child, as well as through the social conditioning girls tend to experience as they grow up. Not only does that mean that it's something men can learn too if we socialise boys differently and encourage men to be more active in parenting their child; it also means that parenting is *work* throughout the child-rearing years, that is only learned with time and effort.

Parenting is work that's unpaid and undervalued.

The truth is that both growing and nurturing a baby is incredibly hard work. A 2018 USA study of working mothers found that they clock about the same as working 2.5 full-time jobs, doing an average work day of 14 hours, so it's not surprising that many 'said the week felt like a never-ending series of tasks to complete.'[24] Positioning parenting as simply a natural, feminine gift belittles the hard work that primary carers do, making it easy to dismiss this 'woman's work', undervaluing the labour involved in child-rearing. Even talking about caring for our own children as *work* and not just an act of love or duty can seem wrong, as if we're saying that it means we don't love our children enough, when of course loving something and it being hard work are not mutually exclusive, as any top sportsperson would attest. According to Professor Jordan Shapiro, 'domestic labour has been historically undervalued, not even counted as productivity by most economic measures,'[25] and this devaluing of the ultimate labour of love means that primary carers carry a heavy practical and emotional load.

Author Eve Rodsky points out that 'for far too long, women have been held responsible for completing an unfair share of work (especially invisible labour) at home. Even if a woman works a full-time job outside of the home, she is often also expected to complete the majority of domestic and emotional labour,'[26] with evidence showing that 'even when the wife is the primary breadwinner, she is spending about one-and-a-half hours more on care and two more hours on housework, while husbands get nearly nine hours more of leisure.'[27] Incredibly, we now know that 'the more economically dependent that men are on their wives, the *less* housework they do,' which may be an attempt to counteract feelings of emasculation that come from them being out-earned. And that happens more often than we may realise, as the share of women who earned more than their husbands is growing, hitting a record high of over 30% by 2021.[28] On average, despite so many women working outside the home too, when a heterosexual couple cohabit in the UK, evidence suggests that women do approximately sixteen hours of household chores a week, while men do six.[29] And although during lockdown, many men were suddenly doing more domestic and childcare duties than they had done previously, working women were still doing more of that additional load, to the point where UK women spent 77 percent more time on childcare overall than men.[30]

And it's not just the washing, shopping, feeding, tax returns, sewing in labels, friends' birthday presents, school-related admin, helping with homework and so on that's the issue; because the emotional and invisible labour, or 'mental load' that's disproportionately borne by mothers is often the most difficult thing to deal with, precisely because it's invisible. A 2023 study found that 71 percent of women feel it's their job to worry and think through all potential scenarios should something bad happen, and 82 percent of millennial women said that 'everyone talks about how overburdened women are, but no one is actually helping them ease the burden.'[31] Millions of mothers continue to take the largely un-credited responsibility for thinking about the immediate issues like nap time and feeding that need to be pre-planned, right through to how best to help their kids navigate friendship difficulties, attitudes to work, mental health and self-esteem. These things are a life's work for the parent who leads the family through these vital tasks, and Rodsky cautions that 'until we really unpack and ask the questions about who is holding the conception and planning - the work behind the work - then the statistics will miss how much more work women are truly taking on.'[32]

Sociologists note that this invisible labour doesn't just tend to fall to the mother because women are more often the primary caregiver; it's also because of the way we raise girls in the first place. 'Girls are really raised to be communal, to think about other people and their needs and concerns a lot of the time' whereas 'boys are raised more to think about their own sense of agency, to be agentic... about their ambitions and their pleasures, and not think about others quite as much.'[33] So in a classic Catch-22, men generally don't recognise the importance of this emotional labour, and so they diminish the mental load that mothers carry, assuming (thanks to the masculine superiority myth) that because they themselves don't value it, it can't be important. And women have to choose between having this important work belittled, or taking on even *more* emotional labour by trying to educate their partner about the importance and value of such work, and then being seen as a bit of a 'nag' for their troubles (a slur, incidentally, which has no masculine equivalent.)

Another factor that contributes to men leaning out and women being frustrated at men's lack of engagement is the dominant social narrative that dads are not really competent and committed parents. This lies behind the language of dads 'babysitting' their children when in fact they're just parenting. It also sets off a vicious circle where fathers are expected to spend less time than mothers looking after the children, which then creates a reality where men aren't as expert at child rearing as mothers are, simply because they're not as well-practised at it, which results in them not being asked to do it as much. Mothers can exacerbate this too when they practise 'maternal gatekeeping' whereby they criticise the dad for not doing childcare and domestic duties 'properly,' when 'properly' just means 'to *my* specifications.' At times this can be justified, when dads simply aren't expert at some parenting tasks or don't see the invisible consequences of the way they're doing things; but more often, it's simply because the mother (who bears the weight of society's expectations and judgements about their parenting) can't quite trust that the dads' different or more laissez-faire approach won't be damaging. This maternal gatekeeping can frequently lead to the fathers taking a step back so as not to get criticised... and so the cycle continues. Men can also exacerbate this vicious cycle by adopting 'weaponised incompetence' where they act as if they're less proficient than they really are, in order to avoid the labour of childcare that's not fun or doesn't feel as heroic and masculine as the domestic tasks they prefer to own, like mowing the lawn or doing DIY. All of this serves to reinforce the gender divide of child-rearing tasks, with the disproportionate burden falling on women.

It's worth noting, of course, that these findings almost entirely relate to straight couples, because in same sex relationships, decisions about who takes on what domestic roles aren't determined by gender. But with straight couples, gendered assumptions and biases about parenting tend to result in both mothers and fathers resenting the way they're judged by society, and each being frustrated about either how much of this unpaid work they're expected to do, or how little they're allowed to do.

The impact of parenting on paid work

When I became a parent in the late nineties and early noughties, like many women, I made a deliberate choice to limit my career ambitions for at least a decade. I understood that 'having it all' was a myth and that if I wanted to take the maternity leave to which I was entitled, and then work three or four days a week while the girls were still young, I'd pay the price in career terms. Back then, there was a mostly-unspoken assumption in industries like mine that if you couldn't be in the pub after work, be working late on a regular basis and generally be one of the lads, you couldn't really expect your career to keep on accelerating once you'd become a mother. Thankfully, the world of work has come a long way over the last couple of decades, but we've not yet reached the promised land of equal opportunities for working parents.

The Motherhood penalty and Fatherhood premium

Logically, becoming a parent ought to be a career advantage for anyone in leadership, as parenting develops qualities that are valuable for successful leaders, such as greater creativity and empathy.[34] That is generally the case for men, as they enjoy a 'fatherhood premium' at work, where they're valued and paid more highly after becoming fathers. However, the opposite is true for women, as working mothers suffer a 'motherhood penalty' where they're valued less than women without children. The hierarchy of how valued you are at work goes: men with children at the top, then men without children, then women without children, and then women with children at the very bottom. In fact, Fast Company reports that even after controlling for experience, education, marital status and hours worked, for every child a woman has, her income decreases by around four percent while a man's income increases by six percent when he becomes a father.[35] That's because women are 'perceived to be less committed to their jobs, less dependable, less authoritative and more emotional when they become mothers (despite evidence to the contrary).'[36]

Fathers, on the other hand, 'are perceived to be more committed to their work than childless men, offered higher starting salaries, held to lower expectations and cut more slack.'[37] Working mothers overall are held to higher standards, less likely to be hired and promoted, and are recommended lower starting salaries; but most worryingly, this motherhood penalty hits lower-paid workers hardest, so 'just like other forms of discrimination, the motherhood penalty disproportionately hurts those who are already most disadvantaged.'[38]

We can see this play out in media portrayals of working dads versus working mums too. US Congressman Jimmy Gomez rightly earned acclaim across broadcast and social media as well as applause from his party when he gave his House Speaker vote with his four-month-old baby strapped to him, proudly saying that he cast his vote 'on behalf of my son Hodge and all the working families.'[39] However, that's in marked contrast to UK MP Stella Creasey's experience. She carried her three-month-old son, Pip, in a baby sling as she spoke about the need for mothers to be supported when returning to Parliament after maternity leave, but received complaints about babies being 'a distraction', so the House of Commons procedures committee ruled that if MP's want to 'observe, initiate, speak or intervene in proceedings' they 'must not bring babies into the chamber or Westminster Hall.'[40] Responses in the press and online were far from universally positive, with ardent support from some quarters but utter vilification from others. Importantly, Creasey was accused of being both a bad mother *and* a bad MP, demonstrating the meme that women are still expected to 'work like we don't have children, and mother like we don't have a job.'

Interestingly, how a man judges women in the workplace is now known to be impacted by his own domestic situation. Studies amongst nearly a thousand straight men and women found that men in 'traditional' marriages (in which women do unpaid work in the household on a full-time basis) have 'primarily negative attitudes towards women in the workplace.'[41] These men were more likely to 'negatively evaluate organisations with higher numbers of female employees and believe they'd operate less smoothly' and were also 'less likely to positively evaluate female applicants than identical ones with a male name.'[42] Traditional gender roles at home even changed the way working men thought over time, as men who married working women who went on to become stay at home mothers were more likely to then develop negative attitudes towards women participating in the workforce, even if they didn't have them before.[43] The exception to this was black men, who had significantly more positive attitudes about women in the workplace, which researchers believe may be driven at least in part by a greater likelihood to have grown up in a family where the woman did paid work outside the home.[44]

The parenting pay gap is gendered.

Taking time out to be a stay-at-home mum is like sitting out of a race for a lap or two, and then having to run carrying extra weight once you get back on the track too. No wonder it's so hard to catch up. Studies have shown that the gap between men and women's pay widens consistently for 12 years after the first child is born, by which point working women in the UK receive 33 percent less pay per hour than men.[45] The years a woman spends out of paid work obviously have an impact on her earnings in those years, but she also misses out on career progression and accompanying salary rises too, so the impact continues even once she gets back. Compared to women who'd had the same hourly wage as her before she left, the wages of a working mother returning to work were on average two percent lower for every year she spent out of paid work, and that figure doubles to four percent lower for more highly educated women.[46]

One result of these inequities is that women over 65 are twice as likely as men of that age to be living in poverty, and 'a lot of that is attributable to how much more time they have spent in their lives to free labour.'[47]

There is something that can be done to address this, though, and that's for men to take more parental leave. Sweden is the model that many look to here, and a study there found that 'for every month of leave taken by men in their child's first year, the woman's long term salary was 6.7 percent higher'.[48] Working mothers are twice as likely to advance in careers when their partner works flexibly too.[49] And as well as the clear benefits to the woman, we know that many dads want to take more parental leave too. For instance, 80 percent of dads said they want more support from their workplace and 46 percent would change jobs for better paternity support.[50] Another report found that remarkably similar proportions of mothers and fathers - 76 and 73 percent respectively - would like to work flexibly to spend more time with children. Yet still, mothers are currently much more likely to work part-time than fathers, with nearly six times as many women as men with a child aged 14 or younger having reduced their working hours for childcare reasons.[51] So if spending more time with the kids is something both mothers and fathers want, what's stopping these men?

Men are allowed but not enabled to take equal parenting leave.

The dominant social assumption that parenting is women's work explains why UK mothers can get statutory maternity pay for up to 39 weeks, but paid paternity leave is just 2 weeks. At the time of writing, the UK government pays an eligible woman on maternity leave 90% of her average weekly earnings before tax for the first 6 weeks, and then the *lower* of 90 percent of her average weekly earnings, or £172, for the next 33 weeks.[52] Shared Parental Leave was introduced in the UK in 2015, where a couple who are having a baby (including those who are using a surrogate, adopting a child, or fostering a child who they're planning to adopt) can share up to 50 weeks of leave and up to 37 weeks of pay between them, whatever their gender.[53] On paper, this sounds wonderful, and we're told that as many as 85 percent of men say they should be 'as involved in caring for children as women', so we'd expect take-up of this to be huge. However, estimates for uptake range from just 0.5 percent to 8 percent among eligible fathers.[54] Why such a huge gap between what UK dads say they want, and what they do?

Affordability is a big issue. The World Economic Forum recently ranked the UK and USA the world's second and third most expensive country respectively for childcare,[55] so the spectre of the costs that parents will face even once they return to work is a huge worry for all but the very wealthiest. The US doesn't discriminate in the way the UK provision does, as it's the only developed country among 41 nations that does not offer *any* paid statutory parental leave, whatever the parent's gender.[56] Instead there's a law that allows 'parents of either sex to take up to 12 weeks of *unpaid* leave without penalty in pay or position', but this apparently-egalitarian system is often unaffordable for one parent to do, let alone both.[57] And while it seems churlish, in the UK, to look our gift horse in mouth, we do need to note that £172 a week equates to an income of less than £9,000 a year, which is why many employers voluntarily top up a woman's maternity pay on the understanding that she will return to work after maternity leave. However, this discretionary topping up of pay is rarely offered for fathers wanting to take significant amounts of leave to co-parent their baby.

A 2020 UK study found that 30 percent of fathers experienced a situation in which the female caregiver of their child had parental pay topped up while they did not,[58] and in 2019, the Court of Appeal ruled that it's perfectly legal for employers who offer enhanced maternity pay for their working mothers to offer nothing more than statutory pay to fathers taking Shared Parental Leave.[59] So we find ourselves in a self-perpetuating cycle where men, who are already likely to earn more than their female partner, can't get their pay topped up in the way that the mother can if *she* takes the leave; so the father returns to work while the woman takes maternity leave alone, reinforcing those gendered assumptions and expectations about parenting. This feels incredibly frustrating to men who want to actively parent, as well as being a missed opportunity because 'if the scheme was incentivised better financially, this could help eliminate the gender pay gap and reverse the trend of women taking the brunt of childcare responsibilities while fathers returned to work.'[60] Instead, the issue of affordability reinforces the status quo of men doing the lion's share of the paid labour while women take on the role of primary caregiver, with the unpaid labour that involves.

Thankfully, some pioneering companies are investing in correcting this issue. Celebrating employers who best support working fathers, The *Working Dads Employer Awards* point to over 40 UK employers, including John Lewis, Vodafone, Aviva and Nationwide, who have 'neutralised their parental leave policies' as well as 'many, many more [who] offer enhanced paid paternity leave for dads.'[61] However, many argue that only passing legislation to make paid leave *mandatory* for both sexes would help level the playing field for men and women both at home and at work, because 'there is data that shows that when companies offer elective paternity leave, men are apt not to take it for a variety of reasons.'[62]

Other barriers to men taking equal parenting leave.

Over the past 50 years, the weekly hours that fathers in the US devote to child care have tripled, and in countries such as Germany, Spain, Sweden and Iceland that have expanded paid paternity leave or created incentives for working dads to take leave, there's been an even steeper rise in fathers' involvement in child rearing.[63] But money alone can't encourage more men to do so, because even when they can afford it, men's disproportionate worries about what other people might think are causing them to spend less time parenting and more time in the workplace than women, despite similar numbers of men and women saying that they'd like to work more flexibly to spend more time with their children.[64] Not realising that the Fatherhood Premium exists, men suppose that taking time out to parent would have a negative impact on their career or their social standing, often mistakenly believing that their colleagues and managers would disapprove if they spent less of their time in paid work. Witness men at the bank Santander, for instance, who thought that one in three of their peers wouldn't encourage male colleagues to work flexibly, while in reality, an enormous 99 percent say they would encourage it.[65] The barrier that needs to be overcome here is what men *think* others might think.

Because of these worries dads have about what others might think, it doesn't take many media stories and social media trolls to really fan those flames. And sadly, judgemental men (and women too) trying to humiliate other men for daring to be loving do appear in the media on a regular basis. Like tech exec and investor Joe Lonsdale, who tweeted in 2021 that 'any man in an important position who takes six months of leave for a new-born is a loser', adding that 'the correct masculine response' to becoming a father was when men 'worked harder to provide for their [children's] future.'[66] Despite the angry outcry from feminist men and women, we can only guess how many men had their worries heightened by comments like this, as well as by the savage trolling that A$AP Rocky received after a 2023 Vogue cover photo showed him lovingly cradling their baby while Rihanna walked ahead, leading him by the hand. The hysteria about Rihanna emasculating her man will no doubt play into worries men may have about leaning into parenting, even though the majority of them do want to do it.

The benefits of more gender-equal parenting.

These fears aren't just stopping men from doing what they *want* to do; they're also stopping them doing what's best for their children, their partners and themselves. Michael Kimmel, one of the world's most respected male academics in the field of gender studies, sets out the many benefits of more egalitarian parenting in his much-watched TED talk, and they're worth quoting at length here: 'When men share housework and childcare, their children are happier and healthier...their children do better in school. Their children have lower rates of absenteeism, higher rates of achievement. They are less likely to be diagnosed with ADHD. They are less likely to see a child psychiatrist. They are less likely to be put on medication... When men share housework and childcare, their wives are happier. ...their wives are healthier. Their wives are less likely to see a therapist, less likely to be diagnosed with depression, less likely to be put on medication, more likely to go to the gym, report higher levels of marital satisfaction... When men share housework and childcare, the men are healthier. They smoke less, drink less, take recreational drugs less often. They are less likely to go to the ER but more like to go to a doctor for routine screenings. They are less likely to see a therapist, less likely to be diagnosed with depression, less likely to be taking prescription medication…. And finally, when men share housework and childcare, they have more sex.'[67]

The benefits of more gender-equal households are so strong that they've even been found to outweigh some external systemic disadvantages: 'Despite experiencing ongoing discrimination, persecution and stigma, gay couples in the United States report higher relationship satisfaction and lower levels of conflict than straight couples'[68] and in Australia, leading researchers found that relative to heterosexual relationships, same-sex relationships tend to have not just more equitable domestic work arrangements and less defined gender roles, but also a greater sense of social connectedness to a community. What's more, 'this joy is contagious and trickles down to the rest of their family unit. The kids of gay couples are happier than those of straight couples despite the fact that they often experience bullying because of their family arrangement.'[69]

It seems that households and families with more egalitarian gender roles are more likely to create even more equality in future too, as a longitudinal study shows that daughters who grow up in households where the mother works outside the home tend to go on to have more senior and better paid jobs than girls from households where the mother isn't in paid work; and boys as well as girls who grow up in such households are more likely to go on to have more egalitarian relationships when they're grown up too.[70] But it takes real effort and energy for men to kick against the dominant socialisation we discussed in *Issue 3: The thing is, boys are just better*. When we teach boys 'that masculinity is defined by men distancing themselves from anything deemed feminine', which includes 'being nurturing, loving, kind, gentle, tender, caring, patient, tolerant'[71], so it takes a lot of work from individual men to overcome this. And as we've seen previously, the current reality is still that 'many people have begun to raise daughters more like sons, but too few people raise sons more like daughters.'[72]

Bringing up boys.

Gendered norms have been identified as a 'core driving factor behind the difference in outcomes between men and women today,'[73] so perhaps one of the most important things parents can do is to actively challenge societal assumptions about how boys and girls should behave around caring and parenting. After all, young boys and girls are surprisingly similar, until boys are taught not to want to be nurturing and empathetic, while girls are taught to imagine themselves as less clever, capable and confident. So it would surely help if we started teaching our children that gendered assumptions, including the idea of a masculine 'boys don't cry' stoicism, is a social construct rather than a biological fact, and that this idea of what's deemed by western culture to be appropriate masculine behaviour ebbs and flows throughout history. For instance, we could highlight how at the very end of the last century, Princess Di's 12 and 15 year old sons Harry and William were expected to show no emotion, just like their father, uncle and grandfather, as they followed their mother's coffin through the crowded streets of London under the glare of the world's media; but compare that with a couple of centuries earlier, and we see that eight admirals carried Horatio Nelson's coffin through London's St Paul's Cathedral in 1806 and records show that 'all of them were in tears.'[74]

I believe that all of the evidence here suggests that we should start teaching children more positive models of masculinity that include caring, nurturing and active, engaged fatherhood. I'm sure it would also help if we moved beyond the reductive ways we think about motherhood too, celebrating a 'motherhood spectrum' rather than the dominant binary of 'natural, valid, legitimate mothers and unnatural, weird, freakish non-mothers,' because 'actually every individual's aptitude and desire for parenthood exists on a spectrum' that's affected by all kinds of things and that can change over time.[75]

Thankfully we've come a good long way since Clause 28 referred to homosexuality as a *pretended* family relationship'[76] and I believe that there's much that straight couples can learn from gay and lesbian parenthood today, as well as from the minority of straight couples and single parents where the father is the primary caregiver. We might also do well to learn from other kinds of families that demonstrate different, equally loving and supportive models of raising children, including communal living, blended families, surrogacy and multi-generational households, all of which challenge the narrow, gendered parenting norms that are no longer serving us.

It's easy to think that progress is linear, that younger generations are naturally more egalitarian and as they grow, so they'll automatically drive positive change in society; and that's certainly how things looked relatively recently, like back in 2017 when we saw that Millennial dads considered childcare and parental leave a much higher priority than the Baby Boomer generation.[77] But that faith in natural progress towards more gender-equal parenting is not necessarily true. In fact, we need to keep actively working to redefine gendered norms if we're to keep making progress, because recent data suggests that we're currently experiencing a significant backlash in this area.

In Britain there has been a rise in the numbers of people who say that 'a man who stays home to look after his children is less of a man', from around one in eight back in 2019 to nearly one in five in 2023.[78] It's no surprise that men are significantly more likely than women to think this, and I find it both disappointing and alarming that in 2023, almost a quarter of men in Britain and 21 percent of men in the United States now say they think that a stay at home dad is 'less of a man'.[79] It's worth noting that 14 percent of women in Britain and 11 percent of women in the US agree with them too.[80] Crucially, this belief is not mostly driven by older generations who are yearning for the traditional values of their youth. It's the youngest generations in the UK who were the most likely to believe that being a stay at home dad is emasculating,[81] and when we look at the global country average across 32 nations included in the survey, Gen Z and Millennials are twice as likely as Baby Boomers to say that a man who stays home to look after his children is less of a man.[82]

The evidence shows that when they've had frequent, regular, positive, engaged and active parenting from their father, young children's cognitive development is better and they display fewer behaviour problems,[83] so a more egalitarian approach to parenting is something we all ought to be enabling. How, then, might we encourage more men to kick against the backlash that we're seeing now and help us achieve this?

WHAT I LEARNED
ABOUT MEN

Pregnancy and childbirth are a brutal business.

All of the men I spoke with who were fathers talked spontaneously and in a very moving way about the bloody, brutal and dangerous process of pregnancy and birth. Each said how heroic their wives or girlfriends were for going through it, how it was not for the fainthearted, and how much respect and admiration they had for them: 'There's no way I could do it. Men aren't strong enough for that!' was a common feeling. A couple of men mentioned how fathers used to be 'made to stay outside the delivery room, pacing and waiting for the news, at which point they'd have a celebratory cigar' and told me that although that was 'ridiculous', 'it's probably because the men weren't able to deal with it.'

The way the dads talked about the moment of becoming a father was incredibly moving too, and a long way from the historical 'ownership' model that saw offspring as something a man possesses and provides for. Instead, they spoke with a heady mixture of love and fear about how humbling it was to have 'co-created this tiny life', and told me of the responsibility they felt to nurture as well as to protect their child for the rest of their lives. Being a grandparent seemed to intensify this feeling too, as 'you're filled with all this love for your own child who's now going through the experience of becoming a parent just like you did; and you're filled with love for the baby too, just like you were for them. It's magical.'

A few told me candidly about the worries they'd had that pregnancy and birth would change their relationship with their wife or girlfriend. 'You know her body's never going to be the same after going through that, and you worry about… is she ever going to want you again, after you've done that to her?' Interestingly, despite traditional narratives focusing on men judging women as unattractive once they're mothers, these men seemed to worry more about whether *she'd* have the emotional and physical capacity to find *him* attractive. There were a few comments, too, about the unrealistic pressure that social media and celebrity puts on new mothers to 'be hot as hell again within about ten minutes, as well as being some kind of super-mum' although a couple did talk with great pride about how their wife or partner is 'still really cool, she's not become all mumsy' or how 'she got her figure back really well - you'd never know she was a mother.'

Not one of my respondents spontaneously mentioned birth control or abortion at all, even when we were talking around the time of the overturning of Row v Wade. When I asked about pregnancy and birth control, they were all quite clear that they'd been taught from a young age that 'not getting a girl pregnant' was of vital importance, but once in more steady relationships, they mostly seemed to see the responsibility for that to fall squarely with the woman. 'It's not an area I think I have any opinion on, it's up to her what she does with her body' was a common response. And while that meant that they thought men's attempts to control women's bodies ranged from misguided to plain immoral, it also meant that they didn't really even consider that there were things *they* could be doing to take more responsibility. Mention of reversible vasectomies or the male pill had most of them turning queasy, and only a couple of the younger men had even had conversations with their partner about birth control options like the pill versus an IUD.

The gay men I spoke with talked fascinatingly about parenthood too. It had never even been an option when one more mature man was younger, but he expressed no remorse about that and seemed incredibly fulfilled by his roles as uncle and godparent, as well as happy that gay men now could become parents if that's what they chose. My younger gay respondents were in an interesting place, in that they felt no real desire to start a family, but also felt a somewhat complicated sense of guilt about it: 'The fact that the community has fought so hard for the rights of gay men to be dads makes me think, you know, am I letting the side down by not wanting to? But then, I don't want that kind of domestic life. That's not really who I am.' For a man who's also not cis, the response was a clear 'that's a complicated question. I really don't know,' along with a desire to move the conversation on to more comfortable topics, away from things that felt too personal. My respondents are a small sample, and we mustn't treat these men as if they represent all of the many, diverse people who are trans, non-binary and/or gay, of course; but nevertheless, it's interesting that the pressures as well as opportunities to become parents can be emotionally complex and nuanced for men beyond the cis-het, just as they are for many women.

They're proud to be more involved than previous generations.

The fathers and grandfathers amongst my respondents all told me that 'most dads are much more involved' these days than previous generations, and without fail, they all saw this as a positive development. 'My dad's generation barely changed a nappy, but most men I know would think you're a dinosaur if you took that approach now.' They were proud of their ability to feed, dress, change, and generally 'keep your child alive and well and happy' in a way that would have been unheard of until quite recently. They were also quick to regale me with stories of their parenting mishaps and messy moments, where they'd missed a nappy change, or been peed, pooped, or vomited on in spectacular fashion. There was, though, a serious side to these 'messing up, but not dangerously' tales, because they often went on to talk about frustrations with the process of learning how to take care of their child - as a baby, toddler and as a young child. 'I guess it's easy to laugh at ourselves because people expect less of dads than they do of mums, but in a way that's quite irritating, because I'm not a completely incapable idiot.' Another bemoans that 'It's like I'm having to constantly prove that I can be trusted to take care of my own kid.'

This sense of being expected to be an incompetent parent seems to come from all around. For instance, 'People at the nursery treat you a bit like a gifted toddler yourself. They're like "ooh, well done dad" when you 've just distracted your son when he's having a tantrum or something. I *know* they don't treat my wife that way, they just expect her to be a capable parent.' Others experience this when strangers praise them for the simplest of parenting skills, 'wanting to give you a medal for being able to push your kid on a swing', or when women they don't even know offer them help they don't need 'as if you're desperate for someone with more oestrogen than you to come and release you from the challenge of wiping your daughter's nose.' A few of them told me that 'you even get it from family too. My wife and I share the childcare, but some of my other family members still think it's a bit weird. I hate it when they talk as if I'm under her thumb just because I can look after my own child.'

Many of these dads talked about how the media can both help and hinder these perceptions of men being competent and committed parents. A couple of them enjoyed telling me about a Netflix documentary that 'showed the science of it, that fathers create oxytocin when they cuddle their baby, just like the mothers do,' really appreciating this unequivocal, scientific proof that men can parent too. Another talked about having seen a nature documentary that mentioned how 'puffins and penguins co-parent equally', enjoying this empirical proof that even beyond humans, dads can be the nurturers. Many explained how frustrating and damaging they thought lazy stereotypes of inept fathers were, from Peppa's 'Daddy Pig' to Homer Simpson to Peter Griffin, as 'they're funny, but really they're just reinforcing really outdated ideas which could make less confident men really doubt themselves.' Some talked about the power of positive examples too, with one mentioning the old Disney classic Pinocchio: 'Someone told me the other day that that was the only Disney movie they could think of that had a man wanting to be a loving father in it. I love Geppetto. He even looks a bit like my dad.' One man, who was a similar age to me, happily recalled 'that Athena poster of a hot guy holding a baby that was on every teenage girl's bedroom wall in the 80's' saying that 'even though the model gave us all major body insecurities as

15-year-olds because he was so ripped, at least it made us realise that women seemed to find men with babies attractive. A mate of mine at school used to walk around the park with his baby cousin when there were girls around that he fancied, thinking they'd think he was like the Athena guy. To be fair, he sometimes did end up with a gaggle of girls around him - although they were usually more interested in the baby than in him.'

A couple of the dads in my sample told me that unlike most media portrayals, they were 'at least equal' in their own parenting, with one saying 'in all honesty I probably take more of the lead in a lot of areas than my wife, because I'm just naturally a bit more patient, more of a nurturer, whereas she's better in some other areas. We each just play to our strengths, and because of the stage our little one is at now, that means a lot of classic parenting stuff falls to me.'

The dads expressed real annoyance with the way that most institutions treated them 'like you're just an assistant to your wife, as if she must be the lead parent.' One tells me that 'at every check-up and doctor's appointment, they assume "mum" is the one in charge and I'm just there for moral support. I know that's probably most common, but if I treated women at work in the patronising way some midwives have treated me, I'd be fired immediately. And rightly so!' One father of older children told me 'The school used to drive me mad. I'd do the drop-off every single morning. And they had my number listed first, as my wife's often in meetings, whereas in my job it's easier for me to be a bit flexible. But if something happened, the girls were ill or whatever, the school would always call her, and she'd have to call me, which would just piss us both off.' The best version they'd had of institutions trying to include them was 'the pretend involvement' they'd experienced when their partner was pregnant, and that was something many found to be 'just cringe'. One dad summed it up by saying he was 'so relieved once the baby was out, because I could join in with the parenting in a real way, not just doing the stuff they made us do in NCT[84] [antenatal] classes that we both found slightly ridiculous, even if it was well-intentioned.'

When I asked those of the younger men who'd said they want a family one day, what kind of father they think they'll be, each proudly told me they think they'll do a good job. 'I don't think I'll be scared of all the shitty nappies and screaming in the middle of the night and stuff. I'm pretty good without much sleep and I'm quite chill as a character, so I reckon I'll be OK at that,' one told me. Another declared proudly 'I think I might be quite good at it, because when I was young my sister would come to me in the night if she got scared, and I was really good at calming her down.' A third talked about having 'great role models in my family of men who were loving and kind, so I hope I'll carry on that tradition.' Similarly, at the other end of my respondents' age range, a grandfather told me how proud he is of his ability to take care of the next generation of little ones in the family: 'I love looking after the grandkids. It allows me to put right some of the things I didn't get a chance to do when my boys were babies.'

Sharing the other domestic work too.

These grandads told me that when their own kids were little they'd split parenting very much along traditional gender lines, them being the ones who were 'out earning a crust' while their wives did 'the lion's share of the childcare and homemaking'; whereas all of the fathers who had children at home now said they were 'as close to equal as possible' in their sharing of the work inside and outside the home - although what exactly that meant in reality seemed to vary. All had wives or partners who also did paid work outside the home, but although all of the wives/partners had negotiated reduced hours since becoming mothers, only one of these men had negotiated anything similar. Instead, they generally told me how they now 'leave work earlier than I used to, and don't go to the pub after work as regularly' so that they could spend more time at home, which they all seemed to think was a significant concession, albeit one they felt good about doing. His paid work having been 'the thing that kept the wolf from the door' throughout his partner's maternity leave meant that each of these men generally didn't do many of the night feeds. 'I needed to be fresh for work in the morning, and you can't do that after being up three times in the night,' said one of the men with a new baby as well as a toddler, before laughing and admitting that his wife 'would kill me if she heard me saying that. She says she can't wait to get back to work for a rest, because dealing with the trickiest clients at work is an absolute breeze compared to managing a baby and a toddler all day.' Beyond the laughter and the nod of recognition for her argument, though, it didn't seem to have an enormous impact on how the night duties were shared, with him saying 'I do take over the night feeds every so often to give her a rest,' reflecting a sense that he was on support duties rather than sharing those duties completely equally 'until she's back at work too.' And this was a pattern that all but one of these dads reflected.

Importantly, just as the analysts and academics note, none of the men I talked to referred to looking after the children in the home as 'unpaid work.' The language that has dominated for generations was still very much alive and well amongst my respondents, where 'work' meant paid work outside the home, and 'being at home with the kids,' was something the women did while they were 'off work' or 'until she goes back to work.'

Unsurprisingly, there was no mention of the economic benefit of that unpaid domestic labour to the household either. One man talked about how because his wife isn't in a high-paying job, 'it barely makes financial sense for her to go back to work, as once we've paid for childcare and a cleaner to help with a bit of housework each week, her salary is pretty much gone', but he told me that they had agreed to do it because 'work is an important part of her identity and good for her wellbeing and sense of self.' A father of school-age children who was divorced told me about how that put pressure on both of them to earn money, as 'running two households isn't cheap', and it meant that 'on the days the kids are with me, I do all the housework and the looking after them. It did make me learn to do some of the things I'd never really been able to do when me and their mum were still together.' But still the language remained that 'work' meant paid work, and domestic labour was simply called 'childcare'.

However, the word 'work' did crop up when other domestic tasks were discussed, partly because the term 'housework' already includes that word, but also because it felt to them more like difficult labour. 'Looking after the kids is tiring and challenging, yes. It's definitely hard work. But it's not *work,* is it? Not like scrubbing the house and doing the washing and stuff. Those are things that you pay other people to do if you're lucky enough to be able to afford to, because it's nasty work.' Their definition of 'work' certainly seemed to rest on being something that people wouldn't do if they didn't get paid to. For them, childcare didn't meet the criteria because, despite its challenges, they all had the strong feeling that 'taking care of your kids is something you do out of love. It's not a job, it's a duty. It's a natural imperative.' More interestingly, when they did talk about paying someone for childcare - whether a relative or neighbour doing some babysitting, or a nanny or nursery doing full-time care - they still didn't really talk about it as difficult 'work'. What they felt they were paying for was not the labour of looking after young children itself, but the 'freedom it bought' them 'when you need it to get back to work or for the occasional night out or whatever.' A bit like with people's appreciation for teachers during lockdown, maybe it's hard to value the hard work involved in some caring tasks and activities because we're so used to them 'just happening.'

Whether or not they had children at home, most of the men said that they and their partner discussed and agreed very deliberately how to share the housework tasks in a way that was fair. For the parents with children at home, since both of them did paid work outside the home too, childcare tasks were included in that 'divvying up of the jobs to be done each week.' Common examples were 'I put the bins out and load the dishwasher; she does the laundry and shopping' or 'I tend to do more of the admin and organisation of finances, holidays, the tech in the house and she does more of the stuff to do with school, health and kids.' Wherever roles were allocated along less stereotypical gender lines, the men seemed proud to point that out to me. One explained 'she does the gardening because that's her passion, so I don't do the classic "man mows the lawn" thing, but I tend to do the washing and ironing as I find it weirdly therapeutic,' while another told me happily that 'I enjoy cooking much more than her, and she's the first to say that I'm better at it, so I tend to do that most nights while she puts the kids to bed and does the tidying up.' I was not surprised to note that none of the men spontaneously mentioned the mental load when talking about this 'fair division' of domestic labour. When I asked them 'what can you tell me about the mental load?' all of the younger men had heard of the phrase, and a few of the older ones too: 'Yeah, that's things like remembering to put the recycling out without being asked, isn't it?' But however confident they were about recognising and explaining the phrase, only one demonstrated a truly deep understanding of all the kinds of things it meant, and he, interestingly, was the partner who tended to take the lead on much of that stuff: 'We are as equal as we can possibly be in our parenting, and really work hard to respect each other's careers, so yeah, we do make sure we share the mental load as well. We divide that up according to our strengths too, so I do more of the thinking about developmental stuff, physical and emotional, because that's more my area, and [his wife] does more of the school-related thinking, intellectual development side as well as things like sleep schedules and life organisation. And then we both talk about things like his little friendship group, his mental wellbeing and stuff, and work out our approach to that together.'

My conversations certainly reflect the broader data that suggests that unless you're the parent who actually does the mental and emotional labour of thinking about everything from the kids' development to friendships to leisure time, much of that work remains invisible. Moreover, I did sense that rather than interpreting it as sharing the thinking ahead, the worrying, strategising and planning, they simply understood it as 'remembering to do the things I've been told to do without too many reminders'; so it's no wonder that some of the men were rather dismissive of the importance of this work and the energy and effort it takes.

She needs to relax a bit as a parent.

In one way or another, each of the dads said that women tend to parent in a way that's different to men, and not necessarily better: 'I'm definitely a bit more relaxed than her. She wants to have everything perfect, have the kids fed on time and clean and make sure everything's tidied away as soon as dinner's over, whereas I'd rather spend more time playing with them.' They justified their approach as superior parenting in a number of ways. Firstly, the benefit to the children: 'Play's good for them, isn't it?', 'They're kids, they don't need to be stressed out all the time about having to do everything right, like an agenda for self-improvement' and 'You can't wrap them up in cotton wool. We weren't when we were kids, and we were fine.' A few talked about the benefit to parents too: 'I sometimes think women put so much pressure on themselves to be this perfect mother, they worry about what everyone else will think instead of just enjoying it', or 'I wish she'd just sit down and relax sometimes instead of needing to finish 72 jobs in the house before bedtime' and 'It's probably the thing we argue about most often, when she stresses out about things not being done to her crazily exacting standards.' I asked some of these men if they discussed this with their partner and, to a man, they laughed and told me that yes, they had, and it hadn't gone well. 'She quoted facts back at me about how much women have to do that men don't understand, and said if she didn't have to spend all her time doing that, she'd be happy to chase a ball around the garden all afternoon' said one. Another told me 'She ripped into me for saying she's a nag and a control freak' while a third said 'I do try and listen when she tells me to do stuff around the house. But the thing is, even when I try, she has a go at me for not doing it her way, so I wonder why I bothered.'

This experience of being 'mumsplained' to was something many of the men found challenging to deal with, and they expressed frustration about 'mixed messages' as well as anger at feeling undermined or underestimated: 'If she's going out and I'm taking care of the kids on my own one evening, she'll give me this long list of instructions like I'm some fool who's never put the kids to bed before, which just feels like she doesn't trust me to be a competent parent; and then she wonders why

I don't volunteer to take the lead more often, but I know she'll just tell me I'm doing it wrong.' 'She says she wants me to be more involved, but then when I dress the kids or even take their minds off things when they're upset, she'll give me that look, like, "that's not how I'd do it", that makes me feel like a bit of a failure even though the kids are fine. It's as if her way is the only way.' Interestingly, when it was one of the first times they were doing something, the men seemed happy to admit they were still learning and often told funny anecdotes where they were the butt of their own jokes. But when they had more experience and felt confident, being made to feel 'not good enough' because they did things their own perfectly effective way was a source of real tension. These conversations made me reflect back on our own years of parenting when the girls were little, and I can see there were definitely plenty of times that Jonny would be doing brilliant parenting his own way but I would stress about it because it wasn't the way I'd have done it; similarly there were times where he'd be inadvertently dismissive of the mental load that I tended to carry, because it was invisible to him or he didn't really value its importance.

I've also reflected on how much I've always appreciated the little moments where he would simply notice and show appreciation for some of that labour that fell to me, such as when one busy December, he sang along with Bing Crosby, but changed the lyrics to 'I'm dreaming of a White Christmas, with every Christmas card my wife writes.' A little thing, but it meant a lot to me in that moment. It made me wonder how often parents show each other gratitude for the things that each contributes, so I asked a few of the men I interviewed about this, and most tended to have a 'women can be a bit over-sensitive about this stuff' response: 'We're all too busy dealing with the regular things to stop and think about the importance of jobs that look irrelevant, or the invisible labour or whatever you call it.' 'She should know I appreciate it without me needing to tell her.' I was surprised, though, by the open-ness of one of my respondents. He thought for a long time, then told me 'I don't notice the extra chores and thinking and planning my girlfriend does a lot of the time, and I probably should pay more attention. But to tell you the truth, sometimes I *do* notice, but it makes me uncomfortable that she does it all and I'm not very good at all of that, so I think I kind of ignore it and pretend it's not happening.' When I asked him to expand, he told me 'It makes me feel a bit useless, a bit inferior, and men don't like feeling that way. So I guess it's easier to pretend it's not happening, or to big up the things I do, to make it feel like we're contributing more than we really are. That's terrible isn't it - it's easier to pretend than it is to say thanks for doing some valuable stuff I don't or can't do.'

The career fear.

Even though most had said they may become fathers one day (if they weren't already), and all of these men had learned about contraception while still at school, not one of the men I spoke with said they'd had any conversation when they were growing up about the prospect of caring for their children, nor of taking a career break to do so. 'I loved hugging and feeding my baby sister when she was born, and everyone used to say I'd make a great dad when I'm grown up. But no one at home, school, or college or even at home really talked about the realities of looking after kids, like the cost or the idea of taking time off work. That's what the mums did in our parents' generation, so we never really thought about the idea of us boys doing it instead.' When I told my respondents that currently in the UK statutory paternity leave is 2 weeks, versus 39 for maternity leave, the men who don't have children in their lives were shocked. 'No, that's outrageous! So much for gender equality!' summed up the feelings of many. One expanded: 'The woman's body takes the physical toll of growing the child, giving birth, but after that it doesn't make any sense to not allow men equal opportunity to do that.'

The men who did have children (and sometimes grandchildren too), or who had close friends or family who'd recently become parents, were more aware of the difference between maternity and paternity entitlements. A few said they'd heard of Shared Parental Leave, but only one mentioned it spontaneously, and this man immediately told me that he'd wanted to take it, but it was unaffordable because his employer wouldn't top up his statutory pay, whereas his wife's company would if she took the time as maternity leave. 'So although the law says we can share it equally, the financial reality says we can't, which is tough for both of us. I wish I'd known about it earlier, because that's the kind of thing that might make men choose certain jobs or companies, if you knew they paid dads like they pay mums when they're on parental leave.' Most were completely unaware that companies would offer discretionary top-ups to mothers' pay but not fathers, and many wondered in exasperation 'is that even legal?' and were shocked to find that it is.

Despite this strong groundswell of indignation about the injustices fathers face if they want to share the parenting equally, when I asked these men how far those feelings would turn into action if they could afford to stay home, just like the national data showed, their fire of indignation was replaced by some hesitancy: 'I definitely think it's wrong that dads don't have the same choices that mothers do. But that said, I don't know if it's something I'd have wanted to do even if I could.' Another told me that 'I don't think in reality that my girlfriend would have wanted me to do that. She's all for gender equality, but I can't imagine her saying "yeah, you take 6 months off now to look after the kids while I go back to work." Not just because she thinks she'd do a better job of it than me (although she does), but because I just think she'd struggle to be away from the kids even more than I did.' When I asked how far he thought that was social conditioning versus a natural biological difference, he said 'I dunno. Maybe a bit of both. But I think because the expectation girls have from everyone is that they're the ones who will do it, kicking against that feels like a really big deal, doesn't it? Like she's a bad mother, letting the kids down in some way.'

A few of the men also admitted, with a wry or guilty smile, that they'd hate the idea of it damaging their careers: 'I'm much more aware of things now, and I really acknowledge [his wife's] sacrifice… but I wouldn't want to take more than maybe three months off at the most. My job's quite competitive and I wouldn't want to get left behind by being out of the game for too long.' Another told me that 'my career is an important part of my self-worth and I'd really struggle to give that up. I know it is for my partner too, but she seems more able to cope with taking a step back and getting passed over for promotions than I would.' A lot of them at least hinted at concerns about other people's judgements too, telling me 'They'd all think it was a bit of an odd decision' or 'it's just not something that men do, in my industry at least.' One went so far as to say explicitly 'come on, people would take the piss, wouldn't they? Even if not to my face, they'd be thinking I've lost my edge if I'm at home changing nappies instead of in the office pitching business.' Many of them also exposed once again that subconscious belief that childcare isn't 'real work' by saying things like 'I'd worry about feeling lazy, like a freeloader if I were to say I'd be interested in being a stay-at-home dad', and a couple of others admitted 'I just think it'd drive me a bit crazy.'

Fundamentally, though, once we got beyond the sense of injustice on behalf of all men to the realities for each of these men, the barrier that came through most consistently and strongly was gendered social norming. 'You'd just feel a bit of an odd one out wouldn't you, hanging out at the park with all the mums. And people would wonder why your wife isn't doing it.'

The future for fathers.

Every one of my dads and grandads told me that fatherhood had changed them for the better: 'It's a love like you've never felt before, when you become a parent. It definitely made me think about the future a bit more, about the kind of world I want my kids to inherit when they grow up.' Another man told me 'I've never been more tired and I've never been poorer, but I've also never smiled and laughed and cried as much as I have since the girls were born', and he echoed the sentiments of many. 'My testosterone's taken a nose-dive since I became a dad, and if you'd have told me that before, I'd have hated the idea, but actually, life feels more peaceful now. I can just enjoy things a bit more instead of life feeling like a never-ending competition.' Many of the fathers of girls were particularly thoughtful about 'not reinforcing the sexist rubbish that kept women in their place years ago' but, as we discussed in *Issue 3: The Thing Is, Boys Are Just Better*, generally that seemed to manifest as encouraging their girls to do things that are perceived as traditionally masculine. 'I coach my daughter's football team, and seeing her and her little mates all charging around getting muddy, being really competitive, it's so great. We've come a long way in a few generations.'

Few of the men talked about encouraging their boys to take on more classically feminine traits, with the only example they really mentioned being a need for greater empathy: 'The world he'll be growing up in is going to be increasingly complex, with LGBTQ issues and social justice and mental health and the environment being so big now, so he's going to need empathy and curiosity to thrive in it.' The black and mixed race fathers talked, of course, about their fears and their hopes for a less systemically racist society in future, but were clear that having 'the conversation'[85] felt like something that was still going to be needed for some time yet, and they instinctively talked more about the dangers young black men face than black women - although maybe that's an anomaly with this particular sample, or simply because they were more likely to talk about the things that they themselves had experienced.

One worry that most of the fathers of white boys voiced concerns about was 'the backlash against men, especially white middle class men, so they'll have a tougher time than I did' and a few men of all races said they worried about 'the whole toxic masculinity thing that's everywhere now. We'll need to work hard to make sure he doesn't think *that's* what a man is supposed to be like, because we don't want him growing up to be an utter dick.' Interestingly, even after all of the conversations we'd had about parenting, none of the men talked about wanting to encourage their sons to be a more active, involved and equal parent than they themselves are. Maybe they just believe that progress in this area is inevitable - although some of the recent data we've explored suggests otherwise.

One final area about the future of parenting that I found really insightful came from an older gay man who wasn't a parent. He told me that he believes things won't fundamentally change for fathers 'until we as a society start to think differently about childless women too. I know from some of the incredible women I have as friends that when a woman gets older and she doesn't have kids, that's frightening to a lot of people. Pity is the nice version of how others treat a childless woman of a certain age.' And he made it clear that, of course, childless men aren't judged in anything like the same way.

It does feel like these conversations about parenting and gender always ended up coming full circle: until dads are perceived to be competent carers and nurturers, women will bear the majority of the labour of love that is parenting. But because most dads *aren't* the primary carer and *don't* take the major career breaks to rear their children, many dads still avoid doing it because that's 'not what men do', even though it's what they *want* to do. And because the primary carer is the one who learns to be more expert, so we keep on reinforcing the belief that women are the ones who are naturally destined to be the primary caregivers, just because they do it more. And then we reinforce the idea that women are born to be nurturers by treating women who don't adhere to these social norms with anything from pity to suspicion, but are nowhere near as judgemental about men who fail to fulfil a biological destiny to become fathers. So how might we escape this Catch-22 where until more fathers do it, more fathers won't want to do it?

WHY MEN MIGHT
WANT TO CREATE CHANGE

The data is clear that more gender-equal parenting has a positive impact on mums, dads and kids. And we know that there are some key behaviours that could accelerate change here: Men leaning into parenting from the moment the child is born would accelerate their bodies' neurological, chemical and hormonal reactions that prime them for parenting, just like it typically does for women in straight couples. Arming boys and girls with practical information about how parenting works, including the financial and career impacts, could help them seek out environments that enable them to do that with less fear of judgement as well as more financial stability. Creating more media representations of competent child-rearing men as well as childless women who aren't to be pitied or feared would help too, particularly in the face of a backlash that positions caring men as emasculated. And we know that there's a benefit to parents encouraging more recognition and appreciation of what each other does too, including dads valuing the mental load women tend to carry, and women appreciating men doing things their way. So, what are the things that men already want, enjoy and do that we could build on, to generate more change and accelerate more egalitarian parenting?

1. Celebrate the science: Telling men that *their* bodies as well as women's bodies do incredible, almost magical things when they become parents feels like a good place to start. We know that fatherhood can make men marvel at the almost super-heroic feats pregnant women's bodies achieve; and we know men often really enjoy both scientific facts and being able to prove they're excellent at things. So, what man wouldn't feel amazed and humbled by his body's secret ability to produce oxytocin, to increase experience-induced brain plasticity, and to generate hormonal changes that enable him to be a 'natural parent' too?

2. Fair for fathers too: We talked in *Issue 4: It's Dog Eat Dog And I'm Nobody's Bitch* about how important the notion of 'fair play' is for men, and how men are often happier using their power to help the vulnerable or the underdog than they are to express their own insecurity and vulnerability. So can we use this to encourage men to fight for dads to have a level playing field on which to parent equally, not just in law but in reality? Can we encourage men to demand an end to the affordability injustice that sees so many companies voluntarily top up a woman's pay but not do the same for fathers? Could we celebrate the dads that take career breaks, heroicising domestic labour in the same way that we do paid work, and salute men when they challenge lazy and misguided assumptions that child rearing is the preserve of mums. And can we ensure that loving, caring fathers feature in the stories we tell too, and that childless women are seen as loving as well as powerful?

3. Strong enough to pull their weight: If masculinity is a competition, a need to prove that you're 'man enough', can we make being strong enough and smart enough to really pull your weight in the *domestic* realm another symbol of winning at being a man? It may sound tricky in the context of the current misogynistic backlash we're experiencing, but instead of treating domestic incompetence as a sign of being a real man, can't we make it feel like a symptom of being a bit of a man-baby? Aren't the 'not involved' guys actually just not tough enough to deal with a really shitty nappy? Aren't the dads who can't get up in the night to do night feeds just delicate little things that aren't resilient enough to cope with a bit of sleep deprivation? Aren't the men who are incapable of planning ahead and thinking about problems before they arise destined to just be foot soldiers not leaders? And as for the men who can't remember the names of their kids' friends or teachers… are they lazy or just a bit dim? Being good at this stuff doesn't need to feel girly. It could feel like being a man rather than a child.

4. Competitive parenting: Evidence suggests that kids with more engaged and active fathers are healthier, happier and more successful; and we know that men are still generally socialised to crave winning. So can we make more egalitarian parenting a winning strategy for competitive men? Instead of heaping pressure on your offspring in order to 'give them a better chance in life' or pressuring them to be 'good kids' so they become a kind of trophy to your achievements in fatherhood, what's proven to give the kids a great chance to succeed in life is you actively caring for them, talking with them, listening to them and playing with them is. That's surely something competitive dads can show off about.

5. The real growth mindset: In our professional lives, the idea of the growth mindset is common. Few would consider a man building on the competence and skills he already has and continuing to learn as being inherently weak. A growth mindset isn't emasculating. If anything, it's aspirational to many. So why should it be any different in the domestic realm? Strategising, planning, thinking ahead and anticipating issues before they arise are all skills that are as valuable in managing and growing the kids as they are in managing and growing a business or a team. If anything, toddlers are trickier. If we position the work of childcare - from learning how to read the signs of a new baby, to shouldering the burden of the mental load - as work that's skilful and difficult, maybe we'll make it more appealing to men. This may even have the added bonus of ensuring that people see time spent parenting as a valuable thing, not just 'time off work.' But note to self: just like at work, we need to trust the people working alongside us to do the job well, but do it their way; not to simply copy exactly what we'd do.

If you have other positive experiences and ideas that have worked to encourage more gender-equal parenting in your family, do share them with us on @MenemiesNoMore. There must be so much we can all learn from each other here. But in the meantime, let's turn to the eighth and final major battlefield in today's gender wars that I explored with my respondents: The world of work.

ISSUE 8:

Danger: Women At Work

How the world of work is still stacked against women.

=============

REALITY CHECK:
WHERE WE ARE RIGHT NOW

When it comes to gender and the world of work, there's a dominant narrative that goes as follows: Gender apartheid has existed for centuries, with women, until very recently, being largely confined to the domestic realm and hardly ever allowed to enter workplaces, except in times of war; and when they *were* allowed to work, women were treated as interlopers, or funnelled into roles that supported or entertained the working men who remained dominant. It is certainly true that this picture of women being 'just a step on the boss man's ladder'[1] has been the reality for generations of women who were allowed to be wartime factory workers, or regular schoolteachers, shop workers or secretaries. The deal was that they could work, but only as long as they posed no threat to their male superiors, and they were largely forced out of the workforce as soon as they became wives or mothers, expected to go back to home and hearth where they were thought to really belong. And we only need look around us to see that's no longer so, as in recent decades women have been entering the paid workforce in droves, thanks to a mix of financial necessity and a desire to have a fulfilling career outside the home, even if they do have children.

But this familiar narrative that has informed middle class white feminism for too long has some significant issues that we must acknowledge before we go any further. Firstly, as we explored in *Issue 7: The Daddy Of All Roles*, it's based on a definition of 'work' that ignores the economic contribution of women's unpaid labour inside their own homes, which is a major oversight when we consider, for instance, that the estimated cost of replacing all this non-market work done in the United States would 'run to at least 44 percent of the country's GDP.'[2] Secondly, it's simply not true to suggest that the *majority* of women have historically been excluded from paid work, as in the UK alone, many millions of working class women have historically undertaken low-paid work outside their own homes, be it in schools or nurseries, farms or factories, or in domestic service in the homes of middle- and upper-class women.[3] In fact, it was the tireless, poorly-paid labour of working class women that enabled those trailblazing privileged white women to make their forays into the world of white-collar men's work in the first place.

Back in the 1800s, domestic service was the single largest employer of UK women, with the textile and clothing sectors coming a close second, although 'women were also found in large numbers in metalwares and pottery and in a variety of petty trades, especially in towns: confectionery, brewing and other provisioning, seamstressing, laundry work, cleaning and retailing' as well as in illicit activities such as entertainment and sex work; and many women often engaged in undeclared paid work within the family trade.[4] In the USA, 'for much of the 19th century, domestic work was a major source of employment, if not the principal occupation, for African American women in the South; for Mexican, Mexican American and Native American women in the West and Southwest; for Asian women in California and Hawaii and for European immigrant women in the Northeast and Midwest.'[5]

Even now, when we talk about women in the paid workforce, too often we neglect to include low-paid domestic labour that continues to support professional working women, and we should recognise that the majority of these domestic workers disproportionately remain immigrant women, and particularly women of colour from formerly colonised nations.[6]

Women (both trans and cis) have long dominated sex work too, and are forced to endure employment conditions that simply don't apply to women with more 'seemly' jobs, even though prostitution itself is legal in the UK. For instance, sex workers are forced to work alone here, a rule that puts these women at enormous risk.[7] It's also worth noting that many women even back in ancient and medieval times in the UK and across Europe were expected to earn their own crust, such as unmarried women whose relatives couldn't afford to support them. These women needed to find paid work, and would often end up with low-status jobs like spinning wool - hence the term 'spinster.'

There has, of course, been a significant shift in recent decades, with legislation seeking to ensure that all workplaces provide a level playing field for men and women; and when I look at the businesses that I've been lucky enough to work in, work with, or even run, I can say without doubt that I personally have been able to come a long way from that 1970s council estate in the shadow of the Dagenham Ford factory, whose activist women workers triggered the Equal Pay Act over 50 years ago. But how far has the world of paid work really come for all kinds of women? Are working women still disadvantaged in reality, despite all the equality legislation? Have we reached the promised land of workplace equality? Or have we even sailed right past it to an equally unfair place where some characteristics are so over-protected that straight, white men are at a distinct disadvantage in the world of work today?

Focus on business performance, not just fairness.

I believe it's vital to root any discussion about the need for gender diversity *in* business by stating the clear commercial benefits *to* business. More equal representation of women in the world of work can't just be an issue of fairness, because it's not a question of women feeling a bit left out and wanting to play too. Businesses that have a better gender balance thrive more; and thriving businesses don't just benefit everyone within that company - they also help drive a more productive economy for all. So let's first recognise that whatever someone's point of view on social justice, the *business* case for creating more gender-equal workplaces is irrefutable.

Amongst the large body of evidence that shows the commercial benefits of gender equality at work, McKinsey data is very often cited, showing that companies in the top quartile for gender diversity on Executive teams are 25 percent more likely to have above-average profitability than those in the bottom.[8] But there's lots more: addressing discrimination against women enhances productivity and work ethic by up to 40 percent according to the World Bank, and promotes a stronger culture of creativity and innovation;[9] bringing more women into businesses increases profitability by as much as 63 percent, according to the ILO;[10] companies with the largest proportion of women on their Exec achieved a 47 percent higher rate of return on equity than those with no female executives;[11] gender equality at work is also good for a business's reputation, which creates value because 66 percent of high-net-worth investors say it's important for them to invest in companies that hire and promote employees of diverse backgrounds, according to a survey by Morgan Stanley;[12] an S&P Global study found that compared to the market average, companies with women CEOs and CFOs drive better stock price performance, with an average 20 percent increase in stock price momentum for women CEO-led companies just two years into the role;[13] Goldman Sachs analysis found that 'even after adjusting for risk, female managed funds outperformed their male counterparts amid the coronavirus-related market swings;'[14] research based on over 84,000 leaders and 1.5 million raters shows that 'female leaders show up more effectively than their male counterparts across every management level and age level;'[15] Daria Burke tells us that women founders are proven to be more cash-efficient (they raise less capital on average so they have less to spend), they make more prudent financial decisions (as investors, CEOs, money managers), they tend to exit faster than the market (generally a year faster) and that BCG found that 'for every dollar raised, these start-ups generated 78 cents, while male-founded start-ups generated less than half that - just 31 cents';[16] and when we consider the costs and challenges of recruitment, where 93 percent, say they experienced skills shortages over the last 12 months (up from 77 percent in 2020),[17] there's a clear economic value to securing and holding on to great talent, so the Boston Consulting Group's finding that employees across all intersectionalities who can be their authentic selves at work are happier, more motivated to give their best, and nearly 2.4 times less likely to quit[18] makes that a hard business argument too.

While we're talking about productivity and the economy, it's also worth remembering that it's primarily women's choices that fuel the consumer economy, with women accounting for over $31.8 trillion in worldwide spending in 2020.[19] According to Catalyst, 89 percent of women across the world reported controlling or sharing daily shopping needs, compared to only 41 percent of men.[20] In the US, for instance, women drive 70-80 percent of all consumer purchasing.[21] Moreover, even in categories we tend to think of as more masculine, women have huge economic power and influence, making the decision or influencing the purchase of 92 percent of holidays, 65 percent of cars, 93 percent of food, 91 percent of new homes and 66 percent of PCs as well as also driving the decisions in more expected categories like groceries and health care.[22] Even when we look at the biggest purchase most people ever make, we see that after married couples, the top homebuyers are single women, making up 18 percent, double the percentage for single men.[23]

The top dog is still rarely female.

Despite the fact that advancing women's employment could add $12 trillion to global GDP and boost some countries' economic output by as much as 35 percent,[24] women still remain underrepresented in positions of power and influence in business. It may *feel* like women are everywhere these days, but the truth is that in most businesses, even when there appears to be a good overall gender balance in the company, women tend to take up more of the roles that have lower status, pay and power, whereas men tend to over-index in the higher status, higher power and higher paid roles. This, then, explains the Gender Pay Gap, which is often misunderstood and is better thought of as an organisation's Gender Leadership Gap. That's because while it's illegal, in the UK and in many countries, to pay a different amount to men and women 'in the same employment performing equal work unless any difference in pay can be justified'[25], it's not illegal to have men dominate the higher-prestige roles that also happen to be higher paid.

For instance, a big retailer is likely to have women outnumber men on the shop floor, but more men than women up in the boardroom; and creative and media companies may well have lots of women in strategy and client service roles, but the most highly respected and influential creative and editorial leadership roles still tend to be more male-dominated. What's more, boardrooms that do have healthy numbers of women in them are still most often run by a male CEO, and the 'power roles' like Chief Financial Officer are still more likely to be filled by a man, while we're likely to see women in the roles associated with 'softer' skills, like HR, that tend to be paid less and aren't considered so much of a stepping-stone to the top job.[26] Looking above the C-suite at the CEO's bosses, we see that Boards can often appear to have a healthy gender balance, but women on Boards are more likely than men to be in the unpaid Non Exec roles, so when we examine beneath the headline numbers, it's clear that the women don't have the same power and pay as the men here either. For instance, more than 90% of the female directors on FTSE 100 Boards are in these Non-Executive roles, and less than 20 percent of these top Boards are chaired by women.[27]

So despite all the positive momentum, 'year after year, surveys from highly-respected institutions including Harvard Business Review, McKinsey, the Global Institute for Women's Leadership and Cranfield' continue to reveal 'stubborn inequalities between men and women in the workplace' which 'often start early, as soon as promotions kick in, but then grow wider the further up an organisation you look - the so-called glass pyramid effect.'[28]

So in 2023, women hold 40 percent of all Board positions in the FTSE 100[29], which certainly sounds impressive (although even this figure still needs to increase by 25 percent to reach gender parity); but the numbers behind that headline figure show bigger gender gaps, as currently, women only occupy 28 percent of Executive roles and a tiny 9 percent of the most senior role, the CEO.[30] Moreover, at the time of writing, not one of those CEO's is a woman of colour.[31] 2023 was the first year in its history that a FTSE 100-listed business had a woman in each of its top jobs: CEO, CFO and Chairperson; but across the FTSE100 companies overall, there are still only 20 female CFOs and 18 Chairwomen.[32] Meanwhile, 85 of the top 100 FTSE companies have executive teams that are 60 percent or more male; and when we look at the Boards, we see that half of the FTSE 100 companies failed to meet the target of having at least 40 percent women in any Board position, with two-thirds not having a single woman in an Exec Director role.[33]

This gender leadership gap exists in smaller businesses and start-ups too. Companies with female leaders 'outperform those dominated by men', and in the UK 'women-led SMEs contribute about £85bn to economic output,' and yet 'only 16 percent of small business employers and one in three of entrepreneurs are women.'[34] Meanwhile generally only around five percent of venture capital funding goes to women,[35] despite, as we've seen, female-founded companies tending to generate better returns in investment; and the figure for women-led tech start-ups is even lower at 2.8 percent.'[36] And despite the enormous cultural as well as economic importance of the tech sector now and in future, in the UK, the numbers of women working in IT reached just 20 percent in 2019, with black women occupying a tiny 0.7 percent of positions, which is 2.5 times below their representation in other occupations, and only around a third the numbers of black men who are currently IT specialists.[37]

No wonder in many areas, women and particularly women of colour are doing it for themselves: back in 2018, women of colour owned 47 percent of all women-owned businesses, generating $386.6 billion in revenues,[38] and now, US research shows that 'women of colour are among the fastest growing group of entrepreneurs,' largely because 'they've faced a double whammy of sexism and prejudice, which has prompted them to go it alone.'[39] Woman-owned businesses in the US are growing on average twice as fast as all businesses nationwide, and women of colour are starting businesses at 4.5 times the rate of all businesses.[40]

In big business too, the US picture echoes the UK, with women holding just 8.2 percent of CEO positions at S&P 500 companies.[41] It's true that in 2022, we saw '72 percent of the incoming S&P 500 class of directors coming from historically underrepresented groups - defined as individuals who self-identify in one or more of the following categories: women, underrepresented racial/ethnic groups or the LGBTQ+ community. However, due to persistent low boardroom turnover, the addition of new directors from these historically underrepresented groups has had little impact on the overall diversity of S&P 500 boards', such that today, only '32 percent of all S&P 500 directors are women and 22 percent are from historically underrepresented racial and ethnic groups, less than half of which are women.'[42]

The 'glass pyramid' is clear to see in the US, just like in the UK, as McKinsey and LeanIn report that women accounted for almost half of the bottom rung of America's corporate ladder, but only make up only around a quarter of C-suite positions.[43] Importantly, these headline figures hide an underrepresentation of women of colour in American corporate leadership that's very much more extreme than for white women: although 29 percent of entry-level employees are white women and 19 percent women of colour, by the time we get to C-suite, white women show up at 72 percent the rate they did at entry level; but women of colour are much more extremely under-represented, present at only a quarter of their entry-level volume, and taking up just five percent of C-suite places.[44]

Interestingly, men of colour experience a 'glass pyramid' whose shape is similar to that of white women, being present in the C-suite at nearly 70 percent of their numbers at entry level, and the only group that bucks this under-representation trend in leadership is white men, who appear in the C-suite at close to twice the volume that they represented at entry level.[45]

So why is all of this under-representation happening? Are white men just much better leaders than women?

Black women face double the discrimination.

We know from the evidence laid out in *Issue 3: The Thing Is Boys Are Just Better* that men aren't intrinsically more intelligent or more capable than women; and only the most ardent white supremacists would try to argue that white folks possess some intrinsic superiority over people of colour (although just like with the masculine superiority myth, we must keep actively working against the biases and prejudices left by centuries of social conditioning that have pushed that lie). So while racism puts significant career barriers in the way of men and women alike, it disproportionately impacts black women at work, who suffer the intersection of both racial and gender inequalities. That's why black women are less likely to interact with senior leadership than any other demographic group; managers are less likely to advocate for black women; black women are more likely than other women to experience a wide range of microaggressions; and black women are more likely to feel excluded and scrutinised than other women,[46] with dark-skinned women reporting how they experience anti-Blackness even from other women of colour who have a more white-adjacent experience.[47]

But there's another area where black women are even more disadvantaged than white women, and that's to do with the way women are expected to behave at work. Data shows that there's a real pressure on all women to be kind, communal, and likeable at work as well as competent; and that women who display competence are deemed to be less likeable, creating a damaging double-bind that men simply don't experience.[48] Women are also penalised for seeming 'overly ambitious' or 'out for themselves' if they express a desire to lead, and these likeability and ambition penalties are exacerbated for black women, who often find themselves 'on the receiving end of racist comments that they are "angry,"' which is completely unfounded as studies show that black women are proven to be no more likely to express anger than any other group of Americans'.[49] This stereotype of the 'angry Black woman' causes real harm as 'Black women who were perceived as angry tended to receive lower performance evaluations and lower recommended raises.'[50] And as if that weren't enough to deal with, black and brown women are often told that the promotion they worked so hard to achieve wasn't one they really deserved, with some accusing them of being 'the diversity hire' rather than recognising the many additional barriers they had to overcome to succeed at work.[51]

So we continue to penalise women, and particularly women of colour, deeming them unlikeable if they're too confident, competent, or ambitious; yet not 'leadership material' if they are not competent, confident and ambitious enough - which becomes even more frustrating and ironic when we look at the leadership qualities that are proven to be most valuable, and see how that maps against men and women.

Women's leadership style is effective but undervalued.

Many who take a social justice approach argue that at work, we should be seeking representation of men and women that matches their proportions in the general population. However, from a purely business viewpoint that may not be the best approach, because according to Professor Tomas Chamorro-Premuzic in his TED talk *Why We Should Be More Sexist*, if we promoted people purely based on the characteristics that are proven to correlate with the most effective leadership, the result wouldn't be 50/50 male/female; it would be at least 70/30... in favour of women.[52] We simply don't know how far that's due to the way we're socialised versus some kind of innate ability, but right now, the evidence is clear that it's women who are statistically more likely to make the better leaders.

However, there is what Chamorro-Premuzic describes as a 'pathological mismatch between the qualities that seduce us in a leader and those that are needed to be an effective leader', and he catalogues these in his punchily-titled book *Why Do So Many Incompetent Men Become Leaders?*, setting out painful truths such as 'all of the aspects of leadership style on which women exceeded men relate positively to leaders' effectiveness, whereas all of the aspects on which men exceeded women have negative or null relations to effectiveness.'[53] He tells us, for instance, that 'whether in sports, politics or business, the best leaders are usually humble,' and that 'arrogance and overconfidence are inversely related to leadership talent'; and yet, despite the prevalence of men in positions of leadership, 'normative data, which includes thousands of managers from across all industry sectors and 40 countries, shows that men are consistently more arrogant, manipulative and risk-prone than women,' whereas 'whether through nature or nurture, humility is a much more common feature in women than men.'[54] Ironically, though, it's more often men who tend to get promoted and rewarded because 'what it takes to get the job is... the reverse of what it takes to do the job well.'[55]

Chamorro-Premuzic isn't alone in these findings. McKinsey also identifies a tendency towards 'promoting primarily on the basis of more traditional types of leadership behaviour, such as authoritative decision making, control, and corrective action, despite those very behaviours being least critical for future success. More likely to drive success are intellectual stimulation (which men and women apply in equal measure), and five other traits that are seen more often in women: inspiration; participative decision-making; setting expectations and rewards; people development; and role-modelling.'[56] And so, as Ruchika Tulshyan & Jodi-Ann Burey explain, 'the same systems that reward confidence in male leaders, even if they're incompetent, punish white women for lacking confidence, women of colour for showing too much of it, and all women for demonstrating it in a way that's deemed unacceptable.'[57]

This over-promotion of people with the least effective leadership characteristics happens because 'self-centred, entitled, and narcissistic [people] tend to emerge as leaders and take control of resources and power in a group' and 'right now these traits... are more common in men than in women.'[58] Hundreds of years of wrong assumptions about what great leadership looks like have created 'unspoken stereotypes of leaders as people - usually men - who seem oblivious to their weaknesses. And we have great tolerance for people - again, usually men - who are not as talented as they think.'[59] That's why Chamorro-Premuzic argues strongly against 'asking women to act more like incompetent men by self-promoting, faking it, or leaning in when they shouldn't', because this approach is 'making the problem worse' and 'will only result in the promotion of incompetent women to leadership roles, and do very little to correct people's unfair stereotypes of female leaders.'[60]

Promoting more women whilst still rewarding an ineffective and damaging leadership model is clearly not the answer, however good it makes the gender-balance figures look. Instead, we'd get better leaders and better businesses if we encouraged men to emulate the qualities that make people more effective as leaders, that we currently see more often in women - emotional intelligence, self-awareness, humility, integrity, and coachability.[61] If we did that, the average male leader too might be more likely to elicit more respect and pride from their followers, communicate their vision more effectively, better empower and mentor their subordinates, approach problem solving in a more flexible and creative way, and be fairer and more objective in their evaluation of direct reports, as more women currently do.[62] He may become as likely as the average female manager to invest time and energy in checking in on his employees' wellbeing, take on mentorship roles and work on diversity initiatives outside his core job;[63] and by doing so, he might help address the fact that only 70% of employees are engaged, when the cost of that disengagement is around $500 billion in the US alone.[64] He might excel in leadership styles which are more prevalent in higher-EQ leaders, such as entrepreneurial or disruptive approaches; and if he bucked the trend of men under-indexing in empathy with a larger gender difference than most other personality traits, he could better see problems from other people's perspectives and become less self-centred and more flexible in problem solving.[65]

If we're to get there, though, we all need to understand the data, refuse to fall prey to the allure of the masculine superiority myth and be particularly mindful of how women of colour suffer exponentially when that myth becomes entangled with the lie of white supremacy too. This is easier said than done, because it's a sad fact that the people who walk through the world with systemic privilege are the very ones who are the most blind to it. Right now, 'men are more likely to live in a world in which their flaws are forgiven and their strengths magnified. Thus, it is harder for them to see themselves accurately', yet this, overconfidence is 'the natural result of privilege,'[66] and it's what can lead people into damaging wars, to collapse economies and make political leadership decisions that damage people's lives and livelihoods. Overconfidence is also what Nobel Prize winner Daniel Kahneman named as the most dangerous bias of all.'[67]

However, I do believe that there is hope, even in this difficult area, and later in this chapter I'll outline what my conversations with men taught me about how we might be able to overcome it.

Other barriers need to be broken too.

Getting more people who embody the right leadership approach into positions of power and influence isn't the only barrier to overcome if we want to ensure successful businesses where people with different lived experiences can all contribute and thrive - which is vital, as 'diverse team members, in general, contribute to a larger output of ideas, leading to a stronger culture of creativity and innovation.'[68] Of course, more empathetic leaders with higher EQ and more flexible approaches to problem-solving may naturally address this more readily, but it's worth outlining here what some other key barriers are that need to be addressed, because however empathetic and creative we are, we can't fix what we don't see.

These issues manifest right throughout businesses, not just at the highest levels - the entire talent pipeline is affected by businesses failing to promote staff according to the qualities that are proven most effective in leadership, with a new study showing that despite scoring better performance ratings, 'women are *consistently* judged as having less leadership potential than their male counterparts, making them less likely to be promoted each year.'[69] We also see women's careers being actively damaged when they behave in ways that aren't so career-limiting for men: 'A woman's perceived deserved compensation drops by 35 percent, twice as much as a man's, when both are equally aggressive in workplace communications. Women are also dramatically more likely than men to be punished for showing assertive behaviours... or for initiating negotiations in the workplace. And high-achieving women are far more likely than their male peers to be described as abrasive in their performance reviews.'[70]

Incredibly, whereas women who express anger are seen as less competent and accorded lower status and lower wages, men who exhibit anger at work in the same contexts actually receive a boost in their perceived status.[71] Moreover, these old biases become exacerbated by the fact that 'women's CV or track record is in large part a product of the opportunities they have or, more often have not had access to', and so 'women interviewing for roles or promotion may not come with the same evidence of success as male peers.'[72] And McKinsey finds that 'while 93 percent of companies take business goals into account in managers' performance reviews, less than 40 percent do so for factors like team morale and progress on DEI goals', even though, as we saw earlier, those qualities are proven to have significant business benefits too.[73] So there's lots more businesses could do to address barriers to promotion and progress for women throughout the workforce.

Another important barrier is that the historically male-dominated world of work generally doesn't accommodate for the 'three M's' that the majority of female bodies go through - menstruation, maternity and menopause - and as a result, businesses as well as women lose out. In the UK, PMS is estimated to impact the productivity of over nine million women between the age of 16 to 45, with businesses losing up to 9.3 days annually as a result of menstruation-related symptoms.[74] Interestingly, due to the stigma that remains around periods, women are nine times more likely to engage in 'presenteeism' (coming to work when in significant pain, but not being able to contribute properly) than absenteeism, but nevertheless, the loss of productivity and lower levels of employee engagement that this creates is estimated to be costing UK businesses at least £6 billion each year.[75] Likewise with maternity, where even before the pandemic, US studies calculated that inadequate childcare was costing employers $13 billion a year in lost productivity, as well as costing working parents $37 billion a year in lost income,[76] and in the UK, the CBI identifies childcare as a business issue that's critical for economic growth.[77] And menopause is costing business dearly too, with one recent study estimating that in the US alone, the annual cost of lost working days related to menopause symptoms for women aged 45-60 is $1.8 billion.[78] All three of these factors contribute to the glass pyramid phenomenon for women at work, with a recent UK study finding that the majority of women said that a gynae or other women's health condition had negatively impacted their career.[79]

The other barrier to gender equality at work that deserves specific attention is flexible working, as the traditional working practices of commuting into a workplace to spend a 5-day working week together may be good for the old-school 'command and control' kind of leadership, but it doesn't work best for many of their employees, nor for overall business productivity. Even before the pandemic, the UK's Chartered Institute of Personnel and Development catalogued the benefits of more flexible working, which include: better ability to attract good talent, including from a more diverse pool of people; improved engagement, job satisfaction and loyalty; reduced absenteeism and improved well-being; better employee retention and progression; improved productivity (with flexibility being an even better motivator to employees' productivity than financial incentives); improving business outcomes associated with a more diverse workforce; and enabling more agility and responsiveness to market change.[80]

Beyond these, though, there's one final barrier to improved gender equality at work that we ought to explore. It's a particularly pertinent one to this project of mine, because it's one that centres on men, and what they're doing - or rather, what they're not doing - to lean in and use their power to create change.

Men over-rate themselves as allies.

2022 research by Token Man & The Hobbs Consultancy found that over half of men (54 percent) are still not engaged with any form of Inclusion & Diversity in their workplace, with only 31 percent of respondents claiming that the majority of men in their workplace fully engage with D&I initiatives.'[81] According to a Catalyst study from 2020, that's not necessarily because men don't *want* to address gender equality in the workplace. In fact, 'an overwhelming majority of men (86 percent) say they are personally committed to interrupting sexist behaviours when they see them in the workplace.' The trouble is, 'only 31% feel confident in their ability to do so.'[82] A 2022 IWL study on Allyship-in-Action supports this: Of all the allyship behaviours they report, 'calling out other men who devalue women' gets the lowest score, with only 15 percent of men overall saying they always/frequently take this action; and this only rises to 38 percent amongst men who claim to be 'participants in allyship communities'.[83]

Catalyst points out that a company culture 'in which silence is the norm' has an enormous impact here, suppressing men's instincts to speak up. They found that 'as organisational silence increases, men are 50 percent less likely to be committed to interrupting sexist behaviour at work.[84] But women's ability to advocate for themselves is limited, as 'the majority of women in the workforce feel excluded from decision making, do not feel comfortable expressing their opinions, and do not feel as though they can succeed.' And only two-thirds of women feel they can voice a dissenting opinion without fear of repercussion, versus 80 percent of men.[85]

Fascinatingly, though, men tend to think they're doing a better job of being a gender equality ally than they actually are. Back in 2013, 92 percent of men said they didn't believe they were excluding women, yet 81 percent of women said they felt some form of exclusion at work.[86] The maths still doesn't add up a decade later, as in 2022, IWL still found there to be a persistent gap between men and women in their perceptions of how men are showing up - or not. Even where the figures for women were most positive, among the executive level of leadership, 77 percent of men believe that most men within their organisation were either 'active allies' or 'public advocates' for gender equity, but only 45 percent of women agreed.[87]

The men who aren't engaged in allyship activity are, unsurprisingly, almost entirely unaware of the biased behaviours that the women in their organisation are suffering; but even the men who participate in their organisation's allyship programmes are much less likely than their female colleagues to notice the biases that are disadvantaging women, such as women being spoken over more often than men; having their judgement questioned in their area of expertise; being overlooked for promotion or stretch assignments; being asked to do the less-valued work like schedule meetings and take notes; and being questioned on their emotional state. And men who consider themselves to be allies are still less than half as likely as women to notice when women aren't given credit for their contributions.[88]

When men are overestimating their own contributions and underestimating the issues women suffer at work, it's no wonder that so many men are failing to engage in initiatives around gender equality. A study that sought to further understand why only 22 percent had actually participated in training found that 'the reasons male respondents gave included that they were too busy; were not invited; did not see the need for allyship; did not know how to get involved; or were more interested in other employee resource groups'[89] Similarly, the 2022 *Masculinity In The Workplace* study found that many men seem to feel that issues of equality are just not relevant to them, with 41 percent of the men in their research sample saying they 'feel they *had to* show active engagement in I&D *despite it not being relevant to their career*' [my italics][90] In fact, many feel that diversity initiatives are a genuine threat to them: 43 percent of male employees said they 'feel less valued because of diversity initiatives;' 49 percent feel they 'will be looked over for promotion due to diversity targets;' and 56 percent think they 'will struggle for another role due to demographic profiles.'[91] These fears and worries aren't exclusive to workplaces, of course; nor are they unique to the UK. It's sobering to note that 2023 research on *The State Of American Men* found that 40 percent of all men say they trust one or more so-called 'men's rights,' anti-feminist, or pro-violence voices from the manosphere, and amongst younger men, that figure rises to nearly half.[92] A majority, 53 percent, of men agree that 'in America today, men have it harder than women'[93], but few feel comfortable talking about it openly, as seven out of ten men say that speaking their minds could destroy their reputation.[94]

So, we have workplaces full of women who are frustrated at the barriers they face, alongside many men who feel like they're the ones who are suffering more now, but who feel scared to talk about how they feel for fear of the repercussions. The irony, of course, is that addressing these issues can drive business performance and benefit the whole workforce - including those men who feel overlooked, excluded and disadvantaged.

Opportunities for business growth.

As we saw earlier, the business argument for a more gender-equal workplace is strong, even for people who aren't motivated by a desire for social justice. As a quick reminder, 'when a business has women at the top, the whole business benefits, not just the other women within it. These businesses are associated with greater profits; better diversity across the company... and better outcomes for employees of all genders.'[95] It even benefits the planet too, because as well as valuing diversity of race/ethnicity and age significantly more than male directors, 'female directors are more likely to see ESG's connection to strategy and to prioritise climate change.'[96]

Men's fears about being the sacrificial lamb in the drive towards gender equality are understandable, and individual men are doubtless experiencing more competition for jobs and promotions from women and other groups who have been historically underrepresented - although it's worth acknowledging that models of leadership that value compassion, empathy, kindness, and consideration would also benefit the many men who don't fit the traditional 'strong man' leadership archetype. We should also note that the zero-sum game assumption that many men hold is simply not borne out, as the IMF explains that 'men's wages will also increase as a result of greater inclusion of women in the labour force since productivity will increase. This is important because these higher wages should strengthen support for removing barriers that hold women back'[97]; and a Canadian study showed that increasing women's workforce participation increased jobs and GDP overall, but not at the expense of men: when the province of Quebec 'increased WWP through parental leave and childcare reform, it had no impact on men's workforce participation.'[98]

There's a huge potential boost to national economies that could be shared my men and women alike, as on average, across countries, 'estimated long-run GDP per capita is calculated to be almost 20% higher if gender employment gaps were closed,' with economic gains through more gender-equal entrepreneurship alone estimated to be $5-6 trillion if women started and scaled new businesses at the same rate men do;[99] and if women were to participate throughout the economy identically to men, that could add an estimated $28 trillion to annual global GDP in 2025, according to McKinsey.[100] That's roughly the combined size of the US and UK economies today.

If we're to achieve this economic growth, we clearly need an approach to gender equality that men can genuinely buy into. However, despite the best intentions and hard work of many DE&I practitioners, and the $8 billion spent on it every year, worrying evidence has emerged that 'these trainings don't work and often backfire, as research tracking the hiring and promotion practices of 830 companies over the course of 30 years found that white men who are asked to go to diversity trainings tend to rebel by hiring and promoting fewer women and fewer minorities.'[101] But beyond making DE&I feel more inclusive for the many cis, straight, white men who feel alienated or threatened by current approaches, there's an additional opportunity that could be seized by businesses that are innovative enough to look beyond their own board rooms and team sheets, and start to explore how the products and services they create could better serve the women who make up their consumers and audiences; women whose influence and buying power are still sorely overlooked and underestimated.

Here, we must start by remembering our tendency to believe that we're being gender-neutral and designing simply for 'people' when, in fact, we frequently take a default-male approach to all kinds of things without even realising it, as we set out right back in *Issue 1: That 'I've Never Really Thought About It' Face*. Recent research in advertising and the media has started to quantify the upside that exists for businesses who lean into these opportunities and better serve overlooked audiences. For instance, System 1's *Feeling Seen* report shows that when 'inclusive advertising was judged by real, diverse audiences [it] proves that brands who get diversity right benefit hugely.' They explain that in the US as well as the UK, 'diverse advertising isn't just about "doing good" - it leads to greater engagement and greater commercial effectiveness.'[102] This is not just because marginalised groups who feel represented by more diverse ads 'react with particular emotion and intensity;' it's also because this Diversity Dividend doesn't come at the expense of consumers who are more used to seeing themselves in ads. The truth is, 'the best diverse ads are popular with everyone.'[103]

Yet despite those clear commercial benefits of better diversity in ads, and the realities of increasing numbers of working women in leadership positions, new data shows that representations of these women is going backwards in online ads, both in terms of their prevalence in adverts and the amount of spend behind those ads. For instance, 'the percentage of women that were portrayed in professional settings decreased from 16 percent in 2021 to just seven percent in 2022' and women with darker skin tones appeared 58 percent less frequently in professional settings than women with the lightest skin tones.[104] What's more, even the ads that did feature women in professional settings received 35 percent less spend than those depicting men in similar roles, and 'ad spend behind darker-skinned women fell by 20 percent last year compared with 2021'[105] While that's a big problem at a societal level, it does present a commercial opportunity for any businesses that's willing and able to address it - and bearing in mind that 66 percent of women still don't connect with what they are seeing in marketing and 60 percent say they think marketing has an outdated view of women'[106], taking heed of the diversity dividend could offer most businesses that advertise a real competitive advantage.

A similar story emerges when we look at news media, where a 2022 report commissioned by the Bill & Melinda Gates Foundation found that 'if the gender gap were to be addressed and women better represented in the news media, the industry could grow female audiences exponentially', estimating that 'closing the gender consumption gap could generate as much as US$83 billion over the next 10 years.'[107] Some brands who've done this in the real world bear this out, such as when The Guardian 'launched the newsletter *Her Stage* to cover issues relevant to women, but in a way that is also accessible to men. The quantitative analysis revealed that the average open rate for *Her Stage* so far has been 65 percent, versus an industry average of between 15 and 25 percent.' And in Norway, 'data scientists found that the most gender-balanced newsrooms, and those that write most about women's issues, deliver the best audience and financial performances.'[108]

The Financial Services sector, too, has a lot of room for growth here, such as in Wealth Management, where a third of assets under management are held by women, and yet McKinsey notes that this 'significantly large' market segment is 'perhaps taken for granted by financial institutions.' And contrary to traditional stereotypes, the opportunity isn't just with single and divorced women, who together hold around 22 percent of assets under management, because 'of the €4.6 trillion in AUM held by women, €3.6 trillion - 78 percent - is held by women who are married or in partnerships and are the main financial decision maker in their household.'[109]

In Europe, women like Olga Miler of SmartPurse and Sam Secomb of Women's Wealth are following the lead of Ellevest (the woman-first US-based financial company that now has $1.5 billion in assets under management) and founding businesses to address this problem, not just because it's the right thing to do, but because businesses that start centring women's needs and wants instead of continuing to under-estimate them stand to benefit financially every bit as much as their clients do. The opportunities are everywhere for those willing to look. A bar, t*he Sports Bra,* opened in Portland in 2022, offering a safe and celebratory space for people, whatever their gender, who love to watch women's sports. It has quickly become a huge success, populated by all kinds of people, including many men. Vogue's Emma Specter noted on her visit: 'more than one table in the place that seems occupied by queer people on a date, but there are also clearly sports-obsessed buddy pairs, middle-aged women sitting solo, grandparents with small children, and every other type of human arrangement that could conceivably be scarfing down nachos and watching women's sports on a Sunday afternoon.'[110]

Motor repair companies could learn a thing or two from Pennsylvania trailblazer Patrice Banks, who 'empowers women to navigate the male-dominated world of car repairs, one wrench turn at a time' through her Girls Auto Clinic repair centre, which is staffed entirely by female mechanics. She's even opened an adjoining mani-pedi and hair salon called Clutch Beauty Bar, where customers can wait while their repairs are done.[111]

And clubbing recently got an overhaul by DJ Annie Mac whose *Before Midnight* series of club nights was inspired by her desire to have a more family-friendly approach to clubbing after she became a mother, but is a huge hit with all kinds of 'ravers who don't want to wreck their sleep,' as the events only run from 7pm til midnight.[112]

Of course there are other enormously successful examples of women-centred product design headed up by famous female founders, such as production company Hello Sunshine, founded by Reese Witherspoon to 'shine a light on where women are now, and help them chart a new path forward'[113] which recently sold for $900m[114]; and Bumble, the dating app created by Whitney Wolfe Herd where 'women are required to make the first move, shifting old-fashioned power dynamics and encouraging equality from the start'[115] which now has a market cap of well over $5 billion.[116] It's my belief that neither of these companies *needed* to have been founded by a woman, because a male leader with the right team and the right research, *could* have sought out excellent stories about and by women; men *could* have understood the vulnerabilities that many women can feel dating, and realised how powerful it would be to for women to be more in control of who can connect with them. But until more men in business start to actively look for these opportunities to better serve women, and consult the right people on how to do that brilliantly, female-founded businesses are going to keep on stealing their lunch.

With all the fear, resentment and backlash we see amongst men in business today, though, we do seem a long way from men feeling able to do that right now. So how do we overcome the barriers that are stopping businesses from capitalising on all of the commercial as well as societal benefits that greater gender equality can bring?

WHAT I LEARNED
ABOUT MEN

Every one of the men I spoke with expressed some kind of concern about the difficulties they now faced in the world of work, although initially, the 'be careful what you say' fear was so profound that it took a while to establish the sense of personal trust we needed in this area. Often, I had to keep repeating my assurances of complete anonymity, including ensuring that their company and sometimes even their whole industry couldn't be identified from their comments. It felt, at times, like I was talking to people in witness protection, such was the concern that a few of these men had about unwittingly 'saying the wrong thing and destroying everything I've spent my whole life working for.' In this area, just like with their worries about false sexual misconduct accusations that we discussed in *Issue 6: Let's Talk About Sex*, the stakes can feel enormously high.

Once they were sure it was a safe space, most of them volunteered at least one recent example of a man they knew who'd 'been passed over by a less qualified woman' at work, and a significant number told me that this had happened to them personally. A couple of the men who were straight and white also referenced how they, or men like them, had 'lost out on opportunities to other men who are more diverse[117] than I am.' Embarrassed as they looked to be saying it, this belief clearly made them feel a sense of real injustice, challenging their idea of 'playing fair' which is hugely important to a lot of men, as we explored earlier in *Issue 4: It's Dog Eat Dog And I'm Nobody's Bitch.*

On a personal level, it doesn't seem fair.

It's important to recognise how difficult many of the men found this conversation, not just because they feared how their comments might be misconstrued and weaponised if they 'got out'; but also because 'I just don't wanna be that dick who bleats on about his own problems, ignoring the fact that men like me have had loads of advantages in life... But it's hard, and it's scary, for men like me when we look ahead.'

Respondents who were from marginalised communities had a specific angle on this issue, where they felt they'd been unfairly 'lumped in with men generally, and written off as part being part of the privilege problem,' which 'really stings, seeing as how I was constantly beaten up as a kid by transphobic and homophobic bullies just for being who I am, and now, finally, I pass as a man, and I'm treated as if I'm the enemy.' Another voiced his frustration with 'basically being told I'm not queer enough' such as when he'd not been considered for an opportunity - for which no one could have been better qualified, - because they wanted 'someone who was "more diverse" - as if one person can be 'diverse' anyway!' And a light-skinned mixed-race man of African heritage told me he'd overheard organisers of an industry event at which he'd been asked to speak discussing using a picture of him where his hair was more visible, 'to make sure people realised I wasn't another white guy! And they were moaning about the fact that they couldn't get hold of a more dark-skinned black man.' He told me, exasperatedly, 'I know diversity's important, but half the time it feels like people are casting for one of those old Benetton ads - doesn't matter what you can do or what your experience really is, as long as it *looks* like a good diverse line-up.'[118]

Beyond these men who suffer other kinds of systemic and personal discrimination feeling ignored by clumsy attempts at increasing diversity, there was a very clear sense that 'it's a hundred percent true that if you're a middle aged, middle class straight white guy, you're right at the bottom of any recruiter's wish list', and 'they're all looking to promote more women and people of colour - which is the right thing to do, but it does mean that men like me are the last people anyone wants to promote now. And I know that's completely fair at a broader level, but it does make me fear for my future, I'll be honest.' Just as we covered in *Issue 2: Aren't We Nearly There Yet?,* this narrative of 'positive discrimination is justified at a broader level but really unfair for me personally' was very commonly expressed, with the apocalyptic vision of 'never being promoted again' and 'being put out to pasture' very prevalent. 'I'm a white man in my 40's who went to public school, for god's sake. I'm basically public enemy number one now, as far as HR people are concerned!'[119]

I'll come back to this being articulated as 'positive discrimination' later, but first, I decided to explore publicly available data on promotions, to see how far the evidence supports my respondents' catastrophic worries that it was 'almost impossible' for men like them to be promoted these days. Promotion rates in the media and entertainment industry were the closest I could find to the 'it's all over for men' doomsday scenario. Here, women are indeed outnumbering men at promotions across a number of levels: as we look through the ranks of seniority that a McKinsey study[120] measured, we see two women being promoted for every one man into both manager and senior manager jobs in media and entertainment, which is no doubt alarming for men working in that sector, but it's worth noting that even here, a third of the people being promoted are men - a significant minority, but not exactly 'almost none'. At the next level up in the media and entertainment industries, we see the proportions flip, with 2 men promoted into VP level for every one woman. It then swings back in women's favour at Senior VP level, with over 3 women promoted for every one man, before reverting back once again at the most senior level, where men in this study have a monopoly on promotions into C-suite.[121]

Outside of the media and entertainment sector, the promotions picture is further from the 'impossible' image held by most of the men I spoke to. Here, fifty percent more men than women make up the first promotion, from entry level to manager - that so-called 'broken rung' that kicks off the glass pyramid for women. Then there are equal numbers of men and women being promoted into the ranks of senior manager and VP; and promotions into the two most senior levels remain quite evenly balanced too, with women just edging a majority of promotions into SVP, at 57 percent; and men making up a similar-sized small majority of promotions into C-suite, at 56 percent.[122]

Another 2022 study, that includes intersectional analysis, found '72 percent of the incoming S&P 500 class of directors coming from historically underrepresented groups - defined as individuals who self-identify in one or more of the following categories: women, underrepresented racial/ethnic groups or the LGBTQ+ community.'[123] Although these proportions are broadly in line with the makeup of the population where this study was done, the fact that we're so used to business being dominated by straight white men can make this representative number feel out of kilter for some.

What you know and what you feel are different.

When I shared these figures with some of the men I talked to, their response was fascinating, often fixing on the areas of the above data where women had the advantage over men and ignoring the areas where the numbers are more equal or where men still get more of the promotions: 'OK it's not *impossible* to get promoted now when you're a man, but our chances are a helluva lot lower than women's though.' They often went on to say that they knew of exceptions to that general rule too, such as, 'those figures may be the case overall, but my mate works at a company where the last three promotions have all been women of colour.' Despite many of these men rationally acknowledging the importance of fairness and balance at a macro level, a visceral feeling of injustice at a personal level often informed their responses. And in many ways that's entirely to be expected - people will of course respond personally to any sense of threat. Moreover, we know from the field of Behavioural Economics that changing our mind about things takes more than simply being presented with some data, and we tend to notice things that confirm our current beliefs, finding ways of rejecting things that contradict our world view.

It's no surprise, then, that almost all of my respondents leapt on the 30 percent figure above, seeing that as 'really low - women in the media have *twice the chance* men of being promoted.' Interestingly, we see how that same number can feel very different to when the boot is on the other foot, as these same men had described around 30 percent of companies' Exec members being women as being 'nearly half.' And so we see smart, decent, thoughtful men ignoring the rational proof that their chances of being promoted are quite often the same as women's, and focusing instead on the areas where it's lower; and we see them think of 30 percent as 'almost done' when it's about the incidence of women in leadership teams, but 'almost none' when it comes to men's promotion rates.

We humans are emotional creatures, so despite the myth of the rational man (sic), the phenomenon of loss aversion is very powerful, prompting men to over-focus on the threats and the losses. We're all hardwired to notice breaks in patterns too, so things that are different simply stand out more, which is why the news that another man gets promoted tends not to be noticed in the way that it is when someone becomes the first woman (or woman of colour, or woman over 50, or mother, etc) to achieve a specific leadership position. This then reinforces the idea that it's women who are disproportionately being promoted over men, with women's celebrations of these firsts further fuelling men's fear that they'll be 'left on the scrap heap' as 'the future is female.' Moreover, these men knowing that 'diversity is supposed to make for more successful companies' didn't seem to help them feel better about it, or stop them saying 'but my company is different though' and 'they just promote women who aren't qualified, who can't do the job, and that's really not helping anyone.'

The masculine superiority myth at work.

It's worth unpacking the language that the men used throughout these discussions too, as we see the myth of masculine superiority wielding its influence here, just like it does in so many other aspects of life. I witnessed the strong sense of entitlement to be leaders in the workplace that many white men in particular unconsciously feel, with more than one saying that 'women are taking men's jobs.' Maybe they only meant 'jobs that used to belong to men' as opposed to 'jobs that should by default belong to men', but I certainly sensed a strong undercurrent that the boardroom is somehow naturally more of a man's domain. Similarly, a lot of the men referred to women being promoted in higher numbers than men as 'positive discrimination' or 'diversity hires,' which suggests that they don't quite believe that these women tend to get promoted on merit. Some voiced this explicitly, telling me that 'women being promoted at twice the rate of men is outrageous really, as they won't be twice as good as the men.' Tomas Chamorro-Premuzic's studies suggest otherwise, of course, because if we promoted people into leadership based on the qualities and attributes proven to make the most successful leaders, women would indeed outnumber men more than two to one right now. But none of the men I talked to had heard of that data, and the assumption remained that men tended to be more qualified for, and more suited to, leadership and promotion; so it's no wonder they feel that more women being promoted somehow goes against the natural order of things and is a form of discrimination where individual good men suffer for the sake of social justice.

Doubtless there are companies who are busy promoting incompetent women to positions of leadership, and a few of my respondents confessed that they were hugely frustrated with their workplaces for 'promoting from within, where they just take the best-qualified woman who's already here even though she might not be best for the job. It's stupid because the men who are more qualified get resentful, and there are women they could bring in who really *are* good enough, but they don't put the effort into looking for them.' The idea that finding competent, qualified women takes more work and effort than finding men may well be true, based on the assumption that 'there are just more men in my industry, so there's bound to be more good ones.'

Interestingly, the 'glass cliff phenomenon' was apparent in my conversations too, where women's failures tended to be seen as symptomatic of a broken system that's unfairly promoting women beyond their capabilities in an attempt to create gender balance, whereas when I asked about men who had failed as leaders, my respondents tended to talk about their individual personalities and characters, not their gender nor the system that supports and promotes them. For most of the men I talked to, when they evaluated other men at work, it was clear that, as Grayson Perry wrote almost a decade ago 'if they achieve something good, it is down to their own efforts. They got the job because they are brilliant, not because they are a Default Man, and they are also presumed more competent by other Default Men. If they do something bad it is also down to the individual and not to do with their gender, race, or class.' And whereas women not succeeding in leadership is seen as a systemic issue of over-promotion and positive discrimination, when men fail, it's simply 'because he is a wrong 'un.'[124]

A few men also criticised their company's *intent* in promoting women, saying that 'they know people will be scrutinising the numbers and the gender pay gap' and 'It's just not a good look is it, these days, to have a senior team without any women in it?' Few spontaneously questioned whether these companies are creating the right conditions for success for women, although one senior man in a typically male-dominated sector did reflect insightfully on a culture-change initiative, saying that 'they're making changes, but not at the highest levels where it could really make a difference; and they seem to care more about how the numbers look than how the culture's changing.' More typically, though, if my respondents discussed culture or models of leadership at all, it was about women's inability to 'fit in' or to 'really hack it,' as 'the culture, especially at the top, can be quite brutal, and I guess a lot of women are just not really cut out for that.' Implicitly, then, many of the men suggested that the traditionally masculine qualities that have long dominated business and leadership are the right ones: 'We're a relatively small company and we have a couple of our senior women away on leave at the moment, so the senior team is almost all men without them. We need them, because they're confident and ballsy and able to stand up to all the guys with big personalities and opinions in a way that most of the more junior women don't.' It didn't seem to occur to him that these senior men could moderate their behaviour, and instead I got the overwhelming sense from many of the men that women ought to be 'ballsy' and 'feisty' and 'tough' and 'stand up for themselves' in order to get ahead, with little suggestion that there could be a different model of leadership that these men might feel they could value too.

They're proud to model more modern leadership.

I didn't yet introduce the evidence about different leadership styles that I've set out in the 'reality check' section of this chapter. Instead, I simply encouraged my respondents to talk about specific examples from their personal lives, asking them 'whose leadership have you most admired in your life so far, in work and in life generally?' The answers were a long way from the ballsy/tough/combative qualities they were talking about before, and could have come straight out of the Chamorro-Premuzic playbook: 'I had a couple of bosses, who were women actually, early in my career, who were brilliant. There was less of the macho bollocks, less like they're trying to compete with you and score points the whole time. They were no pushovers though, they didn't take any shit. But they were more interested in getting the best out of you, and they were smarter than most of us chaps too - probably because women had to be so aware of having to walk the line the whole time between too confident and too meek, too communal and too selfish or whatever, that they were just more aware and more tuned in to other people.' Another talked of his football coach who was 'one of those guys who's not all loud and shouty and full of himself, but he really understood what makes me tick, and knew how to motivate me and get the best out of me - he did for the whole team. He was such a good leader; someone I learned a lot from.'

Many talked like this about leaders, both men and women, in their work life and families, who had qualities of empathy, emotional intelligence, kindness and vulnerability, and then they spontaneously moved into telling me, with a real sense of pride, about these kinds of qualities that they themselves shared, and why they were important. 'I can see the men who went to all-boys schools and probably didn't have sisters, so didn't have a good female role model growing up. They just don't know how to express emotion, to be supportive and nurture people, and to have empathy for others. They charge around like they're still on the rugby pitch, as if that's the best way to make a team work. Fools.' He went on to say that 'knowing how to be around women is a winning quality. If you don't have that these days, you're dead in the water.' Another, a hugely talented and respected man in the entertainment industry, told me with great eloquence that 'I love being around people who are unafraid to be vulnerable because vulnerability is part of being creative, part of the joy of it. That's where I get my kicks - not jumping out of a plane or anything.' He also explained that 'my work is about empathy. We all want to be understood. That's why I'm so interested in emotion, I want people to *feel* things.'

Another man, who's become much more aware of gender and leadership recently, told me about a colleague of his who 'just doesn't understand people are different. He judges everyone according to how far they're like him, and he assumes that if a woman's not driven by the same old-school blokey competitiveness as him, then she can't be really committed or successful. He'll learn... the hard way, probably.' Very few of the men labelled these positive qualities as traditionally feminine, but they did talk about the negative versions in very gendered terms, describing them as 'blokey competitiveness' or 'traditional macho bulllshit' or sometimes even 'a toxic masculine culture.' They often described the positive leadership approaches as 'modern' and 'forward-looking' too, versus 'traditional' or 'outdated', and they were keen to position themselves as being on the side of progress and modernity, looking to the future instead of holding on to a past that's not helpful anymore.

It's important to acknowledge, too, that they were sometimes scathing about women leaders they'd known, vilifying some 'queen bee women' they'd witnessed who were 'much more vicious to other women than any of the men are.' This raised another fascinating point, as 'men wouldn't dare to treat other women like she does, but she gets away with it because of her unassailable position as a senior woman.' Interestingly, the tone here felt like less of a 'powerful women are bitches' narrative, and more about demanding a more inclusive and supportive culture from *everyone*, including women. It also highlights another issue that some of the men talked about, albeit with a strong sense of trepidation in case they 'come over as a tone-deaf idiot.' They said that in their workplace, 'cancel culture and fear has got so bad now that you worry about giving anyone who's in a minority group any legitimate but negative feedback about their performance, in case they tell you you're being racist or sexist or ableist or whatever. I've seen examples where people have used that accusation at their managers when in reality, the manager has been bending over backwards to be properly respectful and inclusive, and the sad fact is, that person is just not good enough at their job. Their protected characteristics have nothing to do with that. And that's a really dangerous territory for us all to be in, where we're all walking on eggshells. We need to fight discrimination, of course, but I wish we could embrace diversity *and* be able to be honest about any individual's performance without so much fear.'

On the whole, we're not that bad though.

My conversations uncovered a few additional sources of resentment about how, as we often hear, 'it's hard to be a straight white man these days.' One was how 'doing things to try and help actually makes things worse.' Just as the broader data shows, a few men had experienced well-intentioned training that they found counter-productive: 'A lot of DEI initiatives are just excruciating when you're a white bloke. I know that's part of it, "sitting with your discomfort" and being made to question your male privilege and stuff. But I've been to a few, and my mates have too, where you come out feeling like they think you're just an irredeemable, evil bastard. I don't think that's true, and it's definitely not helpful. It just makes men feel more defensive and pissed off about it when we know we won't be overheard by the wrong people.' Another told me that 'the language that they [the people running the training session] all use, to make sure no one from any niche gender gets upset… I get it's important, and I honestly don't want to say something that feels transphobic or sexist or whatever by accident because I really do value equality and want to treat others with respect… but when there are 34 different types of gender identity and people will get mad at you if you misunderstand or forget one… it just makes you want to give up.' 'It makes me scared to say anything, in case I say the wrong thing,' another, older man adds, 'so I just show willing, look supportive, and then talk to my [teenage] kids about it when I get home, as that's a safe space where they can help me understand without them telling me I'm the devil and deserve to be fired immediately if I ask the wrong question.'

As well as 'dreading' DE&I training for all these personal reasons, some of the more senior men also surprised me by saying they worried about what it implies about their company, because some of them were concerned that it 'might be seen as a sign that we've got a problem with racism or misogyny' if they have to 'do too much training on anti-racism or gender equality or whatever.' Added to this, these respondents clearly identify themselves and their friends and colleagues as 'good men,' and so they really struggle when they're made to feel judged in the same way as the bad guys are. So then, just as we saw earlier in *Issue 6: Let's Talk About Sex*, most of the time they don't think that there genuinely is that much of a problem, because 'It's not as if we're all shagging the secretaries and taking clients to strip clubs, which is what the bosses before me used to do.'

Invisible issues in a default male world.

This takes us right back to where we started in Issues 1 and 2: the invisibility of the problem and the feeling that we must have achieved gender equality now, or more likely 'gone too far the other way', because 'equality for women at work is commonplace now, or at least it will be soon, at the rate women are getting jobs over men.' A few of the men talked about 'other issues being more on the agenda now, like race and LGBT rights', with a few comments along the lines of 'I think we should get past all this talk about gender at work and just see people as people', without any awareness of the way workplaces are often designed for male bodies, experiences, preferences and traditions. For instance, when I asked about the social events that happen at their workplace, they generally featured traditionally masculine activities including watching football or rugby, go-karting, paintballing and axe-throwing. When I asked the men if their workplace ever offered activities that were more traditionally feminine like going to the ballet or a musical, or watching netball or gymnastics, I got a laugh each time as if it was literally a joke question, followed by some reasons why it wasn't likely, such as, 'Netball's just not as popular as football', 'If grown men went to watch gymnastics people would think we're a bunch of perverts', 'The men here would hate that, whereas the women do enjoy the football once they get there', and even: 'But admit it, the men's stuff is just better, isn't it?'

Similarly, without any of them really noticing it, the very language of work is often based on male bodies, fighting or the military: 'ballsy' women, 'killer' ideas and people 'smashing it,' 'crushing it' and 'nailing it'; people being 'in the trenches' or 'on the front lines'; and super-focused high achievers even being referred to as 'serial killers' who 'destroy the competition' and 'penetrate new markets' to achieve 'aggressive growth targets'. When I asked some of my respondents how they felt about this kind of language being so commonplace in business, they tended to laugh it off with 'It's just a metaphor, it doesn't really matter,' despite there being evidence that this 'military language infused in business systematically elevates traditionally "masculine" qualities and traits as most the valued and important for moving up into the ranks of leadership.'[125] Only one man seized on this idea, but expressed it in the context of the environment: 'The language of business as warfare doesn't exactly set the right tone for more responsible business that respects the planet and other people, does it?' And when I asked how often men in their company used words like 'cute' and 'sweet' to describe something positively, they tended to reply with dismissive, incredulous laughter, and comments along the lines of 'but that would just make you sound like a 12-year-old girl, that's not very professional is it?'

Winning at business is a compelling idea.

So we see that in the world of work, just as in life more generally, the default-male bias and masculine superiority myth combine to ensure that many of the problems women face still remain largely invisible to many men, reinforcing their belief that we must have reached the promised land of gender equality already. That, in turn, exacerbates their frustration at DE&I initiatives designed to solve these invisible issues, which too often leave men at work feeling anything from a bit alienated to actively resentful. For all of these reasons, everything I've learned throughout this project convinces me that having different kinds of conversations with men could be game-changing, at work and in life more broadly. I'm absolutely convinced that it's much more fruitful to start from where men are and build on what already motivates them, rather than focusing on 'changing them,' because that just makes individual men feel (whether for right or wrong) like they're being unjustly positioned as 'the problem'.

What's more, I see enormous opportunity beyond that too, because these men often seemed to really get behind the idea of focusing on how their business might profit from thinking more intently about the women who make up their consumers, customers and audiences. When I shared some of the examples of products and services that I outlined earlier in this chapter, many of the men seemed to come alive, loving the idea of 'doing a Bumble' and making great business success out of 'understanding and solving problems women live with, in a way makes shed-loads of money; and that men can use too. What's not to love?!' Sometimes they were fascinated to realise that products or services that they enjoyed, that didn't make *them* feel alienated, were female-centric in their design: 'I guess it's obvious now you say it, but whenever my wife and I have watched things by Reese Withespoon's production company, I never realised they were all focusing on women's voices or stories. They didn't feel girly, they're just good movies and shows.' And many seemed to enjoy discovering other areas where problems that women face could potentially become opportunities for business growth and competitive advantage: 'I never knew women's feet were a different shape to men's, I just thought they were smaller'; 'I've never really thought about designing flooring and furniture that works for women wearing short skirts'; and 'Imagine how much kudos the social platform that tackles online hate against women would get. I had no idea it was that bad.' And the list goes on…

Identifying innovative ideas that can drive business growth and profitability makes a lot of sense in purely rational terms, but moreover, at a personal, human level, these men seemed to feel a real delight in spotting and solving consumer issues, loving the idea that these ideas could be lucrative and they were largely invisible to their competitors. On top of this, it seemed that the idea of being a *man* who's helping create a more gender-equal world by doing that makes it all the sweeter. Where DE&I talk so often made them feel like the enemy, here they felt like they could take action and be part of the solution, in a way that's a win-win for the business and for society, for men as well as women. 'It's like gender equality becomes a secret weapon in our armoury' (yup, there's that militaristic language again), something that 'helps the company do better at its core business, instead of gender equality feeling like it stands on the side-lines, watching you and judging you the whole time, waiting for you to screw up.' And it feels future-facing, progressive, dynamic and innovative, as well as action-driven and aligned to business growth, all of which have a very different body language and energy to the diversity and inclusion initiatives they said they'd experienced to date. So how do we best motivate more men in business to overcome all of the problems and barriers that currently do exist, and enable them to seize these opportunities that can bring so many personal and business benefits?

WHY MEN MIGHT
WANT TO CREATE CHANGE

It shouldn't come as a massive surprise that the issues and ideas that we've explored in life generally can also drive men's motivations and behaviours inside the world of work. However rational and professional we all claim to be when we 'put our work heads on', we're all still human, so we're driven by deep-seated emotional triggers and desires. No wonder, then, that at work too, we see a misunderstanding and lack of acknowledgement of the issues around gender, as well as a default-male culture, and unchallenged beliefs that make the problems invisible to most; we see the masculine superiority myth in full flow, and a desire to 'kill the competition' in the fight for promotions often focusing on the wrong target; we see men, who still do take up the majority of space in positions of power and influence, worrying about what looks like unfair numbers of women and marginalised groups being recruited and promoted; we even see men *wanting* to understand and help address gender inequality, but fearing how that might trip them up or be weaponised against them. Most of all, we see men experiencing confusion, worry, resentment and anger, while not feeling free to express any of that too openly, for fear of really damaging consequences. But there are some ways forward that we could try:

1. Be informed: Knowledge is power, and both are things that many men like to possess and that can come in very handy at work. So can we find ways of sharing information with men that helps them see the problems and solutions more clearly and insightfully than the other men around them do? We should start with real clarity about the gender balance that currently exists in any workplace, and know how it looks in promotions and recruitment too, across different areas of the businesses as well as at overall level, so that everyone's using fact and not fear as a start-point. We could also celebrate men (and women) who see the folly of looking at this issue as if it's *only* a numbers game about how many male and female bodies are in the room or around the top table. We could arm men at work with information about what qualities and behaviours make the most successful leaders, and encourage them to model those themselves, as well as promote and reward them in others, whatever their gender. After all, that will create better businesses and more inclusive cultures *and* it will naturally lead to more women being promoted on merit too, satisfying that obsession with the optics, but in a way that's more than just cosmetic.

2. Modelling new leadership: Building on the evidence we explored earlier about what best predisposes individuals to be effective as leaders - emotional intelligence, self-awareness, humility, integrity and coachability - can we encourage more men as well as women at work to really lean into these, whether they're leading small group discussions or entire companies? We could help people understand that because of the way we socialise men versus women, these qualities do tend to show up more often in women right now, but make it clear that they're things men can absolutely excel at too, if they have the right attitude, encouragement and environment as well as the right aptitude. We can also remind everyone that these aren't fluffy, feel-good 'soft skills' but business-critical qualities that will bring real competitive edge. Most urgently of all, though, can we stop accidentally promoting, recruiting and rewarding people who display the precise opposite of these qualities and attributes?

3. Be on the side of change: So many men (especially if they're white, cis and straight) seem to feel that gender equality and other important areas of DE&I are external forces that are happening *to* them, powerful pressures that scrutinise them, police them and may just destroy them if they get caught doing something they didn't even realise was a problem. Even men who are pro-equality and believe in social justice often fear, at a personal level, the way the world is going, and can feel left behind, excluded, vilified and unfairly punished. Can we help these men identify a few actions that they can take that feel authentic and positive, and that help them actively lead the change, not just tolerate it? Like my dad's 'lion and trainers' joke, can we help these men see that getting active in driving gender equality will enable them to 'outrun' the men around them? Can we even help them realise that the change we're living through is not some dangerous beast destined to maul them, but a positive force that can bring many benefits to the men who are smart enough to become agents of that change?

4. Find your own personal strategy: when men do understand the scale and breadth of the problems we face, it can feel quite overwhelming. Much like with climate change, or anti-racism, or addressing global poverty, it's easy to feel that one person making a few personal changes is a single raindrop in a lake. What's more, when you're a man in the workplace, especially one with other kinds of systemic privilege, the fear of doing the wrong thing is so great that it feels easiest and safest to make the defensive move of doing as little as possible beyond the set pieces and performative actions you're compelled to do to keep up appearances. But just because a problem can't be solved by one person alone, and just because a few small steps won't get us straight to the destination, that doesn't mean those individuals' steps aren't worth taking. So can we adopt an 'Every Little Helps' approach to accelerating gender equality, each of us identifying just a few areas where we feel best placed to make a difference? Can we concentrate on those positives, rather than all the areas that we're *not* actively addressing? And can we encourage men at work to do as every one of my respondents did, and express motivations and feelings they already have that they can build on and use in ways that aren't self-sacrificial? Of course, the more senior or influential a man is in an organisation, the riskier the world may seem right now, as he'll feel like he's even more under scrutiny and has even more to lose if he makes a mis-step. But building on the qualities and motivations he already has, and just re-directing them slightly, could enable a more comfortable pivot into using his power and privilege to drive gender equality. I strongly believe that we all need to get past the 'menemies' mindset that too often dominates, reach across the gender divide and create more safe spaces where men and women can trust, encourage and build on positives together.

5. Make the changing world a competitive advantage: Lastly, we've seen some examples of how profitable it can be when businesses spend their time, energy and money creating products and services that solve problems for the half of the population that drives over 80 percent of consumer purchase decisions; and we've seen how smart, innovative and powerful the men who lead this change could feel. So can we encourage more men in business to adopt this approach, seeing gender equality in the world beyond their walls not as a cost, nor as a compliance exercise, but as a genuinely powerful commercial opportunity? Of course, it needs to be done with the right expertise, insight and guidance, but it doesn't *only* need to be done by female-founded companies. After all of my conversations with men, I'm so convinced that this is a powerful way forward that I've set up a strategic innovation consultancy of my own, *The Others & Me*, that uses these 'win/win' insights and methodologies to help businesses grow by focusing on the overlooked, undervalued majority in their products and services, as well as accelerating gender equality within their leadership team and culture.

So if your company has an ambitious, male-dominated leadership team who might want to make the most of these untapped opportunities, please do get in touch. And wherever you are, in businesses and in life outside, let's keep talking. Together, I genuinely believe that we can change the world, one product, service, day, and person at a time.

But hang on a minute... What about the future?

Some people are already suggesting that talking about women and gender equality is out of date; that 'the way the world is going, it'll all be non-binary, and men and women won't even exist.'

Which raises the important question - what is the end game that we're seeking here? Is it a world without gender, or one where men, women and non-binary people can all happily co-exist? And what might that look like? That is a question that I explore in the Epilogue.

EPILOGUE:

What's the end game?

Looking forward to a world beyond reductive binaries.

=============

Exploring lives beyond the binary.

Before we launch into talking about what life is like right now for people beyond the cisgender binary, and what the future might look like for all of us, it's important to remember that throughout this book, whenever I've used the words *man* and *woman*, I intentionally include trans as well as cis men and women. As I said at the outset, some issues that I've talked about will be relevant to trans men as well as the majority of cis women, for instance, anything related to having a uterus; whereas many of the issues covered here will apply to trans and cis women alike, such as the threat of sexual assault, which is an urgent danger for trans women, even more than for most cis women. Right now there's a real paucity of data splitting out transgender from cisgender men and women, just as there is for other vital intersectional areas such as race and ethnicity - and often for any gender or sex disaggregation at all.

Nevertheless, as I said at the start, I hope that both cis and trans readers can apply the arguments and ideas here in whatever way is most relevant for them. The same, too, goes for non-binary people, for whom the whole 'men vs women' argument doesn't personally fit. This group is notable by their absence from the data, and yet it's very clear that they suffer many of the issues that apply to both trans and cis women, as well as other barriers and challenges that are specific to their own unique relationship with society's gender norms and expectations.

All of us 'girls, gays and theys' suffer as a result of our gender; all of us are damaged by the intrinsically cis, straight patriarchal system we live in; but the LGBTQ+ community bears an additional oppression too, so I wanted to give some proper space to discussing this more explicitly as we look to the future and reflect on what a more gender-equal world might look like for all of us.

I'd thought this might be a relatively brief discussion, urging inclusion, recognising how cis women can use their relative privilege to lift up our trans sisters too, and celebrating how much we can *all* learn about the experience of walking through the world as a woman, from those who in many ways have been the ultimate test and control: trans women who transitioned relatively late in life. Imagine if we could all emulate Paula Stone Williams' humility as she recognises 'the reality of my male privilege and the fact that I brought some of it with me when I transitioned' as well as 'the frustration of losing much of that privilege… Every week as a female, something happened that reminded me I no longer commanded the respect I once did.'[1] She reflects that when the world treated her as a man, 'we were all sure our successes were because of our hard work, and to some degree, they were. What none of us realised was that we had begun our work lives a lot closer to the finish line than most other people, and miles closer than women and Black and Brown people. I wish I had understood back then just how much of a head start I had been given in life.'[2]

However, when I talked with my male respondents about how they felt about trans and queer people's increased visibility in cis, straight, mainstream society, it revealed a degree of fear and misunderstanding that surprised me a little, as well as some ideas and attitudes that seem potentially damaging for progress on gender equality for cis and trans people alike.

Fear and misunderstanding reign supreme.

One man summed up the feelings of many of these cis, straight men when he said 'Truth be told - and *please* don't say this to anyone else - the whole alphabet soup of gender identity just makes me so confused. Someone said the other day that there are about 30 different genders now! I just can't cope with it all.'

Others admitted to finding the very idea of someone's gender identity being different from the gender they were assigned at birth rather befuddling: 'It makes you wonder, what even is a woman though? Can any bloke down the rugby club just say he's a woman now and we all have to agree? I know we need to respect the way all this gender identity stuff is going, but sometimes, I just don't get it.' Many struggled to, as they put it, 'know which way round it is' and asked things like: 'So is a trans man someone who used to be a man, or who's becoming one now?' and they thought that 'the whole LGBT lobby is so vocal these days that accidentally calling someone who used to be a man a woman can be disastrous.'

Really interestingly, even as they were talking about what they didn't understand, many were unaware just how far these things they *were* confidently saying weren't right, such as describing a trans woman as someone who 'used to be a man.' As we know, being ill-informed is never a comfortable place to be, especially when the stakes are high, so just like when they were talking about gender equality more broadly, many of my straight respondents worried about being 'found out' in this area too: 'It's dangerous, you look like a complete dinosaur for not understanding;' and they had a deep fear of inadvertently 'saying the wrong thing and getting cancelled.'

As if all of that weren't enough, the more we talked, the clearer it became that many of my respondents seemed to have real difficulty reconciling 'the whole LGBT thing' with 'regular gender equality.' It transpired that often, as well as feeling frustrated at the need to 'stay on top of the complications of a million different genders,' they also saw increased LGBTQ visibility as a reason to dismiss gender equality as it applies to cis women: 'Is it even OK to be talking about women now, because trans people don't want anyone to be men and women anymore?' And they seemed even more worried about 'getting it wrong' with the trans community than with cis women: 'I long for the days when we just had to worry about upsetting women! Now we have to beware upsetting the LGBTQ lot too, and that's even more of a minefield.' Frequently, they told me they found it all so overwhelming that they feel like giving up: 'I don't even know if calling someone a woman is a good thing or a bad thing any more... it just feels like an impossible test, it's no wonder men are fed up about the entire bloody gender issue.'

Of course, I understand that when you're a smart adult who's used to being well-informed, it can feel confusing to explore gender identities and sexual orientations beyond the simplistic 'cis straight man and woman' that most of us were taught was the norm from a young age. Nor does it get any simpler the further we go, as the academic literature on gender being a performance can get utterly existential within a few (often very convoluted and highly intellectualised) sentences. So I'll avoid discussing the academic theory and focus on a much simpler and more actionable approach, because unless cis, straight men (and women too) feel confident enough to lean in with curiosity and compassion to learning about life beyond the cis-het binary, we'll never get past the situation we're in right now.

So how might we overcome the twin barriers of 'it's so complicated' and 'I'll be cancelled if I put a foot wrong' that are currently so unhelpful?

Understanding 'the basics'.

I'm sharing here both the understanding that I've gained from generous activists and educators within the LGBTQ+ community, and the clarity that emerged from discussions with my male respondents, so these are simply some ways of thinking about things that seemed to help those confused and quite fearful men to feel like they had a better 'grasp of the basics.' Of course, any attempt to make ideas simpler and more accessible risks over-simplifying them and losing important nuance, and that's a huge danger here where we're talking about a whole diverse range of lived experiences, and unique individuals, so I would urge you to seek out and listen to as many trans and non-binary people as you can, and have them speak for themselves.

Some of the organisations, books, podcasts, TV and films that I personally have found incredibly enlightening include: *Just Like Us*, the LGBT+ young people's charity whose research and School Diversity Week resources are especially accessible; the organisation *Stonewall*, who create resources for workplaces as well as schools and colleges; books including Shon Faye's *The Transgender Issue*[3], *As A Woman*[4] by Paula Stone Williams, Munroe Bergdorf's *Transitional*[5], *None Of The Above*[6] by Travis Alabanza and *Beyond The Gender Binary*[7] by Alok Vaid-Menon, *Outrageous!*[8] by Paul Baker and *Straight Jacket* by Matthew Todd; Golden Globe-winning TV series *Pose* (a real winner if authentic fiction is your thing), or documentaries charting the people and culture that inspired it, including Jennie Livingston's *Paris Is Burning* and Baillie Walsh's *Mirror Mirror*; and just about any podcasts featuring Travis Alabanza, Alok, Laverne Cox, Shon Faye, Paula Stone Williams, MJ Rodriguez and Billie Porter are always enlightening in so many ways.

It's about inclusivity, not exclusivity.

None of the people within the LGBTQ+ community that I've learned from has said that we should all want to get to a place where there's no such thing as men or women. Many do acknowledge, of course, that they'd love to live in a world that doesn't insist everyone should live within the simple gender binary, a world that doesn't make life disproportionately difficult for people who don't conform to those two traditional gender roles; but that's very different from saying that anyone identifying proudly as a woman or a man is somehow intrinsically wrong. On the contrary, each of the queer people I've spoken with, read, and listened to has strongly articulated their desire for a world where women and men, both cis and trans, *and* people who identify as something other than those two genders can all live safely and happily, without telling each other that their gender doesn't or shouldn't exist. Travis Alabanza, for instance, speaks for many when they say 'I do believe we can mention differences without disrespect. That we can lift up our truth without denying someone else's... That no expression of any self becomes a reason why someone may incite harm.'[9] So the idea that, as some of my male respondents seemed to think, 'gender equality for women is old fashioned now because people are just people' really misses the point.

Unless, of course, by 'gender equality' and 'women' they mean a Trans-Exclusionary Radical Feminist approach. And if that's a view you have, I'd encourage you to think again, read on, and particularly explore the *Wait, but what about...* section below, where I debunk some of the fears and myths that feed into this TERF narrative that I consider to be incredibly damaging.

There's another reason why the 'just forget about gender and treat people as people' argument is flawed too, and that's because, as we talked about in *Issue 1; That 'I've Never Really Thought About It' Face*, we all unwittingly tend to think in a default-male way, so we interpret 'people' as men (and cis, straight, white men at that) unless we make an active effort to counter that assumption. We mustn't underestimate the power of this default-male bias. It's so strong that 'we don't even allow non-humans to escape our perception of the world as overwhelmingly male' because, for instance, when researchers in one study tried to 'prompt participants to see a gender-neutral stuffed animal as female by using female pronouns, children, parents and carers still overwhelmingly referred to the animal as 'he'. The study found that an animal must be 'super-feminine' before 'even close to half of participants will refer to it as she rather than he.'[10]

So until we've sorted that issue out, no amount of thinking we can 'just treat people as people and ignore gender' will really help accelerate gender equality, however well-intentioned those remarks might be.

We shouldn't be so categorical, but we do need categories.

The idea that we should 'move beyond any kind of categorisations' sounds utopian, but in reality, this simply doesn't work because the human brain, and even language itself, relies on categorisations to make meaning. Let's get theoretical just for a moment, as this is an important idea to understand: We can all recognise from our own experiences that a dog has some essential 'dog-ness' about it; but we also know from Structuralist linguistic theory that when we think and talk about that animal, we can only *identify* it as a dog because it's not a cat, nor a rabbit, nor a bird, nor any other creatures that we recognise as different from each other. So we need to use categorisations to make sense of the world. However, we should also recognise that even though the meanings and labels we use often *appear* very fixed - we all know what a dog is - they are actually much more arbitrary, nuanced and flexible than we generally admit.

For example, I don't think of foxes and wolves as dogs, even though technically they are, because personally, I determine what's inside or outside the category of 'dog' based on things like character, behaviour and appearance. So I would happily say, for instance, that my old neighbour's Shih Tzu was the epitome of the domesticated pet dog, miles away from big, dangerous wild dogs like wolves; and I was surprised to learn that this cute pooch might be categorised quite differently by biologists, because Shih Tzu's are actually highly genetically similar to the wolf.[11]

The important point is that categorisations and labels are essential for us to make meaning; but they don't just exist as some kind of eternal, existential fact; they are actively created by us, and they have nuance, diversity and flexibility within them. And that matters because how we understand human identity works in this way too, as the great feminist icon Chimamanda Ngozi Adichie explains when she talks about her blackness being a construct, defined in relation to whiteness when she arrived in the USA: 'I wasn't black until I came to America. I became black in America. Growing up in Nigeria, I didn't think about race because I didn't need to think about race. Nigeria is a country with many problems and many identity divisions, but those identity divisions are mainly religion and ethnicity.'[12]

So what exactly does all this have to do with better understanding the LGBTQ+ community and gender equality for all? Well, the parallel is that although I can say I feel utterly sure of my essential woman-ness, it's also true that the idea of *woman* (be it cis or trans) needs the concept of man-ness for it to make sense. And, vitally, the idea of both 'man' and 'woman' changes and flexes in different places at different times, operating on a continuum or spectrum, inhabiting shades of grey rather than absolute either/or, black/white divisions. Most importantly of all, the basis for the categorisation 'man' or 'woman' can be based on different things, from biological to behavioural and even simply aesthetic.

Ultimately, identity categorisations ('I'm this because I'm not that') are important, and we'd struggle to make any real sense of key elements of our identity without them; but high-level categorisations like man vs woman become much more nuanced, multi-layered and rich as we learn more and consider them more fully, as all categorisations and labels do.

We can't learn in a climate of fear.

We're talking here about communities and individuals who are ostracised, misunderstood and often actively vilified, so it's no surprise that this whole topic can be incredibly highly-charged. Clumsily expressing our own understanding or point of view, however unwittingly we may do it, can be very hurtful to people whose very existence is often contested and who face countless difficulties just living their daily lives.

So as I summarise below the framework I developed with my male respondents to enable them to think about 'the whole LGBTQ+ thing' in a way that seems to help, I'm sure there will be things I say that inadvertently cause offence to someone. With this entire project, my hope is that we all hold on to love, openness, respect and constant learning on all sides, and avoid the damaging blame and shame, judgemental culture that is such a big barrier to growth and learning for us all. And that we share positive and helpful learnings and ideas with each other at @MenemiesNoMore.

Disentangling sexual orientation from gender identity.

Personally, I love that the LGBTQ+ community now proudly includes trans and non-binary people alongside people who love in ways that aren't heterosexual, and it makes perfect sense to me that these diverse groups of people stand in solidarity in the struggle against patriarchal, oppressive and restrictive gender norms. However, one unintended side-effect of this is the first level of confusion I often witnessed in my respondents - a lack of real clarity that LGBTQ+ includes two quite different kinds of identity: who you are (your gender identity) and who you love (your sexual orientation). So if we're to make sense of the confusing 'alphabet soup,' let's start by disentangling those two groups. And as it's already a jumble of too many letters for some people's liking, we might as well go the whole hog and use the more complete set of letters that most people agree on for now, to ensure we're properly inclusive: LGBTQIA+

Sexual orientation.

The first way we found to create clarity around the letters LGBTQIA+ was to separate out the 'L', 'G', 'B', 'Q' and 'A', because these all describe sexual orientation - lesbian, gay, bisexual, queer or questioning, and asexual. The precise term 'sexual *orientation*' is important, as we now recognise that who you're predisposed to love is an orientation you're born with, not something that's chosen or learned. (If it were a choice, surely thousands of years of violent oppression teaching people that heterosexuality is the correct way to feel love would have 'worked'?) Talk to any gay person and they'll probably tell you they can no more change their sexual orientation than a straight person can. That's why we no longer use the term 'sexual preference', and why homophobic concerns about 'promoting homosexuality' (as the ridiculous and damaging Clause 28 put it back when I was a teacher in the 90's) are as misguided as they are damaging.

It's also important to register that sexual orientation is not about who you are, nor how you look, nor the interests you may have; so the idea that gay men inevitably look and act 'feminine' while lesbians look and act like men is simply wrong. A man can paint his nails, have an incredibly camp demeanour and be completely heterosexual, just as a gay man can look and act the same as many straight men, or dress proudly in full drag, or present in any way he so chooses - because his being gay is about his sexual orientation, not his wardrobe sense nor his mannerisms. Interestingly too, even though we still often use the term 'gay' to mean men and women, the 'L' in LGBTQIA+ was added alongside the 'G' because the 'default male' bias is alive and well in the gay community, just as it is elsewhere, with lesbians still often having to fight for more visibility and respect.

'B' meaning bisexual is interesting too, as it's one of those categorisations that's often contested. For some, it works to express a sexual orientation that encompasses both men and women; others, though, find it limiting, for instance if they're people who are also attracted to non-binary people, or are still exploring and understanding their own sexuality, or have a gender identity that makes sexual orientation a less simple, binary question. Hence the 'Q' (queer or questioning)[13] and the '+' that always appears at the end, recognising that this high-level categorisation has more nuance in reality than can be set out in any series of letters that the average man in the street stands any chance of remembering and understanding.

Finally, as we discussed in *Issue 6: Let's Talk About Sex*, there are some people who identify as asexual, and they (especially when they're women) can often be pathologised due to a misguided belief that it's essential for all humans to experience sexual attraction to *someone*. The 'A' exists in the sexual orientation group of letters to remind us that, as well as all kinds of men and women who are attracted to their own sex, and people who are attracted to both/any/other genders, there are *also* people who aren't sexually attracted to anyone, whatever their gender.

And if that's what makes them happy, let's recognise that as valid and wonderful, and not treat it like a condition that needs fixing.

Homophobia is often misogyny's bedfellow.

It's worth taking a quick pause to note that while people whose sexuality is on the LGBTQIA+ spectrum suffer specific dangers and difficulties that straight people simply don't, we also see many of the issues of sexism and misogyny play out here. As Shon Faye says 'Misogyny, homophobia and transphobia share much of the same DNA. To the patriarchy, we all do gender wrong.'[14] Lesbian sex, for instance, has long been treated by straight society as if it's not 'real' sex, largely because of the problematic assumptions about phallocentric sex and penetration that we covered in *Issue 6: Let's Talk About Sex.*

Similarly, homophobia directed at gay men is clearly rooted in the 'masculine = active, feminine = passive' bias about sexuality, as well as reflecting how men are socialised to fear being seen as 'girly', as per the masculine superiority myth set out in detail in *Issue 3: The Thing Is, Boys Are Just Better*. It underlies straight men's concerns at gay men displaying feminine dress, body language and interests/attributes. It also explains their fears that being a gay man means embodying the ultimate feminine submission - being penetrated sexually by a man - as well as building from simultaneous, although contradictory, myths about male sexual desire being impossible to control, and oblivious to consent. Homophobia punishes gay men for being both too masculine and too feminine.

This myth of men being unable to control themselves in the face of their sexual desire is of course a social rather than a biological phenomenon, and there's no proof at all to suggest that gay men experience this more than straight men. If anything, evidence seems to suggest the opposite, as the violent oppression of gay men means they tend to worry about and talk about consent much more actively than many straight men have typically had to.

And yet, prejudiced ideas that gay male sexuality is more predatory even than straight men's persists; and it sometimes combines with the general gendered parenting myths outlined in *Issue 7: The Daddy Of All Roles* to create a hysteria about gay men being a threat to children, when there's simply no evidence to support this, and more to suggest that the opposite is true. And so, despite the 'normalisation' of gay relationships that many of us welcome, homophobic attacks - mostly by men[15] - remain far too commonplace, with gay men being abused and attacked for finding men attractive, and lesbians abused and attacked for *not* finding men attractive.

Meanwhile, much like the way 'girly' is still thrown around, I've lost count of the number of times that I've heard good, kind, straight men still use the term 'gay' as an insult, especially when competing with other straight men to be perceived as top dog. No wonder, then, that just like women do in the face of sexist assumptions, gay men too have to constantly correct heteronormative assumptions and microaggressions, correcting everything from 'actually I have a husband, not a wife' to 'actually I'm not really into fashion.'[16] And we know from the data on how everyday sexism damages women that these microaggressions can add up to profound frustrations and barriers throughout someone's life. Even while we celebrate the fact that generally we see much less explicit homophobia than we did a generation or two ago, we must recognise that progress doesn't mean we've made it to the promised land. In fact, like with sexism, a prejudice being less explicit means it's still damaging, but it's often harder to spot and easier to dismiss. What's more, we're seeing evidence of a backlash when it comes to gay rights, in parallel with the one against gender equality, most obviously in the US where at least 36 bills in 15 states are proposing rules that would make it harder even for people to perform in drag, all 'in the name of protecting children.'[17]

Gender identity.

Let's move on from sexual orientation to explore 'T', 'Q' and 'I', the letters in the LGBTQIA+ collection, that describe gender identities: who you are, not who you love. The 'T', of course, stands for trans or transgender - not 'transvestite', nor 'transsexual', which were retired a long time ago. Transgender, as Shon Faye explains, is 'an umbrella term that describes people whose gender identity (their personal sense of their own gender) varies from, does not sit comfortably with, or is different from, the biological sex recorded on their birth certificate based on the appearance of their external genitalia.'[18]

While 'trans' can sometimes be used to encompass non-binary people too, more often it's used to describe a binary identity, someone being a trans man or a trans woman. Interestingly, in the letter line-up there's currently no distinction between trans men and women (unlike with the 'L' and 'G' of sexual orientation), which is slightly surprising given the fact that trans women suffer all sorts of misogyny as well as transphobia... but more of that later. And of course, adding more letters doesn't feel like it's going to help drive clarity and understanding amongst the broader population any time soon.

Despite all of the men I spoke to knowing that 'T' stands for trans, many demonstrated confusion and misunderstanding about trans-ness at the simplest level, saying things like 'I can never remember which way it goes - is a trans woman someone who's transitioned *to* being a woman or *from* being a woman?' Or they talked about trans women being different from 'just women' in ways that managed to both ostracise trans women (positioning them as 'not *really* women') and diminish the experiences of cis women as a whole by suggesting, as we said earlier, that 'we shouldn't even bother thinking about women because society's moved on to the trans issue now.' So let's clear both of these up right away.

Trans women were assigned male at birth.

When someone describes herself as a 'trans woman,' she's telling us the gender she knows she is, not what her body looked like at birth or even what it looks like now. A trans women may or may not have a gender recognition certificate, have changed her gender on her passport, be taking hormones or having surgeries to better align her body's primary or secondary sex characteristics with her gender identity, be using a different name and pronouns to the ones her parents gave her at birth, and/or be expressing the gender she knows she is in all kinds of ways in her day to day life. A transgender woman is a woman, and often (but not always) she says she's always been a woman but was assigned male at birth. That's why saying she 'used to be a man' is inaccurate and upsetting, suggesting a lack of respect for the fact that she may have long known she's a girl in a world that's been constantly telling her that she's a boy.

This split between the gender that someone knows they are the gender that their body and hormones are communicating to the world is undoubtedly a difficult concept for some people to respect, as well as to understand, and we'll come to explore that more fully below. For now, though, let's just accept that suggesting that a trans woman 'used to be a man' or a trans woman 'was born a man' is hurtful, and shows a misunderstanding of how gender identity works. It's both more accurate and more respectful to acknowledge that a trans woman, for example, was assigned male at birth; and that before her transition, she had to go through life with a profound mis-match between the gender she was assigned at birth and the one she knows is her true gender identity.

This disconnect is often experienced by a trans man or woman as distressing 'gender dysphoria' (dysphoria being the opposite of euphoria); so misgendering someone isn't about 'what we're allowed to say these days', it's about respecting someone's identity and not causing them more unnecessary distress.

A trans woman is a woman.

The idea that trans women are 'different from just women' is equally problematic, and has echoes of the way people talk about things like 'football and women's football', 'doctors and lady doctors,' 'bosses and girl bosses' and so on, as if there are 'people' and 'women.' There aren't trans women and women; there are trans women and cisgender women. Moreover, this isn't just a pedantic, semantic issue. If you're a trans woman who's had to constantly struggle to get the world to see you as the woman you know you are, that very woman-ness is going to be incredibly important to you, and so diminishing it because it's a different form of woman-ness and a different lived experience to a cis woman feels unnecessarily cruel to me. I believe there's plenty of space within the concept of 'woman' for both cis and trans women, so let's clarify once more that just like when we think of 'people' we should include both men and women, when we think of 'men' or 'women' we should include both transgender and cisgender men and women.

Identities beyond the gender binary.

There's an important build on all of this, though, because 'people' doesn't just include the two sets of binaries - men (both cis and trans), and women (both cis and trans). Some people have identities or sex characteristics that don't fit into this neat binary. Hence the 'Q', the 'I' as well as the trusty catch-all plus sign.

'Q' in the context of gender identity also means queer, so this one word could be used to describe someone's sexual orientation or their gender identity - it can even be used to describe the whole spectrum of LGBTQIA+ identities. But let's focus for now on queer meaning someone who identifies outside of the exclusive gender binary. These people - the 'theys' of this world - may identify as neither man nor woman, or as both; they might shift along the gender spectrum expressing masculinity and femininity in different ways on different days, or they may refute the whole idea of the binary when it comes to their own gender identity. They may even identify as trans too, or simply describe themselves as 'gender non-conforming.' Alok describes gender identity in these terms: 'A nonbinary person could be bigender, meaning that they're both a man and a woman. They could be agender, meaning that they don't have a gender. They could be gender fluid. Like me. Meaning that my gender shifts in time and space and isn't fixed into an identity. And it's important to understand, that there's as many ways to be nonbinary as there are nonbinary people'[19]

It's crucial that we recognise the extreme challenges faced by non-binary people, who aren't just living as the opposite gender from the one they were assigned at birth, which is challenging enough, but who are living in a way that questions the very notions of our dominant binary system. Travis Alabanza describes the 'constant and consistent ridicule, violence or challenge placed on gender non-conformity' including how they are 'lucky to walk outside and *not* be shouted at, or laughed at, or filmed within the space of a day. This is not an exaggeration: it's a mere fact for those of us who walk through the streets and dare to be gender non-conforming (and feminine) in public.'[20] Non-binary people are often seen to be failing at being either a man or a woman, and can experience marginalisation and vilification even from within the trans community at times.

Interestingly, despite the eye-rolling and outright denial, as well as transphobic attacks that non-binary people receive on a daily basis, many of the cis men I talked to did recognise that 'non-binary people are a thing in a lot of other cultures, aren't they?' Or as Shon Faye puts it, many societies 'do not have the same Western tradition of rigidly forcing people into the two categories of man and woman. The phrase 'two-spirit', for example, has become the most common term in the English language to describe a diverse range of gender-variant ceremonial and social roles among indigenous North American communities. Similarly, examples of third-gender cultures exist across the world, such as the waria of Indonesia, the Samoan Fa'afafine, the hijra in India and the muxe of the Zapotec cultures in southern Mexico.'[21]

And yet still, the largely-unspoken belief still lingers that, as one of my male respondents said rather shame-facedly, 'I know that people who are "they/them" have a difficult life, and [they] genuinely believe they're something beyond just man or woman. But the tricky thing is, should gender really just be about someone saying, "this is what I am" and just ignoring the biological facts? I'm a rational thinker who loves facts and proof, so I can't help but feel slightly concerned about that.' He's not alone. Many of my male respondents seemed to want to prioritise the 'biological fact' of the body over the 'made-up nature of gender.' One young man told me 'It's like science versus arts students isn't it? I'm less about "how does it feel to be you?" and more about "what do the biological facts say?" That's just how I think.'

All of which brings us on to the final letter to explore in our LGBTQIA+ collection: the little-known 'I', people with intersex characteristics.

Intersex.

The 'science versus arts' argument often misses the fact that our bodies naturally exist on a bit of a spectrum of male to female; although when prompted, most of my respondents did recall that women's bodies contain testosterone and men's contain oestrogen. However, none of the men I spoke to outside of the queer community brought up people with intersex characteristics, and most were unaware of what it meant when I introduced the subject, beyond something like: 'That's hermaphrodites, yes? People who are born with a dick and a vagina?'

Erm… no. For starters, unless we're describing plants or organisms, we don't use the term hermaphrodite now. What's more, the term 'intersex' covers a whole range of bodies where someone's reproductive or sexual anatomy doesn't align with what we determine as either male or female. It's estimated that around one percent of the population could be born with intersex variations[22], and this could include 'a person with both ovarian and testicular tissues', or someone having 'combinations of chromosomes that are different…, like XXY.' Additionally, 'some people are born with external genitals that fall into the typical male/female categories, but their internal organs or hormones don't.'[23] These variations in genitalia, hormones, internal anatomy, and/or chromosomes mean that sometimes, a baby's intersex nature may be clearly apparent at birth, but equally, some of these characteristics may only be discovered after puberty or even after someone's death.

It's not widely discussed that babies born with visible intersex characteristics tend to be operated on to align their unconventional body with one gender or another, and this becomes the gender identity in which they are expected to live. We are increasingly hearing from people who've experienced this gender alignment surgery that they couldn't consent to, who later say that they wish they'd been left with the intersex characteristics they had at birth, or that the gender they identify with is not the gender the doctors assigned them as a baby, or that they identify as non-binary; and they may struggle with body dysphoria as a result of the 'wrong surgery' being performed. As with so much in the area of gender identity, and as the final '+' in the collection of letters acknowledges, even when it comes to the biology of the body itself, things are not always as simple and binary as we may believe.

Still, though, many of the men I talked with objected, telling me 'That's different because it's the body *naturally* doing something other than typical male or female. That's Mother Nature, or God deciding that's who you are. That feels more… I don't know, *real* to me than someone saying, "my body's male but I identify as a woman or as a 'they." Bloody hell, I should be arrested by the gender police for saying that, shouldn't I?'

Can you be a woman just by saying you're one?

I believe we need to recognise and listen to this worry, however difficult it might be for some, because it's one that many are exploiting, like when Piers Morgan proclaimed that 'if literally you can now identify in a hundred different ways your gender including two-spirit person and all this other stuff, then I'm entitled to identify as a two-spirit penguin.'[24]

Setting aside the fact that Morgan deliberately misses the fact that gender identity is about humans and not animals, I did witness my well-intentioned, kind and supportive cis, straight male respondents having difficulty with 'some LGBT people wanting to explicitly include every one of thirty or forty different gender identities and sexualities,' which left them feeling that 'it's a bit out of control, and it's inevitably going to trip us up, and cause massive upset for everyone, and that would be really damaging for me.'

Many of the men told me they wished for 'more simplicity, in a way that's not transphobic and that won't get you unfairly cancelled'; and after our discussions that sought to better understand the LGBTQIA+ spectrum, one summed up a kind of comms strategy that many seemed to be seeking too when he suggested: 'Can't we just say that people can be men, women, or non-binary, and leave it at that? As long as we include trans men and women too. Then people can talk about all the different variations beneath that separately, instead of trying to include all of it at the top level.'

But back to the question of 'can people choose to be anything they like, and we all just have to respect that?' When it comes to gender identity, many of the men I talked with (and some women I've discussed this with too) admit to struggling with the principle of people being free to self-identify their gender. It's as if, even if they *want* to believe that trans and gender-nonconforming people can be reliable witnesses to their own experience, something about gender being 'an individual choice or identity' seems really hard for some people to accept, 'like it's opening the floodgates and losing all sense of rational evidence.'

Sometimes that seems to be driven by a deep-seated worry that when someone comes out as trans or non-binary, they may just be identifying that way on a whim, for attention, or 'just for the sheer hell of it.' We can sense some of this in the glib tone of Piers Morgan's 'I'm entitled to identify as a two-spirit penguin' comment, as if trans and non-binary people are all busy inventing elaborate identities just for effect, like they're playing a huge game of identity top trumps while laughing at cis people who don't get it. This is probably about as far from the experience of the average gender-queer person as we could possibly imagine, because having to assert your trans or non-binary identity every day, despite being told you shouldn't exist, is anything but a game. On the contrary, it's something that leaves people more likely to be unemployed, homeless, beaten up, sexually assaulted, and even killed. If a trans or non-binary person risks such difficulties and dangers to be seen as the gender they know they are, I honestly don't understand why we should insist that *we* know best, and that they're just choosing an identity like I might choose a pair of shoes.

Other times, the reluctance to accept someone being able to identify their own gender stems from a fear that some trans people may just be pretending to be their stated gender. This tends to manifest as 'what if trans women are just assuming a fake female identity for nefarious, criminal purposes?' It's a legitimate question, I suppose, as there doubtless have been occasions when this has been the case... but that doesn't mean that we simply shouldn't trust people to identify their own gender. People have pretended to be police, priests or nuns for criminal purposes before too, but we don't use that as a reason to suspect that all cops and clergy are up to no good, or tell them that they shouldn't even exist because some people have used their identity as a cover to do bad things. And yet that's what some people are effectively saying to trans people.

The third struggle that many of my respondents had with the principle of someone identifying their own gender is just a vague discomfort with the idea that a person's essential being is different from their body, and that in cases where the two don't match, we should prioritise some intangible 'me-ness' over the tangible, physical body. It's strange, though, that gender seems to have a unique ability to make us feel this way, because in other areas of life, we're much more comfortable accepting the idea that someone's real, true self is different from and greater than their body.

I have painful but instructive examples of this in the illnesses of both my mum and dad: When dad passed away after years of battling cancer, we'd console ourselves by saying how his frail little cancer-ravaged body simply wasn't able to hold him any longer; and we'd marvel at how dad remained himself, and was bigger than the sick body that was failing him, almost to the end. I've never had anyone challenge our belief that dad's essential identity was something intangible and was neither defined nor constrained by his sick body.

The same is true, in the opposite way, with my poor mum, whose decline into severe Alzheimer's leaves us mourning the loss of *her*, even while we sit with the still-healthy body in which the mum that's disappeared used to live. We say very explicitly that she, her essential mum-ness, is gone, even though her body's still here and strong, and I've heard many relatives of patients with advanced Alzheimer's talk about the pain of their loved one being absent at some vital, essential, human level, long before the body leaves us too. Once again, few people would take issue with this description of what happens with this most cruel of diseases.

So I do wonder what it is about gender in particular that makes so many people struggle to accept that a person's essential identity, spirit, character - call it whatever you will - is bigger than and not defined by their body, when in other situations we can see that so clearly?

Maybe it's a question of familiarity? If so, as trans and non-binary people continue to become increasingly visible and known throughout mainstream, cis-het society, this strange discomfort may well subside. After all, hundreds of years ago, people who adopted a religion that was different from the one they were born into were tortured and killed as heretics; whereas now, we happily respect someone's right to determine for themselves which God their eternal soul belongs to. We're even happy to accept that some people practise no religion at all. Who knows, maybe one day, we'll treat someone telling us what makes them truly *them* while they're alive with as much respect as we do now when they're talking about their spirit or soul.

Finally, if all that deep contemplation fails, and you still feel like a bit of a transgender refusenik, maybe we should just encourage you to watch a load of body-swap movies, from Freaky Friday to Big, Face Off to Superman; Seventeen Again to The Frog Princess...

Then, try telling me that you don't get the idea that someone's essential identity can be different from their body.

Wait, but what about…

There were a few other specific obstacles to fundamental acceptance of trans and non-binary people that arose in some of my conversations with men too, so before I end, I'll quickly address those *whatabouts* here:

What about pronouns & dead names?

My respondents sometimes fixated over changed pronouns, often suggesting invisible quote marks around them. Some did the same to the name of a trans person, or referred to them by their dead name, calling it their 'real name.' Interestingly, they didn't seem to recognise at first how insulting or upsetting this would be for the person they're misgendering, but I found that using examples in everyday life where they happily call people different names or titles from the ones they were given as babies was a way of getting past this that seemed to be quite effective.

When these men acknowledged that they'd never dream of disrespecting Muhammed Ali by calling him Cassius Clay, for instance, or that they happily accepted names like The Rock and Pele even though they weren't the names on those men's birth certificates, they found the idea of offering the same respect to a trans person slightly easier.

When it came to pronouns too, they admitted that they didn't find it at all weird that I changed from Miss Gould to Mrs Meakin overnight just by getting married, and these kinds of everyday examples made them happier to accept that someone changing their pronouns and name is something we can all learn to accommodate with just a little bit of effort.

What about the op?

The degree to which cis people seem obsessed with trans people's genitals is really quite fascinating. We all acknowledged that there are only a few contexts in which you'd ask a cis person about their vulva, uterus, breasts, penis, testicles, or hormone levels, and that would generally be when you're either their doctor or their lover. Trans people surely deserve the same respect; their sex organs are not a matter for public debate and discussion.

Although we have no *right* to know about someone's intimate body parts, Shon Faye wants us to understand that 'genital reconstruction surgery, known colloquially as the op, retains its status in the public mindset as the very core of transition, but... for many trans people it is not the most important aspect of their transition. After all, genitals are the part of the body least likely to be seen by others: many trans people consider body shape, facial hair, voice and facial features to be much more important in daily life, allowing their true gender to be recognized by others', although she does add that 'nevertheless, a great many trans people consider this surgery as vital to being able to live comfortably in their body (particularly trans women, 60 percent of whom will go on to have genital surgery).'[25]

One other fact I found fascinating, disturbing, and not entirely surprising is that trans women who choose gender-affirming surgery encounter the ancient idea that the vagina is defined by its relationship with a penetrating penis, just as cis women have for centuries. For many trans women, 'the clinical reality of gender confirmation [surgery] prioritises depth over sensation, and confirmation over pleasure'.[26] In other words, doctors often construct a vagina that prioritises the pleasure of the person whose penis might penetrate it, rather than the pleasure of the trans woman herself.

What about the children?

Much anti-trans rhetoric focuses on the narrative that trans acceptance is a threat to children who may transition before they can really understand the implications, so it's important to realise that here in the UK, even though surgery is routinely carried out on babies with visible intersex characteristics to align them with one gender or another, gender-affirming surgery is simply *not* given to someone under the age of 18 who identifies as trans. That goes for gender-affirming hormone replacement therapy too, even if youngsters are suffering extreme gender dysphoria -

although in some cases, doctors may make an exception for people over the age of 16, taking into account elevated risk factors for trans boys and girls that include anxiety, self-harm and even suicide.

Children below the age of 16 who identify as trans and suffer body dysphoria might be able to be prescribed medication that delays their body's transition from childhood to adulthood until they're old enough to give consent to gender affirming treatments. The NHS Gender Identity Development Service (GIDS) tells us that the physical effect of these puberty blockers is reversible, which is important for the very rare[27] instances where someone changes their mind about transitioning after they hit puberty.

We should note, too, that 'In England, Wales and Scotland, the Equality Act 2010 prohibits discrimination against transgender children in all schools', and in Northern Ireland, 'guidance issued by the Education Authority says the European Convention on Human Rights may offer some protections for transgender pupils.'[28] Discriminating against transgender children is simply not lawful, any more than it is for adults.

It's interesting too that recently, concerns have been raised that worrying numbers of young girls are now 'identifying as trans men because they're trying to escape the problems of being a girl in an oppressive patriarchal system.' I personally suspect it's unlikely that many people would consider living life as a transgender person to be an easy option, bearing in mind the level of transphobia that exists right now… but if it *is* the case, surely the solution should be to work harder to change the patriarchal system that makes life so oppressive for girls that they want to flee from their own gender? I'd have thought *that* might be a better long-term strategy than making it almost impossible for trans young people with body dysphoria to live more happily as their authentic selves.

What about toilets?

Individual toilets that can accommodate any gender are my personal favourite. They help fix the 'default men/invisible women' queuing issue for cis women that we touched on in *Issue 1: That 'I've Never Really Thought About It' Face*, as well as offering more privacy to all, more gender-inclusive baby-changing facilities that many fathers are crying out for... and they are more easily accessible for trans and non-binary people. But as most public toilets are either men's or women's right now, we often hear concerns voiced about women's safety - or more accurately, cis women's safety - being put at risk.

The argument goes that if we allow trans women into women's toilets, cis women might feel uncomfortable because they know that some of those trans women might still have male primary sex characteristics; moreover, cis women might even be in danger, because predatory men could disguise themselves as trans women and gain access to somewhere that should be a safe space for women.

I have to admit that I struggle to see how a trans woman having a penis under her skirt might affect me if we're both privately peeing in adjacent cubicles with the doors locked. However, when it comes to safety from sexual assault, as a rape survivor myself I would never diminish the concerns that any woman - cis or trans - has in this area. Yet that's precisely why I have an issue with the way these 'women in danger' toilet conversations often play out, because by insisting that trans women and transfeminine non-binary people use men's toilets, we're actually putting *them* at increased risk of sexual violence.

What's more, I believe that banning trans women from women's toilets in order to address the threat that predatory men masquerading as trans women pose is a case of us looking through the wrong end of the telescope. Surely the real issue is with the predatory men who might harm women (both cis and trans), rather than with trans women? Personally, I'd very much prefer us to put our energies into solving *that* problem, rather than banning our trans sisters from the private cubicles and communal washbasins of women's toilets.

Of course, none of these debates is ever perfectly simple, and there are clearly circumstances and spaces where we need to prioritise the safety of many women over the rights of an individual trans woman to inhabit a specific space. Prisons for transgender sex offenders, and hostels that accommodate women who've been victims of sexual violence are just two examples. But even here, I can't help thinking it would be more helpful if we framed the conversation in a way that recognises that the issue is largely about sexual violence perpetrated by men, and not as an issue about the dangers of trans women - particularly because it's trans women who so often end up the victims of that male violence too.

What about sport?

Clearly, a sense of fairness is essential for sporting competition to work, so it's no wonder we're seeing increasingly mainstream conversations about whether or how competitive sport should include trans and non-binary people. Men's and women's categories have long existed in most sports, largely because post-puberty, men's levels of testosterone are understood to give their bodies a significant size and strength advantage over women's bodies[29].

Many argue that this advantage remains for a trans woman even after she transitions, assuming she's done so after puberty. (And bearing in mind that children can't medically transition before age 18, as well as the timescale it takes for young people to access gender-affirming treatments such as puberty blockers, relatively few trans women may have started using female hormones before their testosterone levels started to rise in puberty.)

Surely the answer can't be to simply exclude trans people from pretty much all sport, top-flight or otherwise. So we need to find ways of ensuring the right balance of inclusivity and fairness across different sports, through different rules and/or additional categories.

Strangely enough, we already make accommodations for different sizes and strengths of bodies in some sports, although not on the basis of how much testosterone someone has in their body. We don't, for instance, expect featherweight boxers to get in a ring with heavyweights; and we're happy to separate out bigger versus smaller bodies in rowing, weightlifting, kickboxing, mixed martial arts and wrestling too. But more often, we simply separate competitions into men's and women's, disabled and able-bodied, and see that as the only way to make things fair.

How trans people can fairly compete in sports is by no means a straightforward issue, and I'm certainly not qualified to answer it for sport in general, let alone for each particular sport. But I do hope that experts and governing bodies can start to create ways of providing a level playing field for all kinds of athletes whose bodies don't conform to the precise categorisations of male and female, without giving an unfair advantage to any gender.

And I hope, as ever, that these questions can be addressed in a way that's evidence-based and conducted in a spirit of openness, love and respect.

So what is the gender equality end game that I seek?

All of this begs the question - what exactly does this more gender-equal world that I want us to create together look like?

The honest answer is that I don't know *exactly*. I can no better predict the future than you can; and we know for sure that opportunities and challenges will arise that we've never even imagined; new ideas will emerge that we'll learn from; and some things that we thought were enormously important will turn out to be otherwise. However, I can tell you what qualities I'd love that future to have, and how it would feel.

As I outlined right at the beginning of his book, my ultimate hope is very simple. I want a world where all of us - men, women and people who identify as neither or both - can live more freely, safely and happily, without their gender making life more difficult and dangerous than it needs to be.

We'll never create this world unless we acknowledge the frustrating truth that we're not there yet, that gender inequality is a *big* problem right now, and that it has all kinds of negative impacts on all kinds of women - cis and trans, lesbian and straight, black, brown and white, old and young, and women across every other kind of lived experience.

But that doesn't mean that we should punish, blame, or side-line all men simply because they experience systemic gender privileges that women and non-binary people don't.

We need to stop letting people position feminism as a Hunger Games scenario where the winner destroys everyone else; and instead, we should keep reiterating that a more gender-equal society is proven to work better for all kinds of men too.

We must always remember, as we build this more gender-equal world, that men are not the enemy. Systems and biases and blind-spots and unfounded fears are. So we mustn't be afraid to acknowledge that women as well as men can be upholders of the biases and prejudice that damage us too.

This new world we're building must have space for nuance and flexibility. It must contain more 'and' and less 'versus.' We need to get comfortable holding two thoughts that *appear* contradictory when they actually work together, like the fact that women currently suffer enormously from patriarchal systems of oppression, AND that those systems damage and constrain men too.

Most importantly of all, we all need to build this world not because we think we should, but because we genuinely want to.

Building it cannot feel like a chore, a worthy act of self-sacrifice. It ought to feel like doing it is a pleasure, because it gives each of us more, not less, of the things we love; and because it allows all of us to act in ways that are personally motivating and rewarding for each of us.

We can only achieve this if we stop leaping to judgement, and start understanding each other better instead; if we get past the 'menemies' mindset we've been stuck in for too long; if we create safe spaces that are free from reprisal, shame and worries about being cancelled, so we can openly share ideas, feelings, hopes and fears.

For generations, we'll need to keep on building and developing and growing and nurturing this world. It's taken thousands of years to create the sophisticated patriarchal system in which we currently live, so it'll take more than a couple of years to fundamentally change it. But, as Tesco says, every little helps; and we can all play our part if we start affecting the particular changes that *we* want to and that *are* in our power, and not feel overwhelmed by the millions of things we can't or don't want to do.

As I began this project, I wondered if the strategic approach that worked so well for selling the likes of M&S chocolate puddings and Prime subscriptions could work as well for gender equality. As my work has progressed, I've become utterly convinced that it can, and that it must. I honestly believe that the only way to overcome such a complex and deep-seated set of issues as gender inequality is to do two key things: properly understand the specific problem we're trying to fix; and then build from the motivations men already have, rather than trying to completely change men or do it without them.

Every conversation I've had with these wonderful men, from undergrads to grandads, has left me full of optimism and energy. I only hope that some of what's written in these pages provokes some similarly productive conversations across the gender divide for you too.

I feel more sure than ever that together, we can start to unpick the complex, interwoven threads of the cis-het white patriarchal world we've inherited, and weave a new fabric of society, in our homes and families, schools and unis, friendship groups, businesses, governments and states; a new fabric that has enough richness and texture and colour and shape for each of us to be who we know we are; a society with enough space and support for all of us to grow into the person we might become; a world where we can all find more joy and health and happiness, both for ourselves and for each other.

I hope you're with me.

The Beginning…

No More Menemies, by Lori Meakin

ABOUT THE AUTHOR

Lori grew up on a council estate in Dagenham, and somehow ended up going to three universities: Hertford College, Oxford; Birmingham University; and London University Institute of Education.

After five years as a teacher, she spent a decade working in brand & management consultancy, advertising and at the BBC, before co-founding the brand and advertising agency Joint in 2012, where she worked with clients including Amazon, Vue, Google and Reach.

Outside of the paid day job, Lori has worked with many organisations with gender at their heart including Terrence Higgins Trust, Just Like Us, The English Collective of Prostitutes, My Image My Choice and Women in Journalism, and she's currently on the Exec of Women in Advertising and Communications Leadership (WACL) who work to accelerate gender equality in advertising and comms.

As a result of the *No More Menemies* project, Lori has launched a strategic innovation consultancy, *The Others & Me*, to help ambitious, male-dominated businesses and leadership teams embrace gender equality in a way that works brilliantly for them too.

She's surrounded by a loving family and friends, without whose support and inspiration she'd be lost.

No More Menemies, by Lori Meakin

FURTHER READING

Pragya Agarwal, *Hysterical: Exploding The Myth Of Gendered Emotions*, Canongate Books, 2022.

Travis Alabanza, *None of the Above: Reflections on Life Beyond the Binary,* Canongate Books, 2023.

Hira Ali, *Her Allies: A Practical Toolkit to Help Men Lead Through Advocacy*, Neem Tree Press, 2021.

Paul Baker, *Outrageous! The Story of Section 28 and Britain's Battle for LGBT Education,* Reaktion Books, 2023.

Justin Baldoni, *Boys Will Be Human: A Get-Real Gut-Check Guide to Becoming the Strongest, Kindest, Bravest Person You Can Be,* HarperCollins, 2022.

Justin Baldoni, *Man Enough: Undefining My Masculinity,* HarperOne, 2021.

Laura Bates, *Everyday Sexism,* Simon & Schuster, 2015.

Laura Bates, *Fix The System Not The Women*, Simon & Schuster, 2022.

Munroe Bergdorf, *Transitional: In One Way or Another, We All Transition,* Bloomsbury Tonic, 2023.

Iris Bohnet, *What Works: Gender Equality by Design*, Belknap Press, 2018.

David Brooks, *The Social Animal: A Story of How Success Happens,* Short Books Ltd, 2012.

Tomas Chamorro-Premuzic, *Why Do So Many Incompetent Men Become Leaders? (And How To Fix It),* Harvard Business Review Press, 2019.

Jane Cunningham & Phillipa Roberts, *Brandsplaining: Why Marketing is (Still) Sexist and How to Fix It*, Penguin, 2021.

Shon Faye, *The Transgender Issue: An Argument For Justice,* Penguin, 2022.

Gary Ford, Stephen Koch and Dr Jill Armstrong, *The Accidental Sexist: A Handbook For Men On Workplace Diversity And Inclusio*n, Rethink Press, 2021.

Katrine Marçal, *Mother Of Invention: How Good Ideas Get Ignored In An Economy Built For Men*, Harper Collins, 2021.

Caitlyn Moran, *More Than A Woman*, Ebury Press, 2021.

Caroline Criado Perez, *Invisible Women: Exposing Data Bias In A World Designed For Men*, Penguin, 2019.

Grayson Perry, *The Descent Of Man*, Penguin, 2017.

Liz Plank, *For The Love Of Men: From Toxic To A More Mindful Masculinity,* Macmillan, 2019.

Angela Saini, *The Patriarchs: How Men Came To Rule*, Fourth Estate, 2023.

Mary Ann Sieghart, *The Authority Gap: Why Women Are Still Taken Less Seriously Than Men, And What We Can Do About It,* Doubleday, 2021.

Sophia Smith Galer, *Losing It: Sex Education For The 21st Century*, William Collins, 2022.

Gloria Steinem, *The Truth Will Set You Free, But First It Will Piss You Off! Thoughts on Life, Love, And Rebellion,* Random House, 2019.

Paula Stone Williams, *As a Woman: What I Learned about Power, Sex, and the Patriarchy After I Transitioned,* Atria Books, 2021.

Matthew Todd, *Straight Jacket: Overcoming Society's Legacy of Gay Shame,* Black Swan, 2018.

Alok Vaid-Menon, *Beyond the Gender Binary (Pocket Change Collective),* Penguin Workshop, 2020

REFERENCES

INTRODUCTION: Why am I talking to men about gender equality?

[1] It's important to distinguish between 'masculine' and 'feminine' which are different from 'male' and 'female.' The former, gender, is constructed by society; the latter, sex, describes the physical, biological body (whether it's the one you were born with or not). We all have masculine and feminine qualities despite centuries of socialisation telling us that our gender must match our biological sex and that we should be one or the other. Importantly, even at a biological level, women's bodies contain testosterone and men's oestrogen, and some people are born with intersex characteristics. Some traits that we deem masculine vs feminine may have links to biological differences, and others might not. The extent of nature vs nurture is still very much a subject of debate, but we can safely say that masculinity and femininity as we experience them today are social constructs, even if they don't appear so to many of us.

[2] Apologies to those with a sensitive disposition - I still swear like a sailor, so watch out for the odd profanity in the pages to come.

[3] Less than a third of FTSE 100 executives are women, Board Agenda, March 2023, https://boardagenda.com/2023/03/09/less-than-a-third-of-ftse-100-executives-are-women/

[4] Film Dialogue From 2,000 Screenplays Broken Down By Gender And Age, The Pudding, April 2016, https://pudding.cool/2017/03/film-dialogue/ See also (Geena Davis Institute on gender in media, 2019, seejane.org)

[5] Brandsplaining. Why Marketing is (Still) Sexist and How to Fix It, Jane Cunningham & Philippa Roberts, Penguin, 2021

[6] This isn't an exaggeration. Scientific studies have proven all of these things to be true, even though most of the time men have no idea they're doing it.

[7] Of course, all the above is so much worse for women of colour. Or gay women. Or people who are non-binary or trans, or disabled, or neurodiverse. But it's still almost impossible to find much data on these areas of intersectionality. Moreover, I believe that starting with one primary lens and then exploring intersectionalities helps bring clarity. My primary lens here is gender, but there is lots of excellent work that takes a different primary lens, such as racism or ableism, and we need people working in all of these different ways, not to suggest that only one way is the right way.

INTERLUDE: Getting past the anger

[1] The Authority Gap: Why Women Are Still Taken Less Seriously Than Men, And What We Can Do About It, Mary Ann Sieghart, Doubleday, 2021 p.74

ISSUE 1: That 'I've Never Really Thought About It' Face

[1] Invisible Women: Exposing Data Bias in a World Designed for Men, Caroline Criado Perez, 2019, Penguin

[2] Women's Health Plan, Scottish Government, August 2021 https://www.gov.scot/publications/womens-health-plan/

[3] Women's Health Plan, Scottish Government, August 2021 https://www.gov.scot/news/womens-health-plan/

[4] Our Vision for the Women's Health Strategy for England, Department of Health & Social Care, December 2021, https://assets.publishing.service.gov.uk/government/uploads/system/uploads/attachment_data/file/1042631/dhsc-our-vision-for-the-women_s-health-strategy-for-england.pdf?utm_campaign=Invisiblepercent20Women&utm_medium=email&utm_source=Revue percent20newsletter

[5] Has England Ever Won The Euros?, Metro, March 2023, https://metro.co.uk/2021/07/04/how-far-have-england-got-in-the-euros-in-the-past-14870386/

[6] Mother of Invention: How Good Ideas Get Ignored in an Economy Built for Men, Katrine Marçal, Harper Collins, 2021

[7] *And Woman Created...*, Sandi Toksvig, The Guardian, January 2004, https://www.theguardian.com/world/2004/jan/23/gender.uk

[8] *Why Were Women Written Out of History? An Interview with Bettany Hughes*, English Heritage, February 2016, https://www.english-heritage.org.uk/visit/inspire-me/blog/blog-posts/why-were-women-written-out-of-history-an-interview-with-bettany-hughes/

[9] *The Second Sex*, Simone De Beauvoir, 1949, Random House New York

[10] *An Introduction To Unconscious Bias*, University of Exeter, https://www.exeter.ac.uk/media/universityofexeter/humanresources/edi/equalityanddiversity/equalityanddiversity/edsecurefolder/An_introduction_to_unconscious_bias.pdf

[11] *Invisible Women: Exposing Data Bias in a World Designed for Men*, Caroline Criado Perez, Penguin, 2019, p.5

[12] *What Works: Gender Equality by Design*, Iris Bohnet, Belknap Press, 2018, p.7

[13] *What Works: Gender Equality by Design*, Iris Bohnet, Belknap Press, 2018, p.203

[14] *Invisible Women: Exposing Data Bias in a World Designed for Men*, Caroline Criado Perez, Penguin, 2019, p.5

[15] *What Works: Gender Equality by Design*, Iris Bohnet, Belknap Press, 2018, p.150

[16] *The Social Animal: A Story of How Success Happens,* David Brooks, Short Books Ltd, 2012, p.160

[17] *Her Allies: A Practical Toolkit to Help Men Lead Through Advocacy*, Hira Ali, Neem Tree Press, 2021, p.31

[18] *The Authority Gap: Why Women Are Still Taken Less Seriously Than Men, And What We Can Do About It,* Mary Ann Sieghart, Doubleday, 2021, p165

[19] *Esther Perel on the Paradox of Masculinity*, Psychotherapy Networker, https://www.psychotherapynetworker.org/post/esther-perel-paradox-masculinity

[20] *Understanding Tradition: Marital Name Change in Britain and Norway,* Sage Journals, December 2019, https://journals.sagepub.com/doi/10.1177/1360780419892637

[21] *The Accidental Sexist: A handbook for men on workplace diversity and inclusion*, Gary Ford, Stephen Koch and Dr Jill Armstrong, Rethink Press, 2021, p2

[22] *Her Allies: A Practical Toolkit to Help Men Lead Through Advocacy*, Hira Ali, Neem Tree Press, 2021, p.20

ISSUE 2: Aren't We Nearly There Yet?

[1] *Sea-Change In UK Boardrooms As Women Make Up Nearly 40% Of FTSE 100 Top Table Roles*, UK Government, February 2022, https://www.gov.uk/government/news/sea-change-in-uk-boardrooms-as-women-make-up-nearly-40-of-ftse-100-top-table-roles

[2] Ibid. FTSE 100 has 8 women CEO's none of whom is a woman of colour, and FTSE 250 has 10

[3] *Women Leaders Switch Jobs At Record Rates As They Demand Better From Their Workplaces*, NPR, October 2022, https://www.npr.org/2022/10/28/1132232414/women-workforce-switching-jobs

[4] *8.8% Fortune 500 CEO's Are Women - The Highest Of All Indices - According To The Women CEO's In America Report 2022*, Cision, September 2022, https://www.prnewswire.com/news-releases/8-8-fortune-500-ceos-are-women---the-highest-of-all-indices--according-to-the-women-ceos-in-america-report-2022--301630455.html

[5] *Study: Women Are Underrepresented In Global Fintech Industry*, FinTech, November 2021, https://fintechmagazine.com/banking/study-women-are-underrepresented-global-fintech-industry

[6] *Funding Disparity Widens For UK Female Fintech Founders in 2022*, Bloomberg, August 2022, *https://www.bloomberg.com/news/articles/2022-08-02/funding-disparity-widens-for-uk-female-fintech-founders-in-2022?leadSource=uverifypercent20wall#xj4y7vzkg*

[7] *Are You Two Only Meeting Because You're A Similar Age?* The News Movement, December 2022, https://www.instagram.com/reel/CloFwQKo6ch/?igshid=YmMyMTA2M2Y%3D

[8] *Global Gender Gap Report 2022,* World Economic Forum, July 2022, https://www.weforum.org/reports/global-gender-gap-report-2022/digest/

[9] *Woman And Authority: Mary Ann Sieghart, The Authority Gap,* The Story Of Woman podcast, August 2022,

https://www.thestoryofwomanpodcast.com/episode/replay-woman-and-authority-mary-ann-sieghart-the-authority-gap

[10]Seven In Ten Britons Would Support Making Misogyny A Hate Crime, YouGov, March 2022, https://yougov.co.uk/topics/politics/articles-reports/2022/03/01/seven-ten-britons-would-support-making-misogyny-ha

[11]Misogyny Fuels Violence Against Women. Should It Be a Hate Crime?, New York Times, March 2021, https://www.nytimes.com/2021/03/25/us/misogyny-violence-against-women-hate-crime.html

[12]The Metaverse Has A Groping Problem Already, MIT Technology Review, December 2021, https://www.technologyreview.com/2021/12/16/1042516/the-metaverse-has-a-groping-problem/

[13]*Rape & Sexual Assault Statistics*, Rape Crisis Centre, https://rapecrisis.org.uk/get-informed/statistics-sexual-violence /

[14] Yvette Cooper Warns 300 Women Are Raped Daily And Slams Tories On Charge Rate, Mirror, December 2022, https://www.mirror.co.uk/news/politics/yvette-cooper-warns-300-women-28781553

[15] *Fix the System Not the Women*, Laura Bates, Simon & Schuster Ltd, 2023, p.75

[16]Yvette Cooper Warns 300 Women Are Raped Daily And Slams Tories On Charge Rate, Mirror, December 2022, https://www.mirror.co.uk/news/politics/yvette-cooper-warns-300-women-28781553

[17]*Cressida Dick: Why Is It So Hard To Fix The Met's Toxic Culture?* BBC News, February 2022, https://www.bbc.co.uk/news/uk-60352112

[18] *Police officer called rape a 'struggle snuggle' in messages to Wayne Couzens,* Metro, July 2022, https://metro.co.uk/2022/07/28/police-officer-called-rape-a-struggle-snuggle-in-whatsapp-messages-17086746/#:~:text=Mrpercent20Brownpercent20suggestedpercent20thatpercent20the,consensualpercent20physicalpercent20orpercent20sexualpercent20contact

[19] *Cressida Dick: Why Is It So Hard To Fix The Met's Toxic Culture?* BBC News, February 2022, https://www.bbc.co.uk/news/uk-60352112

[20]*Woman And Authority: Mary Ann Sieghart, The Authority Gap,* The Story Of Woman podcast, August 2022, https://www.thestoryofwomanpodcast.com/episode/replay-woman-and-authority-mary-ann-sieghart-the-authority-gap

[21] Jimson Weed/White Flower No. 1 by Georgia O'Keefe: *O'Keeffe Painting Sells for $44 Million at Sotheby's, Sets Record for Work by Female Artist,* ArtNet, November 2014, https://news.artnet.com/market/okeeffe-painting-sells-for-44-million-at-sothebys-sets-record-for-work-by-female-artist-176413

[22] *List of Most Expensive Paintings*, Wikipedia, https://en.wikipedia.org/wiki/List_of_most_expensive_paintings NB this list is ordered by consumer price index inflation-adjusted value in millions of United States dollars in 2021. Where necessary, the price is first converted to dollars using the exchange rate at the time the painting was sold

[23] *Women Can't Paint: Gender, the Glass Ceiling and Values in Contemporary Art*, Helen Gorrill, Bloomsbury Publishing, 2020

[24] *'Mind-blowing': Why do men's paintings cost 10 times more than women's?* Guardian, August 2022, https://www.theguardian.com/artanddesign/2022/aug/02/painting-gender-pay-gap-recalculating-art

[25] *Women Can't Paint: Gender, the Glass Ceiling and Values in Contemporary Art*, Helen Gorrill, Bloomsbury Publishing, 2020

[26] *Woman and Unbiased Parenting: Virginia Mendez, Childhood Unlimited,* The Story of Woman podcast, June 2022, https://www.thestoryofwomanpodcast.com/blog/e15-woman-and-unbiased-parenting-virginia-mendez-childhood-unlimited

[27]*The Authority Gap: Why Women Are Still Taken Less Seriously Than Men, And What We Can Do About It,* Mary Ann Sieghart, Doubleday, 2021, p.148

[28] *The Authority Gap by Mary Ann Sieghart, review - why men just need to listen,* The Times, June 2021, https://www.thetimes.co.uk/article/the-authority-gap-by-mary-ann-sieghart-review-why-men-just-need-to-listen-jt2hg5sk5

[29] *The Authority Gap: Why Women Are Still Taken Less Seriously Than Men, And What We Can Do About It,* Mary Ann Sieghart, Doubleday, 2021, p.70

[30] *The Authority Gap: Why Women Are Still Taken Less Seriously Than Men, And What We Can Do About It,* Mary Ann Sieghart, Doubleday, 2021, p.168

[31] *Women 32% More Likely To Die After Operation By Male Surgeon, Study Reveals,* Guardian, January 2022, https://www.theguardian.com/society/2022/jan/04/women-more-likely-die-operation-male-surgeon-study?fbclid=IwAR0UG0cmrP5fP-DuYPQK32Ob7tymYrOCTTaT9sFUyiwaY_RNwbjFWo111MA

[32] *Women Are Calling Out 'Medical Gaslighting'* New York Times, March 2022, https://www.nytimes.com/2022/03/28/well/live/gaslighting-doctors-patients-health.html

[33] *24% Of Game Devs Are Female Despite Women Making Up Nearly Half Of Gamers,* The Gamer, June 2022, https://www.thegamer.com/game-devs-women-half-of-gamers/

[34] *Global Abortion Rights, Do Women Worry More? Bees, Matriarchs,* BBC Woman's Hour, July 2022, https://www.bbc.co.uk/programmes/m00194g0

[35] *What Works: Gender Equality by Design,* Iris Bohnet, Belknap Press, 2018, p.115

[36] Adam Grant, LinkedIn, 2021, https://www.linkedin.com/posts/adammgrant_63-studies-women-who-assert-their-ideas-activity-6825129344516595712-B2g3?utm_source=share&utm_medium=member_desktop

[37] *Women Are Happier Without Children Or A Spouse, Says Happiness Expert,* The Guardian, May 2019, https://www.theguardian.com/lifeandstyle/2019/may/25/women-happier-without-children-or-a-spouse-happiness-expert

[38] For the purposes of this argument, it's immaterial at what stage you consider a foetus or fertilised egg to become an unborn person. Nor does the age of the pregnant person make a difference, nor whether she were the victim of rape.

[39] For clarity, I'm not advocating for enforced vasectomies for men. It's simply an interesting illustration of the differing control we're happy to tolerate over men's vs women's bodies

[40] *Opinion: Shock-Value Misogyny Like Andrew Tate's Becoming Increasingly Disturbing,* The State Press, November 2022, https://www.statepress.com/article/2022/11/andrew-tate-shock-value-misogyny-is-disturbing

[41] *Andrew Tate's Misogynistic, Violent Rise To Power, Money And Notoriety,* Le Monde, October 2022, https://www.lemonde.fr/en/pixels/article/2022/10/06/andrew-tate-s-misogynistic-violent-rise-to-power-money-and-notoriety_5999416_13.html

[42] *Big Brother's Andrew Tate Says Women Should 'Bear Responsibility' For Being Raped In Vile Tweets,* Metro, October 2017, https://metro.co.uk/2017/10/19/big-brothers-andrew-tate-says-women-should-bear-responsibility-for-being-raped-in-vile-tweets-7011756/

[43] *New Secret Service Report Details Growing Incel Terrorism Threat,* CBS News, March 2022, https://www.cbsnews.com/news/incel-threat-secret-service-report/

[44] *Top 5 Mistakes Male Leaders Make When Thinking About Gender Equality (Part 1),* [my italics], Forbes, September 2021, https://www-forbes-com.cdn.ampproject.org/c/s/www.forbes.com/sites/afdhelaziz/2021/09/13/top-5-mistakes-male-leaders-make-when-thinking-about-gender-equality-part-1/amp/

[45] They tended to misunderstand the gender pay gap, thinking it meant 'men getting paid more than women for the same job' (which hasn't been legal for half a century), rather than what it is - a measure of average pay across an organisation by gender, which reveals a gender leadership or cultural gap where white men are more likely to be in the highest paid jobs. More on this in *Issue 8: 'Danger: Women at work.*

[46] Only one of my respondents had majority female bosses, and no one reported having a leadership team entirely made up of women, either personally or amongst their close friendship group.

[47] For people of my generation and above, this was the UK's biggest pop show on broadcast TV, that something that just about every teenager watched every week

[48] It's vital that we take an intersectional lens to gender equality too, of course. Here much detailed data is still sadly lacking, but there's more than enough to prove that if you're a woman of colour, or a woman who's also part of another marginalised group, the issues I talk about throughout this book are enormously exacerbated.

[49] There's much more on this in *'Issue 6: Let's talk about sex.'*

[50] 'In winning a 63-year-old bachelor a minor tax refund, Ginsburg "found her foundational argument" against sex-based discrimination', Jane Sharron De Hart, a professor emerita of history at University of California, Santa Barbara *The True Story of the Case Ruth Bader Ginsburg Argues in 'On the Basis of Sex'*, Smithsonian, December 2018, https://www.smithsonianmag.com/history/true-story-case-center-basis-sex-180971110/

ISSUE 3: The Thing Is, Boys Are Just Better

[1] *"A Seat At The Table" Isn't The Solution For Gender Equity*, TEDWomen, 2021, https://www.ted.com/talks/lilly_singh_a_seat_at_the_table_isn_t_the_solution_for_gender_equity [My italics]

[2] *The Authority Gap: Why Women Are Still Taken Less Seriously Than Men, And What We Can Do About It*, Mary Ann Sieghart, Doubleday, 2021, p.14

[3] Ibid, p.15

[4] Ibid

[5] *What Works: Gender Equality by Design*, Iris Bohnet, Belknap Press, 2018, p.183

[6] *Girls Overtake Boys In A-Level And GCSE Maths, So Are They 'smarter'?* Guardian, August 2021, https://www.theguardian.com/education/2021/aug/13/girls-overtake-boys-in-a-level-and-gcse-maths-so-are-they-smarter

[7] Ibid [NB Covid and teacher vs exam board assessment has been a contributing factor in this too]

[8] *What Works: Gender Equality by Design*, Iris Bohnet, Belknap Press, 2018, p.224

[9] *Could you win a point off Serena Williams? Plus, avoiding hen/stag parties, and being naked results*, YouGov, July 2019, https://yougov.co.uk/opi/surveys/results?utm_source=twitter&utm_medium=daily_questions&utm_campaign=question_1#/survey/344ce84b-a48d-11e9-8e40-79d1f09423a3/question/4d73bd62-a48f-11e9-aee6-6742cfe83f15/gender

[10] *Serena Williams Destroyed Five Men Who Tried To Win A Point Against Her*, SportBible, December 2022, https://www.sportbible.com/tennis/serena-williams-tennis-one-point-789713-20221230

[11] *Gender Stereotyping May Start As Young As Three Months, Study Of Babies' Cries Shows*, University of Sussex, May 2016, https://www.sussex.ac.uk/broadcast/read/35272

[12] Ibid

[13] *Are Women Stronger Than Men? Here Are 8 Scientific Facts To Put This Debate To Rest*, Health Shots, March 2022, https://www.healthshots.com/mind/are-women-stronger-than-men-here-are-8-scientific-facts-to-put-this-debate-to-rest/

[14] Ibid

[15] *Women Live Longer Than Men Even During Severe Famines And Epidemics*, The Proceedings of the National Academy of Sciences (PNAS), January 2018, https://www.pnas.org/doi/10.1073/pnas.1701535115

[16] *To Make Orchestras More Diverse, End Blind Auditions*, New York Times, July 2020, https://www.nytimes.com/2020/07/16/arts/music/blind-auditions-orchestras-race.html [NB It's important to note that experts now suggest that because blind auditions don't address other systemic privilege and bias, particularly around race and ethnicity, they may not be the best solution for fuller and intersectional diversity in the makeup of orchestras today.]

[17] *This Orchestra's Blind Audition Proves Bias Sneaks In When You Least Expect It*, Upworthy, February 2023, https://www.upworthy.com/this-orchestras-blind-audition-proves-bias-sneaks-in-when-you-least-expect-it

[18] *How the 'Authority Gap' Between Men and Women Hurts Us All*, Time Magazine, April 2022, https://time.com/6163490/authority-gap-between-men-and-women-hurts-us-

all/?utm_source=twitter&utm_medium=social&utm_campaign=editorial&utm_term=ideas_society
&linkId=159412643

[19] *For the Love of Men: From Toxic to a More Mindful Masculinity,* Liz Plank, Macmillan, 2019, p.201

[20] Ibid

[21] Ibid

[22] *Lego To Remove Gender Bias From Its Toys After Findings Of Child Survey,* Guardian, October 2021,
https://amp-theguardian-
com.cdn.ampproject.org/c/s/amp.theguardian.com/lifeandstyle/2021/oct/11/lego-to-remove-
gender-bias-after-survey-shows-impact-on-children-stereotypes

[23] *The Authority Gap: Why Women Are Still Taken Less Seriously Than Men, And What We Can Do About It,* Mary Ann Sieghart, Doubleday, 2021, p.288

[24] *Like a Girl - Always TV Commercial,* https://youtu.be/5yLXrWLvwAo

[25] *Everyday Sexism,* Laura Bates, Simon & Schuster, 2015, p.89

[26] 'The State of Gender Equality for US Adolescents', Plan International, 2018,
https://www.planusa.org/report/executive-summary-the-state-of-gender-equality-for-u-s-
adolescents/

[27] *Hysterical: Exploding The Myth Of Gendered Emotions*, Pragya Agarwal, Canongate Books, 2022, p.80

[28]Ibid

[29] *Mother of Invention: How Good Ideas Get Ignored in an Economy Built for Men*, Katrine Marçal, Harper Collins, 2021, p.19

[30] Ibid, p.207

[31] *The Gender Pay Gap Starts Early: Boys Get More Pocket Money Than Girls*, Huffington Post, May 2018, https://www.huffingtonpost.co.uk/entry/pocket-money-gender-pay-
gap_uk_5b0532c7e4b0784cd2afd410

[32] *Young Adults Are Biased Against Female Leaders, Survey Shows,* Forbes, December 2022
https://www-forbes-
com.cdn.ampproject.org/c/s/www.forbes.com/sites/kimelsesser/2022/12/15/young-adults-are-the-
most-biased-against-female-leaders-data-shows/amp/

[33] *AI Voice Assistants Reinforce Gender Biases, U.N. Report Says,* Time Magazine, May 2019,
https://time.com/5593436/ai-voice-assistants-gender-bias/

[34]Ibid

[35] *A 630-Billion-Word Internet Analysis Shows 'People' Is Interpreted as 'Men',* Scientific American, April 2022 https://www.scientificamerican.com/article/a-630-billion-word-internet-
analysis-shows-people-is-interpreted-as-men/

[36] *The 'Glass Cliff' Is A Serious Problem For Women In Corporate America. Here's How To Dismantle It,* Insider, March 2022, https://www.businessinsider.com/women-and-people-of-color-
face-glass-cliff-us-2020-7?r=US&IR=T

[37] *The Authority Gap: Why Women Are Still Taken Less Seriously Than Men, And What We Can Do About It,* Mary Ann Sieghart, Doubleday, 2021, p.24

[38] Ibid, p.292

[39] *Why We Should Be More Sexist*, Tomas Chamorro-Premuzic, TEDx Cambridge
https://www.youtube.com/watch?v=VOnNDiOtBgk

[40] *What Works: Gender Equality by Design*, Iris Bohnet, Belknap Press, 2018, p.187

[41] I recognise that this term is derogatory to men, and not in the spirit of a book that's about trying to end the 'menemies' mindset. I used it, though, because it's used in data I quote; and I explore the issue later in *Issue 5: Taking Up Space*

[42]*Data Confirms It: Mansplaining Isn't An Invention Of Women,* Visualeyed, February 2021,
https://www.visualeyed.com/d-stories/article/data-confirms-it-mansplaining-isnt-an-invention-of-
women/

[43] *Three Barriers, Double Burdens And A Restrictive Rule Book: Life For Women In Corporate UK,* Shape Talent, 2022, https://www.shapetalent.com/three-barriers-double-burdens-and-a-
restrictive-rule-book-life-for-women-in-corporate-uk/

[44] *The Girl Who Cried Pain: A Bias Against Women in the Treatment of Pain,* SSRN, February 2003, https://papers.ssrn.com/sol3/papers.cfm?abstract_id=383803

[45] *Pain Bias: The Health Inequality Rarely Discussed,* BBC, May 2018, *https://www.bbc.com/future/article/20180518-the-inequality-in-how-women-are-treated-for-pain*

[46] *When Doctors Downplay Women's Health Concerns,* New York Times, May 2018, https://www.nytimes.com/2018/05/03/well/live/when-doctors-downplay-womens-health-concerns.html

[47] *How Doctors Take Women's Pain Less Seriously,* The Atlantic, October 2015, https://www.theatlantic.com/health/archive/2015/10/emergency-room-wait-times-sexism/410515/

[48] *Hysterical: Exploding The Myth Of Gendered Emotions*, Pragya Agarwal, Canongate Books, 2022, p.277.

[49] Ibid

[50] *Woman and Gendered Emotions, Pragya Agarwal*, The Story of Woman podcast, October 2022, https://www.thestoryofwomanpodcast.com/blog/e21-woman-and-gendered-emotions-pragya-agarwal-hysterical

[51] *How Many Violent Attacks And Sexual Assaults On Women Are There?* BBC, June 2022 https://www.bbc.co.uk/news/explainers-56365412

[52] *Suicides In England & Wales, 2020 Registrations*, ONS, 2021, https://www.ons.gov.uk/peoplepopulationandcommunity/birthsdeathsandmarriages/deaths/bulletins/suicidesintheunitedkingdom/2020registrations

[53] *Provisional Numbers and Rates of Suicide by Month and Demographic Characteristics: United States, 2021,* Center for Disease Control and Prevention's National Center for Health Statistics, 2021, https://www.cdc.gov/nchs/data/vsrr/vsrr024.pdf

[54] *Everyday Sexism,* Laura Bates, Simon & Schuster, 2015, p.332

[55] *American Psychological Association Links 'masculinity Ideology' To Homophobia, Misogyny,* NBC News, January 2019, https://www.nbcnews.com/feature/nbc-out/american-psychological-association-links-masculinity-ideology-homophobia-misogyny-n956416

[56] *The Descent of Man*, Grayson Perry, Penguin, 2017

[57] Interestingly, they tended to position these qualities versus other inferior men rather than versus the women in their lives, who they still generally perceived as being stronger at these skills. More on that in the next chapter, Issue *4: It's Dog Eat Dog, And I'm Nobody's Bitch.*

[58] *Ian Wright, Former Footballer And Broadcaster,* BBC Radio Four Desert Island Discs, February 2020, https://www.bbc.co.uk/programmes/m000fdxw

ISSUE 4: It's dog eat dog, and I'm nobody's bitch

[1] *The Arrest Of Andrew Tate: The 'king Of Toxic Masculinity',* Today in Focus podcast, The Guardian, 5th January 2023 https://www.theguardian.com/news/audio/2023/jan/05/the-arrest-of-andrew-tate-the-king-of-toxic-masculinity-podcast

[2] *What Guys Mean When They Call Someone A 'Chad',* Men's Health, August 2020, https://www.menshealth.com/sex-women/a33499682/what-is-a-chad/

[3] *Man Enough: Undefining My Masculinity,* Justin Baldoni, HarperOne, 2021

[4] Ibid (each of these is a chapter heading from the book)

[5] Ibid, p.17

[6] *The State of Gender Equality for US Adolescents*, Plan International, 2018, https://www.planusa.org/report/executive-summary-the-state-of-gender-equality-for-u-s-adolescents/

[7] *The Descent Of Man*, Grayson Perry, Penguin, 2017

[8] Ibid, p.37

[9] Ibid, p.42

[10] *For the Love of Men: From Toxic to a More Mindful Masculinity,* Liz Plank, Macmillan, 2019

[11] *Mind Reading 2.0: Why Conversations Go Wrong,* Hidden Brain podcast, February 2022, https://hiddenbrain.org/podcast/why-conversations-go-wrong/

[12] *Homicide In England And Wales: Year Ending March 2021,* ONS, February 2022, [Over two-thirds (70percent) of all homicide victims were male and just under a third (30percent) were female]

https://www.ons.gov.uk/peoplepopulationandcommunity/crimeandjustice/articles/homicideinengla
ndandwales/yearendingmarch2021

[13] Ibid

[14] *Guys And Guns: Why Men Are Behind The Vast Majority Of America's Gun Violence,* ABC
News, November 2021, https://abcnews.go.com/US/guys-guns-men-vast-majority-americas-gun-
violence/story?id=79125485

[15] https://giffords.org/lawcenter/gun-violence-statistics/

[16] Ibid

[17] Ibid

[18] *Hysterical: Exploding The Myth Of Gendered Emotions*, Pragya Agarwal, Canongate Books,
2022, p.171

[19] Ibid

[20] *World Cup Football Is A Risk Factor For Domestic Violence,* Lancaster University, June 2014,
https://www.lancaster.ac.uk/news/articles/2014/world-cup-football-is-a-risk-factor-for-domestic-
violence/

[21] Ibid

[22] *For the Love of Men: From Toxic to a More Mindful Masculinity,* Liz Plank, Macmillan, 2019,
p.43

[23] *Being A Man,* Living Well, 2012, https://livingwell.org.au/well-being/being-a-man/

[24] *Being A Man,* Living Well, 2012, https://livingwell.org.au/well-being/being-a-man/

[25] *For the Love of Men: From Toxic to a More Mindful Masculinity,* Liz Plank, Macmillan, 2019

[26] *Ibid,* p.41

[27] *Ibid,* p.41-2

[28] Ibid, p.42

[29] Ibid

[30] *Is Crying Good For You?*, Harvard Health Publishing, March 2021,
https://www.health.harvard.edu/blog/is-crying-good-for-you-2021030122020

[31] *Her Allies: A Practical Toolkit to Help Men Lead Through Advocacy*, Hira Ali, Neem Tree
Press, 2021, p.19

[32] *Men's Friendships Are Different From Women's,* Psychology Today, October 2009,
https://www.psychologytoday.com/us/blog/buddy-system/200910/mens-friendships-are-different-
womens

[33] *Men have fewer friends than ever, and it's harming their health*, Vox, August 2022,
https://www.vox.com/the-highlight/23323556/men-friendship-loneliness-isolation-masculinity

[34] Sheryl Sandberg's seminal TED talk and book *Lean In: Women, Work and the Will to Lead*
urged women to overcome systemic barriers and barriers they were placing on themselves and
'lean in' https://leanin.org/book#!

[35] *What Works: Gender Equality by Design*, Iris Bohnet, Belknap Press, 2018, p.64

[36] Ibid, p.65

[37] Ibid, p.70

[38] *The Duality Of Diva With Mariah Carey*, Archetypes with Meghan, August 2022,
https://open.spotify.com/episode/6S3Y5mKB9nJAk6wvZdbVo8

[39] *2021 Tokyo Olympics: Simone Biles Says She Wears G.O.A.T. Leotards To 'Mess' With Her
Haters,* CBS, July 2021, https://www.cbssports.com/olympics/news/2021-tokyo-olympics-simone-
biles-says-she-wears-g-o-a-t-leotards-to-mess-with-her-
haters/#:~:text='percent20Butpercent20thenpercent20ifpercent20Ipercent20acknowledge,takeperce
nt20itpercent20aspercent20anpercent20athlete

[40] *Serena Williams: 'If I Were A Man,' I Would Have Been Considered The Greatest A Long Time
Ago,* Washington Post, December 2016, https://www.washingtonpost.com/news/early-
lead/wp/2016/12/26/serena-williams-if-i-were-a-man-i-would-have-been-considered-the-greatest-
a-long-time-ago/

[41] *What Works: Gender Equality by Design*, Iris Bohnet, Belknap Press, 2018, p.189

[42] Ibid

[43] Ibid

[44] Ibid

[45] *The Descent Of Man*, Grayson Perry, Penguin, 2017, p.27

[46] *What Works: Gender Equality by Design*, Iris Bohnet, Belknap Press, 2018, p.190 [The Maasai in Tanzania, compared with the Khasi in Northeast India]

[47] *Hysterical: Exploding The Myth Of Gendered Emotions*, Pragya Agarwal, Canongate Books, 2022, p.168

[48] *Hysterical: Exploding The Myth Of Gendered Emotions*, Pragya Agarwal, Canongate Books, 2022, p.xxii

[49] *'What's in it for Men?'*: *Old Question, New Data,* Øystein Gullvåg Holter, Sage journals, November 2014, https://journals.sagepub.com/doi/abs/10.1177/1097184X14558237

[50] *How The 'Authority Gap' Between Men And Women Hurts Us All,* Time Magazine, April 2022, https://time.com/6163490/authority-gap-between-men-and-women-hurts-us-all/?utm_source=twitter&utm_medium=social&utm_campaign=editorial&utm_term=ideas_society&linkId=159412643

[51] A young offenders' institution that has now been abolished, and that has a reputation for being particularly brutal.

[52] https://vm.tiktok.com/ZMFKBxSBk/

[53] *If,* Rudyard Kipling, Poetry Foundation, https://www.poetryfoundation.org/poems/46473/if [NB It's vital that we challenge the dreadful racism inherent in much of Kipling's work whilst acknowledging the power of these specific words as a surprisingly more rounded vision of masculinity]

ISSUE 5: Taking Up Space

[1] *Men vs. Women: Filling Space. or: Why Sidewalk Chicken is a Viable Game*, Live Journal, April 2010, https://issendai.livejournal.com/561611.html

[2] Ibid

[3] *I'm No Longer Moving Out Of The Way Of Men Who Walk Into Me,* Metro, December 2022, https://metro.co.uk/2022/12/05/im-no-longer-moving-out-of-the-way-of-men-who-walk-into-me-17879728/

[4] *Sidewalk Behaviour Exercise*, Feminist Philosophers, October 2010, https://feministphilosophers.wordpress.com/2010/10/30/sidewalk-behaviour-exercise/

[5] Ibid

[6] *Can Playgrounds Be Sexist?*, Visible Women With Caroline Criado Perez podcast, June 2022, https://uk-podcasts.co.uk/podcast/visible-women-with-caroline-criado-perez/2-can-playgrounds-be-sexist

[7] *The Deadly Truth About A World Built For Men - From Stab Vests To Car Crashes*, The Guardian, February 2019, https://www.theguardian.com/lifeandstyle/2019/feb/23/truth-world-built-for-men-car-crashes

[8] *Glasgow Has Become The UK's First Feminist City,* The News Movement, January 2022 Https://Www.Instagram.Com/Reel/Cm9dhrxv6tj/?Igshid=Ymmymta2m2y=

[9] *Where Are The Women In Tech?* The News Movement, January 2023, https://www.instagram.com/reel/CnHv4fnrQhT/?igshid=YmMyMTA2M2Y=

[10] *Women Made Up 20 Percent of Key Behind-the-Scenes Roles in Top-Grossing Films in 2019: Study,* Hollywood Reporter, January 2020, https://www.hollywoodreporter.com/news/general-news/women-made-up-20-percent-key-behind-scenes-film-roles-2019-1265681/

[11] *Women Over 40 Disappear From Television, According To New Study,* Forbes, October 2022 https://www.forbes.com/sites/kimelsesser/2022/10/18/women-over-40-disappear-from-television-according-to-new-study/amp/

[12] *Brandsplaining. Why Marketing is (Still) Sexist and How to Fix It,* Jane Cunningham & Philippa Roberts, Penguin, 2021, p.63

[13] *Hag Horror,* Betwixt The Sheets Podcast, February 2023, ttps://shows.acast.com/betwixt-the-sheets/episodes/hag-horror-older-women-on-film

[14] *Woman & Unbiased Parenting: Virginia Mendez, Childhood Unlimited*, The Story of Woman podcast, June 2022 https://www.thestoryofwomanpodcast.com/episode/15-woman-and-unbiased-parenting-virginia-mendez-childhood-unlimited

[15] https://seejane.org/institute-in-the-news/men-appear-ads-4-times-women-according-research-revealed-cannes/

[16] *Men Appear in Ads 4 Times More Than Women, According to Research Revealed at Cannes,* Geena Davis Institute on Gender in Media, 2017, https://seejane.org/institute-in-the-news/men-appear-ads-4-times-women-according-research-revealed-cannes/

[17] *How To Win The Superbowl,* System 1, February 2022, https://system1group.com/super-bowl-lvii#request-report

[18] *Music Festivals: Only 13 Percent Of UK Headliners In 2022 Are Female,* BBC, May 2022. https://www.bbc.co.uk/news/newsbeat-61512053

[19] *Female Dance Acts Largely Ignored By Radio, Study Says,* BBC, August 2022 https://www.bbc.co.uk/news/entertainment-arts-62395794

[20] *Half Reality, A Quarter Reflected: Women Represent Just One Quarter Of People Featured In Our News - With Little Change In 25 Years,* Reflect Reality, 2020, https://www.reflectreality.internews.org/the-problem

[21] *The News Industry Still Has A Gender Diversity Problem – Here's How To Make It More Inclusive,* World Economic Forum, January 2023 https://www.weforum.org/agenda/2023/01/news-industry-gender-diversity-problem-more-inclusive-davos-2023

[22] Ibid

[23] *Coverage Of Women's Sport Is Pathetic At The Best Of Times - The Lockdown Has Made It Even Worse,* The Conversation, June 2020, https://theconversation.com/coverage-of-womens-sport-is-pathetic-at-the-best-of-times-the-lockdown-has-made-it-even-worse-140593

[24] Ibid

[25] *News Media Still Pressing The Mute Button On Women's Sports,* USC News, March 2021, https://news.usc.edu/183765/womens-sports-tv-news-coverage-sportscenter-online-usc-study/

[26] Ibid

[27] *Correct the Internet,* January 2023, https://www.correcttheinternet.com/

[28] Ibid

[29] *World's First Female Cricketer Sculpture Sees Belinda Clark Immortalised,* Women's Agenda, January 2023, https://womensagenda.com.au/latest/worlds-first-female-cricketer-sculpture-sees-belinda-clark-immortalised/

[30] *Gap Between Male And Female Statues Is Monumental,* Statistica, March 2019, https://www.statista.com/chart/17299/number-of-public-statues-depicting-men-and-women-in-the-us-and-the-uk/

[31] *The Serious Side Of 'mansplaining' Has Been Lost. That's Where The Harm Begins,* The Guardian, February 2023, https://amp-theguardian-com.cdn.ampproject.org/c/s/amp.theguardian.com/commentisfree/2023/feb/09/mansplaining-word-problem-rebecca-solnit

[32] Jessica McCarty tweet, February 2021 https://twitter.com/jmccarty_geo/status/1361332337678639107?s=46&t=7tq3UhuBifZzDQE3uHNZXg

[33] *Boys Will Be Human: A Get-Real Gut-Check Guide to Becoming the Strongest, Kindest, Bravest Person You Can Be,* Justin Baldoni, HarperCollins, 2022, p.193

[34] *Do Women Talk Too Much? (Hint: Science Says No),* All Things Linguistic, June 2016, https://allthingslinguistic.com/post/145374253955/do-women-talk-too-much-hint-science-says-no#:~:text=Whenpercent20Spencerpercent20askedpercent20studentspercent20to,onlypercent2030percent25percent20ofpercent20thepercent20time.

[35] *Women In the Workplace,* McKinsey, October 2022, https://www.mckinsey.com/featured-insights/diversity-and-inclusion/women-in-the-workplace

[36] *Are Men Really Talking Too Much? We've Done The Maths,* Stuff, March 2017, https://www.stuff.co.nz/life-style/life/89851118/are-men-really-talking-too-much-weve-done-the-maths

[37] *Ardern's Exit After 'Unprecedented' Threats Shows Toll Of Burnout For Women Leaders,* Axios, January 2023, https://www.axios.com/2023/01/19/jacinda-ardern-politics-women-threats-government

[38] *Silence, Woman: An Investigation Into Gendered Attacks Online*, Ellen Judson, Amelia Stewart, Josh Smith, Alex Krasodomski-Jones for Demos, October 2021, p.3 https://demos.co.uk/wp-content/uploads/2021/10/Silence-Woman.pdf

[39] *Ardern's Exit After 'Unprecedented' Threats Shows Toll Of Burnout For Women Leaders,* Axios, January 2023, https://www.axios.com/2023/01/19/jacinda-ardern-politics-women-threats-government

[40] *Love Island 2019: Is The Reality Show Affecting Male Body Image?*, Huffington Post, July 2019, https://www.huffingtonpost.co.uk/entry/love-island-2019-is-the-reality-show-affecting-male-body-image_uk_5cf61f85e4b0a1997b702181

[41] *Millions Of Men In The UK Affected By Body Image Issues – Mental Health Foundation Survey, Mental Health Foundation,* November 2019, https://www.mentalhealth.org.uk/about-us/news/millions-men-uk-affected-body-image-issues-mental-health-foundation-survey

[42] *Shouldergate: Why Do We Still Judge Women On What They Wear To Work?*, Yahoo Finance, February 2020, https://uk.finance.yahoo.com/news/shouldergate-why-do-we-still-judge-women-on-what-they-wear-to-work-060005611.html

[43] Why don't more men take their wives' last names? Nov 2022, https://www.washingtonpost.com/lifestyle/2022/11/22/married-men-taking-wifes-name/?utm_campaign=wp_post_most&utm_medium=email&utm_source=newsletter&wpisrc=nl_most&carta-url=httpspercent3Apercent2Fpercent2Fs2.washingtonpost.compercent2Fcar-ln-trpercent2F38654d8percent2F637d02737e2620469f19c976percent2F5f46973eae7e8a549a171430percent2F58percent2F72percent2F637d02737e2620469f19c976&wp_cu=f7c395230cec5e6e6cde7af5b65a45d8percent7CADCBC1A332090E3AE0530100007F15EE

[44] *Why Don't More Men Take Their Wives' Last Names?* Washington Post, November 2022, https://www.washingtonpost.com/lifestyle/2022/11/22/married-men-taking-wifes-name/?utm_campaign=wp_post_most&utm_medium=email&utm_source=newsletter&wpisrc=nl_most&carta-url=httpspercent3Apercent2Fpercent2Fs2.washingtonpost.compercent2Fcar-ln-trpercent2F38654d8percent2F637d02737e2620469f19c976percent2F5f46973eae7e8a549a171430percent2F58percent2F72percent2F637d02737e2620469f19c976&wp_cu=f7c395230cec5e6e6cde7af5b65a45d8percent7CADCBC1A332090E3AE0530100007F15EE

[45] *Can Playgrounds Be Sexist?* Visible Women With Caroline Criado Perez podcast, June 2022, https://uk-podcasts.co.uk/podcast/visible-women-with-caroline-criado-perez/2-can-playgrounds-be-sexist

[46] *One In Three Women Consciously Take Steps To Avoid Being Sexually Assaulted*, YouGov, February 2019, https://yougov.co.uk/topics/politics/articles-reports/2019/02/15/one-three-women-consciously-take-steps-avoid-attac

[47] *She-Hulk Claims She Controls Her Anger Infinitely More Than The Hulk,* YouTube, August 2022, https://www.youtube.com/watch?v=guYVmjX_AZI

[48] *She-Hulk: Attorney At Law & The Power Of Women,* The Female Lead, August 2022, https://www.thefemalelead.com/post/she-hulk-attorney-at-law-the-power-of-women

[49] *What Works: Gender Equality by Design*, Iris Bohnet, Belknap Press, 2018, p.203

[50] Ibid

[51] *Only 40 Percent Of UK Secondary Schools Offer Girls The Same Access To Football As Boys*, Marie Claire, Aug 2022, https://www.marieclaire.co.uk/life/health-fitness/access-to-football-as-a-girl-790926

[52] *Women-Led Startups Received Just 2.3percent Of VC Funding In 2020*, Harvard Business Review, February 2021, https://hbr.org/2021/02/women-led-startups-received-just-2-3-of-vc-funding-in-2020

[53] *UK VV & Female Founders Report,* British Business Bank, 2018, https://www.british-business-bank.co.uk/uk-vc-female-founders-report/

[54] *Ardern's Exit After 'Unprecedented' Threats Shows Toll Of Burnout For Women Leaders,* Axios, January 2023, https://www.axios.com/2023/01/19/jacinda-ardern-politics-women-threats-government

[55] *Silence, Woman: An Investigation Into Gendered Attacks Online*, Ellen Judson, Amelia Stewart, Josh Smith, Alex Krasodomski-Jones for Demos, October 2021, p.3 https://demos.co.uk/wp-content/uploads/2021/10/Silence-Woman.pdf

[56] *Two In Five Britons Think Championing Women's Equality Discriminates Against Men*, The Independent, March 2023, https://www-independent-co-uk.cdn.ampproject.org/c/s/www.independent.co.uk/news/uk/home-news/women-equality-andrew-tate-misogyny-b2296464.html?amp

[57] *Britons Increasingly Scared To Speak Out On Women's Rights, Data Shows*, King's College London, March 2023, https://www.kcl.ac.uk/news/britons-increasingly-scared-to-speak-out-on-womens-rights-data-shows

[58] Ibid

[59] Adam Grant on Twitter, February 2022, https://twitter.com/AdamMGrant/status/1496504345407414276

[60] *How to really know another person*, Hidden Brain podcast, September 2022, https://hiddenbrain.org/podcast/how-to-really-know-another-person/

[61] *Movies Starring Women Outperform Male-Led Titles At Box Office*, Study Finds, Variety, December 2018, https://variety.com/2018/film/box-office/female-led-movies-outperformed-male-box-office-1203086924/

[62] *Why Do So Few Men Read Books By Women?*, The Guardian, July 2021, https://www.theguardian.com/books/2021/jul/09/why-do-so-few-men-read-books-by-women

[63] *Women's Voices Are Missing In The Media – Including Them Could Generate Billions In Income*, The Conversation, January 2023, https://theconversation-com.cdn.ampproject.org/c/s/theconversation.com/amp/womens-voices-are-missing-in-the-media-including-them-could-generate-billions-in-income-196302

[64] *The News Industry Still Has A Gender Diversity Problem – Here's How To Make It More Inclusive*, World Economic Forum, January 2023, https://www.weforum.org/agenda/2023/01/news-industry-gender-diversity-problem-more-inclusive-davos-2023

[65] Ibid

[66] *Demonstrate An Understanding Of Women: 91% Say Advertisers Do Not Understand Them,* Dr John Carlson, September 2017, https://www.linkedin.com/pulse/91-say-advertisers-do-understand-them-d-john-carlson/

[67] *Women Control Only A Third Of Household Financial Assets In The United States - For Now,* McKinsey, August 2020, https://www.mckinsey.com/featured-insights/sustainable-inclusive-growth/chart-of-the-day/women-control-only-a-third-of-household-financial-assets-in-the-united-states-for-now

[68] *Statistics On The Purchasing Power Of Women*, Girlpower Marketing, 2020, https://girlpowermarketing.com/statistics-purchasing-power-women/

[69] Ibid

[70] *What Every Marketer Should Know About Women's Economic Power,* Forbes, October 2022, https://www.forbes.com/sites/bridgetbrennan/2022/10/20/what-every-marketer-should-know-about-womens-economic-power/?sh=4ad3e41c4d4c

[71] *Reputable Retailers Must Prioritise Diversity*, Retail Week, October 2017, https://www.retail-week.com/opinion/opinion-reputable-retailers-must-prioritise-diversity/7026325.article

[72] Ibid

ISSUE 6: Let's Talk About Sex

[1] Cindy Gallop is a figurehead in this area, and any of her talks about Make Love Not Porn are an education. For example *Porn and Social Sex with Cindy Gallop*, I Weigh with Jameela Jamil podcast, May 2022, https://podcasts.apple.com/no/podcast/p-n-and-social-sex-with-cindy-gallop/id1498855031?i=1000559794492

[2] Let's Talk About Sex, by Salt-n-Pepa, August 1991

[3] *One In Three Women Consciously Take Steps To Avoid Being Sexually Assaulted,* YouGov, February 2019 https://yougov.co.uk/topics/politics/articles-reports/2019/02/15/one-three-women-consciously-take-steps-avoid-attac

[4] *Violence Against Women: The Major Problem With Calling Male Violence An 'epidemic'* Stylist, February 2022, https://www.stylist.co.uk/health/women/male-violence-epidemic-language-problem/621828
[5] *Everyday Sexism,* Laura Bates, Simon & Schuster, 2015, p.347
[6] *Rape Case Horror As 300 Women Victims Every Day - And Only Tiny Fraction See Charge*, The Express, November 2022, https://www.express.co.uk/news/uk/1695964/rape-case-uk-statistics
[7] *Quick Facts About Sexual Assault In America*, Plan Street, May 2022, https://www.planstreetinc.com/quick-facts-about-sexual-assault-in-america/
[8] *We Are Writing To Ask You To Urgently Initiate A Statutory Inquiry Into Misogyny In The Police Force,* Women's Equality Party, March 2023, https://www.womensequality.org.uk/policemisogyny_letter
[9] *David Carrick Sentencing - Live: Rapist Officer 'faces Difficult Time In Prison For Many Years', Judge Says As He Gets 36 Life Sentences*, Sky News, February 2023, https://news.sky.com/story/david-carrick-sentencing-live-serial-rapist-police-officer-set-to-be-jailed-for-violent-and-brutal-sex-crimes-against-12-women-12804428#:~:text=Commissioner%20Sir%20Mark%20Rowley%20said,that%20led%20to%20his%20conviction.
[10] *We Are Writing To Ask You To Urgently Initiate A Statutory Inquiry Into Misogyny In The Police Force,* Women's Equality Party, March 2023, https://www.womensequality.org.uk/policemisogyny_letter
[11] *Former Female Inmates Speak About Widespread Sexual Abuse By Prison Staff,* ABC News, December 2022, https://abcnews.go.com/Politics/senate-report-documents-widespread-sexual-abuse-female-inmates/story?id=95157791
[12] *Latest Military Sexual Assault Report Shows 'Tragic' Rise in Cases, Pentagon Officials Say*, USNI News, September 2022, https://news.usni.org/2022/09/01/latest-military-sexual-assault-report-shows-tragic-rise-in-cases-pentagon-officials-say
[13] *Police Watchdog: Give Violence Against Women Same Priority As Terrorism,* The Guardian, September 2021, https://www.theguardian.com/society/2021/sep/17/watchdog-finds-staggering-variation-in-police-use-of-clares-law
[14] *Misogyny Fuels Violence Against Women. Should It Be a Hate Crime?* New York Times, March 2021, https://www.nytimes.com/2021/03/25/us/misogyny-violence-against-women-hate-crime.html
[15] *When Women are the Enemy: The Intersection of Misogyny and White Supremacy*, ADL, July 2018, https://www.adl.org/resources/report/when-women-are-enemy-intersection-misogyny-and-white-supremacy
[16] *Kanye West is the latest - and most famous - example of the misogyny-to-fascism pipeline,* Salon, October 2022 https://www.salon.com/2022/10/19/kanye-west-is-the-latest--and-most-famous--example-of-the-misogyny-to-fascism-pipeline/?utm_source=substack&utm_medium=email
[17] *Statistics About Rape, Sexual Assault And Sexual Abuse*, Rape Crisis England & Wales, September 2022, https://rapecrisis.org.uk/get-informed/statistics-sexual-violence/
[18] Census figures tell us there are 29 million adult men in England & Wales in 2021 of which almost 80 percent (23m) are age 18+: *Male & Female Populations*, Gov.uk, March 2023, https://www.ethnicity-facts-figures.service.gov.uk/uk-population-by-ethnicity/demographics/male-and-female-populations/latest#:~:text=The percent20data percent20shows percent20that percent3A,up percent2029.2 percent20million percent20(49.0 percent25)
[19] *Number Of Forcible Rape And Sexual Assault Victims In The United States From 1993 To 2020, By Sex*, Statista, December 2021, https://www.statista.com/statistics/251923/usa--reported-forcible-rape-cases-by-gender/
[20] *Latest Military Sexual Assault Report Shows 'tragic' Rise In Cases, Pentagon Officials Say*, USNI News, September 2022, https://news.usni.org/2022/09/01/latest-military-sexual-assault-report-shows-tragic-rise-in-cases-pentagon-officials-say
[21] *Losing It: Sex Education For The 21st Century*, Sophia Smith Galer, William Collins, 2022, p.179

[22] *Quick Facts About Sexual Assault In America*, Plan Street, May 2022, https://www.planstreetinc.com/quick-facts-about-sexual-assault-in-america/

[23] *A New Survey Finds 81 Percent Of Women Have Experienced Sexual Harassment*, NPR, February 2018, https://www.npr.org/sections/thetwo-way/2018/02/21/587671849/a-new-survey-finds-eighty-percent-of-women-have-experienced-sexual-harassment

[24] *Four-Fifths Of Young Women In The UK Have Been Sexually Harassed, Survey Finds*, The Guardian, March 2021, https://www.theguardian.com/world/2021/mar/10/almost-all-young-women-in-the-uk-have-been-sexually-harassed-survey-finds

[25] *Misogyny Fuels Violence Against Women. Should It Be a Hate Crime?* New York Times, March 2021, https://www.nytimes.com/2021/03/25/us/misogyny-violence-against-women-hate-crime.html

[26] Ibid

[27] *Women and the Criminal Justice System 2019*, Ministry of Justice, November 2020.

[28] *Sexualized Violence Statistics*, Cal Poly Humboldt, https://supportingsurvivors.humboldt.edu/statistics#:~:text=Anpercent20estimatedpercent2091perc ent25percent20ofpercent20victims,1percent20Thispercent20USpercent20Dept [NB rape in the US was defined by the DOJ in 2012 as "The penetration, no matter how slight, of the vagina or anus with any body part or object, or oral penetration by a sex organ of another person, without the consent of the victim' whereas in the UK it refers only to the penetration by a penis https://www.justice.gov/archives/opa/blog/updated-definition-rape]

[29] Angelina Jolie urges UN peacekeepers to crack down on sexual violence, The Guardian, November 2017, https://www.theguardian.com/world/2017/nov/15/angelina-jolie-un-sexual-violence-speech

[30] *Police Officer Called Rape A 'struggle Snuggle' In Messages To Wayne Couzens*, Metro, July 2022, https://metro.co.uk/2022/07/28/police-officer-called-rape-a-struggle-snuggle-in-whatsapp-messages-17086746/

[31] How Iran's security forces use rape to quell protests, CNN, November 2022, https://edition.cnn.com/interactive/2022/11/middleeast/iran-protests-sexual-assault/index.html

[32] *Locker room talk hurts men too*, Liz Plank's Airplane Mode, March 2023, https://open.substack.com/pub/lizplank/p/locker-room-talk-hurts-men-too?r=nayd0&utm_campaign=post&utm_medium=email

[33] Ibid

[34] *The Secret World Of Incels*, Channel 4, November 2022, https://www.channel4.com/programmes/the-secret-world-of-incels-untold/on-demand/73325-001

[35] Ibid

[36] *MP Jess Phillips In Web Plea 'after 600 Rape Threats'*, BBC News, June 2018, https://www.bbc.co.uk/news/uk-england-birmingham-44438468

[37] *The Authority Gap: Why Women Are Still Taken Less Seriously Than Men, And What We Can Do About It*, Mary Ann Sieghart, Doubleday, 2021, p.264

[38] *Everyday Sexism*, Laura Bates, Simon & Schuster, 2015, p.326

[39] *The Authority Gap: Why Women Are Still Taken Less Seriously Than Men, And What We Can Do About It*, Mary Ann Sieghart, Doubleday, 2021 p.265-6

[40] *'Let's Drown Her Before We Burn Her!!!' Dark Texts Johnny Depp Sent Actor Paul Bettany About Amber Heard Are Read Out In Court As He's Cross-Examined By Her Lawyer*, Daily Mail, April 2022, https://www.dailymail.co.uk/news/article-10739429/Lets-drown-burn-Sickening-texts-Johnny-Depp-sent-Amber-Heard.html

[41] *The #MeToo Movement: History, Sexual Assault Statistics, Impact*, Very Well Mind, April 2023, https://www.verywellmind.com/what-is-the-metoo-movement-4774817

[42] *Eleanor Williams Jailed Over False Rape Claims*, BBC News, March 2023, https://www.bbc.co.uk/news/uk-england-cumbria-64950862

[43] *Eleanor Williams Sentencing: Men Tried To Take Own Lives Over Rape Lies*, BBC News, March 2023, https://www.bbc.co.uk/news/uk-england-cumbria-64943465

[44] *Eleanor Williams: One High-Profile False Rape Case Is Not An Excuse To Stop Believing Women*, Glamour, March 2023, https://www.glamourmagazine.co.uk/article/eleanor-williams-false-rape-believing-women-opinion

[45] *Men Are More Likely To Be Raped Than Be Falsely Accused Of Rape*, 4 News Fact Check, October 2018, https://www.channel4.com/news/factcheck/factcheck-men-are-more-likely-to-be-raped-than-be-falsely-accused-of-rape

[46] False allegations of rape: Briefing Paper, September 2013 https://www.rapecrisisscotland.org.uk/files/false-allegations-bp-170913-1-1.pdf

[47] *Rape Case Horror As 300 Women Victims Every Day - And Only Tiny Fraction See Charge*, Rape Crisis Scotland, November 2022, https://www.express.co.uk/news/uk/1695964/rape-case-uk-statistics

[48] Quick Facts about Sexual Assault in America, Plan Street, May 2022, https://www.planstreetinc.com/quick-facts-about-sexual-assault-in-america/

[49] *A Good Bloke? The Bar Is Hanging Too F-King Low,* Mumbrella, January 2023, https://mumbrella-com-au.cdn.ampproject.org/c/s/mumbrella.com.au/a-good-bloke-the-bar-is-hanging-too-f-king-low-771108/amp

[50] *How Can We Create A Consent Culture? SBS New Docuseries Explores This And More,* Women's Agenda, March 2023, https://womensagenda.com.au/life/screen/how-can-we-create-a-consent-culture-sbs-new-docuseries-explores-this-and-more/

[51] *Britain's Biggest Police Force Is Racist, Sexist And Homophobic - Can It Change?* Guardian Today in Focus podcast, March 2023, https://www.theguardian.com/news/audio/2023/mar/22/britains-biggest-police-force-is-racist-sexist-and-homophobic-can-it-change-podcast

[52] *Misogyny Fuels Violence Against Women. Should It Be A Hate Crime?* New York Times, March 2021, https://www.nytimes.com/2021/03/25/us/misogyny-violence-against-women-hate-crime.html

[53] *Rape Survivor's £3,000 Bill For Lawyer Complaint,* BBC News, November 2022, https://www.bbc.co.uk/news/uk-scotland-glasgow-west-63675793

[54] *Rape Survivor Secretly Recorded Her Abuser's Confession,* BBC News, January 2023, https://www.bbc.co.uk/news/uk-scotland-64248542

[55] *Fight, Flight, Freeze, Or Fawn: How We Respond To Threats,* Simply Psychology, May 2023, https://www.simplypsychology.org/fight-flight-freeze-fawn.html

[56] *Tea And Consent,* Thames Valley Police, YouTube 2015, https://www.youtube.com/watch?v=pZwvrxVavnQ

[57] *Savanta study,* Sophia S Galer, Jan 2023, https://twitter.com/sophiasgaler/status/1620705494339031042

[58] *Fix The System Not The Women,* Laura Bates, Simon & Schuster, 2022, p.161

[59] Ibid

[60] *A UK Judge Just Said That Men Have A 'fundamental Human Right' To Sex With Their Wives',* Stylist, April 2019, https://www.stylist.co.uk/life/judge-men-fundamental-human-right-sex-with-wives/259465

[61] *What Is Sexual Consent?,* Rape Crisis England & Wales, 2023, https://rapecrisis.org.uk/get-informed/about-sexual-violence/sexual-consent/

[62] *UK Sexual Offences Act 2003,* HM Government, https://www.legislation.gov.uk/ukpga/2003/42/pdfs/ukpga_20030042_en.pdf

[63] *What Is Sexual Consent?,* Rape Crisis England & Wales, 2023, https://rapecrisis.org.uk/get-informed/about-sexual-violence/sexual-consent/

[64] *The History of the Clitoris,* Betwixt The Sheets: The History of Sex, Scandal & Society podcast, November 2022, https://podcasts.apple.com/gb/podcast/betwixt-the-sheets-the-history-of-sex-scandal-society/id1612090432?i=1000587439233

[65] *Losing It: Sex Education For The 21st Century,* Sophia Smith Galer, William Collins, 2022, p.69

[66] Ibid p.95

[67] *The Patriarchs: How Men Came To Rule,* Angela Saini, Fourth Estate, 2023, p.153

[68] *What Women Want: Why The Porn Industry Needs To Wake Up To Female Desire,* Stylist, 2017, https://www.stylist.co.uk/people/feminism/pornography-feminism-women-sex-men-make-love-not-porn-cindy-gallop-ask-a-feminist/10451

[69] *'It Stole My Soul': Readers On How Watching Porn At A Young Age Affected Their Life,* The Guardian, March 2023, https://www.theguardian.com/society/2023/mar/10/readers-how-watching-porn-young-age-affected-their-life?CMP=share_btn_tw

[70] *Pornography Survey Results,* YouGov, May 2022,
https://docs.cdn.yougov.com/xfgpv3ng6i/YouGovpercent20-
percent20Pornographypercent20Surveypercent20Results.pdf
[71] *Pornography 'Desensitising Young People',* BBC News, June 2016,
https://www.bbc.co.uk/news/education-36527681
[72] *A UK Survey Shows That A Third Of Women Under The Age Of 40 Have Been Nonconsensually Choked, Slapped, Gagged Or Spit On During Sex. Let's Look Into What's Behind That,* The News Movement, March 2023,
https://www.instagram.com/reel/CqfQg5TI3E_/?igshid=YmMyMTA2M2Y percent3D
[73] Ibid
[74] Ibid
[75] *Young Women And Anal Sex,* British Medical Journal, August 2022,
https://www.bmj.com/content/378/bmj.o1975.full
[76] Ibid
[77] Nonconsensual deepfake porn is an emergency that is ruining lives, The Guardian, April 2023,
https://www.theguardian.com/commentisfree/2023/apr/01/ai-deepfake-porn-fake-images
[78] *Sharing Pornographic Deepfakes Without Consent Could Be Made A Crime In England And Wales – Why Has It Taken This Long?* Glamour, November 2022,
https://www.glamourmagazine.co.uk/article/nudification-intimate-image-abuse
[79] Nonconsensual deepfake porn is an emergency that is ruining lives, The Guardian, April 2023,
https://www.theguardian.com/commentisfree/2023/apr/01/ai-deepfake-porn-fake-images
[80] *Sharing Pornographic Deepfakes Without Consent Could Be Made A Crime In England And Wales – Why Has It Taken This Long?* Glamour, November 2022,
https://www.glamourmagazine.co.uk/article/nudification-intimate-image-abuse
[81] Original source not known, but please let me know if this was you at @menemiesnomore so I can give you credit
[82] *More Than A Woman,* Caitlyn Moran, Ebury Press, 2021, p.113
[83] *Misogyny Fuels Violence Against Women. Should It Be A Hate Crime?* New York Times, March 2021, https://www.nytimes.com/2021/03/25/us/misogyny-violence-against-women-hate-crime.html
[84] *Fix The System Not The Women,* Laura Bates, Simon & Schuster, 2022, p.27
[85] *Nightcap - The Drink Spiking Prevention Scrunchie,* Amazon, 2023,
https://www.amazon.co.uk/nightcap-drink-spiking-prevention-scrunchie/dp/b08rf32y7n?th=1
[86] *Fix The System Not The Women,* Laura Bates, Simon & Schuster, 2022, p.107
[87] *Losing It: Sex Education For The 21st Century,* Sophia Smith Galer, William Collins, 2022, p.6
[88] *Savanta UK,* Sophia Smith Galer, February 2023,
https://twitter.com/sophiasgaler/status/1620707410112552960?lang=en
[89] *U.S. Teen Girls Experiencing Increased Sadness And Violence,* Centers for Disease Control & Prevention, February 2023 https://www.cdc.gov/media/releases/2023/p0213-yrbs.html
[90] Ibid
[91] *Sexual Harassment Is A Routine Part Of Life, Schoolchildren Tell Ofsted,* The Guardian, June 2021
https://www.theguardian.com/education/2021/jun/10/sexual-harassment-is-a-routine-part-of-life-schoolchildren-tell-ofsted
[92] *Girls Asked For Nudes By Up To 11 Boys A Night, Ofsted Finds,* BBC News, June 2021
https://www.bbc.co.uk/news/education-57411363
[93] *Sexual Harassment Is A Routine Part Of Life, Schoolchildren Tell Ofsted,* The Guardian, June 2021
https://www.theguardian.com/education/2021/jun/10/sexual-harassment-is-a-routine-part-of-life-schoolchildren-tell-ofsted
[94] *Fix The System Not The Women,* Laura Bates, Simon & Schuster, 2022, p.52
[95] Ibid
[96] *Losing It: Sex Education For The 21st Century,* Sophia Smith Galer, William Collins, 2022, p.95
[97] Ibid, p.98
[98] Ibid, pp 175, 167 & 169
[99] Ibid, p.6

[100] *Short Kings And Dating,* Curiously Media, November 2023, https://www.instagram.com/tv/CkykVd_Pd2m/?igshid=YmMyMTA2M2Ypercent3D
[101] *'Gay Glass Ceiling': Why More Feminine Men Get Passed Over For Leadership Roles,* The Guardian, January 2023, https://amp-theguardian-com.cdn.ampproject.org/c/s/amp.theguardian.com/lifeandstyle/2023/jan/30/gay-glass-ceiling-why-effeminate-men-get-passed-over-for-leadership-roles
[102] *Heartthrobs,* Betwixt The Sheets: The History of Sex, Scandal & Society podcast, November 2022, https://podcasts.apple.com/gb/podcast/betwixt-the-sheets-the-history-of-sex-scandal-society/id1612090432?i=1000586202231
[103] *Asexuality and Aromanticism with Yasmin Benoit,* I Weigh with Jameela Jamil podcast, February 2023, https://www.earwolf.com/episode/asexuality-and-aromanticism-with-yasmin-benoit/
[104] *Roman Kemp,* Happy Place podcast, October 2022, https://shows.acast.com/happy-place/episodes/roman-kemp

ISSUE 7: The Daddy Of All Roles

[1] *The Patriarchs: How Men Came To Rule,* Angela Saini, Fourth Estate, 2023, p.162
[2] Ibid
[3] *Having A Father Is A Human Right,* Fathers For Justice, 2023, https://www.fathers-4-justice.org/
[4] *Euripides, with an English translation,* David Kovacs, Harvard University Press, line 251
[5] *When Childbirth Was Natural, and Deadly,* Live Science, January 2009, https://www.livescience.com/3210-childbirth-natural-deadly.html
[6] *Maternal Mortality Rises By Nearly 20 Percent In UK, Report Finds,* The Guardian, November 2022, https://www.theguardian.com/society/2022/nov/10/sharp-rise-in-number-of-women-in-uk-dying-in-pregnancy-or-shortly-after
[7] *Black Maternal Health,* House of Commons Women and Equalities Committee, March 2023, https://committees.parliament.uk/publications/38989/documents/191706/default/
[8] *Wealthiest Black Moms More Likely To Die In Childbirth Than Poorest White Moms,* Fatherly, January 2023, https://www.fatherly.com/health/wealthiest-black-moms-more-likely-die-childbirth-than-poorest-white-moms-study
[9] *Doctors Who Want To Defy Abortion Laws Say It's Too Risky,* NPR, November 2022, https://www.npr.org/sections/health-shots/2022/11/23/1137756183/doctors-who-want-to-defy-abortion-laws-say-its-too-risky
[10] *Angry About Roe v. Wade? It's A Threat To Abortion Rights In The UK Too,* Refinery 29, May 2022, https://www.refinery29.com/en-gb/2022/05/10966788/roe-v-wade-abortion-rights-uk
[11] The anti-abortion lobby is on the rise in the UK. We can't get complacent, July 2022 https://www.gq-magazine.co.uk/politics/article/anti-abortion-campaigners-mps-uk
[12] *The Anti-Abortion Lobby Is On The Rise In The UK. We Can't Get Complacent,* GQ, July 2022, https://www.gq-magazine.co.uk/politics/article/anti-abortion-campaigners-mps-uk
[13] *Don't Be A Pro-Choice Softboy, Be A Good Man.* Liz Plank Airplane Mode, August 2022, https://lizplank.substack.com/p/dont-be-a-pro-choice-softboy
[14] *The Rise Of The Stay-At-Home Dad,* Forbes, December 2022, https://www.forbes.com/sites/jackkelly/2022/12/07/the-rise-of-the-stay-at-home-dad/
[15] *More Dads Are Choosing To Stay At Home With Their Kids. Will Covid-19 Accelerate This Trend?* CNBC, May 2021, https://www.cnbc.com/2021/05/07/stay-at-home-dads-were-on-the-rise-pre-pandemic-will-covid-accelerate-the-trend.html
[16] *'parental Leave System Is Broken': Number Of Fathers Taking Paternity Leave Plunges To '10-Year Low',* The Independent, August 2021, https://www.independent.co.uk/news/uk/home-news/paternity-leave-fathers-10-year-low-b1906074.html?r=65638
[17] *Fathers Seek More Home And Flexible Working To Maintain Covid Transformation In Childcare,* Fatherhood Institute, May 2021, http://www.fatherhoodinstitute.org/2021/fathers-seek-more-home-flexible-working-to-maintain-covid-transformation-in-childcare/

[18] *Fathers' Decline In Testosterone And Synchrony With Partner Testosterone During Pregnancy Predicts Greater Postpartum Relationship Investment,* Science Direct, April 2017, https://www.sciencedirect.com/science/article/abs/pii/S0018506X16301015?via percent3Dihub

[19] *Fatherhood Changes Men's Brains, According To Before-And-After MRI Scans,* USC Dornsife, November 2022, https://dornsife.usc.edu/news/stories/fatherhood-changes-mens-brains/

[20] Ibid

[21] *The Myth Of Equal Partnership,* Burnt Toast by Virginia Sole Smith, April 2023, https://virginiasolesmith.substack.com/p/the-myth-of-equal-partnership#details

[22] *Fatherhood Changes Men's Brains, According To Before-And-After MRI Scans,* USC Dornsife, November 2022, https://dornsife.usc.edu/news/stories/fatherhood-changes-mens-brains/

[23] *Primary Caregiver Father And Mothers Are Equally Competent,* National Fatherhood Initiative, March 2022, https://www.fatherhood.org/championing-fatherhood/fatherhood/primary-caregiver-fathers-and-mothers-are-equally-competent

[24] *Study Shows Moms Work The Equivalent Of 2.5 Full Time Jobs,* ABC News, March 2018, https://abc13.com/moms-motherhood-family-working/3238071/

[25] *We Need To Change The Way We Talk About Stay At Home Dads,* Parents, June 2023, https://www.parents.com/parenting/dads/issues-trends/we-need-to-change-the-way-we-talk-about-sahds/

[26] *Even When Women Make More Than Their Husbands, They Are Doing More Child Care And Housework,* The 19th, April 2023, https://19thnews-org.cdn.ampproject.org/c/s/19thnews.org/2023/04/even-when-women-make-more-than-their-husbands-they-are-doing-more-child-care-and-housework/?amp

[27] Ibid

[28] *Women Who Earn More Than Their Husbands Share What Their Marriages Are Really Like,* Buzzfeed News, April 2023, https://www-buzzfeednews-com.cdn.ampproject.org/c/s/www.buzzfeednews.com/amphtml/venessawong/women-who-earn-more-than-their-husbands-marriages

[29] *Fix The System Not The Women,* Laura Bates, Simon & Schuster, 2022, p.41

[30] *Women Providing Two-Thirds More Childcare Than Men During Lockdown, ONS Finds,* People Management, July 2020 https://www.peoplemanagement.co.uk/article/1742891/women-providing-two-thirds-more-childcare-than-men-during-lockdown

[31] *The State of Women… Isn't Working,* The Skimm, March 2023, https://www.theskimm.com/stateofwomen/harris-poll-data-2023

[32] *Even When Women Make More Than Their Husbands, They Are Doing More Child Care And Housework,* The 19th, April 2023, https://19thnews-org.cdn.ampproject.org/c/s/19thnews.org/2023/04/even-when-women-make-more-than-their-husbands-they-are-doing-more-child-care-and-housework/?amp

[33] *The Myth Of Equal Partnership,* Burnt Toast by Virginia Sole Smith, April 2023, https://virginiasolesmith.substack.com/p/the-myth-of-equal-partnership#details

[34] *Why Parenthood Is Good For Creativity,* Ad Age, March 2023, https://adage.com/article/opinion/why-parenthood-good-creativity-why-parenthood-good-creativity/2477151

[35] *Why Working Moms In America Are So Miserable,* Fast Company, February 2023, https://www.fastcompany.com/90843604/why-working-moms-in-america-are-so-miserable

[36] *Stefanie O'Connell Rodriguez,* The Female Quotient, February 2023, https://www.instagram.com/reel/CpLRc8zJKmt/?igshid=YmMyMTA2M2Y=

[37] Ibid

[38] Ibid

[39] *Congressman Wears Baby In Carrier During House Speaker Votes: 'guys Need To Do Our Part',* NBC New York, January 2023, https://www.nbcnewyork.com/news/national-international/congressman-wears-baby-in-carrier-during-house-speaker-votes-guys-need-to-do-our-part/4028919/?amp=1

[40] *MPs Should Not Bring Babies Into Commons, Says Cross-Party Review,* The Guardian, June 2022, https://www.theguardian.com/politics/2022/jun/30/mps-should-not-bring-babies-into-commons-says-cross-party-review

[41] *How Marriage Structure Influences Bias At Work,* The Gender Economy, January 2019, https://www.gendereconomy.org/how-marriage-structure-influences-bias-at-work/

[42] Ibid

[43] Ibid

[44] *Stefanie O'Connell Rodriguez,* The Female Quotient, February 2023, https://www.instagram.com/reel/CpLRc8zJKmt/?igshid=YmMyMTA2M2Y=

[45] *Gender Wage Gap Grows Year On Year After Childbirth As Mothers In Low-Hours Jobs See No Wage Progression,* Institute for Fiscal Studies, August 2016 https://www.ifs.org.uk/publications/8429

[46] Ibid

[47] *The Myth Of Equal Partnership,* Burnt Toast by Virginia Sole Smith, April 2023, https://virginiasolesmith.substack.com/p/the-myth-of-equal-partnership#details

[48] *The Effect Of Own And Spousal Parental Leave On Earnings,* Elly-Ann Johansson, Institute for Labour Market Policy Evaluation, March 2010, p.35 https://www.ifau.se/globalassets/pdf/se/2010/wp10-4-The-effect-of-own-and-spousal-parental-leave-on-earnings.pdf

[49] *Flexible Working Isn't A Perk For Women, It's A Necessity,* Stylist, February 2023, https://www.stylist.co.uk/life/careers/flexible-working-for-women-bill/764044

[50] *Emma Jarvis,* University of Warwick LinkedIn, March 2023, https://www.linkedin.com/posts/emmajarvismba_gender-iwd2023-genderequality-activity-7034799804186550272-Y_LO?utm_source=share&utm_medium=member_ios

[51] *Simply Telling Men That Their Peers Support Parental Leave And Flexible Working Increases Their Intention To Share Care,* The Behavioural Insights Team, June 2021, https://www.bi.team/blogs/simply-telling-men-that-their-peers-support-parental-leave-and-flexible-working-increases-their-intention-to-share-care/

[52] *Maternity Pay And Leave,* Gov.UK, May 2023, https://www.gov.uk/maternity-pay-leave/pay#:~:text=Statutory%20Maternity%20Pay%20(%20SMP%20)%20is,for%20the%20next%2033%20weeks

[53] *Shared Parental Leave And Pay,* May 2023, https://www.gov.uk/shared-parental-leave-and-pay

[54] *Simply Telling Men That Their Peers Support Parental Leave And Flexible Working Increases Their Intention To Share Care,* The Behavioural Insights Team, June 2021, https://www.bi.team/blogs/simply-telling-men-that-their-peers-support-parental-leave-and-flexible-working-increases-their-intention-to-share-care/

[55] *These Countries Have The Most Expensive Childcare,* World Economic Forum, April 2019, https://www.weforum.org/agenda/2019/04/these-countries-have-the-most-expensive-childcare/

[56] *Among 41 countries, only U.S. lacks paid parental leave,* Pew Research Center, December 2019, https://www.pewresearch.org/short-reads/2019/12/16/u-s-lacks-mandated-paid-parental-leave/

[57] *Men Should Take Parental Leave - Here's Why,* Forbes, May 2018, https://www.forbes.com/sites/shelleyzalis/2018/05/03/why-mandatory-parental-leave-is-good-for-business/?sh=599455849ded

[58] *Four In 10 Dads Can't Afford Shared Parental Leave,* Personnel Today, April 2020, https://www.personneltoday.com/hr/four-in-10-dads-cant-afford-shared-parental-leave/

[59] *Employers Can Enhance Maternity Pay And Not Shared Parental Pay,* Personnel Today, May 2019, https://www.personneltoday.com/hr/hextall-v-leicestershire-ali-v-capita-enhanced-maternity-pay-shared-parental-pay-court-of-appeal/

[60] *Shared Parental Leave Uptake Still 'exceptionally Low', Research Finds,* People Management, September 2020, https://www.peoplemanagement.co.uk/article/1747108/shared-parental-leave-uptake-still-exceptionally-low#gref

[61] *Working Dads Employer Awards,* Elliott Rae, April 2023, https://www.linkedin.com/posts/elliott-rae-a3a469144_workingdads-flexibleworking-equalparentalleave-activity-7052608408956366848-0qxJ?utm_source=share&utm_medium=member_ios

[62] *Men Should Take Parental Leave - Here's Why*, Forbes, May 2018, https://www.forbes.com/sites/shelleyzalis/2018/05/03/why-mandatory-parental-leave-is-good-for-business/?sh=599455849ded

[63] *Fatherhood Changes Men's Brains*, Neuroscience News, December 2022, https://neurosciencenews.com/fatherhood-men-brain-21997/

[64] *Simply Telling Men That Their Peers Support Parental Leave And Flexible Working Increases Their Intention To Share Care,* The Behavioural Insights Team, June 2021, https://www.bi.team/blogs/simply-telling-men-that-their-peers-support-parental-leave-and-flexible-working-increases-their-intention-to-share-care/

[65] Ibid

[66] *Anger As Tech Executive Calls Pete Buttigieg A 'loser' For Taking Paternity Leave,* The Independent, October 2021 https://www.independent.co.uk/news/world/americas/us-politics/palantir-founder-buttigieg-paternity-leave-b1947040.html

[67] *Why Gender Equality Is Good For Everyone - Men Included,* Michael Kimmel, TED Women, September 2015, https://www.ted.com/talks/michael_kimmel_why_gender_equality_is_good_for_everyone_men_included

[68] *For the Love of Men: From Toxic to a More Mindful Masculinity,* Liz Plank, Macmillan, 2019, p.118

[69] Ibid

[70] *Learning From Mum: Cross-National Evidence Linking Maternal Employment and Adult Children's Outcome*s, Kathleen L. McGinn, Mayra Ruiz Castro and Elizabeth Long Lingo, Harvard Business School, June 2019, https://www.hbs.edu/faculty/Pages/item.aspx?num=53811

[71] *We Need To Change the Way We Talk About Stay-at-Home Dads,* Parents, June 2023, https://www.parents.com/parenting/dads/issues-trends/we-need-to-change-the-way-we-talk-about-sahds/

[72] *The Truth Will Set You Free, But First It Will Piss You Off! Thoughts on Life, Love, And Rebellion,* Gloria Steinem, Random House, 2019, p39

[73] *Breaking The Norm, Unleashing Australia's Economic Potentia*l, Deloitte, November 2022, https://www2.deloitte.com/au/en/pages/economics/articles/breaking-norm-unleashing-australia-economic-potential.html

[74] *Hysterical: Exploding The Myth Of Gendered Emotions*, Pragya Agarwal, Canongate Books, 2022, p.258

[75] *The Choice Of Parenthood With Ruby Warrington,* I Weigh with Jameela Jamil podcast, March 2023, https://www.earwolf.com/episode/the-choice-of-parenthood-with-ruby-warrington/

[76] *Outrageous! The Story Of Section 28 And Britain's Battle For LGBT Education,* Paul Baker, Reaktion Books, 2023, p.11

[77]*How Millennial Men Can Help Break the Glass Ceiling,* Nov 2017, Boston Consulting Group, https://www.bcg.com/publications/2017/people-organization-behavior-culture-how-millennial-men-can-help-break-glass-ceiling

[78]*International Women's Day 2023*, Global Institute for Women's Leadership and King's College London, March 2023, https://www.kcl.ac.uk/giwl/assets/ipsos-giwl-iwd-survey-2023.pdf p.15

[79] Ibid

[80] Ibid

[81] *Britons Increasingly Scared To Speak Out On Women's Rights, Data Shows,* King's College London, March 2023, https://www.kcl.ac.uk/news/britons-increasingly-scared-to-speak-out-on-womens-rights-data-shows

[82] Ibid

[83]*The Importance of Fathers for Child Development,* Psychology Today, June 2021, *https://www.psychologytoday.com/gb/blog/parenting-and-culture/202106/the-importance-fathers-child-development*

[84] National Childbirth Trust, a UK organisation that runs antenatal and postnatal classes for parents-to-be and new parents.

[85] The conversation that people of colour have with their children that white parents are privileged enough to never have to, about how they'll experience so much more danger and difficulty in the

world purely because of their race; and the effort they'll need to put into managing those micro and macro-aggressions.

ISSUE 8: Danger, Women At Work

[1] Dolly Parton, 9 to 5, 1980, RCA Studios, Nashville

[2] *The Patriarchs: How Men Came To Rule*, Angela Saini, Fourth Estate, 2023, p.172

[3] And of course, millions of women as well as men throughout history have been forced into work with no pay at all.

[4] *Women's Work*, BBC History, March 2011, https://www.bbc.co.uk/history/british/victorians/womens_work_01.shtml

[5] *Desiree Adaway,* Principle at The Adaway Group, https://www.linkedin.com/posts/desiree-adaway-4373265_if-this-month-aint-intersectional-and-liberatory-activity-7045363278184677376-e0wB?utm_source=share&utm_medium=member_desktop

[6] Ibid

[7] *Facts About Sex Work,* English Collective of Prostitutes, 2023, https://prostitutescollective.net/facts-about-sex-work-sheet/

[8] *Companies With Female Leaders Outperform Those Dominated By Men, Data Shows*, The Guardian, March 2022, https://www.theguardian.com/business/2022/mar/06/companies-with-female-leaders-outperform-those-dominated-by-men-data-shows

[9] *Gender Equity For Better Business*, Forbes, January 2023, https://www-forbes-com.cdn.ampproject.org/c/s/www.forbes.com/sites/forbesbusinesscouncil/2023/01/05/gender-equity-for-better-business/amp/

[10] Ibid

[11] Ibid

[12] Ibid

[13] *When Women Lead, Firms Win,* S&P Global, October 2019, https://www.spglobal.com/en/research-insights/featured/special-editorial/when-women-lead-firms-win

[14] *Female-Managed Us Funds Outperform All-Male Rivals*, Financial Times, September 2020, https://www.ft.com/content/021a1b60-a5fa-42ad-83b4-482268cac7ac

[15] *New Research: Women More Effective Than Men In All Leadership Measures*, Forbes, March 2023, https://www-forbes-com.cdn.ampproject.org/c/s/www.forbes.com/sites/kevinkruse/2023/03/31/new-research-women-more-effective-than-men-in-all-leadership-measures/amp/

[16] *5 Reasons Why All Of My Investments Have Been In Women-Founded Companies*, Daria Burke, March 2023, https://www.linkedin.com/posts/dariaburke_startups-funding-investing-activity-7037505356305993728-Abtc?utm_source=share&utm_medium=member_ios

[17] *Difficulty Hiring Staff Hits A Peak With 93% Of Employers Facing Skills Shortages,* SIA, December 2022, https://www2.staffingindustry.com/eng/Editorial/Daily-News/UK-Difficulty-hiring-staff-hits-a-peak-with-93-of-employers-facing-skills-shortages-63855

[18] *How Colorism Affects Women At Work* by Ruchika Tulshyan, Harvard Business Review, April 2023 https://hbr.org/2023/04/how-colorism-affects-women-at-work

[19] *Statistics On The Purchasing Power Of Women*, Girlpower Marketing, 2020, https://girlpowermarketing.com/statistics-purchasing-power-women/

[20] *Women And Money: Busting The Money Myths*, Forbes, October 2021, https://www.forbes.com/sites/melissahouston/2021/10/06/women-and-money-busting-the-money-myths/

[21] *20 Facts And Figures To Know When Marketing To Women*, Forbes, May 2019, https://www.forbes.com/sites/forbescontentmarketing/2019/05/13/20-facts-and-figures-to-know-when-marketing-to-women/?sh=1c1bd3c91297

[22] *Statistics On The Purchasing Power Of Women*, Girlpower Marketing, 2020, https://girlpowermarketing.com/statistics-purchasing-power-women/

[23] *2019 Home Buyers And Sellers Generational Trends Report*, National Association of Realtors, April 2019, p.11,

https://docs.google.com/viewerng/viewer?url=https://www.nar.realtor/sites/default/files/documents/2019-home-buyer-and-seller-generational-trends-04-03-2019.pdf

[24] *Gender Parity Accelerators, 2023*, Accelerators Network, 2023, https://initiatives.weforum.org/accelerators-network/gender-parity

[25] *What Is Equal Pay?*, Equality & Human Rights Commission, July 2021, https://www.equalityhumanrights.com/en/advice-and-guidance/what-equal-pay

[26] *The FTSE 100's First All-Female Top Team Is Shamefully Overdue*, Raconteur, February 2023, https://www.raconteur.net/leadership/tse-100s-first-female-leadership-team-overdue/

[27] Ibid

[28] *The 50% CEO Playbook: Getting To Proportionate Representation In The Top Job And Why It Matters*, WACL, April 2023, https://wacl.info/wp-content/uploads/2023/04/PUBLISHED-WACL_PLAYBOOK_2023.pdf

[29] *Less Than A Third Of FTSE 100 Executives Are Women*, Board Agenda, March 2023, https://boardagenda.com/2023/03/09/less-than-a-third-of-ftse-100-executives-are-women/

[30] Ibid

[31] Meet The FTSE 100 CEOs, Raconteur, May 2023, https://www.raconteur.net/ceo-index/ftse-100-ceos-in-numbers/#diversity

[32] *The FTSE 100's First All-Female Top Team Is Shamefully Overdue*, Raconteur, February 2023, https://www.raconteur.net/leadership/tse-100s-first-female-leadership-team-overdue/

[33] Ibid

[34] *Companies With Female Leaders Outperform Those Dominated By Men, Data Shows*, The Guardian, March 2022, .https://www.theguardian.com/business/2022/mar/06/companies-with-female-leaders-outperform-those-dominated-by-men-data-shows

[35] *Women Still Struggle To Access VC Funds. What Needs To Change?* Vogue Business, April 2022, https://www.voguebusiness.com/companies/women-still-struggle-to-access-vc-funds-what-needs-to-change

[36] *There Are More Black Female Entrepreneurs Than Ever – So Why Do They Struggle To Get Funding?* The Guardian, October 2020, https://www.theguardian.com/careers/2020/oct/29/there-are-more-black-female-entrepreneurs-than-ever-so-why-do-they-struggle-to-get-funding

[37] Ibid

[38] *20 Facts And Figures To Know When Marketing To Women*, Forbes, May 2019, https://www.forbes.com/sites/forbescontentmarketing/2019/05/13/20-facts-and-figures-to-know-when-marketing-to-women/?sh=1c1bd3c91297

[39] *There Are More Black Female Entrepreneurs Than Ever – So Why Do They Struggle To Get Funding?* The Guardian, October 2020, https://www.theguardian.com/careers/2020/oct/29/there-are-more-black-female-entrepreneurs-than-ever-so-why-do-they-struggle-to-get-funding

[40] *Woman-Owned Businesses Are Growing 2X Faster On Average Than All Businesses Nationwide*, Business Wire, Sept 2019, https://www.businesswire.com/news/home/20190923005500/en/Woman-Owned-Businesses-Growing-2X-Faster-Average-Businesses

[41] *Women CEOs Of The S&P 500*, Catalyst, February 2023, https://www.catalyst.org/research/women-ceos-of-the-sp-500/

[42] *2022 S&P 500 Board Diversity Snapshot*, Spencer Stuart, June 2022, https://www.spencerstuart.com/-/media/2022/june/diversitysnapshot/sp500_board_diversity_snapshot_2022.pdf

[43] *Women In The Workplace 2022*, McKinsey, October 2022, Women in the Workplace, McKinsey & LeanIn, October 2022, p.8 https://www.mckinsey.com/~/media/mckinsey/featured%20insights/diversity%20and%20inclusion/women%20in%20the%20workplace%202022/women-in-the-workplace-2022.pdf

[44] Ibid

[45] Ibid

[46] *The State Of Black Women In Corporate America*, Lean In, 2022, https://leanin.org/research/state-of-black-women-in-corporate-america/section-2-support-at-work

[47] *How Colorism Affects Women At Work* by Ruchika Tulshyan, Harvard Business Review, April 2023 https://hbr.org/2023/04/how-colorism-affects-women-at-work

[48] *What Works: Gender Equality by Design*, Iris Bohnet, Belknap Press, 2018, p.25-7

[49] *The State Of Black Women In Corporate America*, Lean In, 2022,
https://leanin.org/research/state-of-black-women-in-corporate-america/section-2-support-at-work
[50] Ibid
[51] Ibid
[52] *Why We Should Be More Sexist*, Tomas Chamorro-Premuzic, TEDx Cambridge, June 2019,
https://youtu.be/VOnNDiOtBgk
[53] *Why Do So Many Incompetent Men Become Leaders? (And How To Fix It)*, Tomas Chamorro-Premuzic, Harvard Business Review Press, 2019, *p.10*
[54] *Why Do So Many Incompetent Men Become Leaders? By Tomas Chamorro-Premuzic*, Harvard Business Review, August 2013 https://hbr.org/2013/08/why-do-so-many-incompetent-men
[55] Ibid
[56] *When Women Lead, Workplaces Should Listen*, McKinsey, 2019,
https://www.mckinsey.com/~/media/McKinsey/Featured%20Insights/Leadership/When%20wome
n%20lead%20workplaces%20should%20listen/%20When-women-lead-workplacess-should-listen-
vF.pdf
[57] *Stop Telling Women They Have Imposter Syndrome*, Harvard Business Review, February 2021,
https://hbr-org.cdn.ampproject.org/c/s/hbr.org/amp/2021/02/stop-telling-women-they-have-
imposter-syndrome
[58] *Why Do So Many Incompetent Men Become Leaders,* Tomas Chamorro-Premuzic, Harvard Business Review Press, 2019, p.13
[59] Ibid, p.14
[60] Ibid, p.173
[61] *Why We Should Be More Sexist,* Tomas Chamorro-Premuzic, TEDx Cambridge, June 2019,
https://youtu.be/VOnNDiOtBgk
[62] *Why Do So Many Incompetent Men Become Leaders? (And How To Fix It),* Tomas Chamorro-Premuzic, Harvard Business Review Press, 2019, p.10
[63] *Women In The Workplace 2022*, McKinsey, 2022,
https://www.mckinsey.com/~/media/mckinsey/featured%20insights/diversity%20and%20inclusion
/women%20in%20the%20workplace%202022/women-in-the-workplace-2022.pdf
[64] *Why Do So Many Incompetent Men Become Leaders? (And How To Fix It),* Tomas Chamorro-Premuzic, Harvard Business Review Press, 2019, p.8
[65] Ibid, pp.94-5
[66] Ibid, p3.4
[67] *Daniel Kahneman: 'What would I eliminate if I had a magic wand? Overconfidence'*, The Guardian, July 2015, https://www.theguardian.com/books/2015/jul/18/daniel-kahneman-books-interview
[68] *Gender Equality For Better Business*, Forbes, Jan 2023 https://www-forbes-
com.cdn.ampproject.org/c/s/www.forbes.com/sites/forbesbusinesscouncil/2023/01/05/gender-
equity-for-better-business/amp/
[69] *Proof Versus Potential: Why Women Must Work Harder To Move Up*, BBC, February 2022
https://www.bbc.com/worklife/article/20220222-proof-verus-potential-problem
[70] *Fix The System Not The Women*, Laura Bates, Simon & Schuster, 2022, p.45
[71] Ibid
[72] *The 50% CEO Playbook Getting To Proportionate Representation In The Top Job And Why It Matters*, WACL, April 2023, https://wacl.info/wp-content/uploads/2023/04/PUBLISHED-
WACL_PLAYBOOK_2023.pdf
[73] *Women in the Workplace 2022*, McKinsey, October 2022,
https://www.mckinsey.com/~/media/mckinsey/featured%20insights/diversity%20and%20inclusion
/women%20in%20the%20workplace%202022/women-in-the-workplace-2022.pdf
[74] *Lack Of Period Workplace Policies Costing Businesses Billions*, HR Review, August 2021
https://www.hrreview.co.uk/hr-news/lack-of-period-workplace-policies-costing-businesses-
billions/137195
[75] Ibid
[76] *Childcare Is A Business Issue,* Harvard Business Review, April 2021
https://substack.com/redirect/5934a580-e35a-479a-bf99-
8ae2a27224be?j=eyJ1IjoibmF5ZDAifQ.iBrqlGceIzjCJ9gV4gUTtyMxBg9_BSdTXqr4gtGBIZU

[77] *Why Childcare Is A Business Issue*, CBI, February 2023, https://www.cbi.org.uk/articles/why-childcare-is-a-business-issue/

[78] *Study Shows The Staggering Cost Of Menopause For Women In The Workforce,* April 2023, https://www.nytimes.com/2023/04/28/well/live/menopause-symptoms-work-women.html?smid=nytcore-ios-share&referringSource=articleShare

[79] *Women's Health At Work, Why It's Time For An Honest Appraisal*, Women's Health, July 2022, https://www.womenshealthmag.com/uk/health/female-health/a40480855/why-womens-health-at-work-matters/

[80] *Flexible Working: The Business Case.* CIPD, November 2018, https://www.cipd.org/globalassets/media/knowledge/knowledge-hub/tools/flexible-working-business-case_tcm18-52768.pdf

[81] *Masculinity In The Workplace 2022 Research*, Token Man & The Hobbs Consultancy, 2022, .https://static1.squarespace.com/static/598d8fb5e3df28d7f216e464/t/640204584e4d6840e63d6871/1677853788167/MasculinityInTheWorkplace2023_Digital.pdf

[82] *Interrupting Sexism At Work: How Men Respond In A Climate Of Silence*, Catalyst, June 2020, https://www.catalyst.org/research/interrupting-sexism-silence/

[83] *Research: Men Are Worse Allies Than They Think*, HBR, October 2022, https://hbr.org/2022/10/research-men-are-worse-allies-than-they-think

[84] *Interrupting Sexism At Work: How Men Respond In A Climate Of Silence*, Catalyst, June 2020, https://www.catalyst.org/research/interrupting-sexism-silence/

[85] *11 Key Diversity & Inclusion Statistics For The Workplace*, Bonusly, Jan 2023, https://blog.bonus.ly/diversity-inclusion-statistics

[86] *Are Women Being Excluded?* Huffington Post, December 2013 https://www.huffpost.com/entry/are-women-being-excluded_b_4377547

[87] *Men Are 'Worse Allies Than They Think' In The Workplace, Study Finds*, The Independent, October 2022, https://www.independent.co.uk/life-style/women/men-women-gender-equality-work-b2198833.html

[88] *Research: Men Are Worse Allies Than They Think*, HBR, October 2022, https://hbr.org/2022/10/research-men-are-worse-allies-than-they-think

[89] *Men Are 'Worse Allies Than They Think' In The Workplace, Study Finds*, The Independent, October 2022, https://www.independent.co.uk/life-style/women/men-women-gender-equality-work-b2198833.html

[90] *Masculinity In The Workplace 2023*, Token Man and Hobbs Consulting, https://static1.squarespace.com/static/598d8fb5e3df28d7f216e464/t/640204584e4d6840e63d6871/1677853788167/MasculinityInTheWorkplace2023_Digital.pdf

[91] Ibid

[92] *State Of American Men 2023: From Crisis And Confusion To Hope,* Equimundo 2023, p.3, https://www.equimundo.org/wp-content/uploads/2023/05/STATE-OF-AMERICAN-MEN-2023.pdf

[93] Ibid, p.4

[94] Ibid, p.20

[95] *The 50% CEO Playbook: Getting To Proportionate Representation In The Top Job And Why It Matters*, April 2023, https://wacl.info/wp-content/uploads/2023/04/PUBLISHED-WACL_PLAYBOOK_2023.pdf

[96] *PwC 2022 Annual Corporate Directors Survey*, PWC, October 2022 https://www.pwc.com/us/en/services/governance-insights-center/assets/pwc-2022-annual-corporate-directors-survey.pdf

[97] *Economic Gains From Gender Inclusion: Even Greater Than You Thought,* IMF, November 2018, https://www.imf.org/en/Blogs/Articles/2018/11/28/blog-economic-gains-from-gender-inclusion-even-greater-than-you-thought

[98] *From Andrew Tate To Jordan Peterson, A Phoney Zero-Sum-Game Argument Sits At The Heart Of Anti-Feminist Backlash*, The Conversation, November 2022, https://theconversation-com.cdn.ampproject.org/c/s/theconversation.com/amp/from-andrew-tate-to-jordan-peterson-a-phoney-zero-sum-game-argument-sits-at-the-heart-of-anti-feminist-backlash-194665

[99] *The World Bank In Gender*, The World Bank, April 2023, https://www.worldbank.org/en/topic/gender/overview

[100] *The Economic Benefits Of Gender Parity*, McKinsey, March 2016,
https://www.mckinsey.com/mgi/overview/in-the-news/the-economic-benefits-of-gender-parity
[101] *How To Design Gender Bias Out Of Your Workplace*, Sara Sanford, TEDx, February 2020,
https://www.ted.com/talks/sara_sanford_how_to_design_gender_bias_out_of_your_workplace/tran
script?utm_id=linkedin.com
[102] *Diversity In Advertising. How To Get It Right?* System 1, July 2021,
https://system1group.com/resources/diversity
[103] Ibid
[104] *The Stereotyping Of Women In Ads Is Getting Worse*, The Drum, March 2023,
https://www.thedrum.com/news/2023/03/08/the-stereotyping-women-ads-getting-worse
[105] Ibid
[106] *Brandsplaining: Why Marketing is (Still) Sexist and How to Fix It*, Jane Cunningham & Phillipa
Roberts, Penguin, 2021, p.79
[107] *Women's Voices Are Missing In The Media – Including Them Could Generate Billions In
Income*, The Conversation, January 2023, https://theconversation-
com.cdn.ampproject.org/c/s/theconversation.com/amp/womens-voices-are-missing-in-the-media-
including-them-could-generate-billions-in-income-196302
[108] *The News Industry Still Has A Gender Diversity Problem - Here's How To Make It More
Inclusive,* January 2023,
https://www.weforum.org/agenda/2023/01/news-industry-gender-diversity-problem-more-
inclusive-davos-2023
[109] *Wake Up And See The Women: Wealth Management's Underserved Segment*, McKinsey, June
2022, https://www.mckinsey.com/industries/financial-services/our-insights/wake-up-and-see-the-
women-wealth-managements-underserved-segment
[110] *At The Sports Bra In Portland, Women Athletes (And Their Fans) Take Center Stage*, Vogue,
June 2022, https://www.vogue.com/article/at-the-sports-bra-in-portland-women-athletes-and-their-
fans-take-center-stage
[111] Breaking Stereotypes And Blazing The Trail For Women In The Auto Industry!, The Female
Quotient, May 2023, https://www.linkedin.com/posts/femalequotient_breaking-stereotypes-and-
blazing-the-trail-activity-7063944501454663680-
NhwK/?utm_source=share&utm_medium=member_ios
[112] Annie Mac Announces Ten 7 Pm To Midnight Parties Across UK For 2023, DJ Magazine,
December 2022,
https://djmag.com/news/annie-mac-announces-ten-7-pm-midnight-parties-across-uk-2023
[113] *Changing The Narrative For Women*, Hello Sunshine,2023, https://hello-sunshine.com/
[114] *Reese Witherspoon's Hello Sunshine Sold For $900 Million To Media Company Backed By
Blackstone*, Variety, August 2021,
https://variety.com/2021/film/news/reese-witherspoon-hello-sunshine-sold-1235032618/
[115] *Make The First Move*, Bumble, 2023, https://bumble.com/en/
[116] *Market Capitalization Of Bumble (BMBL)*, May 2023,
https://companiesmarketcap.com/bumble/marketcap/
[117] This misuse of the term diverse to signal an individual rather than a group was surprisingly
commonplace.
[118] In the 1980s the clothing brand Benetton was famed for creating ads featuring a line-up of men
and women of different races and ethnicities, with the strapline 'United Colours Of Benetton.'
[119] 'Public school' in Britain refers to the most elite private schools, whereas what most other
territories would describe as public schools are called state schools in the UK.
[120] *Shattering The Glass Screen*, McKinsey, February 2020,
https://www.mckinsey.com/industries/technology-media-and-telecommunications/our-
insights/shattering-the-glass-screen
[121] Ibid
[122] Ibid
[123] *2022 S&P 500 Board Diversity Snapshot*, Spencer Stuart, June 2022,
https://www.spencerstuart.com/-
/media/2022/june/diversitysnapshot/sp500_board_diversity_snapshot_2022.pdf

[124] *The Straight, White, Middle-Class Man Needs to Be Dethroned,* The New Republic, October 2014, https://newrepublic.com/article/119799/straight-white-middle-class-default-man-needs-be-dethroned

[125] *Sexist Military Language Infiltrates Business Culture, Making It Tougher For Women To Rise In The Ranks,* Inc, January 2020, https://www.inc.com/soren-kaplan/sexist-military-language-infiltrates-business-culture-making-it-tougher-for-women-to-rise-in-ranks.html

EPILOGUE: What's The End Game?

[1] *As a Woman: What I Learned about Power, Sex, and the Patriarchy After I Transitioned,* Paula Stone Williams, Atria Books, 2021, p.143

[2] Ibid, p.141

[3] *The Transgender Issue: An Argument for Justice,* Shon Faye, Penguin, 2022

[4] *As a Woman: What I Learned about Power, Sex, and the Patriarchy After I Transitioned,* Paula Stone Williams, Atria Books, 2021

[5] *Transitional: In One Way or Another, We All Transition,* Munroe Bergdorf, Bloomsbury Tonic, 2023

[6] *None of the Above: Reflections on Life Beyond the Binary,* Travis Alabanza, Canongate Books, 2023

[7] *Beyond the Gender Binary (Pocket Change Collective),* Alok Vaid-Menon, Penguin Workshop, 2020

[8] *Outrageous! The Story of Section 28 and Britain's Battle for LGBT Education,* Paul Baker, Reaktion Books, 2023

[9] *None of the Above: Reflections on Life Beyond the Binary,* Travis Alabanza, Canongate Books, 2023, p.59

[10] *Invisible Women: Exposing Data Bias in a World Designed for Men,* Caroline Criado Perez, Penguin, 2019, p.10

[11] *The Wolf's Closest Relatives Might Surprise You,* National Purebred Dog Day, June 2018, https://nationalpurebreddogday.com/the-wolfs-closest-relatives-might-surprise-you/

[12] Chimamanda Ngozi Adichie: I Became Black in America, JSTOR Daily, August 2018, https://daily.jstor.org/chimamanda-ngozi-adichie-i-became-black-in-america/

[13] The term 'queer' is also often used to encompass the whole spectrum of sexual orientations and gender identities that sit outside the cis-het gender norms.

[14] *The Transgender Issue: An Argument for Justice,* Shon Faye, Penguin, 2022, p.223

[15] See Issue 4 on sex and Issue 6 on competitiveness for data on how the overwhelming majority of sexual and violent crimes are committed by men, whatever the gender of the victim; and on how men who feel their masculinity is being threatened or questioned often behave more aggressively in response.

[16] Lesbians, of course, face both sexist and homophobic microaggressions

[17] *Why proposed laws targeting drag shows are proliferating in America,* Economist, February 2023, https://www.economist.com/united-states/2023/02/12/why-proposed-laws-targeting-drag-shows-are-proliferating-in-america?utm_medium=cpc.adword.pd&utm_source=google&ppccampaignID=17210591673&ppc adID=&utm_campaign=a.22brand_pmax&utm_content=conversion.direct-response.anonymous&gclid=CjwKCAjwhJukBhBPEiwAniIcNfLaM9NBjtKk8POjVxtLMfeQ9S8 OwlP3C0EQBT5ldW-6yTZ1hFQ8phoCQvIQAvD_BwE&gclsrc=aw.ds

[18] *The Transgender Issue: An Argument for Justice,* Shon Faye, Penguin, 2022, p.xvi

[19] *I Weigh with Jameela Jamil* podcast, June 2020, https://www.earwolf.com/episode/alok/

[20] *None of the Above: Reflections on Life Beyond the Binary,* Travis Alabanza, Canongate Books, 2023, p.38

[21] *The Transgender Issue: An Argument for Justice,* Shon Faye, Penguin, 2022, p.xix

[22] What's Intersex? Planned Parenthood, 2023, https://www.plannedparenthood.org/learn/gender-identity/sex-gender-identity/whats-intersex#:~:text=Intersex%20is%20a%20general%20term,male%E2%80%9D%20or%20%E2%80%80 %9Cfemale%E2%80%9D

[23] Ibid

[24] *LOL: Piers Morgan UPSETS Woke Guy After Saying He Can Identify As A Penguin*, Young America's Foundation, April 2023,
https://www.youtube.com/watch?v=W_n9VdwAQQU

[25] *The Transgender Issue: An Argument for Justice,* Shon Faye, Penguin, 2022, p.86

[26] *The Transgender Issue: An Argument for Justice,* Shon Faye, Penguin, 2022, p.95

[27] *Detransition Facts and Statistics 2022: Exploding the Myths Around Detransitioning,* Gender GP, June 2021, https://www.gendergp.com/detransition-facts/ Studies in the UK, US, Sweden and the Netherlands estimate numbers people who have chosen to detransition (excluding those who did it only temporarily for social, financial or family pressures) ranging from 0.5 to 5%

[28] Gender recognition and the rights of transgender people, UK Parliament, July 2020,
https://commonslibrary.parliament.uk/research-briefings/cbp-8969/

[29] *The complicated truth about testosterone's effect on athletic performance,* Popular Science, November 2019, https://www.popsci.com/story/science/testosterone-effect-athletic-performance/

Printed in Great Britain
by Amazon

25027288R00195